D1083869

KNUT HAMSUN

KNUT HAMSUN
DREAMER AND DISSENTER

INGAR SLETTEN KOLLOEN

TRANSLATED BY DEBORAH DAWKIN AND ERIK SKUGGEVIK

YALE UNIVERSITY PRESS
NEW HAVEN AND LONDON

Copyright © Gyldendal Norsk Forlag AS 2005. [All rights reserved.]

First published in English by Yale University Press 2009

English language translation copyright © 2009 Deborah Dawkin and Erik Skuggevik

Originally entitled *Drømmer og erobrer* (Norwegian title) and abridged from the volumes *Hamsun Svermeren* (2003) and *Hamsum Eroberen* (2004) by Ingar Sletten Kolloen

This translation has been published with the financial support of NORLA.

For information about this and other Yale University Press publications, please contact:
U.S. Office: sales.press@yale.edu   www.yalebooks.com
Europe Office: sales@yaleup.co.uk   www.yaleup.co.uk

Set in Minion by J&L Composition, Scarborough, North Yorkshire
Printed in Great Britain by MPG Books Ltd, Bodmin, Cornwall

Library of Congress Cataloging-in-Publication Data

Kolloen, Ingar Sletten, 1951–
  [Drømmer og erobrer. English]
  Knut Hamsun: dreamer and dissenter/Ingar Sletten Kolloen.
    p. cm.
  Abridged ed. of the author's two volume work published in Norwegian as
Hamsun : svermeren and Hamsun : eroberen in 2003–2004.
  Includes bibliographical references and index.
  ISBN 978–0–300–12356–2 (alk. paper)
  1. Hamsun, Knut, 1859–1952. 2. Authors, Norwegian—19th century—Biography.
3. Authors, Norwegian—20th century—Biography. I. Kolloen, Ingar Sletten, 1951–
Hamsun. II. Title.
  PT8950.H3Z67613 2009
  839.82'36—dc22
  [B]
                                                              2009014229

A catalogue record for this book is available from the British Library.

10 9 8 7 6 5 4 3 2 1

Contents

List of Illustrations   viii
Preface   x

Part I

Before the Iron Nights   3
The Expulsion   4
The Chosen One   10
A Shock   14
Off to America   20
Writing for Dear Life   24
An Undiscovered Genius   27
A Sense of Clarity   31
The Fractional Workings of the Soul   34
The Moment of Triumph   38
Posturing   41
Divine Madness   46
Seducer and Poet   50

Part II

Death to the Prophets!   57
The Sphinx with No Riddle   62
A Charlatan Takes Flight   65
A Literary Thief   68
A Parisian Tour   72
Longing for Edvarda   77
I Beat Ibsen to the Ground   80
Lies   85
Fever-Free   89
Journeying East   93
Prodigal Son – Failed Husband   97

I Shall Spit in God's Eye   99
The Break-Up of Two Unions   104
A Happy House in the Forest?   110
Away from the City   116

Part III

My Only Love on This Earth   121
There Is No Such Things as Harmony   124
Let the Dirt of City Life Go   129
Bjørnson's Throne Is Vacant   132
Putting Down Roots   135
Just Hysteria and Nerves   140
The View from the Hotel   144
War and Murder   149
Myriads of Characters   151
Full Control – But at What Price?   154
I Must Be Rid of This Farm   156
I Am Not Happy in the City   158
A Paradise on Earth   162
Master of Nørholm   165
How We All Struggle   167
Hell Is the City   172
Friends and Enemies in Stockholm   176
To Stockholm with a New Dress   178
Come, Death!   182
Success and Anxiety   184
The Balancing Artist   187
The Wizard's Cold Artistry   190
A Giant Buys Himself   192
Eternal Conflict   196

Part IV

A New Spring?   201
I Shall Write Like a Young Man Again   206
Old Man's Prattle?   211
A Literary Emperor   214
Greatness, What Is That?   218
A Red Streak   223
A Convalescent in Search of Reconciliation   225
A Romantic   228
'Wilkommen, Knut Hamsun!'   229

When the Author Opens Up   234
The World Has Come to the End of the Road   236
Hidden Romance   238
Prostrate before the Incarnation of Power   240
Father and Son in Goebbels's Clasp   243
At the Gates of the Kingdom   246
I Feel Sympathy for the Jew Too   251
I Feel I Am Decaying   255
To Win or Perish   258
I Bring Greetings from Hamsun   259

Part V

Nothing but Reality   265
Yes or No, Herr Reichskommissar!   269
Even If Hitler Himself Invited Me   272
The Web of Destiny   276
He Shall Succeed   279
You Understand Nothing!   282
A Defeated Devotee   286
We Will See Nothing But Destruction Now!   289
The End of the Future   292
I Plead Not Guilty   295
The Stakes in the 'Hamsun Case'   298
The Unshakeable Writer   301
The Clinic   303
Battles and Treacheries   306
A Necessary Diagnosis   309
A Frozen Tap   311
We Have Sinned So Greatly   314
My Conscience Is Clear!   318
A Glimmer of Hope?   321
Strange to Be a Dead Man before I Am Dead   327
The Lion's Claw   331
A Suicide Mission   333
. . . But No Martyr   336
She Came with the Spring   338

Notes   343
Bibliography   361
Index   365

Illustrations

1   Peder Pedersen

2   Tora Pedersen

3   Hans Olsen

4   Sophie Marie Pedersen

5   Knut Hamsun, aged fifteen

6   Coffee at Nicolai Walsøe's house, Tranøy, 1875

7   Drude Janson (photograph by J. W. Taylor)

8   Knut Hamsun, aged twenty-four

9   Cartoon of Knut Hamsun and the leading literary figures of the day

10   Albert Langen

11   Anna Munch (courtesy of H. Aschehoug & Co.)

12   Bergljot and Victoria Hamsun

13   Building Maurbakken, Hamsun's house outside Drøbak

14   Marie Lavik

15   Knut and Marie Hamsun, 1909

16   Cartoon of Knut Hamsun by Jens R. Nilsen from *Hvepsen*, January 1915

17   Jackets for *Rosa* and *Sklaven der Liebe*

18   One of Tore Hamsun's pen and ink drawings of his father (© The Hamsun Estate; agreement made through Gyldendal Norsk Forlag AS)

19   Victoria Hamsun, 1920

20   Johan Irgens Strømme

21   The Hamsun family at Nørholm

22   Marie, Ellinor and Cecilia Hamsun

23   The Hamsun children

24   The Hamsun's farmhouse, Nørholm, near Lillesand

25 and 26 Interiors at Nørholm

27   Knut and Marie Hamsun, August 1930

28   Knut Hamsun and Harald Grieg

29   Knut Hamsun chopping fire-wood

30   Knut Hamsun out in the fields at Nørholm

31   Tore and Knut Hamsun with Josef Terboven at Skaugum, 1941
32   Knut and Ellinor Hamsun
33   Knut Hamsun's visit to Adolf Hitler, Berghof, 1943 (Ullstein Bild;
          photograph by Walter Frentz)
34   Knut Hamsun and Josef Terboven, Fornebu airport, Oslo
35   Gabriel Langfeldt of the Vindern psychiatric clinic
36   Christian Gierløff
37   Sigrid Stray
38   Knut Hamsun at his trial, December 1947
39   Knut Hamsun, Nørholm, 1950
40   Knut and Marie Hamsun, Nørholm, 1950
41   Knut Hamsun, Nørholm, 1950

Preface

With books like *Hunger, Mysteries, Pan, Victoria* and *The Growth of the Soil*, the Nobel Prize-winning Norwegian writer Knut Hamsun (1859–1952) has taken his place in world literature. This poor country boy from the northern-most outskirts of Europe, with only 252 days of schooling to his name, would influence several generations of authors across the continent.

'The Dickens of my generation', enthused Henry Miller. 'Never has the Nobel Prize been awarded to a man worthier of it', Thomas Mann concluded. Herman Hesse called Hamsun 'my favourite author'. Isaac Bashevis Singer declared that 'Hamsun is the father of the modern school of literature in his every aspect – his subjectiveness, his fragmentariness, his use of flashback, his lyricism'.

But Knut Hamsun also joins a list of artists and intellectuals who chose to support a totalitarian regime. While the writer's hand was still active, he raised it in salute to Adolf Hitler. Hamsun stepped outside literature and into poli-tics. When the Second World War came to an end, Hamsun stood accused of being a traitor and was sentenced for his political activities. On the day he received the judgement of the courts he scribbled a final sentence in the manu-script of what would be his last book, *On Overgrown Paths*: 'Midsummer 1948. Today the High Court has passed sentence, and I end my writing.'

The final chapter was complete in the life of an author who had trans-formed world literature, and of a man of politics who had wanted to change the world.

My aim has been to find out how Hamsun became the great writer he was; what it cost him, and those closest to him, to maintain this poet's universe for so many decades; how his political opinions developed, what these were, the contemporary reactions to them, and ultimately their consequences.

My approach has been twofold: first, to bring to light and analyse as many facts as possible; then, to depict as truthfully as possible the life of Hamsun the writer, Hamsun the politician and Hamsun the private person. Along the way I have continually had to ensure that the storytelling urge has not disrupted the factual base. This book has thus been created in the fertile space between the factual and the artistic poles.

As a biographer I stand on the shoulders of many people, from Norway, Denmark, Sweden, Finland, Germany, Russia, France, Croatia, the USA and elsewhere, who in their different ways have all shed light on Hamsun's life and work. This project has lasted five years, and I have had the assistance of a cross-disciplinary research team whose expertise has been invaluable to me.

Professor of Nordic Languages and Literature Harald Næss is the world's foremost expert on Hamsun's letters. For over forty years he has continued to scour the world for them. These have been published and annotated in *Knut Hamsuns brev I–VII* (Oslo 1994–2001), and can also be found in an English condensed version: *Selected Letters I* and *II* (Norvik Press, 1998–1990). Harald Næss was involved with this project from the outset, as was Lars Frode Larsen PhD, who is responsible for much ground-breaking new Hamsun research, presented in the three volumes *Den unge Hamsun* (The Young Hamsun), *Radikaleren* (The Radical) and *Tilværelsens utlending* (Outsider to Society) (Oslo 1998–2001). Professor of Psychiatry Sigmund Karterud was also involved from the beginning, and one of his tasks has been to work up a personality profile of Hamsun. During this work he consulted his American colleague Dr Paul Costa Jr. Professor of Literature Atle Kittang, an internationally renowned Hamsun researcher, has been a useful sparring partner and consultant during the writing process, as has Professor of Political Science Bernt Hagtvet. War historian Odd Vidar Aspheim has generously shared his wealth of knowledge on the subject of the occupation of Norway and the Second World War. My two editors at Gyldendal Norsk Forlag, Hans Petter Bakketeig and Irene Engelstad, have been marvellous. And the Hamsun family, in particular Leif Hamsun, have shown the biographer almost limitless trust and helped open many doors.

The most important discovery has been Knut Hamsun's private archive, containing over five thousand documents, which Hamsun himself claimed to have destroyed. The material dates all the way back to the 1890s, and continues up to his death in 1952. But the biographical team also made other important discoveries of documents, and were the first to have access to the shorthand notes of the psychoanalyst who treated Hamsun in 1926–27.

The main objective in this book has been to follow Hamsun as closely as the source material allows. My wish was to investigate the interaction between his writing, his life and the wider society.

Knut Hamsun: Dreamer and Dissenter is an abridged international version of two volumes, *Hamsun Svermeren* (Oslo 2003) and *Hamsun Erobreren* (Oslo 2004). The biography is built around twenty thousand items of research. These stemmed from a host of archives, books, journals, newspapers, letters and other documents, including school registers, interviews with Hamsun's mother and brother, Hamsun's correspondence with translators and Norwegian, Danish and German publishers, royalties and sales logs from publishers in many countries over almost half a century, accounts and ledgers, the scrap-books belonging to his eldest child, Victoria Hamsun Charlesson, the German interpreter Ernst Züchner's report of the meeting between Hamsun and Hitler, reports from the judicial and psychological assessments, etc.

The original two Norwegian volumes contain a full bibliography and nearly two thousand source references. In this edition, approximately five hundred of the most important ones have been kept.

A biographer has to make many choices. In dealing with individual literary works in Hamsun's considerable output, my primary focus has been on the process of their creation. In the case of a number of Hamsun's books I have tried to focus in on one or several areas where the man and the writer may have crossed paths. Nevertheless, it has to be admitted that a biographer continually risks reducing the work and the creative process.

The greater the writing, the more indefinable the processes of its coming to fruition may seem.

Hamsun used the complex workings of his subconscious in his work, which neither we nor anyone else can have full insight into, while the more rigid, logical workings of his political development are easier to map. If there is something I have learned in this work, it is the following: each of us contains more fateful contradictions than we can ever fathom.

Part I

Before the Iron Nights

The Atlantic cuts deep into Norway, yet no fjord reaches into the heart of this country. It was here, in the mountainous region of Jotunheimen, that Knud Pedersen (as Knut Hamsun was baptised), the fourth of seven children, was born on 4 August 1859. August was an especially nervous time for the peasants here among the peaks, since being so high up, they already had to be on the look-out for the onset of winter. Nightfall could bring with it the most dreadful, harsh frosts, which threatened to destroy all the grain on which their lives depended. The peasants dreaded these 'iron nights' as they called them, and did their best to ward off their effects by lighting small bales of hay to release a dense smoke: if they were skilful enough and lucky with the wind, a veil would settle over the crops and protect them.

Knut's father, Peder Pedersen, battled against just such frosts on the small-holding he rented from his brother-in-law Ole Olsen – a man with a restless nature, an unquenchable thirst for liquor, an unChristian lust for women and a constant cash crisis. God-fearing folk whispered that he was possessed, others that his wild temperament was inherited from his mother, Knut's grand-mother. Several members of her family were known to have either hanged themselves or thrown themselves in the river. Insanity ran in the blood.

Knut was only a few months old when, after years of absence, Ole Olsen suddenly returned to his farm. He had fathered several children in various parts of the country without marrying any of their mothers, and now faced a string of legal proceedings, fines and maintenance orders. The authorities and private individuals to whom he was indebted were threatening him with the forced sale of his property. He needed money fast and intended to sell his farm to the highest bidder.

Peder Pedersen, who had hoped to buy the farm in instalments one day, made a desperate attempt to avert catastrophe. He embarked on the three-week-long journey to Nordland beyond the Arctic Circle to see his other brother-in-law, Hans Olsen, who had emigrated there a few years earlier. Peder hoped he might help the family, but Hans refused to rescue the farm. Knut's father was faced with a choice: emigrate to America, just as so many Norwegians had done and would continue to do in the decades ahead (indeed, only Ireland would give up a greater proportion of its population than Norway);

or, alternatively, rent the little farm in Hamarøy, Nordland, which his well-heeled brother-in-law – a tenant farmer there – had considered purchasing.

He chose the latter course. Just two months before Knut turned three, Tora and Peder Pedersen, who now had five children, left the mountains of Jotunheimen. Their voyage to the land of the midnight sun took them three weeks, first by horse and cart out from the mountains, then along the old pilgrims' route to Trondheim, and finally by steamship northwards. They covered a distance that, if they had travelled south, would have taken them close to the border of Italy.

It was Midsummer's Eve of 1862 when they arrived at their destination.

The Expulsion

Knut's maternal grandparents had also made the long journey to Nordland. Less than four months after their arrival, Knut's grandmother died. His mother, Tora, must have been deeply affected, since her mental health started to deteriorate after the funeral. Two years later, in 1864, she gave birth to her sixth child, a second daughter.

The five-year-old Knut and his younger sister, Anne Marie, fought between themselves and with the newcomer, Sophie Marie, for their mother's lap. Knut often felt left out. He was too old to claim his mother's attention from his two younger sisters, and too young to play with his three older brothers of thirteen, ten and eight.

Tora's health steadily worsened. She was less and less able to take care of the children, or to do the cooking and look after the house, or help Peder in the cowshed and out in the fields. Meanwhile, Peder was working around the clock, not only running the small, labour-intensive farm but also working at his trade as a tailor.

The farm could provide them with enough food, but only if the frosts thawed early enough in spring, if the summer was neither too wet nor too dry, and if the frosts did not ruin the crops in the autumn. Peder's tailoring had to provide enough cash to pay the rent to his brother-in-law, as well as to buy farm equipment and other essentials not produced on the farm. But tailors were plentiful in the parish, which meant Peder had to keep his prices low – added to which, he was not always firm enough with his debtors.

With his wife increasingly bedridden, Peder had to request that the school commission excuse their eldest son, thirteen-year-old Peder Junior, from attending school: 'With sickness visited upon my family almost all year round, it will be very difficult for me to keep all of my many school-age children in education the whole time.'[1]

Meanwhile their newborn daughter, Sophie Marie, screamed dreadfully day and night. There seemed to be something wrong with her hip. In order to lighten the burden on Tora, Sophie Marie was taken before she was even a year old to live with her Uncle Hans in Presteid, the area's administrative centre some 8 kilometres away from the small settlement of Hamsund where the Pedersens lived.

Hans had bought himself a house in the parsonage grounds in Presteid, and worked extremely hard farming an extensive area of church land which he rented, while also leasing out the Hamsund smallholding to his brother-in-law Peder. In addition, Hans traded in cloth and ran the sub-post office as well as a private library belonging to the local study circle.

Hans was financially comfortable and a bachelor; he had brought a house-keeper with him from his home village of Lom. Perhaps the family had only intended for Sophie Marie's move to be temporary, but she never went back to live with her parents and siblings. Instead Hans took over the care of his niece, together with the village midwife whom he had also brought up from the Jotunheimen mountains to Nordland, and who rented accommodation in his house. Indeed, a considerable colony of immigrants from the Gudbrands Valley established themselves in Hamarøy.

The second half of the 1860s brought successive years of crop failure. The snow fell heavily in April and May, and failed to melt. Long after the ploughing and sowing should have begun the fields were still frozen hard and covered in snow. As a result the cows could not be put out to pasture, the herd produced less and less milk, and pregnant cows lay down long before they were ready to calve, often with dire consequences. Fodder was unobtainable. Knut's father was forced to slaughter some of his animals. The grain was sown too late and failed to ripen before it had to be harvested with the approach of the 'iron nights'.

There was not enough food to go round, although in 1867 they had one less mouth to feed at Hamsund after the oldest boy, Peder, decided to emigrate to America. He was just sixteen years old.

Weather conditions were so severe and crops so poor that life was, the adults said, almost as harsh now as it had been half a century ago, at the end of the Napoleonic Wars. Knut often heard his parents and maternal grandfather discussing those gruelling years. Crops had been devastated by the weather then too, and Norwegians had been unable to obtain grain for either food production or planting from their twin kingdom of Denmark, or indeed from anywhere else. The British had blockaded Norwegian ports, leaving Norway's population to starve. And were the British not also to blame for Norway's failure to gain independence in the 1814 peace settlement? Norway had endured Danish rule for over four hundred years, only to be peremptorily handed over to Sweden under the Treaty of Kiel.

Hearing countless tales of Britain's domination of world trade and exploitation of Norway, Knut soon learned to associate the British with hunger and deprivation. It was in these formative years that the seeds of his hatred for Britain and everything British were first sown.

Just before Knut's ninth birthday, in August 1868, his mother had her seventh child, another son. Tora's nerves worsened after the pregnancy and birth. When she found her situation too much to bear, she would simply cease communicating, her eyes would glaze over and her face would stiffen. Sometimes she would dash out of the house into the fields, up into the forest or along the road where her family would hear her screaming loudly and nonsensically.[2]

The young Knut must have wondered why his mother behaved so oddly. Her outlandish conduct and illness would have left him feeling terrified, and bereft of the maternal love and attention he naturally craved. But he may also have felt a certain fascination. His later interest in extreme emotional states, particularly when he worked on books like *Hunger* and *Mysteries*, may indeed hark back to the strange episodes he witnessed as a child.

Was it now that Knut Hamsun began to develop a serious interest in words – the words that eluded his mother in her emotional confusion?

Knut began school just after Christmas in 1868. The local authorities were generally obliged by law to provide children with schooling for a minimum of nine weeks each year, but in Hamarøy they felt unable to provide more than four. The municipality had only limited financial resources, and the few locals who did pay taxes saw little reason to provide the poorer children with more than the absolute minimum of schooling. After all, by the time they reached Confirmation, they were expected to go out to work as fishermen, craftsmen or farmhands, or to emigrate to America, as Knut's eldest brother had done.

Taught by his brothers, Knut could already read and write. A couple of years had passed since he had first scrawled his name on a steamed-up windowpane. He had often sat gazing at the letters on the glass, guarding them from the other children who might try to spoil them. If they succeeded, he would fly into a fury: the words were his.[3]

In time, Knut was transferred to the permanent school in Presteid, staying during the week with his Uncle Hans in the parsonage. Knut often found that instead of being allowed to return home at the end of the school week, he would be expected to stay on and help his uncle by chopping logs, filling up the firewood boxes, fetching water for the animals and household, shovelling manure, fetching hay, and rounding up the animals.

The young Knut was extremely unhappy at his Uncle Hans's house.

Hans Olsen suffered from Parkinson's disease, then known as the shaking palsy, and his symptoms were steadily worsening. When Knut was around twelve years old his parents made a deal with Hans for the young boy to move in with him permanently, so that he could help run both the farm and the sub-post office. From Knut's parents' point of view, this must have seemed an excellent solution. Not only would they no longer have to feed and clothe him, but the capable youngster would enjoy the advantage of moving in his uncle's social circle of parish worthies: the priest, the parish clerk and the sheriff.

Knut's sister Sophie Marie, five years his junior, was still living with Uncle Hans. The household all spoke in the dialect of the Gudbrands Valley, as did the young Knut and the rest of his family when they were together, although Knut soon learned to use the local Salten dialect when he was with the other children in Hamarøy.

Knut did his utmost to sabotage the agreement between his parents and Uncle Hans. He made himself as awkward and ineffective as possible when he was put to work, but achieved nothing more than a stern rebuke. One day, he even put an axe through his own foot, hoping to be sent home; although his mother came to visit him, he was not allowed to accompany her back. He tried making his escape by boat, and when he found the vessel had no oars he simply lay in its prow and let himself drift away; he was discovered and returned to his uncle. Indeed, Knut tried to run away repeatedly. The sheriff caught him early one winter morning on a farm halfway between the parsonage and Hamsund. He had broken in, frozen to the core, wearing no proper outdoor clothes and with no socks in his clogs.

Just below the parsonage grounds flowed the river Glimma, where the ocean tides swept in and out. Conflicting currents clashed twice a day, and then the Glimma would turn into a frothing witch's cauldron. The young Knut would stare down into it. One little movement would be enough to end his suffering.[4]

Knut turned thirteen, then fourteen. He learned hatred, tenacity, and to be utterly obstinate. He had come to his uncle's house to work for both his own and his sister's keep. Hans bullied his young nephew until he did as he was told, and beat him when he made mistakes. If Knut tried to sneak away, his uncle would force even more work onto him. If he complained about the quality or quantity of his food, he was sent to bed hungry. And Uncle Hans's housekeeper knew every miserly trick to make the food go further, not caring for the people she looked after as a wife or mother would.[5]

Hans spent more and more time lying on his daybed in the study or on the improvised bed he had set up in the post office, where he would doze off, only to wake with a jolt, demanding to look at the accounts and records, and poised to lash out at his nephew with the rod.

Sometimes the boy had to bring his uncle's food, and help him with his cutlery.

He must have realised quickly that his uncle could not read his private thoughts.

The agreement had been that Knut would stay with his uncle until after his Confirmation during the summer of his fifteenth birthday, 1874. But he was determined to leave before that. Increasingly helpless and bedridden, his Uncle Hans could no longer stand in his way. The shaking palsy would soon leave the forty-five-year-old a broken man, and when he was forced to hand over the running of the post office to the parish priest during the spring of 1874, Knut saw his chance for rebellion.

He refused to live with or work for his uncle any longer. Neither did he want to be confirmed by Hamarøy's pastor, a man who had ignored his own son's reports of how Hans, across the parsonage grounds, had been beating his nephew. This sense of betrayal no doubt contributed to Knut's negative attitude to priests throughout his life and in his writing, albeit with one or two exceptions. By this point Knut's relationship to God was already deeply divided. In his childhood home he had learned about a mild Jesus; but in his uncle's house he had been introduced to a fierce, punitive God. He lived in terror of this Old Testament deity, while continuing to pray to the Jesus of the New Testament. Occasionally he had felt his prayers were answered, as when he was asked to deliver post bound for Hamsund, a task that took him in the direction of his mother and home.[6]

For as long as he could remember, Knut had listened to tales of his mother's ancestors and their splendid history. The blood of the Norwegian gentry, he had been told, ran in his veins. For his Confirmation, which was obligatory under Norwegian law, he decided to return to the mountain region of Jotunheimen where his parents had come from, and the Gudbrands Valley where he had been born and spent his first two and a half years.

Hamsun wrote to his godfather, one of his mother's well-to-do relatives in the village of Lom, who agreed to pay for his godson's journey and keep in return for him working in his shop.

Around the beginning of April 1874, the fifteen-year-old Knut set off on the long journey south. First he took a small boat to Bodø, then a steamer to Trondheim, and from there, partly on foot and partly by horse and cart, he crossed the Dovre mountains before travelling down into the Gudbrands Valley and up through a branch valley. In his suitcase lay the reports from his schoolmaster, who had awarded him his final grades: 3 for Conduct, which was almost as low as it was possible to get; 1.5 for Writing, an outstanding achievement for the son of a tailor and small tenant farmer; and 2 for Bible and Religious Studies, a middling grade.

Knut, often forced to miss school to work for his uncle, should have received a total of 292 days of schooling over the course of these six years. In fact, the great writer would receive only 252 days of schooling in his entire life.

Before Knut embarked on the journey, his father kitted his son out with two new sets of clothes. His mother imparted various greetings for him to deliver to the grander folk back in Lom, along with instructions on how to behave to please his hosts, her second cousin Tosten Hesthagen and his wife, Ragnhild, who were a middle-aged and childless couple of reasonable means.

Knut's experience of Lom, however, must have proved something of a disappointment. The village was much more ordinary than his parents had described. Their old home, which his mother remembered with such fondness and longing, was being used by its new owner as a smithy. The fields were nowhere near as flat or large as his parents and grandfather had led him to believe, and they contained even more rocks than at Hamsund.

Life at the village shop failed to live up to expectations, too. Knut often watched the Hamarøy tradesmen as they stood rocking back on their heels, thumbs tucked into waistcoat pockets, fingers rapping expectantly, impatiently or enticingly (according to which customer they were serving), or as they leaned over the counter, gossiping with the people with whom they wanted to stay on good terms. But Knut's godfather always kept him busy carrying goods, stacking shelves and running errands.

Knut's godfather soon discovered that the boy could be impressively quick-witted, but could equally easily fall prey to whatever wild notion entered his head. He could behave very arrogantly and insult good customers who would complain and threaten to take their business elsewhere. Or he could decide to be overly generous with customers – as though he owned the shop.

When there were not too many travellers passing through, Knut's godmother ensured he had a small room to himself. He could spend hours alone in this little room, reading and writing. When something sparked his interest he had to scribble it down there and then, often setting aside his book or magazine so his own ideas would not become jumbled with those on the page. After these moments of inspiration he would rush down from his room bursting with excitement and desperate to share his thoughts. If there were other people in the room competing for his godmother's attention, his mood would change and he would become argumentative and surly.

After a little more than six months, the newly confirmed Knut Hamsun left Lom, doubtless satisfied that he had done things his way: liberating himself from his Uncle Hans, and escaping the necessity of kneeling before Hamarøy's pastor, to whom he had taken such a dislike.

The Chosen One

The fifteen-year-old Knut Hamsun returned to Hamarøy in the late autumn of 1874, but he did not return to his uncle's parsonage. Rather, the twists of chance steered him into the employment of one of the most powerful men in Nordland, Nicolai Walsøe.

Throughout his childhood Hamsun had listened to tales of this legendary 'matador of business', as successful entrepreneurs were known at the time. Walsøe was a shrewd businessman who had prospered since the 1860s in the herring industry by taking advantage of his superb location at the northern tip of Hamarøy, facing the fjord and the Lofoten Islands beyond. Hamsun was given lodgings in the garret of Walsøe's house and employed in the general shop.

Laura, one of Walsøe's daughters, was just six months younger than the new shop assistant and, since she received tutoring at home, her and Hamsun's paths would cross several times a day. She had a long slender face, delicate hands, a soft neck, small ears, thick hair, a gentle mouth and a glance that kept Hamsun awake at nights. In a manuscript probably begun at this time, Hamsun described the experience of falling in love – how the heavens parted, an angel appeared, his soul was rocked, and an exquisite charge shot through him each time he came in contact with anything she had touched.[7]

Later, in book after book, Knut Hamsun would revisit those heady Nordland summers when all creation was filled with ecstasy.

Hamsun had arrived at the coastal trading centre towards the end of a record-breaking year. No other fishing community had taken such an enormous haul, which totalled more than a third of the herring catch in the whole of Nordland. It was hardly surprising, then, that the fishermen, when they called in at the general store where Hamsun worked, came gleefully whistling – and that when their wallets were empty and they might usually have tightened their purse strings, the prospect of more good catches kept them spending. The shop assistants were under instruction to be generous with credit.

Nobody could remember business ever having been so brisk. The trading centre was abuzz. It was a convivial and vigorous little township, with not only the general store but a telegraph office, a private pilot station, a shipping company, a sub-post office, an ice manufacturer, a coal depot, extensive fish-processing facilities and a bakery, as well as an inn offering food and lodging. Walsøe employed a seining team and owned his own trading vessel in the fishing grounds. He also ran salting and drying facilities, and owned islets out in the fjord, where eggs and featherdown were collected. Together with locally sourced large game, his produce was transported south in his own steamship.

It seems the young Hamsun was very drawn to Walsøe. Here was a man capable of predicting future fishing seasons and making unimaginable investments, while at the same time having the intelligence and alacrity to alter his course when unexpected opportunities or obstacles arose. A 'matador' like Walsøe needed the gambler's impulsive nerve, as well as the chess player's genius for thinking several moves ahead.

For the first time in his life, the young Knut Hamsun came close to a man he admired unreservedly: the perfect patriarch, a man of mysterious insight and great secrets, unyielding when it mattered, and lenient when it was deserved. More than anything, he was all-powerful. These 'matadors', who held such fascination for Hamsun, would feature in many of his novels.

Hamsun bought himself a heavy, silver-plated watch chain, which he wore dangling between his waistcoat button and left breast pocket. All that was lacking was a handsome watch to match, which he felt sure he would soon be able to afford and which would put paid to the teasing of the local fishermen, who enjoyed staring absently into the horizon and asking if he happened to know the time.

But in 1875 the herring catch failed. Suddenly the seas were empty. Unpaid debts were now a growing problem that gnawed into the community. The once-ascendant Walsøe had to make cutbacks. Hamsun, the youngest man behind the counter, had been at the trading centre for less than a year when he was asked, in that autumn, to leave.

This sixteen-year-old ex-shop assistant found he was not quite as remarkable as in his private moments he had begun to believe. But Hamsun dreamed of becoming a writer and, when he put pencil to paper, he still felt special. When he was writing, even his fantasy of a poor, gifted boy capturing the heart of a rich man's daughter might become reality. Anything and everything seemed possible.

Over the next three years the young Hamsun would achieve a great deal. After a somewhat miserable attempt at being a shoemaker's apprentice, in accordance with his father's wishes, he worked as a supply teacher and a sheriff's clerk, and even tried his hand as a pedlar selling cloth, shoelaces, combs, perfume and other goods along the Nordland coast. Impressions and experiences of this period would be turned to good use later in his novel *Wayfarers*. But most importantly, during this period he published his first book.

Hamsun's supply teaching, travelling to various schools in Vesterålen, lasted for about a year. It meant he was able to brush up on what he had already learned and bolster this with new knowledge. He lived intermittently with his superior from the school authorities, a pastor – though quite unlike the pastor whom he had rejected in Hamarøy. In fact, the pastor and his wife were liberal and kind-natured people who showed great forbearance towards the eighteen-year old's need to assert himself. Most importantly, they encouraged him in his writing.

Hamsun wrote numerous stories between the ages of fifteen and twenty, generally with an identical theme: the poor but gifted boy who, owing to class divisions, struggles and fails to win the girl he loves. He did, however, write one story in which the boy succeeded in winning the heroine's affections, although even here Hamsun had to rely on a neat twist to solve the problem of class: the stranger who falls in love with the squire's only daughter is a pauper in appearance only, having actually inherited a fortune. Hamsun called it *The Enigmatic One: A Love Story from Nordland*.[8]

Mikkel Urdal, a bookseller and publisher of pamphlets for the locals of Tromsø, let himself be persuaded to print *The Enigmatic One*. Around Christmas 1877, aged eighteen, Knut Hamsun held his first published book in his hands. It looked more like a pamphlet than a book, since it was printed on thirty-one pages of the cheapest paper, but to Hamsun that would scarcely have mattered.

He had no doubt fantasised about this magical moment since before his Confirmation. Now, he probably stood on the harbour waiting to rip open the packets of newly printed books the instant they arrived off the steamship. He may well even have tried to persuade people to buy a copy there and then, on the quayside. But neither the author nor the man who had paid for its printing had much luck selling Hamsun's first tome.

Forty years later, anybody passing through Tromsø could still buy *The Enigmatic One* in Urdal's book and stationery store, with the original price of 40 øre still printed on it. Copies now sell in antiquarian bookshops for nearly a million kroner.

Impressed with this gifted youngster and wanting to offer a helping hand, the priest, sheriff and doctor of Vesterålen, who all shared an interest in literature, allowed Hamsun free access to their libraries. Early in 1878, they also offered him the post of sheriff's clerk.

Thus elevated, Hamsun seems to have been at even greater pains to mark the distance between himself and more humble folk. A woman who washed and ironed his shirts described how infuriatingly fussy he could be, handing his clothes back, demanding that every spot be removed and every crease smoothed. After all, men in public office should be immaculate! Yet, according to this same woman, Hamsun was also capable of great kindness; when she had been upset on one occasion, for example, he had come back with a brooch for her.[9]

The young girls who took walks with him gossiped about how staid he was, obsessively brushing the grass from his clothes when they had been sitting in the forest, and wanting to do nothing more adventurous than hold their hands, tell them quaint stories and recite poetry. Little did they know that Hamsun, like the heroes he conjured in his stories, was only ever attracted to women who were out of reach. Indeed, the eponymous central character of his next novel, *Bjørger*, was just such a man. And the book reflected the young writer's life in other ways too: Bjørger's parents were named after Hamsun's own parents, and the businessman's daughter was, of course, named Laura. Hamsun no longer intended to hide his sources. Just as in reality, Bjørger failed to capture the merchant's daughter and, as in reality, the heartbroken young man comforted himself that he could still write.

Entrance to and absorption in the personal libraries of the doctor, sheriff and priest had had an almost miraculous effect on Hamsun as a writer. In *Bjørger*, his style is much more accomplished, containing sensuous detail and precise language, as well as the introduction of truncated sentences and a greater directness of tone which more closely reflected his own speech patterns. Although he still confined himself to the peasant milieu and repeated the theme of the poor boy and the rich man's daughter, this time Hamsun captured the wildness of sexual passion. And most remarkable perhaps in a young man of only nineteen was his insight into the mind of an emotionally unstable man: the fear of insanity, and the euphoria of creativity.

The triumvirate, suitably impressed with this new work, recommended Hamsun to Nordland's wealthiest businessman, Erasmus Zahl.

One Saturday in the spring of 1879, Hamsun wrote a letter that would alter the course of his life. As he would do so often in the years to come, he chose to reach for something seemingly unobtainable. He asked Zahl to lend him a sum of money that was equal to his teaching salary for two hundred weeks.

The letter, probably drafted with the help of his three supporters, was a careful balance of boastfulness, flattery and religiosity. He would, Hamsun explained, use the money to travel to Copenhagen where he intended to present himself to Frederik Hegel, the director of Gyldendal.[10]

Hamsun did not for a moment contemplate that the leading Nordic publishing house of the day, which boasted none other than Ibsen on its list, would do anything other than welcome him with open arms. He also seemed to have conveniently forgotten the fact that he had paid local printing houses to publish *Bjørger* and a long narrative poem, *A Reconciliation*,[11] and that interest in his works so far had been minimal despite his own strenuous efforts to sell them to the locals. Additionally, he failed to mention in his letter that the magazines he had approached in Oslo had all refused to print the poems he had sent them.[12]

The letter nonetheless succeeded in opening Zahl's door to Hamsun. 'The giant of Nordland' invited the nineteen-year old to visit his business premises on the island of Kjerringøy, just outside Bodø. One early June day, Hamsun's long legs carried him up the jetty that crossed the shallow sound to Kjerringøy. The buildings here were more numerous and more impressive than at Tranøy, and at the heart of this trading centre was a garden with a white gate: the epitome of luxury in these northern climes.

After welcoming Hamsun into his home, Zahl walked over to his safe and removed 1,600 kroner. This was an enormous sum of money – a farmhand would earn no more than 200 kroner a year[13] – and it was all for Knut Hamsun. He must have left Kjerringøy with his confidence sky-high. He was the great Zahl's golden boy. The businessman known for his unerringly good judgement had invested in his talent as a writer.

Hamsun spent his twentieth birthday, 4 August 1879, back home in Hamsund, Hamarøy, helping with the haymaking. He showered his family with money and gifts. Then he carefully selected some books, manuscripts, clothes and other possessions that he wanted to take with him from his old life into his new. Nobody could have guessed that twenty years would pass before he would visit again.

A Shock

Hamsun arrived in Bergen in the middle of August 1879, whence he intended to travel on by steamship to Copenhagen. But here, in Norway's second largest city, he walked into a well-stocked bookshop for the very first time in his life. He was shocked. It suddenly dawned on him how hopelessly inadequate his reading had been. Until now he had only ever read books he took a fancy to, in particular so-called peasant tales. But in leading literary circles this genre had long since passed out of vogue, superseded by the demand for realism.

Hamsun's response was to spend about a third of his remaining fortune on new books. Reading these led the twenty-year-old to see the imperfections in his own work. He realised that he had to make drastic improvements to his poem 'Sverdgny' and his story 'Frida', yet another tale of a poor boy trying to court a wealthy man's daughter, before he could think of presenting his work to Frederik Hegel. With this in mind he retreated to Øystese, a small coastal village deep in the Hardanger Fjord.

Hamsun was increasingly preoccupied with the way he spoke. Neither the mountain dialect of his parents nor the coastal dialect of Hamarøy quite corresponded to his literary and social aspirations. It was important that his written and spoken language should be as one. He began constructing a persona and cultivating a certain air of mystery.

The inn where he stayed was frequented by the liberal and politically engaged young people of the area. Hamsun held forth so opinionatedly on books and authors that tempers were sometimes lost. Proudly he showed off his private library of over a hundred books. Did they, he boasted, know anyone else who had the two-volume work on Lord Byron by the German Karl Elze?[14] The bombast almost certainly concealed doubts that troubled him privately. Was he really good enough?

A weakness in Hamsun's character was now surfacing that would prove an affliction for years to come: a complete lack of monetary control as soon as he had cash in his hands. After little more than three months he had spent the greater part of the pile of banknotes Zahl had lent him. He was now desperate and impertinent enough to ask his patron for a further loan of 400 kroner. One kroner was a good day's pay for a worker. Amazingly, he received the money.

He wrote back, expressing his thanks in lavish terms and vowing to bind Zahl's name to his own, which, he was sure, would one day be famous.[15]

Just before Christmas 1879, Hamsun finally boarded the steamship to Copenhagen. As soon as he arrived he made his way to Klareboderne in the city centre, where Gyldendal's offices were situated. He took lodgings close by and early the next morning put on his best clothes to proceed to the publishing house with his manuscript.[16]

He asked to speak to Frederik Hegel himself, and was shown into a waiting room. The publisher had not yet arrived that morning. Standing behind a counter, deliberating over a manuscript, was an elegantly dressed young Dane with melancholy eyes, of a similar age to Hamsun. Hamsun would get to know him nine years later: his name was Herman Bang.

Finally Hegel appeared. The publisher was in his early sixties and had, to Hamsun's eyes, a priestly appearance. They talked briefly. Hegel was friendly enough, but failed to lift the counter to invite this young man, who had travelled so far, into his office. Instead he asked Hamsun to leave his manuscript and return the following day.

But it was in vain that Hamsun waited at the publishing house for Hegel to reappear the next day. Eventually he was obliged to identify himself and explain to a secretary his reason for being there. He was promptly handed a parcel. When he asked what this signified, he was informed that his manuscript had been refused. There was not one word from Hegel accompanying the script and the indomitable publisher was nowhere to be seen. It was Christmas 1879.

Hamsun went straight to Hell – 'Helvede', that is, an inn where he might drown his sorrows. He toasted the landlady and played at being a man of the world. The twenty-year-old author was all alone in Copenhagen.

Until this point Hamsun had inhabited a world as far removed from the literary scene as it was possible to be. He had never met a writer, and only in the last couple of years had he come into contact with people who discussed literature in any depth, and who were familiar with both classical and contemporary authors. He rarely read the literary reviews in the national newspapers, and had never attended a lecture or visited a theatre. He had only stepped into a real bookshop for the first time in Bergen.

His elementary grasp of literature, of which he had been so boastful, was still riddled with holes. He was hopelessly ignorant in comparison to the majority of young hopefuls who delivered their manuscripts to Hegel and other publishers. Well educated and widely read, these young men had often already had articles printed in newspapers. The young Dane Herman Bang, whom Hamsun had seen in the publisher's waiting room, was one such case. Two years Hamsun's junior, he had published a collection of articles that year entitled *Realism and Realists*. In it, he discussed contemporary literary shifts and the controversy over the appointment of the radical Georg Brandes as a professor at the University of Copenhagen, as well as the rise of new writers such as Zola and Balzac who demanded greater realism in literature.

Hamsun, by comparison, had sauntered up to the publisher of the illustrious Ibsen himself, offering a manuscript largely influenced by and imitative of the early peasant tales of his literary hero, Bjørnstjerne Bjørnson. But these novels had been written over twenty years before. It was clear that Hamsun had failed to acquaint himself with the new and progressive fashion for social realism – the literary genre that both Ibsen and indeed Bjørnson himself had been key in developing among Scandinavian writers.

Henrik Ibsen's latest play, *A Doll's House*, was being performed at Copenhagen's Kongelige Theatre at around this time. The middle-class marital conflict of Nora and Helmer belonged to a world of which the young Hamsun knew nothing. Wide-eyed, he wandered around the theatre foyers observing the throngs of well-to-do men and women who talked and behaved with such an air of superiority. He must have asked himself if he could ever be a part of this life. Undeterred, however, Hamsun continued his approaches to publishing houses in Copenhagen, and even paid a visit to Andreas Munch, the now elderly Norwegian national Romantic poet, in the hope of securing a recommendation. Those publishers who bothered to respond to the aspiring writer explained that his manuscripts were poor imitations of an outdated genre, but it seems Hamsun refused to accept their reasoning. According to a letter he wrote to Zahl, Hegel had rejected 'Frida' because he saw in it a defence of Bjørnson, a writer who (according to Hamsun) seemed for the moment to be beleaguered by enemies in Copenhagen.[17]

Hamsun resolved to bring his case before his literary hero, Bjørnstjerne Bjørnson himself. Surely he must recognise his genius.

Bjørnson and Ibsen had vied for some time, and with increasing animosity, over which of them could claim to be the greatest Norwegian writer. In terms of his contribution to and place in Norwegian civic life, Bjørnson reigned supreme; there was not a single issue on which he had failed to express his opinion. He had also engaged with the international scene, travelling back and forth between his native Norway and various places around Europe. Ibsen, by contrast, had not set foot in his native land since his acrimonious departure in 1864.

Leaving Copenhagen at the beginning of January 1880, Hamsun travelled back to Norway, calling on the great Bjørnson at the magnificent farmstead he had procured for himself near Lillehammer. Hamsun handed over his manuscript and stood awaiting the usual request for him to come back in a day or two. Instead, Bjørnson took the bundle and glanced through it on the spot, leafing through the pages, reading short sections and skimming the rest. Then, shuffling the pages together, he handed the manuscript back, declaring it worthless.[18]

He suggested that Hamsun might pursue a career in acting rather than writing, and furnished him with an introduction to a well-established actor in the capital, Jens Selmer, who gave Hamsun free tickets to performances. Hamsun now had the opportunity to teach himself about the theatre, a subject on which even he had to admit he knew little – although this had not stopped him voicing the strongest of opinions on the plays of Ibsen and others.

Meanwhile, Hamsun continued to feel an enormous urge to express himself in writing, but the newspapers and journals to which he applied showed no interest.

In those first months of the new decade in Oslo, Hamsun pawned one possession after another: his watch, his winter clothes and a number of his one hundred books. Sometimes he would even attend the auctions himself. It somehow seemed less painful when he saw his things go to good homes.[19]

He approached Bjørnson again, this time with a letter asking for assistance not as a hopeful writer, but simply as a man who needed to make a living.[20] He must have made a favourable impression: Bjørnson took the trouble of putting the young man in touch with Olaf Skavlan, a professor of European literature at the university in Oslo. Skavlan read through what Hamsun had to show of poetry and prose and, for the first time since leaving his home in the far north of Norway, Hamsun received some encouragement. In a written assessment, the professor concluded that Hamsun had 'an undeveloped, but enormous literary talent'.[21] Indeed, he urged those who had money at their disposal to offer this youngster their support so that Hamsun might buy some private tuition and perhaps take his Middle School examination.

One man who offered Hamsun assistance was Harald Thaulow, an apothecary of some social standing. Thaulow gave the aspiring writer some copying work and, through him, the young man gained access not only to the Thaulow family sphere but also to the more select circles of Oslo society.

It did not last long. The higher echelons – among them businessmen, government officials, academics and senior officers – gradually lost patience with young Knut Hamsunn, as he now spelled his name.[22] His lack of education soon became apparent, which was only to be expected. But his strident opinions could be a real source of irritation. His conceit was sometimes intolerable, even for the most generous. The women felt he possessed a certain unpolished charm but seemed unaware of what an unsuitable match he was. Added to which, rumours of his excessive spending soon saw doors closing to him. In less than a year he had spent what his former job as sheriff's assistant might have earned him in eight. He now had creditors and debts in Bodø, Oslo and Copenhagen.

People in Nordland had sometimes warned him against living in the city.

Hamsun had grown up in a farming community, where the highest and lowest lived cheek by jowl; where owner and tenant, farmhand and parish pauper ate at the same table; where every person was dependent on everyone else because they tilled the same earth. Now he was in the city where the struggle for survival was inconceivably more savage, first and foremost because it was possible to rise and fall so fast.

Hamsun had presented his very best work to Frederik Hegel and other publishers in Copenhagen, and they had smiled good-humouredly and turned him down. His manuscripts described a world these Danish and Norwegian publishers knew little of: the farming communities north of the Arctic Circle. It undoubtedly began to dawn on Hamsun that he could not continue in this vein. He must write about the modern world, about the lives of the city-dwellers. The reading public wanted to read about themselves.

The cleft in Hamsun's existence was most apparent in the evenings. Leaving the elegant theatres and bourgeois homes behind him, he would stop off at lower-class taverns on the way back to his wretched lodgings, where he would stuff balls of newspaper in his ears to block out the sounds of other people's tawdry lives. He tried to put this double life down on paper.

He showed some of this writing to the wife of his patron the pharmacist. Nina Thaulow was a well-read woman who was acquainted with many well-known writers and artists, including Bjørnson himself. Hamsun felt sure that she must recognise what he had within him, but she was far from impressed.

Writing to Bjørnson later, she complained: 'I tried to work my way through his writings, but was left utterly perplexed. I found them utterly bombastic, unnatural and unclear.' Neither did Bjørnson have any belief in his talent.[23]

Ten years later, in *Hunger*, Knut Hamsun would put the experiences of this period to good use. Little did the pharmacist's wife know what a sterling misjudgement she had made.

Hamsun, still in need of gainful employment, approached another member of the capital's elite, this time the Norwegian highways commissioner. But instead of offering him clerical work, the commissioner sent this young man of dubious reputation to work where he no doubt thought he belonged: a road-side ditch. Hamsun had no choice but to accept employment on a road construction project on the north side of Lake Mjøsa, Norway's largest lake, where he began work in May 1880.

Hamsun stood out from the crowd from day one. He towered above most, and his red-blond hair almost reached his shoulders. He owned no work clothes, but wore the tatty garments of a man who had once had means, and he spoke in an elegant voice with hints of both the Gudbrands Valley and Nordland dialects.[24]

He was soon promoted from manual labourer to on-site administrator. Now he stood at the head of the new road with a pen and paper counting gravel loads. Once more his writing skills had given him access to a higher social status, but that did not change the grim reality: Hamsun was in a rut, with neither savings nor potential creditors on the horizon. He was having to wear all his four shirts at once with newspaper between them as insulation, and his food and lodgings were abysmal.

At the beginning of 1881, however, Hamsun suddenly found the doors of the well-to-do flung open to him again. As he was making his way back to his lodgings one day, an elegant man stopped his horse and cariole to ask if he would like a ride. Nikolai Frøisland, the thirty-year-old director of the match-stick factory, had heard rumours about this literary man who worked on the highway in his tatty but elegant clothes.

In the course of their short journey together, Hamsun intrigued the businessman so much that he was invited to visit him at his home. The shabby aesthete, peeling away the four layers of newspaper-padded clothing, spruced himself up as best he could and walked the short distance to Frøisland's house. Frøisland offered him some clerical work. Now, as Hamsun counted gravel loads by day and mixed with higher social circles in his free time, an idea began to take form.

Hamsun determined he would go to America. And to this end, he set about persuading the factory director and other contacts to assist him.

Off to America

In January 1882, along with 28,000 other Norwegians that year, Knut Hamsun set out for America. The journey took him through Hamburg, where he had his first taste of the legendary generosity of the German people towards Norwegian artists.

An acquaintance had given him a letter of introduction to a shipping company in Germany. Hamsun described his meeting with the company director years later:

> He was extremely friendly. I explained that I was a young, unknown writer who wanted to go to America and make something of myself. I told him I had family there, and asked if he could help me with cheap passage . . . I shall never forget that man. He sat and looked at me. Then he asked: Where do your relatives live? – In Elroy, I said. – I'll give you free passage and a train ticket to Elroy, he said. [. . .] I didn't understand his English too well, and he probably didn't understand much of mine either, but he explained that he was doing it because I was a young Norwegian writer.[25]

Hamsun would never forget the kindness of the German company director who gave him free passage and a ticket to the Midwest.

On Wednesday, 1 February 1882, still seasick, the twenty-two-year-old Hamsun took his first shaky steps in the New World.

From New York he took a train inland to Chicago. He bragged in a letter to a friend that he had seen nearly the entire world since leaving Norway, also mentioning having delivered some poems to a magazine for Scandinavian immigrants. The editor had promised he would print several of them.[26]

It was therefore with some confidence that he met a Norwegian-American professor whom he hoped would become his mentor. But once again Hamsun's sense of his own importance did not meet with agreement. The professor cast an eye over Hamsun's manuscripts and delivered his verdict: the distance between ambition and ability was unbridgeable.

Hamsun's reunion with his older brother Peder, who had been living in America for fifteen years, stripped him of many illusions. Here, Hamsun witnessed the misery caused to country folk by relocation to urban places. Things had not turned out well for his brother, a tailor by trade, who increasingly preferred to wander around with a violin in one hand, a bow in the other and a bottle of liquor in his pocket. His wife and children had to get by as best they could. It was a theme Hamsun would return to repeatedly in his novels: the plight of country people who moved to the cities, tearing up their roots to no avail, only for those roots to drag behind them for the rest of their miserable lives.

Hamsun took work on farms in Elroy. He soon longed for home, complaining about the unsympathetic nature of the farmers' wives who had emigrated from Britain. But life improved significantly when he moved in with a German immigrant family; the farmstead was well kept and the lady of the house lavished on him the attention he craved so badly.[27]

He soon settled down in the little town, working for the chief businessman in the area who also managed the bank and post office. Hamsun was rapidly promoted to the position of clerk, and donned a pair of shiny black leather shoes. He developed a slight infatuation with the twenty-three-year-old daughter of a Norwegian immigrant, but as soon as she showed signs of reciprocating his interest his euphoria evaporated. Hamsun liked women to pay attention to him but they must not come close enough to disturb his thoughts.

In November 1882, in a schoolhouse outside Elroy, Knut Hamsund, having newly taken the name of his parents' farm, gave his first lecture. His subject was Bjørnstjerne Bjørnson. The precocious twenty-three-year old praised Bjørnson's contribution as a writer and politician, while lamenting rejection of any belief in Heaven or Hell and denial of the divinity of Christ.[28]

Hamsun lectured several times in various Norwegian immigrant communities. As time passed he relaxed his criticism of freethinking, to such an extent that a priest ultimately warned good Christians against attending his lectures. This did not make it easier for him to gain a platform for his ideas.

By day he earned his living as a clerk, while in the evening he would try to concentrate on his writing in the cramped garret he shared with an American friend, Willy Ager. When he failed to make headway with his writing he would occasionally draw. On one wall he stuck a portrait of himself in profile with a motto alongside it in English: 'My *life* is a peaceless flight through all the land, my *religion* is the Moral of the wildest Naturalism, but my *world* is Aesthetical literature.'[29] One Sunday he began to sketch directly onto the ceiling above his bed. Soon an angel of death had spread its eerie presence across a third of the ceiling and the two young men living under it.

Late one evening, Willy Ager returned to find the Norwegian sleeping, the lamp still lit on a chair beside him. Next to it lay a cigar, a knife and the following instructions: 'Smoke the cigar and stick the knife into my heart. Do it quickly, decisively and as a friend, if you value my affection. Knut Hamsund. PS This note will be your defence in court.'

The American had cause to wonder on several occasions whether the aspiring writer was joking or serious in wanting such an end, since this dismal request was repeated in various forms.[30]

It is unlikely that Hamsun was suicidal. He was, however, certainly experiencing a crisis of faith. Hamsun had long since rejected his Uncle Hans's harsh, punitive Old Testament God. But he had also begun to question the divinity of the mild Jesus of the New Testament, to whom his mother had taught him to turn in prayer. He shared his beliefs and doubts with another Norwegian who had emigrated to America, Svein Tverås, admitting in a letter dated 29 February 1884: 'Let me tell you, I have doubted the truth of Christianity in its entirety for a long time.'

What he failed to mention to his friend was that only two days previously he had accepted the post of combined secretary and deacon to Kristofer Janson, the Norwegian educationalist, author and Unitarian Church Society pastor in Minneapolis. Hamsun moved into the Janson home at 2419 Nicollett Avenue in March 1884.

Janson saw a lot of himself in the young man, as did his wife, Drude. Once again Hamsun found himself living in close proximity to a married couple. The arrangement, with the head of the house as his employer and the wife a kind of surrogate mother, was one with which he was familiar. But Drude Janson was different. When she and Hamsun were alone in a room she would find a dozen ways to convey to him that she was a woman with strong, unfulfilled desires.

Janson was away a lot. Hamsun and Drude shared long conversations. She even cried in front of him. They opened up to each other more and more.[31]

But the relationship between Kristofer Janson and his young assistant also flourished. Hamsun helped him with correspondence, organised church events, gave lectures and did some translation work, although his unreliable grammar and limited English vocabulary sometimes resulted in an appalling scramble.

Hamsun could spend entire days in his employer's rich library, giving the other members of the household many an opportunity to observe his rather eccentric methods of study. He rarely sat down to read a book in any depth, instead spending hours standing in front of the shelves, taking books down and glancing through them. When Janson and others asked whether there were any books he felt the need to look at in more detail, he explained that he had a peculiar intuitive capacity to come directly to the essence of a book's content and its author's ideas.

For Janson, a pastor and writer, the ideological message of a book was paramount. That had never been the case for Hamsun. He was not looking to books to expand his knowledge or reinforce his own opinions. More than anything, he wanted to be touched emotionally.

Drude Janson understood this.

She was working on several manuscripts herself, and she too felt that words should elicit feelings. It was in reading each other's work that they had grown so close. She was enthralled by Hamsun's writing, telling him that she had never before experienced such a vibrancy of colour and sense of beauty. Yet she advised him to delay seeking to publish the manuscript he was currently working on. The book must be allowed to reach full maturity. Hamsun had never met a woman like Drude before, and he followed her advice.

The Jansons frequently held open house in Nicollett Avenue. The rooms would fill with people playing music, debating, giving talks and generally conversing. It was not long before the newcomer found his natural place – at the centre of events.

Hamsun was pushing himself relentlessly. Secretary and deacon by day, lecturer, popular party-goer, close companion to Drude and author by night. He was constantly coming down with coughs, colds and even fevers.

One evening in June 1884, he acted as auctioneer at a bazaar. Experiencing increasing difficulty in calling out the descriptions of the various lots, he eventually doubled up in fits of coughing. Then something seemed to loosen in his chest. His handkerchief filled with blood.

Drude insisted he be examined by a doctor. He was diagnosed with galloping consumption, now known as tuberculosis, and given two or three months to live.

Drude nursed him, sitting at his bedside, wiping the sweat from his fore-head. He took in her womanly smell, the weight of her breasts as she leaned over him to straighten the sheets, the arch of her neck as she stretched across the bed. And lying there almost naked, he found himself intensely aroused.[32]

Throughout his life Hamsun had been strict with himself, and yet there he lay, only twenty-four years of age, dying. He was obsessed with the thought that he might never possess a woman. There was a brothel in town that he had kept well away from, though he lacked neither desire nor oppor-tunity. The wish to save himself and the fear of disease had prevented him from surrendering to his cravings. Such restrictions seemed an irrelevance now. He wanted to go to the bordello, sin, whisper his ecstasy and expire in the act.

Hamsun confided this last wish to Drude. She told him that she understood.

He organised with a member of the household for his watch to be sold; a carriage was to be ordered with the proceeds since he was too weak to walk. He waited, but no carriage arrived. Instead, Drude came into his room. She told him she had cancelled the carriage.

Evening turned to night and night to morning. Drude continued to nurse him. Hamsun's sexual desire did not wane, neither did his determination to hire a prostitute. So Drude, thirteen years his senior and a mother of six, made him a proposition. That afternoon, according to a letter Hamsun wrote four years later to the author Erik Skram, he was offered the chance to sin under that very roof. There was no room for misunderstanding.

He refused her.

It was high summer and Hamsun asked Drude to pull open all the curtains. He demanded she light some lamps, many lamps. He could not fill the room with enough light. He loved the light, he told her.

She no longer understood him. Everything was different between them now. She wondered if he had gone mad.

One night he set fire to the curtains.

Writing for Dear Life

A few weeks later, at the end of July 1884, Hamsun was on his way back to Norway, travelling via New York, Belfast, Liverpool and Hull. Being a man of great kindness, Kristofer Janson had initiated a collection of the necessary funds. Hamsun turned twenty-five during the journey. If he was going to die, he wanted to die writing – and in his home country.

In Oslo he was granted a stay of execution. A renowned doctor told Hamsun that he would survive the winter, although the spring would be critical. The doctor advised his patient not to work or put himself under any physical or mental strain, but to eat healthily, breathe plenty of fresh, dry air, and rest. The doctor also recommended several sanatoriums in which people with pulmonary disorders had made satisfactory recoveries.

Hamsun did not have sufficient means to stay in a sanatorium, but since several were located in Valdres, just west of his birthplace in the Jotunheimen mountains, he decided he would take lodgings there.

But complete rest was out of the question. Without work he would simply starve or freeze to death. However, he reasoned that if he could be frugal during the winter without his health worsening, he might be able to scrape enough money together to take a partial rest in the spring.

Before leaving Oslo, he made the rounds of the capital's newspapers and magazines. This time, unlike four years before, the editors did at least listen to him. The articles about his stay in America with which he now presented them were a great deal more interesting to them than any of his fiction had been.

Taking accommodation with a widow in Valdres, he began quite literally writing for dear life, knowing at the same time that his very writing could kill him. The doctors had told him that if he followed their advice, the tuberculosis would be restricted to his lungs and he could expect to add months or even years to his life. But he did not, could not listen to them. When the waves of inspiration took him, he rode them until he collapsed over his papers, utterly spent or worse – wet with fever, shivering and bent double from coughing. And every time he coughed something seemed to come loose. He was unable to prevent it.

He reworked lectures and writings on America, selecting this and that from his piles of manuscripts. He composed articles on a huge variety of subjects, including Seneca, St Paul, Kristofer Janson, the unique pulse of New York, the inventor of a hymnbook with electric illuminated letters, and a man named Broad Shoulder, the progeny of a French painter who had raped an Indian chief's daughter.

Writing these articles was undemanding. He could have produced several per week at a leisurely pace and still had time to rest, but instead he dashed them off so he could clear time for his more creative work.

He rejected almost everything he wrote, as he had done so often since his humiliation in Copenhagen and Oslo almost five years before. He had come to the realisation that he could never compete on the same terms as the literary sons of the well-to-do. He would never have all their advantages: their high-school examinations and university education, the connections they had forged in their student days, the foreign trips, their opportunities to read widely, the visits to museums, concert halls, theatres and opera houses from an early age, even the simple day-to-day cultural refinement when they conversed at home. Hamsun could never hope to emulate the unsurpassable elegance that emanated from them whatever the circumstances. It was a self-confidence instilled from birth.

Hamsun realised that if he was ever going to outdo these young men he had to write like nobody had ever done before. His writing would have to scale new heights. Rapturous visions came to him of how his work would spark such excitement that it would illuminate the skies above him, and how as the crowd's cheers swelled to ever greater heights he would slip away, only to reappear, bearing yet another masterpiece aloft, while his wide-eyed public marvelled, 'Who is this man?'

As winter approached he fantasised about all the incredible things that might happen – if he survived. He was convinced he possessed exceptional talents. Writing to a friend, he confided: 'nothing is beyond my comprehension. And things other people struggle with, theories and rules and figures, I grasp in a flash – things just seem to reveal themselves to me. It is these flashes that occasionally give me a premonition of the future.'[33]

Doubled up with violent coughing fits, Hamsun was rarely able to forget his physical state, and it became increasingly difficult to maintain the division between author and subject. The result was a short story about a dying man who tries to convince himself of the absurdity of clinging so tightly to this bitter satire called life.

Just before Christmas 1884, the editor of the newspaper *Dagbladet*, Lars Holst, wrote to Hamsun to tell him he would be printing his short story 'A Fragment of Life' and praising his talent. Hamsun was ecstatic.[34] Was he finally on the verge of a breakthrough? Were the editors, publishers, chattering classes and literati at this moment pondering the real identity of the 'unknown author' to whom this piece was credited? It was unthinkable to stay holed up in the mountains when he was on the brink of fame. Hamsun travelled post-haste to Oslo.

Only to discover that nothing had changed.

Hamsun had experienced many a dismal Christmas, but that of 1884 was the most desolate of all. The city air was damaging to his lungs, and he had left himself without funds to travel back to Valdres since he had been certain Holst would pay him for more work. Eventually Hamsun had no choice but to swallow his pride and seek financial assistance from some of the people who had helped him during his last stay in the capital.

Now, he was doubly determined to show his benefactors that he could write, despite the fact he lacked the advantages of their background.

In the short story that he was currently working on, Hamsun had given the central character a happy, wealthy childhood home and a loving mother, a woman who resembled the mother of Nikolai Frøisland, the matchstick factory director. Fru Frøisland had been so taken by the aspiring writer that she had been among those who had lent him money for his trip to America. In one letter Hamsun unburdened his heart to Nikolai Frøisland: 'Hello to you – and to your mother! My goodness, what a woman! If only I had had such a mother, Nikolai, my talents, which were partly killed off by my upbringing, would have made me into something exceptional. I am sure of it.'[35]

Hamsun seemed to attract mother-figures. Perhaps he courted them. The widow Kari Frydenlund, who ran the hotel and coaching inn in Valdres where he was staying, was another such. It was here that the twenty-five-year old now attempted to write and survive the spring that the doctors had warned might be his last.

He was halfway through his twenty-sixth year when, at the beginning of 1885, he began to sign letters with the name by which he would one day be internationally known: Knut Hamsun. With the fear of death gradually receding, and writing as he had never done before, his new name was his and his alone, free of association or attachment to any particular place: a name to be filled with his own genius.

For the whole autumn of 1885, interrupted only by occasional article writing, Hamsun worked flat out on a novel that he hoped would change his life. By New Year, he was burned out once more. His nerves were frayed and he was rocked by depression. His thoughts were occupied again with his childhood and all that seemed beyond his reach. Once more he confided his despair to his friend Nikolai Frøisland: 'You spoke with your mother, what did she say about me? God help me! What a life to be born into. And what an upbringing – one that never brought the slightest order to the disorderliness of my soul! So I am gripped by reckless impulses, ill-conceived actions, and then I am left with the most earth-shattering regret. But then it's too late. I have had to educate myself step by step: I have had to scramble my way up in life, rather than walking. Which is why one is left with so many regrets. And then my head bursts with ideas of how to mend my wrongs, to meet some of my obligations, but making any of these ideas into a reality goes so painfully slowly.'[36]

Now that his work was populated with urbanites rather than the farming communities he was so familiar with, Hamsun was continually confronted with everything he was not. He continued in his letter to Frøisland: 'In fact my book is intended to be about bohemians; about the tragedy of people going to the dogs – and it is imperative I have some sort of grasp of my material. One day I see the whole picture, I feel full of courage, knowledge-able, as though I have my finger on the pulse of my subject; the next I feel downhearted again over my ineptitude, and I work in vain, I work for dear life.'

An Undiscovered Genius

As the spring of 1886 approached, the twenty-six-year-old Hamsun again ran out of money. He was also growing restless; he had been living in the mountain valley for more than twelve months. Occasionally he had given lectures to the inhabitants of Valdres about the authors he had discovered recently: Balzac, Flaubert, Hugo and Zola, as well as Bjørnson and Ibsen. It had been suggested to him that he tour these lectures, and to this end he prepared two new talks, on the Norwegian poet Alexander Kielland and the Swedish playwright August Strindberg.

His tour began promisingly on Saturday, 8 May 1886 at a school in the tiny settlement in the mountain valley. Turnout was good. His next venue was Gjøvik, near Mjøsa, where he had been a roadworker five years earlier. Only five people turned up. Hamsun attracted pitiful audiences in three villages around the Oslo Fjord before giving up.

He took himself to Oslo and tried to hide away.

For nearly eight years, Hamsun had been writing and rewriting innumerable versions of the novel he hoped would change his fortunes. Thus far, he had not made the slightest dent on the public consciousness. But despite adversity, Hamsun had not lost his gritty sense of humour. He described himself as a 'young genius with a name so unknown that not one single editor knows how to spell it correctly; a name that nobody remembers having read, and one of the worst names in the world to make famous'. With few omissions, but with some blatant exaggerations – having taken a close look at Mark Twain's technique – he wrote 'On Tour', a short story based on the experiences of his own disastrous lecture tour.[37]

Hamsun was taking his final, decisive literary step forward. He would no longer need or use fictional characters as screens to hide behind or mirrors in which to reflect himself. He was in the process of developing a technique that allowed him to give free rein to the whole of his own contradictory and highly strung personality. His was a technique distinguished by fracturing the first-person narrator into several voices placed in peculiar dialogue with each other, alternately observing, reflecting and commenting on each other. Other characteristics of his writing now included the impulsiveness of his characters, the richness of their thought processes, abrupt mood swings, explosions of emotion and, creeping between the narrative voices, a self-effacing irony that left no room for self-pity.

Early that summer in Oslo, the twenty-seven-year-old Hamsun experienced moments of pure elation as he realised he was on the point of an extraordinary artistic breakthrough. But the unique qualities that were already germinating in 'On Tour' still failed to receive recognition. Yet it was these qualities that would soon propel his novel into the limelight and make *Hunger* world-famous.

After several refusals from newspapers, Hamsun approached the author Arne Garborg with 'On Tour'. Eight years his senior, Garborg was one of the most respected young writers in Norway. He promised to read Hamsun's short story, but not for a few days. Hamsun, at the end of his tether, was deeply offended; his behaviour necessitated an apology to Garborg the next day: 'For almost five years now I have been met with "come back in a day or two" – for five years. So I could not take more yesterday.'[38]

Hamsun described to Garborg his pride at having replaced hackneyed phrases with fresh expressions, and thus how dispirited he had felt when manuscripts were returned with editors' corrections. One of them, for example, had told him it was impossible to write 'the filthy wind'.

Hamsun appealed directly to the older writer, whose opinion he must have deeply valued, and laid his head on the block: 'I have come to you for a *final* answer. And you must give it to me. I can see how dangerous it is to pursue this occupation for which I bear such a passion, for anything more than pleasure. If you say that I should stop, then I shall – I shall stop.'

Garborg did not go that far, though he did find the style of 'On Tour' outlandish. He suggested Hamsun had imitated the works of Dostoevsky and other Russian authors. Hamsun's first reaction was to protest, and then to feel wounded. But it soon dawned on him what a wonderful, if unintentional, compliment Garborg had paid him: Hamsun was being compared to the Russians – without ever having read them.

But the full-length novel he was working on refused to take shape. Hamsun found his waves of inspiration dried up too quickly and did not carry him the distance.

Late in the summer months, when newspaper editors were finding themselves short of material, *Dagbladet* printed 'On Tour'. Still the reaction Hamsun was hoping for failed to materialise. Nobody hailed the arrival of a new literary genius. The few who commented at all wondered how he could be so recklessly self-revelatory.

In rural communities, it takes time to climb or fall, a lifetime or even several generations; in the city, it can take just days or weeks. In the summer of 1886, after exerting himself beyond all limits, Hamsun attempted a breakthrough in the capital for the third time, but it was still not sufficient. Nothing, he complained, was ever good enough for these city folk. The sense of there being a dreadful remorselessness to his life set in. Hamsun was spiralling downwards, yet even now he did not stop writing.

Hamsun had just passed his twenty-seventh birthday. He could no longer afford his rent, was registered homeless and given a bunk in a cell in the police station. It was scarcely possible to sink lower. He persisted in his writing, but knew that he had come to the end of the road. He would not be able to continue with his work in Oslo.

On 19 August 1886, Hamsun boarded the *Geisir*, bound once more for America. Feverish, drenched with sweat and extremely weak, he gazed back towards land and bade farewell to the capital city that had never welcomed him, where the lights shone so brightly from the windows of its many homes.

Having already visited America two and a half years previously filled with hope, this time Hamsun was under no illusions that the Norwegian immigrant community, or for that matter anyone in the New World, wanted his writings. But then again, neither did anyone in Norway.

He travelled to Chicago, but did not go further inland as he had done before. He had no intention of returning to Norway until he had made enough money to pay off all his debts as well as some to put aside. Furthermore, he was intent on having the book, which he felt sure would change his life, finished and stowed in his suitcase. 'Yes,' he told a friend, 'we shall most probably meet again. I will not give up my dream to have my book completed one day.'[39]

Wrestling with thoughts of this unfinished novel, and of his pawned collection of books back in Valdres which he feared in his absence might be sold, he spent his days lugging railway sleepers, cement and boxes of outsized bolts. Chicago's city railway was in need of continuous expansion. Hamsun worked like a pack-horse in 40°C heat for $1.75 a day. He kept his spirits up with the thought of improving his circumstances, working as a reserve conductor on the cable cars, which would earn him $50 to $60 a month, and from there progressing to a permanent job earning perhaps $25 a week.

Hamsun had to wait longer than he would have liked, but eventually got a job as a conductor – although initially it was only on the horse-drawn streetcar, a route that was being discontinued as a part of the modernisation of Chicago.

Christmas came. He worked nights and, just as he had done when super-vising the road construction in Norway, insulated his clothes with layers of newspaper. The horses trotted along slowly enough for him to see the street signs in time to call them out to the passengers. Tempted by higher wages, however, he applied to be transferred to the Cottage Line, on the newer, faster cable trams that ran through one of the nicest areas of the city.

He did not keep his job for long.

Street signs had to be deciphered. Stops had to be announced, and this sometimes meant yelling something out to his passengers even when, in the fog and dark, he was unsure where they really were. He frequently made mistakes: being a conductor proved difficult for a man whose eyesight had already been weakened by years of reading and writing in poor light, and whose concentra-tion was less than reliable.

Hamsun's meagre savings soon ran out. Having read somewhere about Chicago's uncrowned king of the meatpacking industry, Philip Armour, Hamsun located the offices and handed a begging letter to an employee to pass on to the boss. Surprisingly the office clerk soon returned, bringing him the $25 he had requested and a note from Armour saying his letter was well worth it. Hamsun spent the money on a train ticket to Minneapolis, and he was soon looking for employment again.

It was a gruelling time for Hamsun, as he explained in a letter to Janson. He took a succession of trains across the prairie lands to different towns looking for jobs on farms and the railways, but found nothing. He carried his belongings in a bag on his shoulder and slept in disused boxcars, meeting and travelling with other men. It was in a town called Casselton, Dakota, in an abandoned wagon, that Hamsun spent Independence Day: 'Then came the 4th of July. We – there were three of us – celebrated as best we could with a bottle of beer and a large rye loaf. On the 5th, we broke camp and tramped 36 miles inland, found some work on a so-called "bonanza farm", but were chased away two days later because we refused to put up with being bawled at. So back down to Casselton again, and then another 6 miles out, where we got more work and where we are staying now.'[40]

For three months Hamsun worked on one of the gigantic farms owned by city-based shareholders. He had of course grown up on a smallholding and worked on a number of modest farms back in Norway, where it was only through day-to-day toil and seasonal labour surges that families and communities survived the winter. People shared a general mistrust of machinery. In America, he saw how independent farmers were being ousted by investors who employed foremen to manage the farms, and presided over their enormous ranches from their boardrooms in Chicago and New York. Farming and capitalism: surely it was impossible, against nature. The earth should be farmed to sustain people's lives, not to drive up the price of shares. Now, great iron monsters could plough twenty-two furrows at a time, and took fifteen minutes to thresh an area that in Norway would have taken a week by hand. The prairies were full of machines. There was no arguing with them. They were inheriting the earth.

Big business and its foremen had stripped the individual of almost all responsibility. Any reciprocal dependence had been blown apart. Life was reduced to a question of pay, and it seemed to Hamsun that the layabouts were reaping the rewards. Those who tried to maintain their dignity were ground down. In due course he would write about these people – the silk shirt-wearing Evans, Huntley with his unfaithful wife, the cook Polly who served her enemy his own finger – and of course Hamsun himself.

A Sense of Clarity

Hamsun was growing increasingly critical of American society.

He followed very closely the case of the so-called Chicago Anarchists, which reached its climax in 1887. A month before Hamsun had begun his miserable career on the streetcars in 1886, seven workers had been condemned to death for their part in the Haymarket Affair. The growing workers' movement had organised action across the USA demanding an eight-hour working day. Police in Chicago had shot at a group of striking workers, killing some of them. The following day at a protest meeting a bomb had been thrown, and police had fired shots into the crowd; a number of protesters were left dead and many policemen injured. Only one of the men who went on trial had actually been present when the bomb had exploded, and he had been on the speakers' podium. Nonetheless, four of the Anarchists were hanged on 11 November 1887.

Hamsun was one of the few citizens of Minneapolis who, that Friday, showed their solidarity with the stigmatised Left in their disgust for the authorities; he fastened a black ribbon to his buttonhole. The admiration for America's democracy that Hamsun had expressed in articles he had touted to Oslo's newspapers three years previously had been replaced by a deepening distrust of what he would soon term the despotism of democratic freedom.

When he was in company, Hamsun railed against what he called the 'democratic mob' of the New World, but in solitary moments his attention was focused on the writers of the Old. Despite the upheavals of constant relocations in Minneapolis, at the beginning of 1888 Hamsun was preparing for a new eleven-lecture series which he planned to give on modern European literature. For the first time, Hamsun consolidated his fragmentary reading of a dozen years, supplemented with books borrowed from the city's central library, into coherent lines of thought. Thus, during these few weeks, the direction of his own writing grew even clearer to him.

The lectures focused on one writer after another. Starting with Balzac, whose writing was, Hamsun emphasised, different from that of any writer before him, he moved on to Flaubert, who he asserted provided a link between Balzac and Zola, the master of darkness. He then considered the four best-known contemporary Norwegian writers: Bjørnstjerne Bjørnson, Jonas Lie, Alexander Kielland and Henrik Ibsen. Hamsun described Bjørnson as a standard-bearer for ideas, but criticised him for being overly moralistic. Lie, on the other hand, was primarily a writer about marriage, not one of the greats, but admittedly an important elder. Kielland was caught between ethics and aesthetics, while Ibsen was a sceptic with too great a fondness for riddles. Moving on to the Swedish playwright August Strindberg, Hamsun described him as having an occult insight in his language. Hamsun rounded off with two additional lectures about literary criticism and Impressionism, a style that, according to him, required the writer to turn psychologist, reaching truth through uncompromising subjectivity.

For years Hamsun had described himself as a literary man, but only now was this becoming a reality, as much to himself as to the wider public. His lectures had to be moved to a larger hall than originally planned, and then to an even larger venue. A journalist friend reported on the whole series. Suddenly his praises were being sung across the city, week after week.

Some of his audience commented on the contrast between the speaker's appearance and his rarefied aesthetic ideals: 'He wears rough shoes on his feet with thick grey woollen socks that hardly reach his short, tight and very worn trousers. His shirt, like his trousers, is also short and tight, and well buttoned-up. His lorgnette is attached to an unusually long, rough, dark blue cord.'[41]

Hamsun was clearly pushing himself to his limits. Between lectures his friends often found him cold, hungry, confused and in a state of exhaustion. Yet he would still triumphantly present them with newly minted pages for the novel that he still insisted would change everything. To one acquaintance he exclaimed that he had been chosen to tell the world something new, and in a new way.

Nights were spent hard at work too, and his nerves were being subjected to colossal strain. 'It's hell. [...] Here I am, with a body that could topple mountains, and muscles like cable rope, and yet, God damn it, my nerves are as sheer and delicate as gossamer!' He recognised that his heightened state was creating a 'fanatical self-criticism' in him that sometimes caused him to reject ideas and passages 'that, God strike me down, were genuine *finds*'.[42]

But the texts that emerged from this harrowing process were unlike anything he had written before.

The spring of 1888 brought Hamsun great gains in artistic clarity. His eleven lectures made no mention of his own artistic evolution and journey – this was not their purpose. But in preparing for them, he began to map out his own literary inheritance. Bjørnson's work had demonstrated the effectiveness of dismantling traditional sentence structures. Strindberg had confirmed to him that one could not simply study to be a writer, but had to wage a war in which one's sanity was at stake. Mark Twain had awoken him to the literary potential of colloquialisms and the colourful exaggerations that came from the oral traditions of his native Nordland. Dostoevsky had shown him that the imbalance of the mind is the writer's principal tool, and that great art could emerge from the secret struggles between pride and feelings of inferiority.

Now he felt he could and indeed must return to Europe with a manuscript he was sure of completing. In one lecture he took an arrogant farewell of America: 'I understand that Kristofer Janson is writing a book called *Mysteries of Minneapolis*. I have not read this book, but judging by its title I would rather swallow an umbrella than read it!'[43]

For some artists, the ore of their talent lies in a shallow seam; life needs merely to scratch the surface to reveal it. For others, it has to be blasted from deep shafts – a painful, protracted task that can be undertaken only by the artist himself, and that is accomplished only at great risk. Knut Hamsun was just such an artist, and he knew it. For twelve years he had spent every spare minute writing and, as he stood on the deck of the *Thingvalla* on 30 June 1888, watching the harbour workers cast off the great ropes of the ship that would carry him back to Europe, he could imagine that the riches within him were almost in reach.

The ship's first port of call was Oslo, but Hamsun did not go ashore. If he had, it is not altogether certain that he would have become the writer that was soon to emerge. Oslo's narrow-minded cultural elite had already forced him to flee twice. The city was not kind to revolutionary artists; fellow Norwegians Henrik Ibsen and Edvard Munch had also felt compelled to leave their native land to find the freedom necessary for their art. After almost three weeks at sea, Hamsun finally disembarked in Copenhagen – gateway to a European world that he would now conquer.

The Fractional Workings of the Soul

It was 17 July 1888, the height of summer in Copenhagen.

Hamsun pawned his raincoat for 6 kroner, rented a room for 5 kroner a month in the workers' quarter of Nørrebro, and began making plans for launching his literary career. He felt time was running out; three weeks after reaching Copenhagen it would be his twenty-ninth birthday. He resolved to tell people he was a year younger than he was; the circles he was hoping to mix in were up to ten years younger than him in any case.

Gaining acceptance into the literary circles of Scandinavia's cultural centre, particularly the youthful cliques, was Hamsun's first step. He knew where to find them. At Janson's house he had come across a new literary journal called *Ny Jord*, which had been launched at the start of that year and was already attracting a host of young writers.

His second step would be to make contact with the capital's literary elite. He had followed events well enough to know that the Brandes brothers had secured a reputation as the gatekeepers of the literary world. The forty-six-year-old Georg had recently triggered a huge debate with his lecture tour on Nietzsche. Edvard, his junior by five years, was an author, politician and editor of the newspaper *Politiken*.

The third step in his plan was to find a publisher for the manuscript that was on the verge of completion.

One August day, Carl Behrens, the twenty-one-year-old editor of *Ny Jord*, arrived at the offices of the journal's publisher, P. Hauberg & Co. The secretary told him that a man had already attempted to see him several times, and was now waiting for him. It was Hamsun, proffering an article on Kristofer Janson in exchange for cash. Usually Behrens cited *Ny Jord*'s tight finances as the reason he could offer contributors no payment, or at best a nominal sum. But the Norwegian who confronted him now was clearly of humbler means than the young middle-class men whom Behrens usually dealt with, and he offered Hamsun a respectable fee.

The article certainly fulfilled the literary journal's declared aim: agitation. Hamsun's premise was that Janson was more educationalist than author, having sacrificed the quality of his writing for the sake of making it accessible to the ordinary man. The importance of language as an artistic object in itself was a subject upon which Hamsun would wax lyrical throughout his whole career. Later, the astounded son of a consul described how this Norwegian had come with his rough worker's hands, calling for a new, highly aesthetic writing: 'Language must possess all the scales of music. The writer must always, unfailingly, use a word that pulsates, that conveys a thing, that can wound the soul so it yelps.'[44] A writer must sense the hidden power of words, 'give his language sudden effects. It should have a hectic, tormented energy that rushes through one like a wind, it should possess hidden intoxicating tenderness that nestles into the senses, it should be raucous like a sailor's song in a storm, or sigh with the intensity of a person overcome with tears.'

When Hamsun told Behrens that he had lived in Janson's house in America, the young editor saw this as a golden opportunity to conduct a literary patricide in his columns. It was in step with the journal's questioning and over-turning of conventional writings and attitudes. Behrens introduced his new find to his circle of friends who included writers such as Sophus Claussen, Johannes Jørgensen, Sophus Michaëlis, Viggo Stuckenberg and Valdemar Vedel – writers whose main thrust was to challenge the literary and political bastions of their parents' generation.

Copenhagen was proving kind to Knut Hamsun, and for the first time he entered a highly literary and intellectual milieu: 'How pleasant this country is for me. I assure you, its whole being, the pattern of life here is in absolute harmony with my spirit, my nature! This is Europe, and I am a European, thank the Lord! People have the time to live here – they take time to do so – they take the time to stand at a bookshop window and read the titles – and they're not only bookworms like myself', he reported back to his Minneapolis clique.[45]

Indeed, the book that he was working on would be imbued with this European spirit. It was very unNorwegian, he said: 'I no longer feel or think like a Norwegian, but like a European. Maybe that is a weakness in me, but my life has been so very multifarious.'[46]

Hamsun spent the autumn after his twenty-ninth birthday reading, listening to and learning from his new intellectual sparring companions. Behrens lent him a copy of Georg Brandes's study of literary history. Hamsun promoted himself as the champion of two main causes: originality of language and the need for the inner lives of characters to be drawn in greater depth.

Psychology, particularly the subconscious, neuroses and pathological states, was a new area of scientific enquiry and the latest literary vogue, capturing the interest of writers and literary critics across Europe. Like others in the circle, Hamsun had read a good deal in the press about these subjects and was fascinated by them. He must have mulled over his mother's appalling breakdown for some time; over the last few years he had noticed that he seemed to have inherited her nervous disposition. But with his diverse life experiences, wouldn't it manifest itself differently in him? Was the fragility of his nerves proof of his being a more highly developed human being? And that being so, should he abandon rationality and reason in favour of instinct and the subconscious? Dostoevsky, whose works Hamsun had read in America, allowed his characters to challenge reason. Had Hamsun not already begun to do the same?

Of the writers Hamsun now met, Valdemar Vedel was the most systematic in his approach to the new psychological writing. The twenty-three-year old was working on a doctoral thesis on the subject of the writers and critics of the Danish Golden Age, and had made his manifesto public. The modern, complex psyche had ceased to move in great waves of simple emotions like love, hate, sorrow, anger and joy. The voices that surfaced in us now were profoundly richer, stranger and infinitely more varied. The new literature had therefore to enter a pact with this modern life of the psyche, and a precondition of the creation of a psychological literature was, Vedel maintained, above all a strong individual voice.[47]

A precocious, highly schooled son of a government official and a tailor's son with 252 days of village school education, embraced one another.

The *Ny Jord* circle's interest in the psychology of modern city-dwellers was as influential on the twenty-nine-year-old Hamsun as Bjørnson's peasant tales had been on him in his teens. It seemed everything he read and everyone he spoke to helped him formulate a sense of his own identity as a writer. And the more he discovered, the more eager he was to put it to use. 'I feel a desire to create that beats in my breast like a bird, that beats its wings desperately', he wrote ecstatically to his pharmacist friend, Yngvar Laws, in Minneapolis. 'A new spring is bursting, new forces are shooting up – an eternal renewal – a spring morning for every generation! Our time has come!' He was intoxicated with ideas; over and over again he explained his intention to examine the very 'mimosas of thoughts – the delicate fractions of feelings – I want to burrow down into the finest weave of our souls – delicate observations of the fractional workings of the soul'.[48]

Hamsun set aside the manuscript he had brought with him from America. His encounter with the young writers and literati of Copenhagen and their call for a deeper account of the psyche had possibly been the most revelatory experience of his life. He explained to Laws that he wanted to begin a completely new work. 'A longing to begin screams inside me! – I have no time to lose – the devil of creativity gives me no peace! The time is ripe! Surely my book must come now!' he bellowed across the ocean.

He had tried his hand at describing characters different from himself and had never been satisfied with the results. All too often he had felt his own persona stood in the way. Now, books and articles were being published in which Hamsun recognised his own irrationality and split nature, his own strong and sudden impulses which sometimes led to unexpected actions.

'I simply want to present my wild theory of this mathematics of the psyche in a novel!' Hamsun continued in his letter to Laws. 'This is what I long for! I cannot get it out of my mind! My book! – My book! About these delicate manifestations. I want to unearth the spirit's most extreme manifestations – I want to let them listen to the breath of the mimosa – each word like dazzling white wings – a spoken mirror of movement.'

Hamsun's elation was tempered by financial anxiety. Necessity forced him now to pawn his carpetbag with its numerous red and green railway labels charting his travels in Norway and America. As he walked away from the shop, he felt as though the bag sat watching him go like a faithful pet. But he felt gloriously, emphatically ready to write an entire library of psychology-driven books – it was merely a matter of continuing where he had left off.

Sitting in his attic room at 18 Sankt Hansgade, Copenhagen, in the autumn of 1888, he wrote the words that would eventually become the opening lines of *Hunger*, words that would make him famous: 'It was at that time I wandered starving through the streets of Kristiania [Oslo], that strange city which no one leaves without being marked by it.'[49] In this work, Hamsun was determined to show his readers more than the narrow middle-class world of Ibsen's *A Doll's House*.

His narrator was, like himself, a writer who had been working on yet another article for a magazine and, like himself, was living hand to mouth: 'I was hungry, very hungry; sadly my 10 kroner had lasted all too short a time; two, almost three days had passed since I'd eaten anything and I felt faint, slightly exhausted from guiding my pencil.' Sitting on a bench, this character makes a little paper cornet out of a clean page, folding it at the top so that it seems to contain something, and after first pretending to himself that it is filled with coins, he fools a police constable into picking it up. 'I laughed and laughed and slapped my knees, laughed like a lunatic. And not a sound issued from my throat, my laughter was frenzied and mute, with the passion of tears.' The constable shakes him back to the despair of still being alive:

Here I was with a better head than anyone in the country, and a pair of fists which, God help me, could grind a porter into a pulp, and I was starving myself into freakishness, right here in the middle of Kristiania! Was there any rhyme or reason to this? I had slaved in the harness and toiled day and night, like a mare carrying a pastor; I had read 'til my eyes popped out of my skull, and starved all reason from my brain – what the hell did I have to show for it? Even the prostitutes begged God to save them from the sight of me!

Sobbing and swearing, he head-butts a lamppost, drives his fingernails into the backs of his hands, bites his own tongue from sheer madness, and laughs at the pain:

> Yes, but what should I do, I say to myself. I stamp on the pavement again and again, repeating: What shall I do? – A gentleman walks past and remarks, with a smile:
> 'You'd better go and get yourself locked up.'
> I watched him walk away. He was one of our famous lady-doctors, known as 'the duke'. Even he didn't understand my condition, a man I recognised and whose hand I had once shaken. I fell silent. Locked up? Yes, he was right; I was crazy. I felt insanity in my blood, felt it chase through my brain.

'Psychological writing': Paul Bourget and the Goncourt brothers, Dostoevsky, Ola Hansson and Valdemar Vedel could call it what they wanted. Who knew more about the troubled modern mind than Knut Hamsun? And who had worked harder to find a more precise language in which to describe it?

Having completed what would soon be known as 'the *Hunger* fragment', Hamsun paced the streets around where Georg Brandes lived, not daring to make himself known. On the third day he gave up. He decided instead to seek out Brandes's brother, Edvard, an author himself and editor of *Politiken*. The latter promised to read the fragment for the following day. As Hamsun left the editor's office, memories of the last time he had left a manuscript behind in Copenhagen, nine years earlier, must have come flooding back.

Frederik Hegel had not even bothered to turn up on that dreadful winter's afternoon. Edvard Brandes, however, was there the next day as promised.

The Moment of Triumph

'You have a great future ahead of you!'[50]

Edvard Brandes finally gave Knut Hamsun the acknowledgement he had been waiting for for nearly ten years.

However, the piece that Hamsun called 'Hunger' was, Brandes explained, too long to be printed in two parts and too short to be serialised in *Politiken*. In any case, the excited newspaper editor felt Hamsun's text deserved an altogether different fate than to be chopped to pieces for the daily papers.

Brandes contacted his publisher, Gustav Philipsen, urging him to secure Hamsun's story for the journal *Tilskueren*, which he also owned. Brandes also recommended that he pay Hamsun an advance to enable him to complete the full-length novel, to be published by P.G. Philipsens Forlag the following year. Philipsen trusted Brandes's opinion wholeheartedly, and immediately made contact with the Norwegian author. They met in October 1888. This time it was Hamsun who was declining an offer; he had already given the fragment to *Ny Jord* and his friend Carl Behrens. Philipsen was not to be dissuaded, however. What did Hamsun require as an advance for his book? One hundred, 200, 300 kroner? More?

The director of a reputable Danish publishing house was offering Hamsun an advance without even seeing the extract. Hamsun was so taken aback that initially he declined, and then mumbled that 100 kroner would suffice.

As the bewilderment and numbness wore off, Hamsun's eyes lit upon a vellum-bound book lying on the table between them. He pictured what it might be like to have his novel presented so extravagantly, and found himself sharing his thoughts with Philipsen: Oh, how he would love to write a book that would be bound like that! To sit in a deep chair in a room with dark-green wallpaper and no pictures on the walls, but a large silk paper shade over the lamp, together with some ten people, reading aloud from his luxurious volume. The room would be so hushed that every member of the rapt audience could hear the mimosa whispering within them.[51]

Philipsen remarked on the importance of keeping one's audience in mind when writing in order to reach the largest readership. Hamsun retorted that he did not intend to write for the masses.

There had been times when Hamsun had gone for days on end without a morsel to eat. There had been times when he had gnawed ravenously on matchsticks. Recently it had grown bitterly cold; there was no fireplace in the attic he was renting, and he had pawned all his winter clothes. A tiny window in the roof was his only source of daylight, and that had been dwindling rapidly as September moved into October. Hunger, biting cold, gloom and the pressures of writing were tearing at his nerves.[52]

Nevertheless, flaunting the same poor man's pride as his primary character in *Hunger*, Hamsun assured Philipsen that 100 kroner would be quite sufficient and he had no need for more.

The *Hunger* fragment was to be published anonymously in *Ny Jord* in November 1888, signed by an 'unknown author'. On the day it reached its hundred or so subscribers, the celebrity Danish-Norwegian literary couple Amalie and Erik Skram were holding a party at their home. Among the guests were the writer Herman Bang and his Norwegian colleague Gunnar Heiberg. After dinner, the assembled group called for some readings. One of the guests had come across a piece in *Ny Jord* that had made a strong impression on him. Since the hostess and several of the guests were Norwegian, and the piece was set in Oslo, it seemed doubly appropriate to have a reading of 'Hunger'.[53]

The author and playwright Gunnar Heiberg cleared his throat and began. An hour later he finished.

Nobody was in any doubt: Scandinavia had a new author. A queue formed before Amalie Skram's desk of literary guests, all eager to express in writing how deeply affected they were by the words they had heard.

The author must be informed immediately. But who was he?

Amalie and Erik Skram knew *Ny Jord*'s editor, Carl Behrens, personally. Amalie's persistence soon wore him down and he revealed the name of the author to them. No longer anonymous, Hamsun soon received a letter from the Skrams and sent them his thanks in return: 'it made me so happy, it was so unexpected – and unexpectedly joyous! Perhaps things will brighten up now. I have been a little held back in my efforts, I am twenty-eight years old and have received a few knocks, but have lost neither strength nor desire.'[54]

Within a week of its publication the thousand copies of *Ny Jord* had sold out. Behrens had to print more; it had been years since anything like this had happened. Here, in Scandinavia's cultural epicentre, anybody who wanted to be anybody had to read Hamsun's piece. Its style as well as its subject matter, which was presumed to be the author's own reckless self-revelation, were both shocking and fascinating.

The hysteria spread quickly to Norway. Olaf Thommessen, the editor of the Norwegian newspaper *Verdens Gang*, commented that this anonymous author's story 'deserves our attention as evidence of a very unusual literary talent, with an outstanding capacity for description and acute powers of observation. If this is a new author who has appeared, then without doubt we have another gifted writer.' Ironically, Thommessen did not realise that he had himself turned down a great deal of this gifted writer's work in the past.

In Copenhagen, Hamsun made every effort to stop his name from being leaked. He pleaded with the Skrams not to give him away but, inevitably, a few days later he was outed by the Norwegian newspaper *Dagbladet*. Not one of the editors of the newspapers or journals in Norway had guessed that the unknown writer was Knut Hamsun, despite the fact that all of them had rejected texts that bore an enormous stylistic resemblance to the extraordinary piece in the Danish journal.

All at once the scores of editors, professors and publishers in Oslo who had been turning Hamsun away for the last eight years began to quarrel over who had spotted his talent first. Their boasts eventually reached him, and he decided to exploit this new interest. He chose his target carefully.

On 2 December 1888, less than two weeks after the furore had broken out, Hamsun wrote to Johan Sørensen, publisher of *Library for the Thousand Homes*, the most popular and widely read series of affordable novels in Norway. That morning another article had appeared in the Danish newspaper *Morgenbladet*, reporting that there was almost as much excitement in Oslo about Hamsun's short story as there was over the publication of Ibsen's latest play, *The Lady from the Sea*. According to the article, 'Hunger' had revealed how poorly Norway nurtured its young talent: 'Still, a generation after Ibsen's youth, a talent of Dostoevsky's calibre has nearly starved to death on the streets of Kristiania.'[55]

He was still too short of money, Hamsun explained in his letter to Sørensen, to finish the three pieces that would complete his book. 'I was forced to go to print with the section that has gone public. [. . .] I can't work well, not properly. I sit here in an attic, with the wind blowing though the walls, I have no wood burner, almost no light, only one small window in the roof. I can't even go out now since it's turned so cold, my clothing's inadequate.'[56]

He could not lie to the Norwegian publisher outright, so admitted that he had signed a contract with P.G. Philipsens Forlag for *Hunger* when it was completed. But he tantalised Sørensen with the promise of another book, 'a novel that I feel people will read, I am sure of it. But I am not in a position to work on it without interruption, *Hunger* must be finished first.'

Sørensen promptly sent him 200 kroner. It was enough to buy a thousand cheap meals, or to pay the rent on his attic for nearly four years. The man who had published the majority of the great contemporary authors in his series described 'Hunger' as a masterpiece and made Hamsun an offer that must have filled him with joy: Sørensen would guarantee him the same royalties as Ibsen.

That same day, Hamsun sent a long letter in which he repeatedly tried to express his gratitude, but constantly ended up elaborating on the hardships he had endured until now – as well as the extreme frailty of his nerves: 'During the last six weeks, I have had to wrap a kerchief round my left hand while I wrote because I couldn't even bear the sensation of my own breath on it; and neither have I been able to strike a match, apart from *under* the table, where I wouldn't see the flare.'[57]

Posturing

It was Advent 1888 in the Danish capital. Dipping straight into his advance, Hamsun released his carpetbag and other possessions from pawn and bought himself several new outfits. He had accepted an invitation to give a lecture at the Students' Union, 'and there will only be intelligent people there, so it's a good thing I don't have to be ashamed of my clothes. The rest is no problem, I'm an old hand up on the lectern', he wrote with some self-assurance to his new prospective publisher in Norway, Sørensen.[58] Hamsun might well have been more circumspect had he been aware of the qualms Kristofer Janson expressed to Edvard Brandes at this time. Impressed as he was by 'Hunger', Janson had little confidence in the opinionated young writer, who according to his observations suffered from the autodidact's classic lack of in-depth knowledge and understanding.

At 9pm on 15 December, a well-turned-out Hamsun mounted the podium. He launched into a derisive attack on America's lack of culture. Admittedly, in two centuries the new lands had reformed Europe's worst scoundrels into upstanding and employed citizens – but he criticised what he saw as their raucous self-congratulation for their own accomplishments, which according to Hamsun drowned everything else out in America. The country had failed to achieve any cultural advancements beyond the din of steam-hammers. Americans used their brash self-satisfaction to cow visiting Europeans. Their literature dealt only with love and gun battles: it was devoid of emotional scope and subtlety. It lagged behind Europe by three developmental phases. Hamsun tore Walt Whitman's almanac poetry to shreds, and made a scathing attack on the Yankee philosopher-guru Ralph Waldo Emerson.[59]

The atmosphere in the hall crackled. This was radical stuff – a slap in the face for all those cultural and political commentators who had lavished such praises on the United States. Long live the Old World! Long live Europe! Long live Copenhagen! Long live the new generation of writers, the spiritual aristocrats!

As soon as the applause had faded, members of the public made their way towards the lectern, Hamsun's Danish publisher Gustav Philipsen among them. Philipsen had shown interest in publishing the lectures, but Hamsun was concerned that the publisher might have got cold feet now that he had heard how controversial his ideas were. Philipsen, however, joined the queue of admirers and, when he eventually reached Hamsun, he reassured the speaker that he was still extremely keen to print the texts.

Everybody wanted a closer look at Knut Hamsun now. They all wanted to know just how eccentric the author of the *Hunger* fragment really was. He rarely disappointed, and anecdotes about him soon proliferated.

Fired up by the attention, Hamsun proceeded to play one publisher against the other. He wrote to Sørensen in Oslo, describing how dejected he had felt when Gustav Philipsen had talked of accommodating the masses. It would, Hamsun told Sørensen, go against the grain to write even one such line; he would never simplify the psychology of his work. He promised Sørensen that as soon as Philipsen had had his two books from him, he would transfer to his publishing house in Norway.[60]

Two days before Christmas, Hamsun was able to write a letter thanking Sørensen for a further 200 kroner.

Hamsun finally had the opportunity to see one of Strindberg's works, *Miss Julie*, in performance. The notion that after completing his psychological novel he might write a modern drama of the mind began to take root. He was certainly no stranger to dramatic extremes of temperament, behaviour and emotion, he assured Erik Skram: 'I have smuggled some of them into *Hunger*, and now everybody assumes "Andreas Tangen's" crazed actions are all caused by his starvation. But that's not true. Unfortunately. And people also probably think I'm mad. But I'm damn well not mad!'[61]

Skram was a kind-natured and accommodating man, erudite but rarely didactic, and in conversation inclined to listen rather than impose his opinions. He was fascinated by this Norwegian, twelve years his junior, who was so determined in his struggle to perfect his talents.

Hamsun spent that Christmas at the home of the Skrams. At one point the conversation turned to his severe illness at the Jansons' four years earlier, when he had seriously contemplated death. The Skrams wanted to know what feelings had been aroused in him by the prospect of dying. Hamsun's conversation became disjointed. Thoughts of Drude made him tongue-tied and, as Amalie knew Drude, Hamsun omitted a great deal. He could not talk openly about the stirrings that the scent of death had provoked in him.

Later that night back in his room, Hamsun fell into a peculiar mood. The next day he awoke with the taste of blood in his mouth. A surge of inspiration swept over him, so overwhelming that he wrote ten pages in just a few hours. It was a creative epiphany. Returning to reality, he found he had written some 'marvellously useful things here and there. Wordings and sentences I wouldn't sell for my life', he reported to Erik Skram ecstatically.[62] Hamsun described feeling the 'interconnectedness of my nerves with the universe, the elements'.

In this letter Hamsun also shared his secret with Skram: his uncontrollable desire in Drude Janson's house. How she had given him the opportunity to sin under her roof, and how he had refused her; and how, if she had not offered herself and he had been reduced to begging, he dared not imagine what would have happened.

For years Hamsun had held women at a distance but that had not stopped him fantasising about them. Now, single and married women alike were flocking round him. He could make them laugh and make them marvel, holding forth with lofty speeches or passing them little notes meant for their eyes alone. Many promised to come to his next lecture shortly after New Year.

Hamsun's tendency towards exaggeration – and at times downright fantasy – was applauded around Copenhagen's café tables, where the robust, bustling atmosphere called for such dramatic posturing. But in the salons of the cultural elite Hamsun often met with raised eyebrows. People soon discovered that this Norwegian's reading was far more inconsistent, and the gaps in his education far greater and more numerous, than he gave pretence to. A sharp-witted opponent could easily expose his weaknesses and back him into a corner. Hamsun learned to dread the discussion sessions that followed lectures.

On 12 January 1889, Knut Hamsun held his second lecture on America in the Students' Union. Georg Brandes's presence must have made the man on the podium even more nervous. The renowned critic and lecturer had already registered Hamsun's academic deficiencies, and had even murmured a little poisonously about the fuss that was being made of this bandy-legged Norwegian. Nonetheless, he wanted to take a closer look at this young man for himself.

As the applause died down, Brandes took to the floor and gave a speech of thanks, 'which was the warmest recognition I could ever wish for. Were I to prove worthy of just half his praises, then I would be great indeed', Hamsun boasted in a letter to a journalist friend in Minneapolis the following day.[63] Hamsun also thanked Brandes: 'If I could be even a little deserving of your good will, of a nod of recognition, I will never regret that it took so many hard days to achieve.'[64]

The ensuing relationship between the two men worked tolerably well so long as the apprentice knew his place and was willing to learn. Brandes belonged to Copenhagen's Jewish community. Circumstances had led him to forge a path as a freelance intellectual, outside the walls of that city's academia. Perhaps Knut Hamsun and Georg Brandes recognised something of the exile in each other.

The task of assembling his lectures in book form required more time and effort than Hamsun had expected. He comforted himself with the fact that it would earn him easy money as well as opening readers' eyes to his literary powers. At the same time he was also aware of the controversy his book would attract.

Hamsun tried to give the contents page of *On the Cultural Life of Modern America* a thesis-like appearance, and interspersed scholarly intimations within the text too. As the publication date loomed, Hamsun also furnished his text with a foreword defending his approach: 'Truth is neither two-sided nor objective, truth is selfless subjectivity.'[65] Shielded by this device, Hamsun pulled no punches.

After pouring scorn on America's literature, painting and theatre as well as the general state of its cultural life, he turned to its wider negative impact. As a guest in America, he had felt it impossible to express his opinions in the face of 'the despotism of freedom – a despotism, made all the more intolerable because those that enforce it are a self-satisfied, unintelligent people'. In his urge to criticise, Hamsun failed to mention the works of Mark Twain, whom he still admired. Forgotten, too, was his wide-eyed astonishment at the beautiful buildings and magnificent bridges built by American architects and engineers; now even the finest palaces in Chicago's Michigan Avenue possessed 'no more refinement than a negro's head'.

Neither was the modern American woman to his taste; for the most part she busied herself suffering from nerves, reading *Uncle Tom's Cabin* and taking evening strolls. The American was 'an upstart, who is self-educated in culture and etiquette', Hamsun wrote, without seeming to reflect how many people had passed a similar judgement on him.

There had, he accepted, been signs of a cultural elite in the American South, but the kind of democracy championed in the northern states had led to this budding aristocracy's demise. The Civil War, Hamsun felt, had made the negroes into the masters of the southern plantations, and this he could not accept: 'Negroes are, and always will be, negroes: a primitive human from the tropics, creatures with intestines for brains, rudimentary organs on the white body of society.' Europe should stop applauding the political democracy of the New World and look upon its consequences with dismay: 'Instead of creating a cultural elite, what has been created in America is a stud farm of mulattos.'

Shortly after his arrival in Copenhagen, Hamsun had written to an emigrant friend vehemently denouncing what he saw as the farce of democracy and people's representation.[66] Nine months later he had given birth to a book in which every sentence crackled with antipathy towards this modern New World.

Nietzsche was very much in the air at this time. Brandes had introduced the German philosopher to the Nordic countries in a series of lectures in the spring of 1888, and these had drawn considerable public attention. The journal *Ny Jord* was dedicating large amounts of column space to Nietzsche, and certainly the philosopher's thoughts on the masses, mediocrity and the superman were recurring themes in the discussions between Hamsun and Brandes in early 1889. The final chapter of *On the Cultural Life of Modern America* reveals Hamsun's fascination with Nietzsche's call for the ideal of equality and its inherent slave mentality to be supplanted by a natural morality of the superman.

On the Cultural Life of Modern America came out in 1889; it was almost ten years since Hamsun had held a freshly printed book in his hand.

Despite the furore over the *Hunger* fragment, Hamsun told a friend in April that he was not going to admit publicly to having written the piece: 'It is bad enough to expose oneself as nakedly as I have. And it will be worse in the forthcoming sections. But I imagine it will cause quite a stir when it appears.'[67]

Hamsun frequented popular drinking establishments such as Bernina in the centre of Copenhagen. In fact, it was not until he started socialising with the *Ny Jord* circles that Hamsun had begun to drink alcohol; now he was making up for lost time, and preaching to anyone who cared to listen of a miraculous cure for hangovers – the coffee bean.

He craved attention and spent lavishly to achieve it, growing quite cross if anybody refused his offers of generosity. Some people whispered accusingly that he was simply a social climber trying to ingratiate himself. Some commented on his obvious need to prove himself financially viable after having lived beholden to others for so long. Others wondered why Hamsun always behaved as though he needed to buy his way out of something.

Divine Madness

During the Easter week of 1889, Knut Hamsun returned to Oslo.

It was almost three years since he had been forced to leave his homeland, but now, as he stepped off the train at Østbane Station on Good Friday morning, he was met with a warm reception. The Norwegian publisher Sørensen had invited Hamsun to stay with him in his villa just outside Oslo, where a huge welcoming party was to be held in his honour. Guests included notables from Norway's Parliament, not least the president of the Lower House and several professors from the university. The Left-wing press were represented by both *Dagbladet*'s Lars Holst and *Verdens Gang*'s Olaf Thommessen.

After dinner the guests separated into smaller clusters. Hamsun and his host sat apart from the rest of the group and were left largely undisturbed, particularly as their conversation grew more heated. After several refills of his brandy glass, Hamsun attacked Sørensen for what he called his worship of Bjørnson.

By Easter Sunday, Hamsun was lamenting his plight to his Danish publisher, Philipsen: 'I'm half wrecked. It's hell for my nerves here. A host that's killing me by degrees with his prattle. [. . .] Besides which, the air – I mean the air of life – in which these people live is the reverse of the air I require. You cannot imagine how backward the most prominent people are here at home.'[68]

The editors of the Oslo newspapers and journals were all busily sifting through their rejection piles looking for the articles and short stories that Hamsun had previously sent in. Now, of course, they were deemed to be publishable. The hypocrisy revolted Hamsun: 'People come and tell me to my face that they <u>always</u> knew that something extraordinary would come of Hamsun. [. . .] God, how it revolts me', he complained in the same letter to Philipsen.

It was with almost malevolent delight that he refused these offers of publication. So too all party invitations. Hamsun also declined the offer of accommodation in Oslo made by Sørensen, who still laboured under the misapprehension he would be Hamsun's next publisher. The writer now longed to return to Valdres and the Jotunheimen mountains, so that he might nurse his nerves and continue work on the novel that was to be *Hunger*.

Dagbladet was the first of the Norwegian newspapers to review *On the Cultural Life of Modern America*. In a favourable write-up, Hamsun was praised for his eminent skills of persuasion. But Hamsun's good mood evaporated when the review in the Danish *Politiken* appeared; like many other critics, Edvard Brandes flagged up various mistakes and obvious misinterpretations. Edvard's brother, however, was more generous. Norway's newspaper *Verdens Gang* carried a review by Georg Brandes that bolstered Hamsun's ego and pleased him greatly. Georg suggested that Hamsun's nature had been too sensitive and aristocratic to adjust to America, and that his disillusionment must have been born of his yearning for a smaller, more select community with a liberal-minded and cultivated elite. Norwegian readers would no doubt assume that Georg Brandes had Oslo in mind, but Hamsun understood it differently: it was the glittering literary circle of Copenhagen to which Brandes referred, and to which he was welcoming the newcomer. Brandes concluded firmly that Hamsun was 'a new and exceptional Norwegian novelist, a real writer, who thinks independently, with strong aims, talents, who is already a force, and who will go far'.[69]

Hamsun decided to remain in Oslo until he could deliver his manuscript for *Hunger* to his Danish publisher ready for printing in the spring of 1890. He needed cash to do so, but it only required a hint from Hamsun that he was actively writing for the editors of the two main rival Norwegian newspapers, *Dagbladet* and *Verdens Gang*, to reach for their chequebooks. Among various texts he sent out was 'Hazard', a short story about an obsessive gambler.

It was an action he would regret.

Since his first rejections in Copenhagen ten years ago, when his early stories had been censured as being simplistic and outmoded, Hamsun had been wracked by the fear of not being original enough. With his *Hunger* fragment, he had finally won the recognition of the literary elites of Copenhagen and Oslo for which he had fought so hard. He had not imitated anybody. The fragment signalled what would become his own unique style. But Hamsun was well aware that his reputation for originality – a reputation crucial to his sense of pride as he struggled to complete *Hunger* – could be destroyed by the merest accusation of plagiarism. It was this that he feared when, only days before Christmas 1889, he came across a Norwegian translation of Dostoevsky's novella *The Gambler*. Seeing similarities with 'Hazard', he requested that Olaf Thommessen, editor of *Verdens Gang*, return his story. It had not yet gone to print but, Thommessen apologised, it was too late to back out; the story was going to fill three whole pages of the eight-page Christmas edition. Thommessen reassured Hamsun that they both knew the genesis of 'Hazard', and that if need be, his testimony would refute any suggestion that Hamsun had plagiarised the Russian.

In fact, nobody drew any parallels between 'Hazard' and Dostoevsky's novella. At least not at the time. That would come later.

During the first three months of the new decade, Hamsun worked on completing *Hunger*.

With its narrator resembling the author so closely that Hamsun described his book as self-revelatory, the book charts a writer's desperate struggle for survival. The main protagonist has no history since, for Hamsun, people living in the cities had none. In the country there is a sense of belonging, of interconnection with family and a shared past within a community. But in the city a man's identity and sense of worth are transitory.

The narrator of *Hunger* does have an identity as a writer, an artist, and this he clings to. After he has pawned his waistcoat, the man behind the counter expresses surprise when the narrator returns to fetch a little pencil from its pocket: 'As trifling as it seemed, that pencil stump had made me what I was in the world, you might say it had given me my place in life. [. . .] So it shouldn't really have surprised him that I wanted my stubby little pencil back; it was far too valuable to me, almost like a little person.'[70]

Hamsun's original intention had been to describe the unstable, shifting emotions caused by the experience of hunger. By the time the book was complete, he had explored the subtler underlying reasons for his character's hunger, and his motives for denying himself satisfaction. Hunger is an appalling experience, but not fatal to an artist capable of channelling it; hunger might make him capable of the thing he craves most.

Hamsun describes the fevered rush of creativity when words tumble out, 'arranging themselves coherently, forming themselves into situations; scene after scene, actions and words welling up in my head and a marvellous pleasure gripping me. I write as though possessed, filling page after page without pause.' Making a clean copy of his work, the character recognises it as the best he has ever produced. He kneels and thanks God for 'a wondrous heavenly intervention in my soul, and an answer to yesterday's cry of despair. It is God! It is God!' The protagonist is not just momentarily saved. He achieves something much more important. The creative human being has overcome all obstacles, even the physical demands of his own body.

The most important battles of *Hunger* are not fought in the narrator's disturbed encounters with the haunting young woman Ylajali, or with other characters in the novel. The truly decisive struggles take place between the earthly demands of the body and the divine needs of the writer's aspiration.

Hamsun's protagonist is no ordinary man, but a poet whose future achievements are of such potential magnitude that even the fates have entered a wager over him: 'Up in the heavens, God kept a watchful eye on me and saw to it my downfall followed all the rules of art, evenly and slowly, without pause. But down in hell's abyss, the angry devils' hackles were raised because it took me so long to commit a cardinal sin, an unforgivable sin, for which God in his righteousness would be forced to cast me out.'

Pacing the streets of Oslo, having constantly to devise new methods to suppress the growlings of his stomach, the narrator is led by hunger and its accompanying temptations to commit one minor sin after another – quite a number in total. But the cardinal sin for an artist – the sin of writing without the spark of God and exclusively for survival – he resists every time. The novel is a forthright statement against hack-writing. On one occasion, however, the character wavers – 'I scribble away at my play, writing everything that occurs to me, just to be finished quickly and move on. I wanted to convince myself that I had had another inspired moment, I lied to myself, deceived myself shamelessly and wrote as though I didn't need to search for the words' – but then calls upon what is left of his willpower. Just as the Bible commands the believer caught in temptation to cut off the part of his body that offends him, Hamsun's character snaps his pencil with his teeth, and in so doing overcomes his final test and saves himself.

The only thing left for the narrator is to make his sacrificial offering. Of all the impressions most indelibly inscribed on the writer's peculiarly delicate sensibilities during these weeks in Oslo, one stands out: the little boy who sat on the pavement outside the hostel playing with paper strips, and the red-bearded man who leaned out of his window and spat down on his head, jeering at him. Overcoming his own ravenous hunger, Hamsun's character keeps a resolution to give the last of his six biscuits to this child.

The relationship between child and monstrous adult was one Hamsun knew only too well from his own formative years.

The previous autumn, Hamsun had confessed to his Danish publisher why work had been progressing so painfully slowly: 'It's natural of course that everybody thinks I'm going to produce a masterpiece, when the published piece was so successful, which is why I never feel anything I do is good enough.' Six months later, however, the manuscript was almost complete. His fear of failure had not got the better of him. 'I believe this is a book the like of which has never written before, at least not here in our country', he declared.[71]

Seducer and Poet

At Easter 1890, Hamsun left for Copenhagen with his nearly completed novel. He had spent a year in Norway – much longer than planned.

His publisher, Philipsen, was getting understandably impatient. He practically wrenched the manuscript out of Hamsun's hands as he disembarked from the ship and passed it straight to the typesetters, thereby increasing the pressure on Hamsun to produce the remaining pages. What probably had a greater impact on the writer, however, were Philipsen's constant reminders about the line of creditors who were queuing at the door. Hamsun had only succeeded in shaking off the most persistent of them by referring them to Philipsen. Now the list was so long that he could barely remember how much he owed each one.

His female acquaintances, however, he kept tabs on.

At about two o'clock one Monday afternoon, some time in May or June 1890, Knut Hamsun was sitting in a modest café in Copenhagen. A man walked in and sat at the neighbouring table. He was in his mid-forties, a literary historian, translator, encyclopaedia editor and author of numerous popular science books. Hamsun had been a guest in his house on several occasions; they had attended the same parties and dined out together. Now, they pretended not to see each other.

There was good reason for Hamsun to be unsettled by this chance encounter with Erhardt Frederik Winkel Horn. He had been having an affair with his wife.

Hamsun was prepared for anything, from threats and angry accusations to angst-filled confessions and desperate pleadings. But Winkel Horn did not utter a word. Time passed and Hamsun began to find the situation increasingly intolerable. Calling the waiter several times, he demonstratively ordered the bill, as if to hint to the other man that time was running out if he intended to confront him – which he surely must after recent events.

The waiter took his time. Winkel Horn maintained his silence. Not even a flicker crossed his face to reveal that he had noticed the presence of the man who was rumoured to have made him a cuckold. Hamsun considered making the first move. The other man's silence was causing him, despite himself, to cringe with shame. Finally, he managed to pay and leave.

Two hours later, still somewhat shaken, Hamsun related the details of this encounter in a letter to Erik Skram, the person in Copenhagen to whom he felt closest. Furthermore, Skram already knew of the affair, and had been asked by Hamsun to speak with Winkel Horn; Hamsun's uncertainty as to whether this conversation had taken place was one of the reasons he had not approached him in the café.

'So why the hell doesn't anything happen when he has every reason for revenge,' he asked Skram, 'why the hell doesn't anything happen, when the opportunity is so good? By God I'm not putting up with this. My sincerest plea, Mr Skram, is that you ask W.H. to bring all this to a close. Under no circumstances do I want to be in the presence of that man again for more than a minute without something happening. I'm fond of the man, I was on the verge of speaking to him, I cannot take any more of this silence, I want to know what I'm dealing with.'[72]

Hamsun asked Skram to explain to Winkel Horn that he wanted to be punished, but not just in any way, and certainly not with silence. He would be unable to remain calm if a similar situation arose again. 'Perhaps it suits him to act proud et cetera. Tell him straight that if he wants to play his stupid games with me I shall take him by the throat the next time I see him. Just so he knows. I have insulted this man gravely, and I'm minded to demand my fate for it, and immediately.'

Just like the central character in *Hunger*, Hamsun had a propensity for sudden mood swings, and now he was overwhelmed by pity for Winkel Horn: 'I've never seen anything more laughable than this damnable business – I'm fonder of the man than his wife. When I saw him again now – he'd grown greyer, older – I could have thrown my arms round him.' Yet, as with the protagonist in *Hunger*, beneath his compassion lurked aggression: 'And if he comes up with something about forgiving me, I shan't stay calm, he can stake his life on that.'

It was Skram's task to make Winkel Horn understand immediately that Hamsun could not even walk around Copenhagen for fear of meeting him. 'If he doesn't – to his own satisfaction – take his revenge, then I shall spit God's salted torment in his miserable eyes when I meet him. That is my final word.' In the margin he added: 'He said he was going to do something, so why doesn't he get on with it?'

Hamsun, it seems, either would not or could not see that Winkel Horn had already exacted his revenge.

Hamsun sent copies of *Hunger* hot off the press to numerous critics in Denmark, Sweden and America, with an accompanying note explaining that this was *not* a novel about marriages, picnics and balls – indeed, it was not a novel at all. 'What interests me are the eternal stirrings, below the smooth surface of my soul, the strange peculiarities of the mind, the mystery of the nerves in a starving body. This book consciously plays on a single string, but attempts to draw hundreds of notes from this string.'[73]

He had to bend the ear of the press before Brandes, who had such influence in Scandinavia, had a chance to sway opinion. Brandes's review of *On the Cultural Life of Modern America*, in which he had affirmed the author's epic talent and true aristocratic nature, had held the literary door ajar for Hamsun. But recently Brandes had slammed that same door shut again. After only briefly leafing through *Hunger*, he proclaimed he had found the novel too monotonous.

Brandes's rejection was the worst thing imaginable: 'Not only do I feel utterly alone without you, but if you withdraw your understanding from me, there is naturally no use in my continuing. [. . .] I have nobody else but you', Hamsun lamented.[74] He felt sure that Brandes could not have read enough: 'I do not think, if we counted them, that we would find a greater variety of emotional states in Raskolnikov, for example, than in my book.'[75]

But Georg Brandes did not send any more encouraging words to the author of *Hunger*. He was at heart a rationalist, and although he did not object to a little madness, he believed that a sense of proportion should be maintained; in *Hunger* the protagonist came far too close to a neurotic on the verge of disintegration. A radical thinker, Brandes may have raised the banner against God, the priesthood and politicians, but never against reason itself. He had no desire to identify with a literary figure with whom he could not engage intellectually.

On Wednesday, 4 June 1890, four days after Hamsun had pleaded with the St Peter of Scandinavia's literary gates, he was on board a ship again. But this was not the voyage he had begun to discuss excitedly with friends – travelling to Tunisia, Piraeus, Smyrna, Sevastopol and Odessa and back again over the Balkans and St Petersburg. He still did not have the money for this dream trip. His fee for *Hunger* amounted to a handsome 2,100 kroner, but a large portion had been swallowed up immediately by debts, and he was still being pursued by impatient creditors.

However, Hamsun saw a way of providing himself with some speedy economic elbow room: knock out another book over the next two or three months, and then set out on his great journey across the Orient. This next book, he explained, would contain three or four psychological short stories.

The boat he had boarded was set to take him back to Oslo, the city with which he had such a strained relationship. But he had no intention of lingering to endure the curious gazes and gossip that would surely erupt as soon as the Norwegian newspapers published their reviews, which would almost certainly speculate on how autobiographical *Hunger* was. Less than a week later Hamsun set sail on a boat that would take a winding route along the south-east shoreline of Norway, calling in at all its coastal villages. The journey suited him perfectly. He was banking on it inspiring a creative spark to launch him on his new project, an approach he had often relied on before – not least in America – with amazing results.

Something made him land at Lillesand, a village close to the southern tip of Norway. Its 1,500-strong population made a good living off the sea and the forest behind it, which provided the shipbuilding yard – the pride of the village – with excellent timber.

He was still in a fragile state as he came ashore.

Brandes's words had been as wounding to Hamsun as a broken bottle brandished by a hooligan. The last months of work on *Hunger* had been like rolling in splintered glass. And the jealous drama played out between Frederik Winkel Horn, his wife and himself, had caused him to bleed some more. He confided to a friend how weary he was of being alone, of not having a lover or wife, of travelling from place to place, of living temporarily in wretched conditions with nobody to say goodbye to or to long for at home.[76]

In Lillesand, he took lodgings in a converted boathouse. From his large veranda he had a view inland towards the village square and out across the harbour and shipping lane. The highlight of his days was the arrival of the steamships in the afternoon. He soon made friends and acquaintances.

But there were those who gossiped about him, saying that *Hunger* was a blasphemous and shamefully erotic book, that his behaviour was improper towards young ladies and, not least, that he had turned the head of one of the town's many grass widows.

This was, Hamsun confessed to several correspondents, quite true.[77] Elise Dorothea Jahnsen was twenty-six years old and still childless after three years of marriage to a naval officer, who was away at sea. In such a small town it was impossible to keep anything secret for long.

Some months previously, Hamsun had carped about Winkel Horn's failure to stand up to him, scoffing at his refusal to retaliate. In Lillesand, he was soon acquainted with a *real* man. On his return, the naval officer paid the writer a personal visit, making it abundantly clear that he should stay away from his wife. There was no mistaking this man's meaning.

The truth, however, was that Hamsun's excitement had already dulled. It was the thrill of the chase that filled him with passion. The more unobtainable a woman was, the more overwhelming his desire. And when he was in this state, there were no limits to what he imagined might, or must, happen. Being in love was like the rapture of writing: he rode the waves until he collapsed exhausted.

When, after receiving a telegram, Hamsun, carrying only the lightest luggage, boarded an eastbound steamship to a nearby village, gossip about him reached unprecedented levels. His curiosity had been aroused by an eccentric Englishwoman, Mary Chavelita Dunne. She was a writer, and the same age as Hamsun. Of Australian, Irish and Welsh extraction, she had also lived in both Germany and America, settling in Norway with an alcoholic lover who had recently died.

From the moment he entered her room one Sunday evening in September 1890, she was lost. She was travelling the next day, but they agreed to exchange letters until her return to Norway, when she hoped very much to see him again.[78] Armed with further experiences to be transformed into art, he returned to the close village atmosphere of Lillesand to work on the book that he hoped would achieve everything that *Hunger* had not.

Part II

Death to the Prophets!

Knut Hamsun had long dreamed that he might one day be measured against Henrik Ibsen and the other major Norwegian writers of his day. In the summer of 1890, he realised the extent to which the established generation of writers actually stood in his way. But as far as he was concerned, the fault lay not with his writing or with his novel *Hunger*, but with the critics who had been fed for years on the platitudes of the old guard, the four grand old 'prophets' of Norwegian literature: Bjørnstjerne Bjørnson, Alexander Kielland, Jonas Lie and Henrik Ibsen.

Despite many favourable reviews, *Hunger* had not been hailed as a great work of genius. The Danish newspaper *Avisen* had suggested contemptuously that Hamsun apply to be a corpse-bearer at the asylum of modern literature. In *Politiken*, Edvard Brandes took Hamsun's verisimilitude to task, questioning whether it was believable that a starving man would waste his last coppers as willingly as the central figure in *Hunger*. Some were critical of the erotic scenes, others of the book's fierce denial of God, which Hamsun had advertised proudly beforehand. Here and there he was accused of being coarse, cynical, even an abomination, but such criticisms were in the minority.

Among the first Norwegian newspapers to come out in praise of *Hunger* was *Verdens Gang*. Hamsun, it proclaimed, was an extraordinary literary talent and an artist of the highest order. *Dagbladet* saw in Hamsun a virtuoso heralding a new voice and literary style. In Copenhagen, *Københavns Børs-Tidende* praised the meticulous precision of his artistry. Meanwhile, *København* recognised his artist's temperament and delicate poetic sense. Indeed, the first round of reviews, appearing mainly in the Left-wing press, proved both balanced and positive.[1]

Yet, though he registered the words of praise, it was the negative criticism that Hamsun ruminated on. Perhaps he needed it to stoke the fighting spirit upon which he depended. 'I am crammed full of ideas and as strong as a lion', he assured Erik Skram. 'God strike me, I shall write so these four grand prophets here at home are forced to take notice!'[2]

He abandoned the idea of writing a collection of psychological short stories. 'I am turning ideas over in my head for something which will be among the most impressive stuff ever written on this earth', he promised Skram, who had reviewed *Hunger* for *Tilskueren* in Denmark and *Samtiden* in Norway, and was convinced that it was comparable to the very best of European literature.

But there was a review that rankled with Hamsun. The reviewer felt that the central character's withdrawal from Ylajali after his stormy flirtation made him seem somewhat impotent. This reviewer implied that there might be personal reasons for what he interpreted as Hamsun's incapacity to depict the erotic. Hamsun was deeply insulted and promised to 'write a song in praise of love, to make Allah and Bjørnson quake!' Hamsun was indeed convinced the unkind words originated, albeit indirectly, from his old idol and the doyen of Norwegian literary life, Bjørnstjerne Bjørnson. He was determined now that his next book would be a novel of substance, proving beyond question that nobody was better equipped for life or writing than Knut Hamsun.[3]

Although Hamsun had found himself welcomed, at least partially, into Scandinavia's literary and political circles, he was already at odds with both Edvard and Georg Brandes in Copenhagen, as well as the influential Bjørnson clique, the conservatives in Norway and substantial sections of the Left.

The experience of being in a tight corner, from which he could leap into the attack, made him dangerously hungry for a fight.

Just as he had done after the publication of Hamsun's lectures, Philipsen tried to convince his author that the reviews of *Hunger* were in fact far more balanced and positive than Hamsun complained they were. Philipsen clearly had little notion of the extent to which Hamsun lived according to his own subjective perceptions. When the publisher hinted that the first print run of two thousand copies was unlikely to sell out, and that Hamsun was therefore being absurdly impatient in asking for a further advance so soon, Hamsun took umbrage. Yet the 400 kroner he was demanding represented an enormous sum: 3 kroner at that time was a good day's wages for a craftsman.

Hamsun repeatedly reminded Philipsen of the uniqueness of *Hunger*. It was, he said, 'a book never written before, it is exceptional, and exceptional books are, of course, rather rare'.[4] Some of the strongest endorsements Hamsun had for the unique quality of his book came from Germany. Hans Kurella, a doctor who published an international psychiatric journal, wanted *Hunger* to be translated as a scientific work. Two German magazines had also already written about him. And only two weeks after the book's publication, Ibsen's German translator, along with Samuel Fischer, his German publisher, had telegraphed Hamsun asking for the rights. Hamsun told Philipsen that another publisher had also signalled strong interest.

It soon emerged that the magazine *Freie Bühne* intended to serialise *Hunger*. *Freie Bühne* was owned by Fischer, who had also decided to publish the full novel in the following year. Hamsun was going to be published by the same house in Germany as Ibsen.

Encouraged by the response in Germany, Hamsun wrote to Hans Lien Brækstad, an ardent promoter of Norwegian literature in Britain, urging him to contact Ibsen's British translator, William Archer.[5]

Hunger's reception convinced Hamsun that he had to lead the way in clearing a path for a new literary form: psychological literature. Hamsun saw the outright rejection of his novel by large sections of the Right-wing press, and the partially negative reviews of the Left, as evidence of the inadequacy of what he scornfully described as Norwegian moralistic, character, and quack literature – literature that failed to describe the unique psyche and emotional life of modern man. 'The emotions in Norwegian literature lack variety and are too rigid', he complained to a Swedish colleague, Gustaf af Geijerstam. He wrote a manifesto on this new literary form, entitled *From the Unconscious Life of the Mind*, which he sent to the new Norwegian magazine *Samtiden*.[6]

Well over half this article was taken up with describing how two of his stories had been written in his sleep. He explained that, in using techniques of free association, he was investigating the connection between his experience of reality and his subconscious actions. In this article, Hamsun hoped that by elucidating his own emotional experiences and modes of writing, and thereby indirectly those of *Hunger's* central character, he would demonstrate the need for a new literary form. It was a clarion call for books by authors who could shed light on 'the secret stirrings that happen unnoticed in the remotest regions of the soul, the unpredictable chaos of perception, the delicate life of the imagination held under the microscope; the meanderings of these thoughts and feelings in the blue, trackless, traceless journeys of the heart and mind, curious workings of the psyche, the whisperings of the blood, prayers of the bone, the entire unconscious life of the mind'.[7]

Hamsun was attracting attention in Germany and Austria, and was receiving a growing number of letters from publishers and translators. One letter was from a German translator, Marie Herzfeld, to whom Hamsun had already sent his short story 'Hazard' (without, it seems, any sign of his earlier concern about its similarities to Dostoevsky's *The Gambler*). Now he sent her his article on the life of the subconscious. Herzfeld was clearly well connected, since Hamsun's article soon appeared in the major German newspaper *Frankfurter Zeitung*.

The young eagle had begun to build what would turn out to be a powerful nest in Germany. Ibsen had better take heed.

The idea of swooping down from a lectern onto Bjørnson and the other literary prophets of Norway and their overrated books seemed increasingly alluring. Hamsun chose Bergen as the location to try his hand again as a speaker in his homeland, following the collapse of his lecture tour six years earlier.

His lecture dates were repeatedly postponed during that autumn and, unsurprisingly, he began to get more nervous as the time approached. Would anyone come? Would the Norwegian public, brainwashed by their four prophets, even show any interest in him?

Almost two weeks before he was due to speak he arrived in Norway's second largest city. By the time he stepped out the podium on Thursday 19 February 1891, he had bombarded the population of Bergen with no fewer than twenty-seven notices in the city's three major newspapers.

The hall held three hundred people. Several had advised Hamsun to rent a smaller venue. But by a quarter past seven, the room was overflowing. People were even standing along walls and in doorways. By half past, many had been turned away. A noticeably large number of women were present. Now the speaker gazed down on four hundred Bergen residents, cleared his throat and, with a greeting designed to thwart convention from the outset, began: 'Gentlemen and ladies! My subject today is Norwegian literature, and what I have to say will probably cause offence.'[8]

He would, he explained, attack Norwegian literature so as to clear the way for something that was so far lacking. He intended to concentrate on the four main Norwegian writers of materialist literature, the four prophets who, according to Hamsun, comprised a mixture of democratic utilitarianism, English 'housekeeping' morals and a dash of European realism. In Norway, he argued, they were still producing an old-fashioned literature, aimed primarily at social reform, with overly simplistic characterisation where the characters had dominant traits that guided their actions. Meanwhile, in France, an aristocratic, psychological style of fiction was emerging that overshadowed Zola and other socially orientated writers. These new writers had become friends with the people rather than remaining their observers.

Bjørnstjerne Bjørnson was an educationalist in his sympathies and abilities, and a farmer and democrat by temperament. His books were like household medicine cabinets, in which wisdom was stored in little nuggets. An educator of grown-up children. Alexander Kielland was a man with an interest in the rudimentary traffic of life that far exceeded his feel for human psychology. His books exuded a busy cheerfulness. Jonas Lie was no leader, but an excellent foot soldier; not a shining star, but a bright candle and good-humoured, like a kindly uncle.

Finally he came to Henrik Ibsen, the most famous of them all. Ibsen had, Hamsun railed, been content more than anybody else to produce the most simplistic psychological portrayals. This, Hamsun pronounced, was a result not only of the limitations of dramatic form in conveying the inner life of characters, but also of Ibsen's rigidity and lack of nuance in his understanding of the human psyche.

An hour and a half later Hamsun's lecture met with a lengthy ovation.

With the rest of his lecture series already well prepared, he had plenty of time now to celebrate his success during the four-day break between the first and second of his talks. Bolette Pavels Larsen, an author, translator and critic for the Bergen newspaper *Bergens Tidende*, had become good friends with Hamsun after writing an effusive review of *Hunger*. With motherly pride she now introduced him to her various circles in Bergen. During their diligent correspondence before he came to the city, Hamsun had given her some insight into his relationships with women – and she now witnessed at first hand the effect he had on them. The ladies in Bergen simply could not get enough of him. Reporting back to another, rather envious writer, Larsen wrote: 'Goodness, he has conquered them all. All the women, all of them, were at his feet.'[9]

Hamsun had to rent a hall double the size of the original one for his second lecture, and still the gallery and main hall were filled to bursting. The audience numbered at least seven hundred.

He began his lecture provocatively. In his view, the books with which his audience were no doubt most enamoured contained nothing but the crudest, cheapest and most superficial characterisations. This was, he stated, because Norwegian writers, and in particular the four so-called 'prophets', had failed to explore the complexity of modern man. The modern psyche, he explained, was a world in which everything shifted and nothing was as it appeared.

Now, like a prophet himself, Hamsun addressed his disciples, offering them a parable: visiting Hamsun's home during the previous winter, a fellow author had been moved to tears by a blind old man who had allowed his grandchild to ride him like a horse. Without a murmur, the old man accepted this little rider's whippings as they played in the back yard. For Hamsun's colleague, this scene was the most beautiful example of human goodness he had ever encountered. But Hamsun, who had watched the family living below him for some time, knew this was a shallow misinterpretation. In fact, the old man had stolen some cheese from his daughter, and she was now observing this humiliating game from the window. Basing his understanding on conventional character types, the visiting author had misunderstood the dynamics of the situation. The old man allowed the child to hit him across his hands and generally torment him because he wanted to put himself in the stocks, he needed to suffer, driven by a maudlin cruelty towards himself. At that moment the blind old man was an extraordinary psychical being, of whom the writer of 'character types' had no understanding.

Hamsun's third lecture was rather an anticlimax for much of his audience. Turning his attack on what he termed fashionable literature, or light reading, he spent almost half his lecture pondering a book that few of his audience were familiar with: Guy de Maupassant's *Notre Coeur*, which had recently been translated into Norwegian. He used populist writers like Maupassant to demonstrate their instinct for the *Zeitgeist*. Then revisiting Ibsen and other Norwegian and Nordic authors, he concluded that neither the authors, nor indeed their readers, measured up.

So was there no glimmer of hope for contemporary literature?

Certainly. Halfway through his series, in the middle of his second lecture, Hamsun had signalled his hope for the future: 'There is one writer here in this country who brought a book out recently, unlike any other book, partly because it dealt with a highly emotional character. The book was not great, it didn't sell; but two months after its publication the author had already received fifty letters of thanks from various Norwegian men and women, strangers, people whom he had never met, as well as acquaintances, among them a few celebrities.'

The author to whom he was referring was, of course, himself. The book was *Hunger*. And those people who had sent him their praises were privileged enough to be counted among the few not brainwashed by the four prophets and their devotees.

The Sphinx with No Riddle

Throughout the spring and into the early summer of 1891, Hamsun lectured in many towns. Neither Ibsen nor any of the other writers whom he had attacked attempted to defend themselves publicly. Their silence served only to fuel Hamsun's wrath. And his mood was not lightened when he saw the enormous international success Ibsen was enjoying.

On 16 July, Ibsen returned to Norway after twenty-seven years living abroad. The Right- and Left-wing press competed to claim him as their champion. He had not returned to settle down, Ibsen insisted, but merely to take a boat trip along the Norwegian coastline. When he returned to the capital, having visited the northernmost part of Norway, Hamsun snarled to a friend in a letter: 'That creature has arrived back in the capital. According to the news agencies he has declared he is "satisfied with the North Cape". Satisfied with the North Cape! Imagine that creature, nodding his head, assuming a profound pose and declaring himself "satisfied" with the Orion Nebula. Allow me to fall about laughing!'[10]

Just a month after turning thirty-two, Hamsun would have read in the newspapers that Ibsen, bedecked with all his honorary medals, attended the one-hundredth performance of *The League of Youth* at one of Oslo's theatres. Ibsen's accomplishments were hard to ignore.

But on 2 October, it would have been Henrik Ibsen's turn to read in the newspapers of Hamsun's forthcoming lecture, to be given in Oslo in less than a week. Shortly afterwards the famous dramatist received a written invitation from the speaker himself.

The sixty-three-year-old Ibsen was increasingly obsessed with keeping abreast of what younger writers were up to, and this was undoubtedly an opportunity to do just that.

On the evening of Wednesday, 7 October, the famous Hals Brothers auditorium was packed. All the young authors were in attendance, as well as other cultural figures and a few political notables. Even the polar explorer Fridtjof Nansen was present. In the front row Edvard Grieg, Norway's most eminent composer, sat with his wife, Nina, the concert singer. Just before eight o'clock another couple arrived to join them: Henrik Ibsen, together with a younger woman who, nobody could fail to notice, was not his wife Suzannah. Ibsen had been quick to re-establish contact with his landlady's daughter from his Bergen days, but had soon discovered that his landlady's granddaughter, Hildur Andersen, a twenty-seven-year-old pianist, made much pleasanter company. They took their seats close to the podium.

Hamsun had placed Ibsen at the very front, in seat number one.

The young writers applauded expectantly as the speaker mounted the podium.

'Gentlemen and ladies.'[11]

Not until thirty minutes later did the lecturer utter the name that everybody had waited with bated breath to hear. Hamsun began expounding on the emotional rigidity and lack of subtlety in Ibsen's work. Minutes later he attacked Ibsen's choice of form itself, the play: 'this psychology that is supposedly so clear, that is to say: so shallow that it can be understood and enjoyed all the way from the stage, is an indefensibly coarse and artificial psychology.'

Hamsun reduced Ibsen to a sphinx with no riddle. 'We have grown so used to believing what the Germans say about Ibsen that we read him assuming we will find words of wisdom, convinced we shall find it excellent throughout. And if we happen to stumble upon some strange comet in his book, then it is not a comet at all, but a riddle, and even if it seems utterly implausible, then it is not the fault of the author, we have simply failed to understand him. And it must be admitted, this man has a remarkable inclination to talk – deeply.'

Ibsen sat unruffled throughout the entire lecture, and stared up at the man on the podium with what seemed like great interest. Not even when the speaker elicited laughter from his audience at the great playwright's expense did he show a flicker of emotion.

The applause went on so long that there was time for the speaker to withdraw and return to the podium. The majority of the audience relished Hamsun's nerve, but others found his disrespect troubling, and some were deeply dismayed. One of the latter was the editor of *Verdens Gang*, Olaf Thommessen, who shared his indignation with Ibsen after the lecture. Had they lived in a civilised country, Ibsen broke in, the students would have dashed the fellow's brains out that very night.[12]

Many people had to be turned away from the second lecture. But Norway's political elite, not least the prime minister and minister for justice, were guided to the seats that had been reserved for them close to the podium. As indeed was Ibsen. When his female companion asked with surprise why he should want to hear the 'shameless man' once again, his response was: 'But surely you must understand, we must go in order to learn how to write.'[13]

Ibsen's ironic stance may have disguised a more serious intent than his young friend understood. In his second lecture Hamsun would present his own thoughts on 'psychological literature'. Ibsen was not unaware that his plays were regarded by some as dealing with society rather than the workings of the soul. In fact, it was a view he had heard from several quarters over the years. Only months before, George Bernard Shaw had characterised him as being primarily a social rather than a psychological writer. In August, he had visited Copenhagen to take a closer look for himself at the 'dramatist of the soul', August Strindberg. And now, in October 1891, he was toying with ideas for his next play.

The hall was already remarkably hot: 160 gaslights from five chandeliers and approximately eight hundred people generated a considerable temperature. And the man on the podium offered his audience scant opportunity to cool off.

But Hamsun met rather more opposition in the newspapers after this second lecture. They felt he had vastly overstated the barren conditions in which psychological writing existed.

After his third lecture, which also played to a packed house, the newspapers published less extensive articles, preferring instead to print readers' letters about the event. Many who wrote in felt that, in applauding Hamsun, the Oslo public had behaved despicably towards Norway's greatest writers, including Ibsen. Generally Hamsun could sweep such criticisms aside. But the attack levelled at him by one editor, Olaf Thommessen of *Verdens Gang*, was deeply wounding.

A Charlatan Takes Flight

Knut Hamsun left Oslo a marked man once more.

He had suffered starvation, cold and humiliation in this city before, but never had he been the target of an assassination. Yet that was precisely what Olaf Thommessen, whom Hamsun had portrayed with such tenderness as the Commander in *Hunger*, now seemed intent upon. On Thursday, 15 October 1891, Thommessen's lead editorial in *Verdens Gang* would make this one of the darkest days of Hamsun's life:

> The great man [Hamsun] has spoken. He has left for Trondheim with his psychological insight. People without any critical faculty have been enthralled by his critique. Harsh perhaps: but it seems his audience are nearly as ignorant as Hamsun the great soul-seeker is himself. They certainly equal him in refinement and tact. This psychologist heaped abuse on Henrik Ibsen in his very presence; the audience went into raptures and clapped – not least those who only recently applauded the author of *Ghosts* and *The League of Youth*. Excitement over this psycho-critical charlatanism reached its peak at the start. But a three-hour course in ignorance, superficiality and impertinence is *too* much. And now – in retrospect – the excitement has dampened and waned. Mr Hamsun has slammed the greatest writers of Europe, just as he slammed the United States of America a couple of years ago – about which he knew little more, aside from the fact they could survive tolerably without Mr Hamsun. America still stands – as do our writers.

The only person who defended Hamsun was his new champion in Bergen, Bolette Pavels Larsen. She wrote a warm, supportive article and sent it to *Dagsposten* in Trondheim, where his next lecture series was to be held. She argued that Hamsun displayed both revolutionary power and modesty, pointing to his never having sought a government stipend. She painted a picture of a genius who, driven by an irrepressible urge to forge his own path, was forced to take the podium – despite his aversion to putting himself forward. Nobody should be in any doubt, she said, that Hamsun would triumph in the end.[14]

Her article lay waiting for him to read when he reached Trondheim, no doubt easing his arrival. He lectured in Trondheim to packed houses once more.

Afterwards, Hamsun took the coastal ship south again to Kristiansund, a neighbouring town, where he intended to settle for a while and continue work on his psychological novel.

There were no grass widows here, as in Lillesand. Instead, there was a twenty-one-year-old piano teacher, Julie Amanda Lous. She was charming and had strong eyebrows for which Hamsun had something of a weakness. But it was when she perched on her stool before the piano that he felt a rush of excitement and an overwhelming desire to be a part of her world, the world of the educated bourgeoisie where tea was served in cups bearing the family's coat of arms, and where each piece of furniture and object had a story to tell.

Friends called her Lulli. Soon she allowed Hamsun to call her Lulli too. Then she allowed him greater liberties. Lulli fell for him. She had never met anybody like Knut Hamsun, although she had read about a man very like him – in *Hunger*.

She had also attended his lectures, as had all the people Hamsun came to know in Kristiansund. They had all listened to him describe how, as a modern psychologist, he investigated and illuminated the soul in sorrow and joy, in wakefulness and sleep: 'I walk at its side as it moves with rational steps through reality down here, and I pursue it zealously into other worlds, chasing it on its journeys through space, climbing up into the fairytale-blue, playing with the stars, greeting the sun-spirits, transgressing the limits of the world and floating down to settle by a golden castle behind the mountains at the gate of the Occident. All this I do, and I do it with the conscious aim of illuminating a soul deep into its very mystery.'[15]

Soon after his arrival in Kristiansund, the inhabitants of the little town noticed Hamsun behaving rather eccentrically. What they did not realise was that his behaviour correlated with that of his latest protagonist, Johan Nilsen Nagel.

When an old lady died in the room next to his on the day after Christmas, Hamsun claimed he was able to see ghosts, and that he had received a visit from her; she had come into his room several times, he said, once looking for an old umbrella and insisting that it must be among his things. The only grief she (and he) felt was that she was to be buried the next day.[16]

Hamsun was in a somewhat overexcitable and impressionable state. When he read Dostoevsky's *The Insulted and Humiliated*[17] he was so deeply affected that he had to take a long walk. He passed a blind man on the road, whistling to himself with all his might. A small incident, yet one that left a peculiarly deep and lasting impression on him; Hamsun worked it into a passage about blind angels which he added to the growing pile of sketches that would form his next book, *Mysteries*. He was experimenting with a new method of work, slowly collecting disparate scraps that he would then piece together.

Hamsun had thousands of thoughts in his head but complained he was unable to follow any of them.[18] Ultimately, though, he succeeded in bringing the strands together. *Mysteries* began: 'In the middle of last summer, a little Norwegian coastal town was the scene for the most remarkable events. A stranger appeared in town, named Nagel, a peculiar and remarkable charlatan who did many extraordinary things, and then vanished as suddenly as he had arrived. This man received a visit too, from a young and mysterious woman, who came on God knows what errand, and dared not stay more than a few hours, before leaving again. But all this happens later.'

Hamsun's Nagel is defined, if one could call it thus, by his continual instability. It is as though his dominant characteristic is his very lack of character. A glimpse of something, a vague smell, a thought or a single word are sufficient to trigger a dramatic change in his mental state. Alone, in his better moments, he can apparently hold a dialogue with his various personalities. In the company of others, his often contradictory and unpredictable behaviour fascinates some, but also leads to confusion, disdain, laughter, aggression and ultimately rejection. In the end Nagel's potential diminishes, and with it everybody's attention. It is a short road to disappointment, followed by anger, which causes guilt and ends in shame.

This was familiar territory for Hamsun. And as he worked on *Mysteries* he gained ever-greater insight since he himself was the primary object of investigation. He invested this central character with his own opinions on authority-figures, power and the masses, his disdain for the urban bourgeoisie, the British and the bigoted Gladstone, and even his hatred of Henrik Ibsen.

But at some point Hamsun decided, or discovered, that there was a fundamental difference between himself and his creation. Much like his creator, Nagel dreams of accomplishing great things, although he ends up as 'a wanderer whose path is blocked [...] an outsider to existence'. But where Nagel's stream of thought drives him ever deeper into chaos and madness, his creator brings order to it: he is a poet. Nagel lacks the ability to transform his ideas into anything more than impetuous action. Hamsun's mother had run from the house yelling things that nobody understood; her son had been obsessed ever since with the search for the right words, and for a way of setting them down on paper.

A cripple, known to the locals as Minutten or 'The Midget', stands at the centre of *Mysteries*. Hamsun had grown up with two cripples himself, his sister and uncle, and living with them he had experienced a whole gamut of contradictory emotions, from compassion to jealousy and bitterness.

In *Mysteries*, Hamsun has Nagel spend a great deal of effort trying to rescue Minutten from his slavish frame of mind – and succeeding temporarily. Did Hamsun try to wean his sister from that same slave mentality, instilled in her by their uncle and his housekeeper? Sophie Marie, despite the problems with her hip, had in fact graduated from teaching college and found a placement at the college in Vadsø, in the far north of Norway. But in *Mysteries*, the sight of the cripple dancing in the town square to the amusement of the locals under-mines any belief in the purpose of life that Nagel might have had. Hamsun also describes how Nagel is visited by a terrifying ghost, born of his own childhood memories of living so close to the graveyard in his Uncle Hans's house.[19]

Hamsun clearly mined his own experiences, emotions and opinions for his art. He has Nagel pronounce: 'Do you know what a great poet is? A great poet is a man that feels no shame, who is shy of nothing. Other fools have moments when they blush from shame in private, but the great poet does not.'

A Literary Thief

In April 1892, Knut Hamsun boarded a coastal ship bound for Copenhagen via Bergen. He had extracted enough impressions and experiences from Kristiansund for his work and, as with all the other little towns where he had stayed, he had no further need of it.

Hamsun had almost finished his book – but the people in whose lives he had become entangled were not finished with him. In Sarpsborg there had been an affair with a hotel maid, in Lillesand a liaison with the wife of a naval officer and now, in Kristiansund, there was Lulli. Over the last months of his stay Julie Amanda Lous had fallen desperately in love with Hamsun, and on Easter Sunday night, just before his departure, she had given herself to him. But now, upon his return to Copenhagen, Hamsun wanted nothing more to do with her. He refused to write to her and sent her strict instructions not to contact him, telling her that he needed absolute peace to finish his book. When Caroline Neeraas, a mutual acquaintance from Kristiansund, wrote defending her friend's honour and expressing hope for a reconciliation between them, she unleashed Hamsun's worst venom. 'I'll tell you just one thing,' he wrote from the room he was renting from a widow in Bredgate, 'and this is my final word: her power over me last winter was largely the result of her having absolutely no competition. That is likely to change now!'[20] To another corre-spondent in Kristiansund, he snarled: 'Hah, I have to laugh, when I think how she made me feel so damned fond of her during long stretches of the winter. But she's such a dreadfully stiff example of an utterly non-erotic woman, who can *never* really fall in love.'[21]

Hamsun had grossly misjudged the strength of the piano teacher's feelings. Lulli would never forget him. For her, the failed relationship would be her life's tragedy, and it would come back to haunt Hamsun a quarter of a century later.

In Copenhagen, Hamsun had no shortage of women eager to please him. 'God damn it, I rode a young thing seven times one night, the last time down in the restaurant on the morning we parted. She comes to me as often as I want, she's studying to be a doctor', he bragged gleefully.[22]

And somewhere out in the wide world, Mary Chavelita Dunne was also prepared to come running at the click of his fingers. The two had continued their correspondence since meeting in the autumn of 1890 in Arendal. Now, when they finally met again, Hamsun realised that the woman standing face to face with him was very different from the paragon he imagined he had been writing to and about. He chose stubbornly to hang onto his romantic ideal, discussing Tolstoy's ideas on celibacy, Ibsen's *Hedda Gabler*, Strindberg's depiction of women as she-animals, and Nietzsche. They then went their separate ways, promising to burn each other's letters. Mary was dejected, but comforted herself with the notion that she had fallen for a genius. She told him she would turn her experiences into literature.[23]

Hamsun had already done just that, in his novel *Mysteries*.

By the beginning of June 1892, just before his thirty-third birthday, Knut Hamsun had finished *Mysteries* and sent the final manuscript to the typesetters. He was satisfied it resembled nothing that had ever been written before.

Only weeks later he was accused of being a literary thief.

Marie Herzfeld – with whom Hamsun had previously corresponded, sending her his short story 'Hazard' as well as his article on the subconscious, which she translated – had suddenly stopped answering his letters. She had agreed to translate *Mysteries* into German, so Hamsun was eager to remain in contact. Having written to her several times, he finally received a letter with devastating contents: a clipping from the Berlin magazine *Freie Bühne* of an article by the theatre director and critic Felix Holländer. Holländer had read 'Hazard' and publicly accused Hamsun of plagiarising Dostoevsky's *The Gambler*. A formal note from Herzfeld accompanied the article, curtly informing Hamsun that any future correspondence should be addressed not to her, but to Holländer.

Neither the timing nor the location of this public accusation of plagiarism could have been more damaging. Hamsun's German publisher, Samuel Fischer, also oversaw *Freie Bühne* and was thus immediately aware of the serious indictment levelled against the author whose first novel he had so recently published.

For two years, German publishers and translators had courted Hamsun, enquiring eagerly after his next book. Now they ignored him despite his efforts to engage them in discussion. Nobody in Germany wanted *Mysteries*.

Hamsun wrote a lengthy letter to Marie Herzfeld, explaining how upset he had been when he had discovered the similarities between his and Dostoevsky's texts three years ago – as well as how he had desperately tried to stop his story from appearing in *Verdens Gang*. He did not, however, offer her any explanation for his decision to send her the story a year and a half later without any amendments to reduce those similarities. Hamsun urged her to pass the contents of his letter on to Holländer, and to ask him to contact Olaf Thommessen to verify his account.[24]

The editor of *Verdens Gang* had, of course, recently lambasted Hamsun for his treatment of Ibsen and labelled him a charlatan, but Hamsun trusted that Thommessen would nonetheless be true to his word and endorse his version of events. When Hamsun saw a translation of Holländer's entire article, it was clear that one of his fellow Norwegian writers must have fed the critic false information.

With only a hope that someone would come to his rescue and absolve him of these malicious allegations, Hamsun left Copenhagen.

Again he abandoned any plans of travelling to the Orient since he had already squandered much of his advance for *Mysteries*; perhaps even more persuasive a deterrent was that cholera was rife in the countries he planned to visit. He decided instead to travel to Gotland in southern Sweden, but his progress was abruptly halted on the Swedish border when he saw the front page of that day's edition of *Morgenbladet*. The Norwegian newspaper, which had persecuted him for so long, had printed a reworked version of Holländer's article, spiced up with a few additional untruths.

It was imperative that the editor of *Verdens Gang* step forward to vouch for him now.

Hamsun changed plans again and travelled to the Danish island of Samsø, fully intending to transform an enormous pile of notes, including some older ones, into yet another book. For five or six years he had toyed with the idea of portraying the lives of degenerate bohemians and pseudo-artists; he had doubtless used elements of this theme in his work already. But as he envisaged it now, the new book would depict writers who were not true artists but mere trend-followers and parasites. The action would take place in Oslo, and he planned to have it finished by spring.[25]

But once again Hamsun's intentions were thwarted. He developed an alarming skin infection, which affected him so badly that he looked increasingly like a leper. He was forced to travel back for treatment to Copenhagen, where surgeons at the county hospital twice had to lance his boils. With his face covered in scalpel wounds, Hamsun barricaded himself in a hotel room.

Simultaneously, the critics were let loose on *Mysteries*.

Hamsun's genius was again left undeclared. *Dagbladet* and *Bergens Tidende* (for which Bolette Pavels Larsen wrote) were the most favourable of the Norwegian newspapers. But *Mysteries* antagonised most critics: *Morgenbladet*

noted that the author had not abandoned the mentally disturbed hallucinations of *Hunger*; *Aftenposten* dismissed Hamsun in the same breath as
Edvard Munch for their 'unnatural' evocations of drunken delirium, feverish
hallucinations and twisted fantasies.

In Denmark, Edvard Brandes wrote in *Politiken* that he thought *Mysteries*
left a rather childish impression, and described Minutten as 'a very Russian
character'. 'Minutten lives in Lillesand', the exasperated author wrote to his
publisher after reading Brandes's review; 'I've not spared the man. He caught
my interest, and I took lodgings in the same house as him in Lillesand, and I
talked to him every day.'[26]

Hamsun could tear apart the reviews of Edvard Brandes and others, piece
by piece, he griped to Philipsen, but it was not worth the trouble. There were
so many traces of the people in his own life reflected in the characters of
Mysteries: there had to be, since the psychological poet has to study the real
world. Hamsun had lectured on this very subject thirty-six times in twelve
different locations during 1891. But this had made no difference. The accusations of plagiarism, charlatanism and humbug dominated the reviews in
Norway and Denmark.

The review that upset Hamsun most was, without a doubt, the one that
appeared in Olaf Thommessen's newspaper, *Verdens Gang*, which described
Hamsun as a pitiful but opportunistic imitator of modern Russian literature,
who had written a book about a mentally disturbed and abnormal figure who
bore a striking resemblance to the author himself.[27]

Not only had Thommessen broken his word by refusing to speak out against
the allegations of plagiarism, but he allowed the newspaper of which he was
editor to pile abuse on Hamsun. All of the author's fury was now targeted at
Olaf Thommessen. Hamsun decided he would exact his revenge in the best
way he knew how: his next book would be a scathing attack on an editor
bearing all the characteristics of Thommessen.

The book, *Editor Lynge*, was intended to be politically devastating, exposing
all the weathercocks and fly-by-nights as well as the cynic in the editor's
chair. It would be a wake-up call in election year, and in that sense incendiary
stuff.

Hamsun was on the offensive, and now he had his old foe Ibsen in his sights
too.

Just before Christmas 1892, the old sphinx published his play *The Master
Builder*. In a key scene in the first act, the ageing artist confides his fear of
becoming obsolete, of the changes that will displace him: 'I can sense it's
getting closer. Someone is going to demand soon: step aside, let me through!
And then the others will rush after, threatening and screaming, give way, give
way, give way!'

Could Solness's dread of the younger generation have been shared by his creator? The outwardly aloof Ibsen had perhaps been more affected by Hamsun's rebellious attack than had appeared.

Symbolic, abstruse, with bewildering actions performed by its characters: critics did not know what to make of *The Master Builder*. Confused as to the correct interpretation, several of the reviewers indirectly admitted that Hamsun, in his previous lecture series, had a point. So it was with renewed energy, that Hamsun accepted an invitation, at the beginning of 1893, to address the Students' Union in Copenhagen. *Editor Lynge* had been hurried through the press and would be published in the spring, and the lecture would be a fresh opportunity to get his claws into Ibsen. Hamsun felt in a position to attack with vigour.

During his lecture tour of Norway eighteen months before, Hamsun had consistently refused to round the evenings off with a discussion, and this time he again gave strict instructions that this practice of non-debate should be adhered to. He had learned from bitter experience, particularly in the bourgeois drawing rooms of Copenhagen, how difficult it was for him to hold his ground in verbal duels with academically competent combatants.

There were many familiar faces in the big hall just before Easter. Georg Brandes was one such. For one and a half hours Brandes, an Ibsen scholar himself, heard Hamsun's attempt to tear the myth of Ibsen's genius to shreds. For twenty years, Hamsun bellowed, Ibsen had concocted a sense of his own worth, and cultivated the public's belief in his depth of vision. Such potbellied hypocrisy was hard to equal.[28]

Hamsun was interrupted twenty times by applause.

Feeling very pleased with himself, he was on his way out of the hall when Brandes took the floor. As eloquently as he had poured unction into the young eagle's beak four years previously, Brandes now plucked his feathers one by one. Hamsun tried to gather himself for a counterattack. Standing demonstratively before Brandes, he challenged the doctor of literature, pointing out that even the Brandes brothers themselves disagreed fundamentally on how *The Master Builder* should be interpreted. But before he could say more, Brandes retorted: 'And, so what?' There were howls of laughter in the hall. Hamsun's nose had been put firmly out of joint, and he beat a swift retreat from his dangerous opponent.[29]

A Parisian Tour

Hamsun left Copenhagen's Students' Union with his head hanging low. Brandes's attack had again underscored his inadequate schooling and working-class background. Although the idea of his making a cultural tour of Berlin, Rome and Paris was not a new one, now seemed a good moment to act on it. After postponing his journey several times, he finally sat on a train bound for Paris in mid-April 1883, having toasted his departure with a typically dissolute drinking binge.

Drinking sessions for Hamsun would generally begin at Bernina's with a whisky fortified with a splash of even more potent Danish schnapps. When Hamsun was in an extravagant mood, as he was now with his advance for *Editor Lynge*, he would order a 'Norwegian', a tray of ham and fried eggs, washed down with more schnapps and rounded off with huge cigars. Then a 'Legbreaker', a large glass of port mixed with raw egg yolk, might be brought to the table, after which a favourite drinking game would commence. Starting with the host nation's schnapps, competitors would see who could drink their way furthest around Europe, imbibing Norwegian aquavit, Scottish whisky, English Old Tom gin, Dutch curaçao, French cognac and Italian certosa. For anyone still capable of lifting a glass after all that, there was genever to be washed down with a sweet anisette, a spiced maraschino, a raunchy chartreuse, a calming benedictine and a crisp kirsch. The landlord would likely be heckled by those still in the game if he couldn't then serve up a shot of Russian vodka or Japanese sake. At other times they would see who could drink the most 'devil punch', a concoction of seventeen alcoholic ingredients invented and christened by Hamsun himself.

Hamsun was extremely adept at spending money but, as one of his Danish drinking companions, the journalist Frejlif Olsen, attested, he was also very accomplished at getting it. Shortly before leaving for Paris, the two friends had been sitting in a Copenhagen café, hungry, hung over and completely penniless, when Gustav Philipsen walked in. 'We're saved!' Hamsun declared, dragging his publisher into a corner for a lengthy conference.[30] He returned to his drinking companion waving four 100-kroner notes triumphantly in the air. Olsen wondered how on earth he had managed to squeeze such a fortune out of the publisher, who had been under the impression that Hamsun was already on his way to Paris with the aid of a travelling advance he had given him only days earlier. Hamsun had, of course, sworn once again that he would be taking the train that same evening.

He did not. He did, however, dispose of the 400 kroner.

Money is power. Hamsun demonstrated his power in both getting his hands on more cash and his reckless waste of it.

Eventually arriving in Paris, Hamsun and Sven Lange, his travelling companion and fellow author, took lodgings at a boarding house at 8 rue de Vaugirard, close to the Luxembourg Gardens. They were soon introduced to the Scandinavian colony at the Café de la Régence opposite the Théâtre Français. The café stocked a plentiful supply of Nordic newspapers, and Hamsun could confirm for himself that nobody had been able to criticise his latest book for being too removed from reality.

Far from it, in *Editor Lynge*, Hamsun fires off his version of political developments in Norway from the 1888 split of the Left-wing Venstre Party up to events in the spring of 1893. He does little to disguise the identities of any of his characters, or that of the newspaper *Verdens Gang*. Hamsun had backed the radicals in their fight for a freer intellectual climate, as well as their increasingly robust stance on Norwegian independence from Sweden. Olaf Thommessen was very different. Over the years Hamsun had watched him switch sides whenever he or his paper stood to gain. It seemed to Hamsun that in the chasing of subscriptions, journalism had become increasingly ruthless, and that the editor of *Verdens Gang* was the worst offender. He was quite determined that it should be obvious to the world who his cynical editor had been modelled on; in fact it took Hamsun's publisher some persuasion to stop him using Thommessen's real name.

In *Hunger*, Hamsun had described his first meeting with an intrepid editor who displayed both strength and brilliance in his battle with the conservatives. Now, in *Editor Lynge*, Leo Høibro (who voices many of Hamsun's opinions in the novel) describes the editor as 'a peasant student like the rest of us, internally damaged by being transferred to an alien soil and atmosphere, he's a country bumpkin who wants to act the freedom fighter and gentleman, neither of which he was born to. The man lacks sophistication of the heart, his blood runs false.' Weaving a tender love story into his plot, Hamsun also shows how cynical modern man destroys the finest thing of all: the trusting intimacy between a man and a woman. Høibro has given his heart to Charlotte Ihlen, but she allows herself to be seduced by the farming student Endre Bondesen, a man who idolises Editor Lynge. A throwaway mentality taints everything in the book, and the source of this infection is the editor and his newspaper.

Editor Lynge caused as much sensation as if an incendiary device had been lobbed at a public figure; people were vociferously eager to dissociate themselves from the scandalous crime, and yet pushed forward to gawp. The book had been on sale for no more than a week when Philipsen announced the excellent news that a second printing was necessary.

A few days later, sitting in Café de la Régence leafing through the newspapers, Hamsun could see from the scorching reactions to his book just how precisely he had hit his target. Olaf Thommessen selected a reliable marksman to avenge Hamsun's vilification, appointing the poet and author Arne Garborg to review Hamsun's book for *Verdens Gang*. Already a bitter rival, Garborg declared that, by passing moral judgement on others, Hamsun had merely pointed the finger at himself and at his own 'compulsion to cause a stir, to surprise, to shock, to play the big shot, to be on everybody's lips, the centre of attention by whatever means possible, hated perhaps, but at least feared'. In conclusion, Garborg spat: '*Editor Lynge* is written for the mob.'[31]

Hamsun was not happy in Paris. Each time he left his lodgings during the summer and autumn of 1893 he was reminded of the deficiencies that would always remain with him, no matter how much he read, lectured or wrote. He was constantly confronted by everything he could never be, from the company of his fellow educated Scandinavians, to the numerous students in the Latin Quarter on their way to and from the Sorbonne's many buildings, supported by parents, relatives or patrons.

The writer whose father had forced him to become a shoemaker's apprentice confided these feelings of inferiority to Erik Skram, hoping perhaps that Skram might visit and make his stay more enjoyable. 'You speak the language, you've read about the art and life here, you have it all at your fingertips. Things are different for me, you see: I'm a barbarian, I lack the education.'[32]

But, at the same time, Hamsun could not help doubting their superiority. Everybody, it seemed, thronged to Paris, presenting themselves as artists and writers, overly self-assured and raucous; most of them were impostors, and always would be. Hamsun had seen it all before in Oslo and Copenhagen. Parasites, all of them, gorging themselves on things that were not their own, only to regurgitate them as if they were. The women, Hamsun thought, strove to be so modern and fashionable that they lost any charm and became calculating, cold and manipulative. He had depicted such a woman in *Mysteries*: coquettish, always after something, forever playing games.

He had of course fallen for such women too.

Almost against his will, he pulled out the manuscript that he had been working on for a long time, but that he had repeatedly pushed aside. It was set in the artistic milieux of Oslo that Hamsun held in such contempt – an atmosphere of which Paris had reminded him.

From notes and passages he had already written but judged imperfect, a new novel was taking shape. It would make fresh attacks on cowardly politicians and contemporary trends that corrupted the naturalness of life – not least in women. And each time he fell into bed with one of these modern types, his contempt deepened. 'Our young woman has lost her power, her rich and precious simplicity, her deep passion, her breeding, she is no longer devoted to one man, her hero, her God, she has developed a sweet tooth, and nuzzles up to anybody and gives everybody that willing gaze', he wrote in the novel that he would entitle *Shallow Soil*.

Hamsun had tired of the pseudo-artists, charming and deceiving both themselves and others. The private tutor Coldevin is his mouthpiece in the book: 'Our young writers do nothing to raise the standards, leastways not in my opinion. They lack the drive [. . .] nothing comes to them.' Another of Coldevin's speeches shows that Hamsun's anger towards Thommessen and his paper had not yet abated: 'No. One should not forgive, never. One should take revenge. Forgiveness is dastardly. It turns everything rightful on its head. A kindness should be repaid with greater kindness, but a wickedness must be avenged.' Hamsun meted out vengeance and malice in equal measure.

The only two characters to remain largely uncorrupted in the book are both businessmen, merchants, of whom Hamsun had met quite a number in the last fifteen years. Here, he described how the artists' clique repaid their generosity by corrupting their women. The man who had generally written so slowly in the past was now churning out page after page.

At the end of October 1893, just as Hamsun had sent the last instalment of *Shallow Soil* from Paris to his publisher in Copenhagen, he had a breakdown. The conservative newspaper *Morgenbladet* had launched another scathing attack on him, again accusing him of being the worst possible charlatan – the living embodiment of everything hollow in Norway's civilisation.[33]

Hamsun's right hand, with which he wrote, had started trembling when he was upset. After some hours lying on the sofa, he had calmed himself sufficiently to write to his faithful friend Bolette Pavels Larsen in Bergen. Did she, he asked, know of anyone else who had been treated so badly by their own country? He could not understand it: 'I pour my heart's blood into every chapter – I have spent nights on end crying and suffering with my characters over the summer, and did the same for *Mysteries* and *Editor Lynge*.'[34] Was it, he wondered, because he did not ingratiate himself with the reviewers like the parasites he had described in *Shallow Soil*? He quoted numerous examples as evidence of his persecution. Hamsun felt sure there was a pattern to it – some ghastly lie had to be circulating about him. He pleaded with Larsen to use her influence with the editors in Norway and Denmark to put a stop to such false rumours.

Hamsun was convinced that he was the victim of malicious fabrications. Those around him tried to persuade him otherwise, but it was no easy task. Even the positive reviews of *Shallow Soil* in both *Verdens Gang* and *Dagbladet* did not diminish Hamsun's conviction that he was being persecuted. However, he seemed to give some credence to Bolette Pavels Larsen's rationalisation that he had simply fallen victim to the cultural elite's arrogance towards anybody without qualifications: 'I am self-educated. I can't do a thing about that now anyway; but when I am old, and can no longer write or be a blacksmith, I can always take that Examen Artium, since presumably I will have plenty of money. And surely nobody believes I <u>couldn't</u> take the diploma. That would be too ridiculous.'[35]

But Hamsun was soon to experience a boost to his confidence. In Paris he made the acquaintance of the twenty-four-year-old Albert Langen, the wealthy son of a German sugar manufacturer in Cologne. For some time this ambitious young man had been toying with the idea of setting up his own publishing house. Now, after being greatly impressed by *Hunger*, and hearing about the boycott of *Mysteries* by all the German publishers, he saw an opportunity and decided to make his dream a reality. On 1 December 1893, he established Albert Langen Buch- und Kunstverlag, which would have offices in Paris and Cologne. He secured the rights to translate all of Hamsun's books into German and French. In exchange, the new publisher was obliged to open a generous advance account.

Meanwhile the largest publisher in Poland had commissioned a translation of *Editor Lynge* and *Shallow Soil*. A Polish translation of *Hunger* had been published the previous year.

All efforts at being translated into English, however, remained fruitless.

Longing for Edvarda

During those painful months in Paris in the late autumn of 1893, Hamsun started work on a new book. One of the ideas he had carried southwards with him was for a novel set in the far north. Life in Nordland was what Hamsun knew best. And he understood it in a different, more intimate way than the author Jonas Lie, who had achieved great success with his writings about the nature and people of northern Norway. Lie was now permanently based in Paris and, in the absence of Bjørnson, was revered as a king in the Scandinavian artists' colony.

Hamsun had steered clear of the gatherings at the house of Lie and his wife, Thomasine, on the avenue de la Grande Armée. He had heard rumours, even before his arrival in Paris, that Thomasine had blacklisted him as a result of the critical remarks he had made about her husband in his lectures.

In November 1893, the Scandinavian colony in Paris held a huge party for Lie's sixtieth birthday. Hamsun did not attend. He had far more important things to do: 'By God, I'm going to write a magical and intense book now, believe me, I'm giddy with it. [. . .] Bolette Larsen, I shall astound you with my book about Nordland next time, by God I will. It will be exquisite.'[36]

Hamsun had recently contributed an essay about August Strindberg to a collection in honour of the Swede's forty-fifth birthday. In it, he compared

Strindberg to an animal who longed to escape civilisation and return to nature. As Hamsun sat in his Paris room facing a neatly manicured park, it suddenly dawned on him that he had could just as well have been describing himself. He had touched on this craving for nature in *Mysteries*; now he was determined to explore it further.

Notes accumulated, but Hamsun found himself unable to shape his ideas and sketches. Eight weeks into 1894 he had only completed one and a half pages. Whereas his two previous books had called for him to write with clenched fists, delivering blow after blow, this novel required an altogether gentler approach. He had to venture deep into the landscapes of his childhood to rediscover the feelings and sensations of a time when he had felt at one with nature.

He locked himself in his room, stopped answering letters, covered sheets of paper with writing only to rip them up, throw himself onto the sofa and howl in despair. His task seemed impossible. Not only was Hamsun grasping for descriptions of nature, words that would do justice to the landscape; he was also facing the challenge of capturing the experience of love – a man feeling tenderness and violent passion at one and the same time – in its totality. But for years Hamsun had only fooled around with the women he desired. Possession had always afterwards filled him with remorse.

He called his new female central character Edvarda, and pictured her before him. A tanned face, an equally tanned neck. The apron she knotted a little low on her belly, to lengthen her waist. Her mouth large, her smile dangerous. She was the daughter of a successful businessman and had been given some characteristics that were undeniably those of Hamsun's first love, Laura, in Tranøy – although the twenty years that had passed had offered up many other women upon whom Hamsun could draw.

Hamsun was finding it increasingly difficult to stay in Paris.

And the intensity with which he wanted his Nordland novel to pulsate was evading him. As so often in the past, he sought comfort in Bolette Pavels Larsen: 'My dearest, pray to God to give me the strength to write my book!'[37]

Whether they were earthly or heavenly powers that convinced Hamsun he must return to his homeland, he did not let on, but barely two weeks later, in early June 1894, he left Paris for Norway. First he invested in a handsome new wardrobe – at the expense of his new international publisher, Albert Langen.

In the event, Hamsun did not need to travel all the way back to Nordland and his childhood home to find inspiration for his book. Seasick from the boat trip from Antwerp, he came ashore at Kristiansund. It was far enough north for his purposes, and the powerful coastal landscape soon demonstrated its power in the writing that was to become his novel *Pan*: 'From my cabin I could see a jumble of islands and islets and skerries, a little of the ocean, some hazy mountain peaks, and behind my cabin lay the forest, a vast forest. I was filled with joy and gratitude at the smell of roots and leaves, of thick smoke from the pine, reminiscent of bone marrow; not until I was in the forest did everything within me come to rest, my soul filled with harmony and strength.' Hamsun began to draw on his experiences and the people he had met in Nordland as a young man: his stay with the businessman Walsøe on Tranøy, his visit to Erasmus Zahl at Kjerringøy, and other tradesmen along the Nordland coast. *Pan*'s central character, Thomas Glahn, is a huntsman, fisherman, lieutenant and guest at the home of the powerful tradesman Mack. And, just like his creator before him, he lives alone, able to glimpse the trading centre's enormous white buildings, its wharfs and general store, from the cabin he rents at the edge of the forest.

Nordland, the Sami people, superstition, mysteries, the midnight sun and a Rousseau-like stranger who meets a free-spirited Nordland girl – these were the principal ingredients of *Pan*. Sitting on those long Nordic summer nights in Lillesand, he wrote about the even brighter summer nights beyond the Arctic Circle: 'The nights were growing shorter, the sun would scarcely dip into sea before it rose again, red, replenished, as though it had descended for a drink. Nobody believes the strange things that happened to me during those nights. Was Pan sitting in a tree expectantly watching my next move?'

Edvarda, the tradesman's daughter, beautiful with her long slender legs, meets Glahn in the harbour. She throws herself about his neck and kisses him on the lips. Edvarda says something, but Glahn does not hear her. He is entranced by her dark, burning eyes, her high-arching eyebrows, and the rise and fall of her delicate bosom.

Edvarda tells Glahn that when he looks at her it is as though he is touching her. She comes to him in the night. The local doctor tells Glahn that Edvarda is a child who has been spared the rod too often – a temperamental woman, too rigid to cry, irrational yet calculating. She needs to be disciplined, concludes the doctor. There are times when Glahn is convinced that nothing good can come of their relationship. And, as the summer nights slowly lose their magical glow, Glahn realises Edvarda has weakened him. His hunting prowess deteriorates. He becomes the prey that Edvarda toys with and mauls adeptly and heartlessly.

On 15 October, Hamsun sent off the manuscript and boarded a ship bound for Copenhagen, whence he would take the train back to Paris.

Hamsun had set *Pan* in 1855, with Glahn relating the story two years after the event – probably a conscious attempt to curb criticism that he only ever wrote about himself.

It was an effective device.

Two newspapers carried critical reviews of *Pan*: *Verdens Gang*, whose reviewer detected a shallowness that he felt characterised all Hamsun's work; and *Morgenbladet*, Hamsun's bête noire. But these were in the minority. *Dagbladet* filled several columns with the praises of a well-known critic, and soon one enthusiastic article followed another in the Norwegian and Danish press.[38]

In Copenhagen, Philipsen again had to order a reprint. Hamsun's new publisher, Albert Langen, published *Pan* in both German and French. *Shallow Soil* was translated into Russian, and *Mysteries* into Dutch. It was clear that Hamsun's fortunes were turning. Doubtless this thrilled him in private, yet he refused to admit it to others. A fellow Norwegian author commented on his perpetual desire to present himself as the persecuted man, reminding Hamsun of all the good reviews he had received: 'you're not the hunted game any longer. You must allow that to have its effect on you.'[39]

The appeal was made in vain. Despite excellent sales and reviews, Hamsun continued to perceive himself as unfairly treated by the literary establishment. He began 1895 exhorting Philipsen to persuade Norwegian newspapers to publish a notice that *Pan* was in its second printing. In Hamsun's eyes, his enemies in the press were attempting to smother all interest in the book by what he saw as a systematic silence. Yet of all the major newspapers, only one had overlooked Hamsun and his latest literary offering.

I Beat Ibsen to the Ground!

Hamsun had written verse, novels, short stories, essays and lectures. There was only one genre to which he had not yet turned his hand: the play. The theatre held an enormous attraction for him, despite the fact he often spoke derogatively about it. There were large financial rewards to be gained when plays were produced, and the transition would be easier now that he was beginning to give more attention to dialogue in his books.

Hamsun nursed a secret dream to outshine his old foe Ibsen, and at his own métier. He began to develop ideas for an ambitious theatrical work.

Shortly after his return to Paris, Hamsun met the playwright who had revolutionised the dramatic form and, in his opinion, stood head and shoulders above all others: August Strindberg. During the next few weeks they spent a great deal of time together. The numerous members of the Scandinavian community who had already fallen out with the unpredictable Swede, and who also knew of the eccentric Norwegian, put wagers on how quickly they would come to blows.

Early in 1895, Hamsun started writing a play in four acts. As usual, he thought big. This play was to be the first in a trilogy about the rise and fall of a man with an unyielding nature, Ivar Kareno.

Hamsun was unshifting in his antipathy towards Ibsen looking more and more like outright hatred. He seemed to draw energy from the discord. Ibsen, he railed in one letter, ought to have followed his advice to stop writing; he would have avoided blighting a life's work with talentless, senile prattle. The grand prophet's latest crime, according to Hamsun, was his play *Little Eyolf*. When *Hunger* received glowing praises in the Paris magazine *Le Journal*, Hamsun gloated to Philipsen: 'I am a great man in Paris, I'm beating Ibsen dead. Bury him!'[40]

During the spring of 1895, Strindberg was admitted to hospital suffering from increasing mental health problems. A notice appeared in Scandinavian newspapers warning that Strindberg risked complete breakdown if he was not helped home to Sweden and relieved of his financial worries. Hamsun was behind this appeal, as well as a similar campaign in Germany launched with the help of Albert Langen. Money and offers of assistance began streaming in.

But Hamsun's kindness backfired. The unstable Strindberg placed counter-statements in the newspapers claiming that Hamsun's appeal had been launched without his knowledge and that he did not need money.

Those who already saw Hamsun as a bombastic self-publicist now had further grist to their mills. Hamsun tried desperately to explain that he had acted with Strindberg's full consent – which was true – but his protests were useless. The patient continued to denounce his aide, who grew so depressed that he became bedridden.[41]

Langen invited Hamsun to stay with him in Germany, as he had done the previous Christmas when Hamsun had got as far as the station and then changed his mind. Langen did not persuade him this time either.

But Hamsun could not continue living in Paris. At the end of May 1895, he left the city in which he had spent seventy weeks of the last two years.

With his nerves in a bad state, Hamsun returned to Norway. He booked himself into one of the many guesthouses that had sprung up in Lillehammer during the last decade, The little town, situated next to Lake Mjøsa and the entrance to the Norwegian mountains, was a popular destination for those seeking a remedial getaway to heal body and mind.

Dr Torp's sanatorium was a well-known treatment centre for people with nervous disorders and, one Sunday, one of its guests paid Hamsun an unexpected visit. Hamsun had come to the attention of the Swedish poet Gustaf Fröding as a result of his scathing tirades against Ibsen. Fröding's own review of *The Master Builder* concluded that the play was a gallant reply to the younger generation's recent attacks on the playwright, spearheaded of course by Hamsun, and he wanted to take a closer look at the Norwegian for himself. Fröding left with the impression that Hamsun possessed the zeal and ferocity of a lay preacher.[42]

At the Gates of the Kingdom, the first play in Hamsun's trilogy, was politically pertinent. It was written in response to the Norwegian Parliament's decision in summer 1895, under threat of Swedish military force, to abandon its demands for independence in favour of negotiations for a separate Norwegian consular service. From confrontation to conciliation: it was a move that prompted protest from Hamsun and many others.

In the play Hamsun attacks those who abandon the burning ideals of their youth. The central character, twenty-nine-year-old philosopher Ivar Kareno, remains steadfast in his beliefs, no matter how they clash with the opinions of the day. Kareno espouses obstinacy, vengeance and hatred as his ideals. Even peace between nations may not always be desirable. 'Let war come', declares Kareno, 'it matters less to preserve this or that number of lives; since life's source is boundless in its supply, what matters is to keep humankind standing tall within us.'

Kareno's sentiments reflect almost verbatim those that Hamsun expressed in a letter to an American friend during the autumn of 1888 in which he discusses his lack of faith in elections, democracy and parliamentarianism. Kareno declares his belief in 'the born leader, the natural despot, the commander, the man who is not elected but crowns himself leader of the masses on earth. I believe in, and hope for, one thing: the return of the great terrorist, the essence of man, Caesar.'

Kareno's best friend betrays his ideals. His wife, Elina, is seduced by Bondesen, the sort of journalist and opportunist whom Hamsun had previously described so unfavourably in *Editor Lynge*. Kareno himself, however, remains firm – as indeed Hamsun always had.

Hamsun's disdain for weak, wavering politicians was growing steadily deeper. During Christmas 1893, while in Paris, he had written a poem, 'The World Tilts':

> For nights and days I have seen and felt it:
> We are ground down into the earth, all of us. [. . .]
> But deep in the whirl of human life
> The eternal and latent powers slumber
> Aroused during historical times,
> Geniuses, as yet unrecognised,
> Waiting for the call from people and country,
> Oh, great, radiant geniuses.[43]

Not long after his thirty-sixth birthday, Hamsun travelled to Oslo and to a guesthouse some 10 kilometres south of the capital, where he continued work on the second part of his trilogy about the stubborn genius Kareno.

Here, during the autumn of 1895, Hamsun began another affair with a married woman. When she had to leave for Vienna the following spring, Hamsun decided to accompany her to Germanic lands; they probably kept company through most of Sweden, Denmark and large stretches of Germany.

Hamsun's affection for the German people had begun twelve years earlier, when the shipping director had granted him free passage to America; Hamsun had never forgotten this man's tremendous generosity. More recently, he explained to Albert Langen, his sense of himself as being unambiguously Germanic had become more intense the longer he had spent in France.[44]

Finally, after numerous invitations, the prosperous publisher received Hamsun in Munich where he was now settled with his new wife. Langen's wedding was an extraordinary affair: he and his sister had married two of Bjørnson's children, Dagny and Einar, in a double ceremony. Hamsun waited until after the great day to turn up, but upon his arrival Langen introduced him to various literary circles in the city, including those connected to his satirical journal *Simplicissimus*. The publisher's new father-in-law, Bjørnson, was also still in Munich.

Twenty years before, north of the Arctic Circle, Hamsun had studied Bjørnson's peasant tales in minute detail, aspiring to write like him one day; now he and Bjørnson were exchanging compliments at the foot of the Alps. A good many years had passed since they had last spoken. In the interim, Hamsun had publicly criticised the older man time and again – and occasionally written conciliatory letters to him.

Bjørnson's latest play, *Beyond Power II*, Hamsun praised unreservedly, being rather more aware now of the challenges of writing effective drama. And Bjørnson also had something to share with the younger man: an article he had written on contemporary Norwegian literature. In it, despite some reservations about aspects of Hamsun's writings, Bjørnson said that 'behind it all is a warm-hearted, impish face laughing at us, which is now unmistakable. And in his recent works a sense of conscience and integrity seem to guide the action and events of his stories.'[45] Bjørnson had singled out *Mysteries* as one of literature's great books, and pointed to the descriptions of nature in *Pan* as the most magnificent in Norwegian literature.

During meals and other gatherings, Bjørnson took every opportunity to make grand gestures signalling his paternal fondness for Hamsun. There was a measure of pride in the way he referred to the young artist, as if to exclaim: 'Look what I have brought forth!'

Bjørnson headed home while Hamsun continued courting his new admirers.

Munich was a European cultural centre, effervescent with significant figures whose influence stretched across and beyond Germany to neighbouring countries. It maintained close ties with newspapers, journals, publishers and theatres internationally. Bjørnson's article, for example, appeared simultaneously in the Norwegian magazine *Kringsjaa*, the German journal *Zukunft* and the New York magazine *Forum*. People were eager to know which of Hamsun's works were already in translation. And new translations and theatre productions were being considered. The author Arthur Holitscher wrote an extremely positive article about Hamsun for the Vienna newspaper *Neue Freie Presse*.

Bjørnson had not yet reached Norway when he came across a copy of *Basta*, the Norwegian edition of Langen's magazine *Simplicissimus*. Its front cover carried a daring illustration of a young woman standing in a doorway with her lover, while behind them a dead man lies in an open coffin. Inside the magazine was a story, 'Life's Voice', written by Hamsun. The lover, discovering that the corpse in the adjacent room is the husband of the woman he has just made love to, reflects frankly: 'I sit brooding for some time. A man has a wife thirty years younger than him. He suffers a lengthy illness, and one day, he dies. And the young widow breathes a sigh of relief.'[46]

Bjørnson's morals were outraged. He sent a serious threat to its publisher. Langen had, in Bjørnson's view, prostituted both himself and his father-in-law. This was utter pornography, and Langen must either change his editorial direction or Bjørnson would publicly denounce him.[47]

Hamsun, who was still in Munich, received this outpouring of revulsion through Langen. Even more hurtful was the fact that Bjørnson had expressed his dislike of the second part of the Kareno trilogy, *The Game of Life*, which had just been published.

The apprentice urged the master to read his play again. 'By talking about it without understanding it, you have prevented its publication in German. It is the deepest book I have ever written, I have poured all my hard-gained ruminations into it, and believe me, I ruminate a great deal.'[48] Hamsun also informed him, somewhat spikily, that he had written the play 'with all my soul, and I'm perhaps not entirely ignorant of what great writing is. *The Game of Life* will have its day.'

The reviews arrived. *Dagbladet* slated it for being as trite as a noisy minstrel show. *Verdens Gang*, on the other hand, found it rich in beautiful effects, deep insights, dazzling images, sharp paradoxes and flights of imagination.[49]

In *The Game of Life* Kareno returns to his childhood landscape of the north and takes work as a private tutor. Ten years have passed since his wife left him for the journalist Bondesen. Kareno is as unyielding as ever and spends his spare time building a tower where, by means of glass and prisms, he intends to unravel the deepest secrets of light. He is soon drawn away from his scientific investigations into the diversions of love.

Beautiful Teresita exhibits the same mesmerising contradictions as Edvarda in *Pan*; both are attracted more by the game of erotic power itself than by any sense of harmonious fulfilment. The consequences are as fatal for Kareno as they are for Glahn.

Hamsun might have gained a great deal from staying in Munich, like Ibsen before him, or indeed like any author wishing to cultivate German contacts. But he was unable to rest. He had finally found his princess – a certain Bergljot Bech Göpfert – but he was not sure if he could capture her.

Lies

Lecturing on strange states of mind and writing about emotionally unstable characters, Hamsun was bound to attract a few eccentrics. One in particular was now growing increasingly persistent, and her obsession was starting to threaten one of the major relationships of Hamsun's life.

Anna Munch made her first appearance during Hamsun's lecture tour of 1891. She had a faraway look in her eyes, wore a pince-nez, and carried a small round mirror in her left palm, as if it were attached to her. She had followed Hamsun to Copenhagen, Oslo and Paris, where it took all of his efforts to keep her at bay, and had also shown up at the guesthouse in Lillehammer. She believed she and Hamsun were destined for each other and her letters grew in intensity.

In the summer of 1896, shortly before his thirty-seventh birthday, Hamsun returned to Norway. Anna booked herself into the same guesthouse in Oslo and, once more, tried in vain to establish contact.

Hamsun had populated his works with numerous characters exhibiting strange irrational urges and twisted perspectives on life, but he could steer the characters of his own creation; Anna Munch was totally beyond his control. She was ruled entirely by her obsession, which took a more sinister turn in the autumn of 1896. In the guesthouse in Oslo, she witnessed Hamsun seducing a married woman.

Friends and acquaintances of Hamsun began receiving anonymous letters. Soon the recipients included residents at the guesthouse, staff at magazines and newspapers, people involved in the theatre, bookstore owners, restaurateurs. The letters warned them against Hamsun, a man who exploited everyone he came in contact with, particularly women, whom he robbed of both money and honour.

If Hamsun had once been noncommittal and devious in relationships, it was no longer the case. During his stay in Paris the rumours that he thought were being spread about him had been a figment of his imagination. This time, however, lies really were being circulated, and they were lies that threatened the relationship with the woman he had set his heart on.

Hamsun now wrote the first letter in his life in which he used the pronouns 'we' and 'us'. He had never included anyone else in his existence before. Suddenly he was imagining what it might be like to share the rest of his life with a woman. If he won her.

Bergljot Bech Göpfert was the daughter of a wealthy shipmaster and inventor from Nordland. She was nineteen when she met her husband, an Austrian two years her senior, at a trading centre on the Helgeland coast owned by her mother's relatives. He had come for the hunting and, unlike Glahn in *Pan*, captured his Nordland girl. They married, had a daughter named Maria Bergljot (but who was soon called Vesla by her mother), and set up home in Vienna.

The new bride soon discovered that her husband's hunting instincts extended to the pursuit and ensnarement of other women.

Bergljot came to Oslo to take care of her mother when she fell ill. When her mother died in a guesthouse outside the capital in 1895, aged only fifty-two, Bergljot stayed on with her father, a formidable man. Such were the circumstances that framed the encounter between her and Hamsun.

He was famous and worldly-wise, and told her she would make an emperor of him. She was young, beautiful, rich – and belonged to another man. He desired her more than any other woman he had known. She aroused in him both enormous tenderness and a dangerous lust, which demanded her complete subjugation.

Soon Bergljot was spending more time in Oslo than Vienna. It grew increasingly difficult for her to distinguish her reasons for coming: whether she was escaping her husband; fulfilling her filial duties to her widowed father; or being lured by the forbidden longing for her lover.

One woman between three powerful men. And one of them so powerful that escape was impossible.

Bergljot mused over what was real and what was fiction in Hamsun's books. And he listened avidly to her story. The more she told him, the more he wanted to hear. Everything concerning her and her husband, whom he had now begun to refer to as the 'Austrian Dog'. Bergljot was an abducted princess and he was going to rescue her.

Since the publication of his first book he had described many love affairs – but never a happy one. Nagel, Glahn and the central figure in *Hunger* had all failed to capture the women they loved. And any of his characters who had been either affianced or married had always suffered betrayal. In *Pan*, he had described a scene between Glahn and the blacksmith's wife, Eva:

I tell her I am thoughtful and sad tonight. And out of compassion she remains silent. I tell her I love three things, I love a dream of eternal love I once had, I love you and I love this plot of land.
'And which do you love the most?
'The dream.'

Hamsun moved from guesthouse to guesthouse in the capital. It was increasingly difficult for the couple to meet. The poison-pen letters were being sent to a growing number of people; Bergljot's husband received several in Vienna, as did her father and siblings. The letters told the readers to refuse any dealings with Hamsun.

But Bergljot Bech Göpfert was undeterred in her affections, and applied for a divorce from her Austrian husband. In the winter of 1896, formal proceedings began in the divorce drama of which Hamsun was the cause, just as the curtain rose in Oslo on *At the Gates of the Kingdom*.

Five weeks later, at the beginning of January, *The Game of Life* received its premiere. Audiences streamed to see both plays and now, at last, Hamsun received praise from *Morgenbladet*: its regular theatre critic was enthralled. But the paper's previously noxious stance towards Hamsun had not been entirely eliminated; within days the editor published a contradictory critique, resulting in the theatre critic's resignation, and causing a scandal.

Further scandal was awaiting Hamsun. Just before Christmas, twenty-six members of the public signed a petition in *Morgenbladet* and *Aftenposten* protesting against the portrayal of Teresita's immoral behaviour in the stage version of *The Game of Life*.[50] It quickly gained support. Suddenly Hamsun was under pressure from every side.

Professors, headteachers and priests were among Oslo worthies who publicly condemned his work. And now Zahl, the giant of the north, called in the loan he had made to Hamsun seventeen years earlier, and threatened legal action. Göpfert was refusing to relinquish either his wife or his child. The anonymous letters were spreading poison everywhere.

And worst of all, though perhaps unsurprisingly, Hamsun was unable to write.

The sixty-eight-year-old Ibsen, however, was still managing to put pen to paper. Much to Hamsun's annoyance, Ibsen's new play, *John Gabriel Borkman*, appeared just before Christmas 1896. Hamsun decided to take the podium at the Students' Union in Oslo, and fired another broadside at the old literary guard: 'For years they have hoodwinked us. [...] These are books written by old men, scraped together with quivering hands, written from a state of emptiness and lack of inspiration.'[51]

Resolving to make a head-on attack on the lies that were threatening to destroy his relationship with Bergljot, Hamsun went public. In May 1897, Oslo newspapers reported that for the past eighteen months he had been the victim of a shameless, anonymous persecution; the head of police special investigations stated that inquiries were ongoing, and announced a reward for information leading to an arrest.[52]

Hamsun borrowed a large sum of money which he made available to the police, demanding that Anna Munch be apprehended, subjected to mental examination, charged and punished. But now he also felt as though he himself was under surveillance. The police had to gather their evidence.

Curiously, Anna Munch published a book of her own in the spring of 1897. Her description of a woman obsessed with an author, pursuing him to Oslo, Copenhagen, Paris and Lillehammer, seemed a little close to the bone. Yet the accused still denied any wrongdoing: 'Personally I regard my book – in which I acquit him, making myself the "nuisance" – the best proof of my innocence.'[53]

The stress was affecting Hamsun. For the first time in his life, he drank alone. In the autumn of 1897, he confided to Larsen: 'I drank a lot of whisky this spring and summer. In three months I drank sixty bottles on my own, all on my very own at night. I was so broken, it was the only thing that held me up.'[54] 'The best thing would probably be to shoot oneself. But, alas, that takes courage, and I don't have much', he wrote to another friend. He wanted to run away somewhere, far enough for the lies not to affect him: Tibet, Africa or Tunisia, where Nagel had gone in *Mysteries*.

But Hamsun went no further than to another guesthouse outside Oslo.

Here, by a lake on the edge of a forest, Hamsun could write a little again. It was late summer and he was about to turn thirty-eight. He had not been able to concentrate in any depth since completing *The Game of Life* a year ago. Now at last he got a proper grip on the third play of his trilogy.

The spring of 1897 saw the publication of *Siesta*, but this was little more than a collection of short stories that had already appeared in newspapers, as well as a few pieces that had been lying around. The collection also contained stories that perhaps contributed to the whispering that maybe Hamsun himself was the perpetrator of the anonymous letters: 'The Queen of Sheba' tells of a person who pursues a woman, and in another tale, 'Secret Pain', the narrator – uncannily similar to Hamsun – is pursued by a man who provokes him into reporting him to the police.

Siesta was published by Gyldendal instead of his usual publishers, Philipsen. Philipsen had recently joined forces with two other publishers to create a new publishing house that proved less susceptible to Hamsun's charms; and whose proposed advance was rather less generous than Hamsun had come to expect. That was, however, unsurprising, given the fact that seven thousand copies of Hamsun's work remained in storage. *Mysteries* had been a financial disaster. *Hunger* had still not sold out seven years after publication. Hardly anybody bought Hamsun's plays. The full retail value of these remainders was 30,000 kroner but, seeing no great future in Hamsun, the new director offered the lot for a third of its value. Hamsun was naturally hurt and, eighteen years after he had been turned away by Frederik Hegel, he switched to Gyldendal.

Hamsun was also rebuffed by the authorities, being refused a state subsidy of 1,200 kroner proposed by the Norwegian Writers' Union. The official reason was his short story 'Life's Voice', which Bjørnson had found so offensive and which had been banned by the director of public prosecutions.

Almost every author, young and old, united in public protest on Hamsun's behalf; the only really notable absence was Henrik Ibsen. A collection brought in 600 kroner. The recipient was disappointed. But once again Hamsun found friends in Germany, where his reputation was growing rapidly. There was a steady flow of new translations of his books into German, and his short stories found a place in various journals and newspapers. When Albert Langen heard that Hamsun had been refused a stipend, he voiced his outrage together with others affiliated to his magazine *Simplicissimus*, including Thomas Mann and Frank Wedekind. Langen printed a declaration of support, as did his brother Martin, who ran the Berlin paper *Welt am Montag*. Soon Hamsun was receiving donations from Germany that exceeded the entire amount collected in Norway. Germany had recognised Hamsun very early in his career, and it was something the author would never forget.

But there was one thing he was beginning to wish he could forget: his vow to marry Bergljot.

Fever-Free

In November 1897, Bergljot Bech Göpfert received her divorce from her Austrian husband. To marry again she had to apply for permission from the Norwegian Justice Department.

Bergljot would celebrate her twenty-fifth birthday at the start of 1898, when her daughter would be three years old. She longed to begin anew, to make the home that she and her lover had talked about together over the past two years. But lately Hamsun had grown unwilling to talk. From this brooding mindset he crafted the final play in his trilogy, *Evening Glow*, which undoubtedly drew on his life with Bergljot.

The play focuses on Elina, who had previously been seduced by Bondesen. In this new work, she has returned to the apparently unyielding Kareno with another man's child. Kareno demands that the child should live with its grand-father, but when Elina's father dies, the child comes to them. Kareno's irrita-tion and jealousy mount, and Elina offends his pride when she reminds him that, with her inherited wealth, he will be fortunate enough no longer to need a stipend. 'Shall I be your scholarship boy then?' he bursts out bitterly.

Having let this woman back into his life, Kareno seems to relent on one point after another, until Leo Høibro from *Editor Lynge* (granite-hearted and uncompromising) makes an appearance. He works on Kareno, reminding him of his own once-unbending views on life. 'Fie! To go around knowing [. . .] That fundamentally one is married to the remains of a human being. [. . .] And to be forever doomed to breathe the scent of failure. The odour of another with every breath.'

Hamsun was himself beginning to see his fiancée through Høibro's jaundiced eyes. Bergljot was a 'used' woman, used by the Austrian dog. Hamsun's passion had not merely cooled; with the thrill of the chase over, it had died. He asked Bergljot to reconsider their engagement, suggesting they both give themselves more time. She made it clear that she was not to be delayed or dissuaded.[55]

With the continuing spread of slander against him, Hamsun was finding it increasingly difficult to separate reality from fantasy. One December day in town he counted eight men spying on him, and reported it in a letter to Norway's prime minister, beginning: 'Your Excellency, you will surely not refuse to use your authority to assist me in my anguish.'[56]

It was a desperate plea for help. The prime minister did not reply.

When Hamsun now became the prime suspect in the investigation, he demanded that it be closed; unsurprisingly, this did nothing to allay police suspicions.

Hamsun wrote a long letter to the Speaker of the Norwegian Parliament, the second most powerful man in Norway after the king, pleading with him to take up his case: 'In this last anonymous letter I was informed in no uncertain terms that this persecution will never end. It tells me that my persecutors are numerous, and will hunt me down as long as I live, and know where to find me in whatever country I stay.'[57]

Hamsun felt trapped. It was impossible for him to escape from his promise to marry Bergljot once her divorce had been finalised. If he did, the 'lies' that Anna Munch had propounded about his being a cheat and womaniser would all be proved true.

Bergljot's previous marriage made it difficult to find a priest willing to marry them, but eventually they did, and they were officially declared man and wife in May 1898. The witnesses were friends of Hamsun's: author Hans Aanrud and bookseller Christian Dybwad. Bergljot presented Hamsun with a tiepin with an oriental pearl that went perfectly with the frock coat he had had made. They held the reception at a hotel in Oslo. Quite a crowd had gathered in the hope of seeing the celebrity author and his beautiful bride. When the couple appeared on the corner balcony, cheers erupted – but the groom did not look particularly happy.

The next day the couple left Oslo for a little house outside the capital. Bergljot supplied a rich selection of glasses, crockery and table linen from her first marriage. Her new husband bought champagne, wine and other drinks in the city.[58]

Bergljot had a tidy fortune at her disposal: an inheritance from her mother, as well as assets from her previous marriage to Göpfert, and she was set to inherit yet more when her father died. The bridegroom's own finances were in the best shape they had been in for a long time too. His debt to Zahl had been written off, admittedly by a sleight of hand that somewhat undermined Hamsun's insistence that he was always so upright. Asserting that, since he was under age when he signed the loan agreement, he was therefore exempt, Hamsun took Zahl to court and won; he was released from a debt totalling some 2,000 kroner plus nigh-on twenty years' interest, as well as all legal fees, leaving Zahl to pay the costs for both sides.

But Hamsun was paying a heavy personal price. He was resigning himself to a passionless marriage and family life, just as the former firebrand and hitherto-unbending Ivar Kareno did in *Evening Glow*, which Hamsun finished that spring.

Hamsun took his new bride with him to Valdres and set about writing his next novel. If he felt powerless in his life, at least in his writing he could direct everything down to the least detail. His subject was a love that would never fade because it was never realised.

In *Hunger*, *Mysteries* and *Pan*, Hamsun wrote of men who destroyed everything once their desires were satisfied. They did not seek fulfilment itself, but the dream of fulfilment. In his new novel, love would be kept potent through fantasy and poetry and, in turn, that ideal of love would fuel words and art.

By late autumn 1898, in less than four months, Hamsun had completed his next novel, *Victoria*. In the meantime he had also dispatched his new bride back to the capital.

Victoria is the first of Hamsun's books to give his characters a past. At the opening of the novel, Johannes, the fourteen-year-old miller's son, falls in love with Victoria, the daughter of the lord of the manor. He fantasises that one day she will throw herself at his feet and beg to be his slave. Johannes eventually travels to the city and becomes a famous writer. His ideas of love are his source of inspiration: 'Love is God's first word, the first thought that floated through his mind. When he said: Let there be light! There was love. And he saw that everything he had made was good, and he wanted nothing to change thereafter. And love was the world's origin and the world's ruler; yet all its paths are full of flowers and blood, flowers and blood.'

When they meet in town, Victoria is wearing an engagement ring. He confides to her that merely knowing that she might love him just a little will make a great man of him. The following night he falls into a creative trance and exhausts himself scribbling down his ideas. In the early hours of morning he flings open his window and cries out in jubilation. To his irate landlord he explains: 'It was like a long fork of lightning. I watched a flash of lightning that followed a telegraph line once and, God help us, it looked like a sheet of fire. That's how it streamed through me last night.'

Time passes. Johannes deals with humiliation and celebrates literary triumph, but the thought of Victoria always fuels his writing. One day he meets her old tutor who tells him about his own youth spent chasing unhappy love. Clandestine writings were born of it but no life. Now he has settled down, marrying a woman who has been married before and who already has a child. He explains to Johannes why he has abandoned his dream of love: 'Have you ever, even once, seen a man with the woman who was right for him? [. . .] So a man is obliged then to take the best love he can, and he needn't die from this compromise. Let me tell you, nature has arranged things so wisely that he endures it perfectly. Just look at me.'

He tells Johannes that Victoria is dead and gives him a letter that she wrote to him on her deathbed: 'I will never see you again, so I regret never throwing myself at your feet and kissing your shoes and the earth you walked on, and never showing you how inestimably I have loved you. [. . .] Dear God, you should have known how I loved you, Johannes. I have not been able to show you, so many things have stood in my way, most of all my own nature. Daddy was similarly cruel to himself. [. . .] Victoria writes this to you, and God reads it over my shoulder.'

Hamsun suffered a crisis of self-loathing during the writing of this book. 'Oh God, how this writing sickens me. I am tired of the novel, and I have always despised drama, I have begun writing poetry, the only form of writing that is not both pretentious and meaningless, only meaningless,' he complained to a friend.[59]

The gap between his writing and life had grown too great.

The newly married couple could not agree about where their lives should go next.

Bergljot, with four-year-old Vesla to consider, wanted a new home: the child could not grow up in guesthouses. But Hamsun vetoed any plans for a house or apartment. His nerves were bad, he told several people, and one reason for this was the presence of his stepdaughter. He felt he had to get away, 'to get some sleep, away from the little one'.

Having failed to create the home of which the couple had once spoken, Bergljot made a further sacrifice for the sake of her husband, sending Vesla back to Austria to live with her father.

Yet Hamsun's version of events was that he 'stood and screamed that I wanted her'.[60]

Journeying East

When it became clear by the late autumn of 1898 that he was to be offered the state funding he had been refused the previous year, Hamsun made up his mind. He would take the trip to the Orient that he had dreamed of for so long – with or without Bergljot. He would set off in the summer, and in the meantime they would live in Helsingfors, Finland. This would make an excellent starting place for a journey eastwards, it would not present the same linguistic challenges as Paris, and the couple could also escape their persecutors. Hamsun knew many people there – literati whom he had met in Paris and Copenhagen, including the German-Swedish author Adolf Paul, the writer and diplomat Birger Mörner, and authors Elias Kuhlefelt and Karl Adolf Tavastjerna.

At the beginning of November 1898, the couple booked into the Kleineh Hotel in Helsingfors. It was here that Hamsun read *Morgenbladet*'s review of *Victoria*.

The conservative newspaper had hardly been receptive to Hamsun's previous work, and in reviews of *At the Gates of the Kingdom* and *Evening Glow* had been particularly critical of his portrayal of Elina, suggesting that a man of Hamsun's inferior background did not have enough insight into upper-class women to describe them accurately or well – let alone (so it was implied) to marry one. The same censure was now trotted out in a scathing review of *Victoria*. Once Hamsun had cooled down a little, he wrote a curt note to the editor, comprising a single brief sentence: 'Thank you for your recent extraordinary rudeness.'[61]

Hamsun wrote to Georg Brandes in Denmark, the only man with enough clout to limit the damage of such a devastating review. Hamsun and Brandes had not corresponded for several years but the situation was becoming desperate; the influential *Morgenbladet*'s condemnations were convincing the book-buying Norwegian middle class to steer clear of Hamsun's works. If Brandes were to stand up for Hamsun's talent in an article, all could yet be saved. The Norwegian made a plea from the heart of one writer to another: 'I am thirty-eight years old now, I have been writing for ten years and published eleven books, but I sit here today wondering if it is worth it for me to continue.'

Brandes's answer was even more hurtful than *Morgenbladet*'s review. The Dane called attention to both Hamsun's uneasy relationship to criticism – which he himself had witnessed – and his indisputably narrow cultural background as the son of a tailor.

That Christmas, a furious Hamsun replied to Brandes, spitting with sarcasm. He could see clearly now that, in order to be counted among the cultured, one would have to have taken countless trips abroad, to have read countless books and seen countless paintings; whereas to lack culture was 'to have had parents who did not make one a student or a doctor of this or that, to lack culture is to be forced to travel to America, to do manual work on the prairies, and to eventually find oneself incapable of taking on the opinions of most educated people about the recognised canon, despite one's sincerest and most determined efforts at convincing oneself to do so'.[62]

Just before Christmas, Bergljot and Hamsun moved out of the Kleineh Hotel and into a house at Råholmen just outside the centre of Helsingfors. Bergljot was still set on realising her dream of making a home. A great deal of carpentry work was needed, and Hamsun, who had not used his practical skills since his time in America, bought himself an enormous store of tools.

At last the couple, now married for six months, could invite their fast-growing circle of acquaintances to visit them in their home. Hamsun's closest friends were the bookseller and writer Wentzel Hagelstam, and Alexander Slotte, also a writer. Jean Sibelius, however, had not been charmed; the composer did not like Hamsun's lack of refinement, which manifested itself in surliness and eccentric behaviour that sometimes went well beyond what he considered proper.[63]

Nobody who visited the Hamsuns could avoid noticing the tension between the Norwegian couple. One minute Hamsun could introduce Bergljot proudly, and the next ignore her or show irritation towards her. Bergljot must have hoped that their past difficulties, not least his violent mood swings, had been caused by the stress of his being stalked, and the pressure of his finishing his novel. Here in Helsingfors it became evident that she had married another man she did not know. Added to which, there was the winter to contend with; as she confided to her sister Alette: 'God, it's dreadful here, we are both going mad from this indescribably crazy winter – sickness and misery.'[64]

Halfway through the spring they rented a second modest house at the back of 23 Kaserngatan in the centre of Helsingfors. Hamsun kept on the little house at Råholmen so he could work there. He produced a short story, 'The Conqueror', about a writer driven into disturbing states of mind as he tries to capture women. The more unobtainable the women are, the stronger his desire and belief that the relationship will last for ever – until the moment he possesses them.

With a financially successful year behind him – two editions of *Victoria* in Denmark and Norway and translations into German, Swedish and Finnish; *Editor Lynge* and *Siesta* published in German; productions of *At the Gates of the Kingdom* in Stockholm and Bergen; and various short pieces published in Finnish, German and Austrian journals and magazines – Hamsun now had the means to consider his long-planned journey to the Orient which the couple would undertake later that year.

Early in the summer Bergljot took a trip to Oslo and Vienna to visit her father and then her daughter. Hamsun had a merry time of it as a grass widower in her absence. But when Bergljot returned in the autumn, so did all his feelings of inadequacy. Even the thought of their travels failed to cheer him. In a letter to Bolette Pavels Larsen, he wrote: 'By the way, I do not care if I return from Turkey alive or not. Hell and damnation, what a life this is!'[65]

On 2 September, the couple left for St Petersburg via Vyborg. Hamsun took a notebook with him, planning to write a travel sketch or perhaps an entire book. In a restaurant in Moscow, he jotted down: 'I sit here feeling quite at home, that is to say remote, and consequently in my element.'[66]

In Russia he observed the pervasiveness of the master–servant relationship. 'One obeys a man who knows how to give a command. Napoleon was obeyed with joy. It is a pleasure to obey. And the Russians still know how to do this.'

Memories were constantly being aroused in him as he travelled. When he saw farmhands threshing their crops in the old style, he realised why there had always been grit in the Russian grain his father and neighbour had ground in their little mill in Nordland. The journey through the Caucasus, which he had read so much about, was made by horse. Reaching Mount Kazbek, he wrote in his notes that he felt as though he stood face to face with God, and simultaneously mused on the fatalism of the East. It was so simple, tried and tested, as strong as iron.

The British were everywhere, and the way Englishmen seemed to stare through him so arrogantly did nothing to allay his prejudices. Observing their domination in Turkey, Hamsun wrote in vehement defence of the Sultan – a man generally lambasted by the European press.

From Constantinople, husband and wife journeyed through Bulgaria and Serbia into Austria, where Bergljot was to see her daughter again. Hamsun had travelled through a fairytale land with a beautiful woman at his side, but time and again he was reminded that she was not the princess he had imagined. Worst of all, perhaps, she had snooped in his notes and objected at his writing what she judged to be the most blatant lies.

Six weeks later, in mid-October, they reached Copenhagen, where they rented an apartment on the outskirts of the city. Hamsun confessed his unhappiness to his Finnish friend Wentzel Hagelstam; he was 'more and more convinced that life's content and meaning is in drink. God damn it! Not because it tastes good, but because the sky grows a little higher. And then the Caucasus! I never in my wildest dreams imagined anything so vast. It had such a powerful effect on me that it made me cry. – But sitting here, writing books. It's just too vile.'[67]

Bergljot travelled back to Oslo to visit her father. Hamsun stayed in Copenhagen, needing to be alone to write his travel sketches, as well as a new collection of short stories he was planning, and some articles. He was broke again. Bergljot said they could use her money. He objected, but was repeatedly obliged to relent.

The peasant life he had seen in the Caucasus had brought back vibrant memories of his childhood – the good times when he was living in Hamsund and Hamarøy. He began to weave these memories into the book he was working on, which he entitled *In Wonderland*: 'In good weather I lay on my back on the heather and wrote with my finger across the entire sky and lived enchanted days. And I let the animals wander wherever they pleased for hours, and when I had to find them again I'd climb up a hill, or clamber into a tall tree and listen with open mouth. [. . .] I think about all these things, as I roll along in a wagon down a wide Caucasus road. Everything seems so wondrous, I feel as though I could put down roots here and be blessedly removed from the world. It would have been a different matter if I had been cultured enough to really benefit from my present life; but I am not.'

Hamsun sat in an apartment in Copenhagen leafing through the notes he had made during his journey through the Caucasus, adding new passages here and there – passages that intertwined his childhood experiences of the north with the fairytale land he had just travelled through.

Prodigal Son – Failed Husband

In the late spring of 1900, Hamsun made the journey back to Nordland and his childhood home in Hamarøy. He had been gone for twenty-one years.

Many of his family and other people from his childhood had died or moved away, but his mother and father were still alive; Tora had turned seventy in January and Peder had just celebrated his seventy-fifth birthday. They lived in a small cottage in Hamsund, so small that Hamsun had to bend to get through the door of the attic room in which he slept; he measured it to be no more than 1.3 metres high.

Hamsun observed the changes in village life from the simple existence he remembered. Those farming the land now had to produce more and more in order to pay back the loans forced upon them to purchase modern tools and machinery. The fishermen had to make much larger investments. People were buying more readymade goods in the shops.

His parents' cottage and brother Ole's hut, situated on a smallholding separate from Hamsund, both needed repair. Hamsun engaged labourers and wrote to Bergljot for money. She sent 500 kroner, as much as two farm labourers would earn in a year. She also sent presents for Hamsun's little nephews, which he had asked her to buy.

Bergljot, in turn, wanted to know what he intended to do in the autumn after he had finished writing as he had planned. Where, she wondered, were they going to live? Hamsun told her she should simply be pleased that, at long last, he was writing again. But in another letter to her just a week later the cracks were starting to show: 'We must both hope to God that I don't dry up completely. Oh, but I shan't – sadly I shan't probably be finished for the autumn after all. Oh my God, what an agony this all is!'[68]

He was finding it impossible to live in such close proximity to his parents, his brother's family and other relatives, and soon moved into a *jordgamme*, a traditional Sami turf hut, 3 or 4 kilometres away.

Even there, he only held out for a couple more months.

Returning to Oslo, Hamsun found lodgings in a boarding house, while Bergljot continued to live with her father. He would visit occasionally to spend some hours with her, but she was far from happy with the arrangement.

With Hamsun still struggling to write, the couple travelled together to Copenhagen in the autumn and rented an apartment in the Frederiksberg quarter.

Hamsun read the newspapers avidly. Reports of Paul Kruger, the despairing president of the Boer Republic of the Transvaal, had him transfixed. Kruger was attempting to galvanise major European powers into action against the British. In the face of uprisings, Britain had sent 400,000 troops to the

Transvaal, and there were shocking stories of so-called concentration camps in which the British were accused of starving women and children to death. Hamsun's New Year's wish was that the Russian tsar would intervene in the Boer War: 'Then England will answer: Take your hands off, boy! And then perhaps there will be a little world war, which might change things significantly.'[69]

Meanwhile Hamsun's writing was still in crisis. He had not written anything satisfactory for two years. He confessed to a friend: 'I brood my characters into oblivion, and make no progress. It has been like this for a long time now. I have often found myself unable even to write a few lines like these, due to boredom, disgust, fatigue. That is the way things are. We shall have to see!'[70]

These feelings were no doubt also clouding his marriage. Hamsun was aware of his behaviour and, at times, could be contrite. After one of his meetings with Bergljot in Oslo it had been a repentant man who had written to her:

> You have endured a great deal with me, I have been impossible so often in the past. So if you feel perhaps you were less than cheerful and pleasant in town today, you mustn't blame yourself – you are still very much in credit. I remember a time out in Råholmen in Helsingfors when I castigated you for having bought 10 øres' worth of tallow for the birds. And you said nothing. I think back on it now and it makes me deeply sad. I do certainly feel that I am better than I was, and I'm not just saying it. And if I get I worse again, it is nothing more than a sickness inside me. I suffer like a dog because of it, Bergljot.[71]

Bergljot left Copenhagen to spend Christmas in Oslo. Six weeks later Hamsun wrote to ask if he should join her there. He had to press her for any answer since, as so often, he left her confused as to the reply he really wanted. She would have to pay for his travel, and he made clear his objection to her withdrawing more of her money on his behalf; but he also made no secret of the fact that he was stuck in Copenhagen without a penny. He had pawned some possessions, and nursed some vain hope that his next lottery ticket might provide the money for his fare.

If Bergljot agreed to his coming to Oslo, he would take lodgings close enough to visit her and her father after he had written himself empty. 'Not every evening of course, but now and then. And you and I could sit in my hotel in the evening once in a while and take a glass.'[72]

Bergljot finally sent money, and at the beginning of February Hamsun packed his dirty clothes, removed the nameplate from his front door for fear of his neighbour stealing it, and boarded the train.

They had been married for almost three years but still had no permanent home to speak of. Bergljot finally persuaded Hamsun to put down roots in Oslo, and in the spring of 1901 travelled back to Copenhagen to pack up the apartment. Her husband, true to form, bombarded her with detailed instructions on how the carpets should be rolled, the legs of the daybed unscrewed, his bed taken apart, the wicker chairs tied together. He had also decided on the distribution of the rooms in their new apartment in Bygdøy Allé 7: Bergljot's bedroom and sitting room would face the garden, his and the dining room towards the back yard.

Meanwhile, Hamsun was reworking 'Hazard', which he called 'Father and Son', this time making the storyline less like Dostoevsky's *The Gambler*. The thought of gambling at the roulette table was beginning to obsess him.

His wife had no idea.

I Shall Spit in God's Eye

Knut and Bergljot Hamsun had discussed travelling north during the summer of 1901. Bergljot would visit family in Nordland first and then follow him to Hamarøy. As it transpired, only Bergljot travelled: Hamsun announced he was going to write.

As soon as she had left their apartment Hamsun retrieved Bergljot's bankbook, which his wife had insisted should be in both their names, visited the bank and withdrew a large sum of money. Then he took the boat and train to Antwerp, and from there continued to the coastal town of Ostend – a town famous for its casinos.

He did not intend to quit until he had achieved his aim: to make himself financially independent of Bergljot. Hamsun set out to buy himself free of his marriage.

But soon he found himself issuing a distress call to Wentzel Hagelstam. 'I don't dare travel home again, Hagelstam; salvage my good name and my life. I have suffered such dreadful mental torment since I came here that I can't bear it any more, and my soul is without balance.'[73] He begged the Finn to contact his rich friends and ask for a loan. 'I am not dishonest, I shall repay it all. Please forgive my making this huge request!' Hamsun assured his friend. He had lost a fortune of 13,000 francs.

Concealing the true extent of his gambling debts, Hamsun begged Bergljot for forgiveness – and duly received it by telegram. 'My God,' he replied, 'these are the worst weeks of my life, apart from the year before we were married. I am just skin and bone and my eyes have sunk deep in my skull. Never mind. God bless you, my Bergljot, for never being angry with me for anything.'[74] But despite his contrition, Hamsun explained that he would not come home yet. He was going to try his luck at another casino further south in Belgium, in Namur.

There he received another letter from his wife enquiring whether everything taken from the account had been lost. He denied it. 'Dear God,' he confided to Hagelstam, 'I would have preferred her to hurl abuse at me and call me a dog and a wastrel.' Hagelstam managed to persuade his friends to forward the requisite funds in record time. 'I have never really been that *terrible*, but I am inclined to go too far, I am not the most temperate person', Hamsun admitted.[75]

The money from Helsingfors was the result of an astonishing fundraising effort organised by Hagelstam among the Finnish-Swedish community. Hamsun took it straight back to the roulette table. Soon this small fortune was reduced to no more than a few francs. His adversary was too powerful, he lamented to his wife, whom he was in the process of ruining: 'Our heavenly father has, in his mercy, sunk me deep in wretchedness, and now he sits no doubt rubbing his merciful hands, since he has done such an excellent job. More than once I turned to him on my knees in the streets of Ostend, for a whole month, for five weeks perhaps. And he heard me just as much as he hears everybody. Now I shall spit in his eye, for the rest of my life. He made me who I am, and bears the responsibility.'[76]

Bergljot could no longer have had the least doubt that she had married the man that Hamsun described in *Hunger*. Perhaps most painful of all for her was his next suggestion: he begged her to come to the casinos with him. A couple of weeks would suffice. 'This is how it is; I can put down just 20 francs and in seven minutes these can easily turn into 100,000 francs.'[77]

Bergljot did not come. Neither did his prayers bring salvation. The blackguard of the heavens ignored him.

The weather grew colder. Hamsun had to wear his shirts in layers as his summer coat gave no warmth and the soles of his shoes were completely worn. Bergljot sent him money to travel home, but he was nervous that he might meet her seaman brother on board the ship. One Friday afternoon towards the end of October, he wrote a farewell note, put Bergljot's new address on the envelope, and posted it from Antwerp: 'Dear Bergljot, I shall go aboard now, and will never come ashore again. Farewell. God bless you, and thank you. Your Knut.'[78]

But Hamsun did not take his life that October of 1901.

Instead he returned to Bergljot and created new life; Hamsun's wife fell pregnant.

Hamsun now began working on several projects: a collection of short stories; a thin but promising manuscript of poems; a collection of articles; his travel sketches; and his poetic drama; all of which were meant to ameliorate his financial position. He had been making promises to his publishers for months. They were perhaps beginning to ask themselves if he had already given his best. Hamsun had to prove them wrong.

Halfway through Bergljot's pregnancy, around her twenty-ninth birthday, Hamsun thrust the problems and practicalities of yet another move upon her. They were to be a proper family now and live in respectable style. The couple rented the ground floor of a large two-storey villa with a front garden, set well back from the street, in a good district.

Nonetheless Hamsun continued to spend most of his time in lodgings outside town.

By June 1902, he had finished the poetic drama that he had been struggling with for three and a half years. The intention was that this should mark the beginning of another trilogy. The first part would depict a revolt against God, the second resignation, and the third faith.[79] He called it *Friar Vendt*. Its similarities to Ibsen's *Peer Gynt* ran deeper than merely the title. Hamsun's eponymous hero presents himself to the audience: 'I should have been a priest, / but truth be told, I am strangely grafted; / at my birth a wolf entered my blood, / he lies growling under my waistcoat.'

But Hamsun did not create a gentle Solveig to rescue Friar Vendt, who is brought down by drink and deception, and the betrayal of a woman. In the dead man's wallet a piece of paper is found bearing the seal of the king, testament to his having atoned for his sins.

Having spent a few days around midsummer with Bergljot and having felt the seven-month-old foetus move inside her, perhaps Hamsun felt a glimmer of hope. He too had suffered enough from life and maybe his fortunes were changing. He drew the rest of Bergljot's money out of the bank and travelled back to the Belgian casinos, where he threw himself on God's mercy again.

He gambled away the remainder of his wife's fortune. He felt sure that all that was left to him was further degradation and punishment. But perhaps the fates were smiling on him after all. He chanced upon a painting of Christ on the Cross with St Francis at his feet, which an Antwerp art dealer was offering for sale at what seemed an extremely reasonable price. The more Hamsun looked at it, the more he was convinced that it was a Goya – and in his present state its subject matter particularly appealed to him. He felt sure he would be bringing a valuable treasure home to his wife and child.

On 15 August 1902, Hamsun became a father. He decided the baby should be christened, as was one of his literary progeny, Victoria. The birth had gone smoothly and Bergljot was doing well – and so too, surprisingly, was the new father. Granted, he stayed mostly at guesthouses since his nerves could not stand the baby's screaming, but Hamsun's writing flowed more easily and better now than it had for years.

He tried to persuade Gyldendal to forward him some money as an advance on future books. He asked for 25,000 kroner. It was an astronomical amount, equivalent to the total funds allocated to helping orphan children by the city of Oslo that year. It would have covered the rent on a spacious Oslo apartment for almost thirty years. But the fortune was intended for one purpose only: to replenish Bergljot's bank account and transform Hamsun from an unhappily married writer into a divorced and productive one.

Jacob Hegel at Gyldendal in Copenhagen refused to give Hamsun the loan. He was all too aware of the mediocre sales figures for Hamsun's books, and recently had heard rather a lot about his excessive expenditure and numerous creditors. But he did stretch out a helping hand, printing 2,500 copies of *Friar Vendt* despite the fact that only Ibsen's plays ever sold in book form.

Friar Vendt was generally well received by the critics, but was not hailed as a work of genius. Hamsun was deeply disappointed. There was also a concern that his Goya was not a Goya. This seemed to be the consensus opinion of those who had seen it thus far.

Hamsun approached Albert Langen, petitioning the German publisher to mobilise some of his wealthier friends if he was unable to provide the entire sum himself. Langen made three approaches without success, but he tried to comfort Hamsun: 'Is your position really that desperate? A writer with a gambling debt! You're not an officer with status and honour on the line! You have been reckless, of course – but you still have your talent, your genius.'[80]

Langen's solicitations had sparked off rumours about Hamsun's wellbeing. German newspapers went further and reported that the Norwegian author had disappeared without trace. The news was picked up by the Norwegian papers, and it was not long before a source claimed that Hamsun had committed suicide.

Towards the end of 1902, Hamsun found himself having to issue a public denial of his own death through a news agency. The truth was that he had been admitted to hospital with a bad case of bleeding haemorrhoids. An itchy behind had plagued him periodically for years and had grown worse. It was a legitimate, albeit embarrassing, excuse for his absence from Bjørnson's seventieth birthday celebrations, to which guests from home and abroad were invited.

Bjørnson was overwhelmed when he was presented with his *Festschrift*, within which Hamsun had dedicated a poem to him. Bjørnson tracked him down in hospital to thank him.

The visit from Norway's grand old national bard energised Hamsun enormously. Soon he sent Christmas greetings to Gyldendal bragging that certain critics who were still working against him should be aware that 'in the future it will be difficult for them to get around me. I still have great, heavy irons which I plan to make red-hot.'[81]

Before Christmas he was discharged and, back home, Hamsun commented proudly on how well Victoria ate, belched and gained weight. He also liked to tell guests about how he had saved her life by holding the baby close to his bare chest when she was ill so she could absorb what he called 'animal warmth'. Loyal Bergljot also boasted to everybody about her husband's rescue of their little girl.

Three weeks into 1903, Hamsun had to return to hospital for a follow-up operation. His suffering was not only physical. Lying on his belly, he bemoaned his situation to Bjørnson, divulging the stories of his gambling trips, the bank account he had stripped of 25,000 kroner, and his debt to the Finns. Hamsun begged Bjørnson to use his huge influence with their shared publisher, Gyldendal, in Copenhagen.

Hegel lent Bjørnson a sympathetic ear, indebted as he was to the man who had been instrumental in convincing two generations of Norwegian writers, most notably Ibsen, to publish with the firm. But it was doubtless Hamsun's own threat to leave Gyldendal for the Norwegian publisher Aschehoug that made Hegel sit up and listen. Hamsun's growing status among his Norwegian colleagues had become apparent after he had been elected chairman of the Norwegian Writers' Union for 1903, a post that Hamsun had in fact turned down twice before. Hegel feared that should Hamsun leave his publishing house he might take other Norwegian writers with him. Hamsun and Hegel came to an agreement, and Bergljot's bank account was reimbursed.[82]

Hamsun himself was far from solvent, however. Part of the agreement with his publisher was that his advances and fees would be reduced. In addition to feeding his old creditors, he had to pay his debt to the Finns. Before the agreement was signed, Hamsun hassled Gyldendal for a rise in royalties. Was it his age, he asked curtly, that hindered him from earning as much as Ibsen? It could hardly be a question of talent.

In March 1903, Ibsen celebrated his seventy-fifth birthday. Nobody entertained the notion that Hamsun, who had persecuted the world-famous playwright for almost fifteen years, would contribute to the *Festschrift* or make a speech. But then, neither did anybody imagine that he would choose this moment of celebration to launch yet another attack on Ibsen in his next book. And in a travel book no less, his *In Wonderland: Lived and Dreamed in the Caucasus*:

For years Henrik Ibsen made a habit of sitting at a certain time sphinx-like in a certain chair in a certain café in Munich. From then on he had to persist with this act; wherever he went, he had to sit sphinx-like for the people, at a certain time and in a certain chair. People expected it. It may have been an awful bother for him sometimes; but he was too strong to give up. Oh, what powerful characters the two of them are, Tolstoy and Ibsen! [. . .] But had they been a little greater they might not have taken themselves quite so seriously. They would have smiled a little at their own vanity.

Ibsen was written about and discussed everywhere, and his characters peopled the stages of Europe. Not a single theatre director in Scandinavia or even Germany was interested in putting on a production of Hamsun's *Friar Vendt*. Neither had his earlier trilogy of plays aroused as much interest as he had hoped. He realised that he had to put his plans for two more verse dramas aside – at least temporarily. He did not, however, give up hope of writing a play that would make him money, as well as elevate his reputation as a playwright to equal, or preferably surpass, that of Ibsen.

During the late winter and spring of 1903, Hamsun's friends glimpsed the unhappiness of his marriage while Hamsun himself worked on a new play called *Queen Tamara*.

Prince Giorgi, husband of Queen Tamara of Georgia, is a man of unparalleled accomplishments in the kingdom, yet he remains inferior to his wife because she possesses the economic and political power he lacks. He betrays her and is forgiven, causing him to suffer greater humiliation. In the end he seeks his own destruction, but fate plays its eternal game in his favour: love finally makes the prince ruler of his wife-queen.

Hamsun had not stopped believing in love's power in his writing. This was not the case in his life. Deep inside him, he confided to Bjørnson, darkness was looming. He turned down Bjørnson's invitation for the couple to spend the summer at his home, Aulestad. Bjørnson could not help Hamsun with this particular agony.

The Break-Up of Two Unions

Bergljot's bank account may have been restored, but her relationship with Hamsun was not. He partied hard, wrote little and rarely slept at home with his wife and daughter.

Around midsummer of 1903, he left Norway for Copenhagen, financed by another stipend. The city was full of people he knew, and he was full of self-hatred: a dangerous combination for his nerves as well as his wallet.

When he decided, three months later, that he should at least pay his wife and daughter a visit, he had already squandered the whole of his substantial grant and had to pawn some of his possessions to raise money for the fare.

Hamsun returned home that autumn to huge political tension.

When Sweden used the threat of military action to prevent severance of the Norwegian-Swedish union in 1895, it had caused widespread resentment in Norway. The discontent had been further fuelled by events across Europe. The Norwegian Parliament had given indications of its desire for independence, including the rejection of the union flag, the erection of statues of Norwegian national heroes, the launching of armoured ships, the opening of an ammunition factory and the construction of new fortresses. Hamsun had scoffed at the proposed compromise presented by Norwegian and Swedish negotiators, but Bjørnson saw the situation differently. After years of being in favour of independence, he now came down on the side of the unionists.

In 1903, the Swedes offered Bjørnson the Nobel Prize. In previous years he might have turned it down in political protest, but in December he travelled to Stockholm to accept it, much to the fury of Hamsun and many others. In their eyes Bjørnson was a traitor: 'That bastard went over to the Swedes in his seventy-first year, for 140,000 kroner. I might have done it, all his followers might have done it, since they are mere Bjørnson offshoots – but not the man himself, he owes something to his past, to his whole past.'[83] The only thing that could have been worse, in Hamsun's view, was if Ibsen had received the prize.

Two of Hamsun's books had been published that year: his travel sketches in March, and *Queen Tamara* in September. Now a collection of short stories, *Brushwood*, was issued in time for Christmas 1903, containing old material, partly reworked.

The critics were gradually becoming more sympathetic towards him. But Hamsun still craved the attention of Europe's theatre directors, and the acclaim and high earnings he dreamed of. Seven years after it had been premiered in Oslo, *At the Gates of the Kingdom* had still only received performances in Bergen and very minor theatres in Stockholm, Munich and Berlin.

Hamsun could never settle at home for long, and suggested once more that he might spend the following year travelling. This time Bergljot had her own demands and refused to be overruled: while he was away, she wanted to take a one-year midwifery course at the Rikshospital in the capital. She would live close by and on free weekends visit Victoria, who would have to stay with Bergljot's widowed aunt in the nearby town of Lillestrøm.

Hamsun agreed, but only grudgingly, referring contemptuously to Bergljot's aspiration as a whim. He insisted that it would be absolutely out of the question for her to practise her skills; he did not want to fuel rumours that he was unable to support his family.

In the interim before the start of Bergljot's training and Hamsun's return to Denmark, the family moved to Drøbak in the Norwegian countryside, some 30 kilometres south of Oslo, where they rented an apartment. Before Hamsun's gambling spree they had considered buying a small house near the capital; the money having been spent, they could now just afford to rent apartments on half-year contracts. Only now with the Gyldendal cash in the bank could they entertain the idea of buying once more, and Hamsun promised that, after the year was over, they would build a house of their own.

Hamsun was still broke, and tried in vain to get a loan against a collection of poems he was bringing out, *The Wild Choir*. Reviews were favourable, but not ecstatic.

Hamsun turned forty-five as he packed for Denmark in the autumn of 1904, although publicly he still knocked a year off his age.

Rather than staying in Copenhagen itself, he chose to reside in the small town of Hornbæk on the northern Zealand coast. It was an attempt to avoid the daily temptations of the capital's public houses and eateries but, with the city only a couple of hours away by train, he found it impossible to keep his distance.

His escapades grew increasingly bizarre and stories abounded. Everyone had an opinion on why his behaviour was so outlandish: he was playing God; his need for attention was insatiable; he was prey to the same forces as his own invention Nagel – a highly strung man at the mercy of his impulses.

On one occasion his behaviour became particularly extravagant. Hamsun insisted that the wife of Holger Drachmann, his favourite Danish poet, should accept his beloved gold watch as a gift; the following day he was obliged to ask for its return through a mutual female acquaintance, offering another watch and a brooch in exchange. On another occasion, carousing in Bernina, Hamsun stopped short in the middle of a rant about the follies of the age and stared at the barmaid. No longer in the first flush of youth, she looked weary and rather miserable; and no wonder, when Hamsun and his cohorts had sat guzzling food and drink worth at least ten times more than she earned. This woman deserved flowers! The bar should be weighed down with roses. Hamsun dashed outside, waved down a coach driver and gave him some money to go to Tivoli, where flowers would still be on sale. Fifteen minutes later, the coach driver banged on the window and Hamsun returned with an enormous armful of roses. He walked up to the woman at the bar, declared the roses were for her, gave a deep bow and departed into the night.[84]

One evening he decided to drop in on the poet Johannes V. Jensen in Larslejstræde. The Dane was notoriously sullen and terrifyingly taciturn. He never laughed, yet the two men seemed to share an understanding few could comprehend. Hamsun was standing in Jensen's little apartment performing a monologue in honour of his Danish colleague.[85] Eventually needing a breather, he looked about the room. His eyes alighted not on a comfortable chair, but the ceramic stove. He leapt over to it and, taking measure of its strength, raised his right hand and brought it crashing down in a single powerful, well-aimed blow, breaking the stove in two and scattering the glowing coals and ash across the floor. Suddenly embarrassed, Hamsun shoved the coals back underneath the collapsed stove. Jensen looked him in the eye and remarked drily that Knut Hamsun was always welcome, with or without fire in his wake.

Jensen had numerous opportunities to observe this unpredictable Norwegian. He recorded his impressions in a poetic sketch, describing his drinking companion's titanic sense of humour, wild spirit, sincerity, hunger for life, warmth and wit, but also his deep and vast loneliness which, when Jensen glimpsed it, sobered him instantly.

In a poem about Hamsun, the poet Holger Drachmann observed the same thing: 'deep in the forest sat a child, / – a lost and tearful child.'[86]

While Hamsun wreaked havoc in Copenhagen, Oslo was hit by an earthquake. On Sunday, 29 October 1904, a quake registering 5.5 on the Richter Scale struck. Some saw it as an omen of the tremors that threatened the Norwegian-Swedish union. Earlier that spring, the government had presented proposals detailing how an independent Norwegian consular system might function. During the summer and autumn, Norwegians had waited in suspense to see how Sweden would react. It was rumoured that there were strong divisions of opinion in Stockholm, both within the government and in the wider Swedish parliamentary sphere. It was also claimed that Crown Prince Gustaf was pressuring King Oscar II, now in poor health, to take a firmer stand against the Norwegians.

Towards the end of the year Hamsun launched an explosive attack on Bjørnson, now the leading figure of the pro-unionists. 'You have grown old, master, that is the problem. If only you hadn't grown old! [. . .] For seventy years you stood strong on one side, and in your seventy-first you find that your rightful place is on the other. Old age thinks it grows wiser and wiser, while in reality it tends to become increasingly stupid', he growled in one newspaper article.[87]

These caustic words were quoted in numerous papers and attracted several rebuttals, including one from the Norwegian composer Edvard Grieg.

With the approach of the Christmas season Hamsun hit the bottle. His drinking bouts were punctuated with failed attempts to regain his self-control. During one such momentary attack of remorse he wrote to a friend that he had been on a seven-week bender, commuting between Hornbæk and the capital. He swore he would stop, admitting he was once again in debt. He confessed to feeling like a fraud because he had done so many awful things and behaved like a swine.[88] It was 12 December 1904.

Not even two weeks later, Hamsun seemed to be acting with rather less contrition. He met the author Ragnhild Jølsen in a Copenhagen restaurant. She had been engaged to Thomas P. Krag, one of the few men who could rival Hamsun in the art of flirtation. Now, on the day before Christmas Eve, Hamsun had no competition. It was just the two of them.

A day previously, Hamsun had written a letter to her that was laden with seductive promise. He described how he imagined her to be tall and slender, with delicate hands and hair like Cleopatra: 'And I think there must be a touch of Satan on your lips and in your eyes and as you walk.'[89] He warned her that he would need to catch the last train from Copenhagen to Hornbæk, 'but if I am with you and the café is filled with light and music and such, I might well lose my head again. I do not understand it. Good night then, my child. You must understand, I could be your father', flirted the forty-five-year old.

Jølsen was twenty-eight and had just published her second novel, about a woman who sacrifices everything for her family. She herself was the daughter of a Norwegian landowner who had been forced that year to sell the estate that had been in the family for almost three hundred years.

For a few hours, Ragnhild Jølsen seemed like a living, breathing Victoria, the daughter of the lord of the manor. But Hamsun was no longer a bewildered Johannes, as in the novel, who chooses to write instead of taking what life offers. Neither was he the same writer he had been then.

And the following day he was no longer the same husband.[90]

As Hamsun grew more distant from Bergljot, the woman he had loved and won, he was beginning to generate a greater distance between himself and his characters. He had often employed irony in describing things that were painful to him, but now it became a more pervasive tool. This new distance diminished the need to describe his characters' every thought or impulse, and made the process of writing less painful. His writing became more reliant on a subtle playfulness that ran beneath the text.

When he maintained this ironic distance, the speed with which Hamsun could write astonished him. His next novel, *Dreamers*, was completed in just two months, appearing before Christmas 1904.

Hamsun had never arrived at words easily. But this new approach at least meant he could maintain distance as well as focus. It was as though he had grown long-sighted, able to scrutinise his characters with greater objectivity. And in *Dreamers* the characters were numerous. The housekeeper Marie van

Loos. The telegraph operator, charmer, tough guy and inventor Ove Rolandsen. The sexton's daughter Olga, with eyes like twin souls. The religious Enok, who always wears a handkerchief around his head, and his eternal enemy, Levion, who tore Enok's ear off. Ragna, the girl at the fish-glue factory owned by Mack at Rosengård; Mack's brother, who lives in Sirilund (from Hamsun's earlier novel *Pan*); and his daughter, Elise, tall, tanned, beautiful and unobtainable.

It is a wild, heady Nordland spring that seems to push all creation to its limits. A young parson's wife, naïve and gullible, arrives at the village. 'It is ill-treatment of your eyes even to look at me', Rolandsen tells her, serenading her until she flushes with emotion.

Indeed, Rolandsen knows how to make every woman blush. He falsely admits to a theft of Mack's property in order to claim the reward, and with the money finishes work on his own glue invention. With the first hint of autumn, Rolandsen presents Mack, the local big shot, with an ultimatum. He engineers the situation to get things exactly as he wants them – and Mack's beautiful daughter into the bargain.

Whereas everything went awry in the space of a spring, summer and autumn in Sirilund in *Pan*, in *Dreamers* everything turns out well in the end and is wrapped up neatly. These characters do not on the whole suffer fraught, desperate emotions, and when they do they are sketched with reassuring distance and a certain indulgence. Everything resolves itself, and for once the man gets the woman he wants. The impossible is achievable. Rolandsen proves to be master of his own fate and Hamsun rewards his ingenuity, boldness and bubbling humour.

Hamsun had been persuaded to write *Dreamers* by Gyldendal's literary director Peter Nansen, who had been uneasy with the author's recent output. It had been six years since his last novel, *Victoria*, had been published. The plays and hastily assembled collections of short stories and poetry that had filled the void had done little for Hamsun's reputation or his pocket.

Nansen requested that Hamsun deliver a book of no more than one hundred pages for his popular series *Gyldendal's Nordic Library*. With the promise of a broad readership and 2,000 kroner, Hamsun put his plans for a comedy – and, to a certain extent, his own literary qualms – aside. The only reservation he outwardly expressed was that he had been prevented from depicting the passionate seduction of the parson's wife.[91] It was to be a book suitable for the whole family and must offend nobody: the very kind of literature Hamsun had once expressed so much contempt for.

By enticing him to contribute to this series, Nansen was trying to set Hamsun on a more reader-friendly path. He succeeded, but at the expense of any critical acclaim. Sven Lange of the Danish *Politiken* was merciless: the characters and scenes in the book were mere regurgitations of Hamsun's previous creations; the irony, wit and charm left no strong impression on the heart.

After a six-week-long drinking binge in Oslo, Hamsun finally travelled back to Norway in February 1905.

He booked into a hotel in Drøbak. It would be a further six months before Hamsun, Bergljot and Victoria would attempt to live together as a family. He did not want to abandon all hope that it might be possible; ironically, his unfaithfulness had made it harder than ever to give up on the relationship. Years later he would describe his feelings about his infidelity: 'In the sixth year I had a stipend and had to go abroad, she [Bergljot] wanted to be "independent" and started doing *her* things – consequently not *ours*. That was when it happened. I cheated nobody but myself. It is the lowest, most wretched thing one can do. No love, no tenderness, just ruination. Inside you condemn yourself. [. . .] [I]t is no proof of love, only a release. And afterwards I wished myself far away, without a thank you, without a kiss.'[92]

Hamsun had found a means of survival as a writer: greater distance. As a husband this approach had failed completely.

A Happy House in the Forest?

Just as Nagel in *Mysteries* had dreamed of hiding himself away with Martha in a little cabin in the forest, Hamsun wanted to build a little house on the edge of the woods above Drøbak. In the spring of 1905 he was making detailed drawings for its construction. It would be in Empire Style, with a curved roof and bay windows. It would have an entrance with a porch, hallway and stairway, which he had designed himself, a kitchen, a dining room and a living room facing out towards the fjord. On the first floor they would have the maid's room, Bergljot's and Victoria's room and his own. There would also be an outhouse with a storeroom for firewood, a laundry room, a small brewery, the lavatory and a workshop.[93]

As Hamsun built himself a house, Norway armed itself for war. Negotiations had broken down, so hopes were now pinned on pressuring Sweden to accept a peaceful dissolution of the ninety-one-year-old union. On 7 June 1905, Norway's Parliament passed a unilateral resolution declaring that its union with Sweden was terminated. In August, 85 per cent of men eligible to vote went to the ballot box; there were 368,392 votes in favour of dissolving the Norwegian-Swedish union, and only 184 against. Norway's women, who did not yet have the vote, added their voice to the argument, submitting 250,000 signatures in favour. This young nation's united desire for independence made a strong impression on the rest of Europe.

Sweden and Norway were soon back at the negotiating table, but the points of contention were numerous and talks collapsed after a week. It was not until well into September that discussions were resumed again. In the meantime the Norwegian government ordered partial military mobilisation.

Hamsun positioned himself on the most radical wing, writing militant poems for one of Oslo's newspapers and even joining a gun club. The other side of the border also saw significant military expansion, while sections of the Swedish press stoked up national pride and rallied the Swedish public with memories of ancient greatness. In London, *The Times* ran articles by the renowned Norwegian explorer Fridtjof Nansen, which aroused enormous sympathy for the Norwegian perspective in Britain, even after the appearance of a rebuttal by the Swedish explorer Sven Hedin in the same newspaper. It was clear now that neither Britain nor Germany saw any point in a war and they advised Sweden to negotiate.

Later that autumn, delegations from the two countries finally reached agreement: Norway was to be independent.

The Norwegian people were now faced with a decision as to whether Norway should be a republic or a monarchy. The electorate came to the ballot box for the second time in three months. No longer was the nation united. In parts of Norway, support for a republic was extremely strong, but ultimately the monarchists were victorious, with 260,000 votes to 70,000. Prince Carl of Denmark was a popular contender for the Norwegian throne: he had close links with other European royal families which might strengthen Norway's security in times of unrest, and he had also already fathered an heir. He also gained enormous popular sympathy when he demanded a referendum be held before eventually accepting the Norwegian Parliament's offer.

In November 1905, Europe's only elected king arrived in Norway's capital city. He took the new name Haakon VII, and his son, Alexander, took the name Olav, although his wife, Maud, daughter of the British King Edward VII, kept her own.

Hamsun meanwhile was preparing to move his family into their new house.

It had all proved more expensive than he had planned. In total, he noted, it had cost 9,931 kroner.[94] Raising the money had been hellishly difficult. The previous year had been reasonably successful financially – *In Wonderland* had been published in German, together with *Friar Vendt* and *Evening Glow*, while *Pan* and *Victoria* had come out in Russia and *Dreamers* in Sweden – but Hamsun had frittered away a great deal of the money earmarked for his new abode.

He had been fortunate in having a number of his short stories and poems appear in newspapers and magazines across Europe since his return to Norway in February 1905. In May, he sent out another collection of short stories, *Striving Life*, based mainly on his experiences in America and aspects of his travels in the Orient. One hundred and sixty-two extracts were translated into German, and Albert Langen, as always, stretched himself financially and provided Hamsun with several thousand marks. Gyldendal lent him the greater part of the money needed to build his house, secured against the two new novels that Hamsun was working on. In one, he would continue depicting the lives of the people of Nordland as he had in *Dreamers*; the other would be a first-person narrative, but this time maintaining the distance he now needed to write.

He called the house Maurbakken – 'Ant Hill'. A place to grow old and wise.

Hamsun wrote to his best man, Hans Aanrud, describing his dreadful state of turmoil and declaring that no one should ever get married.[95] It was not the most optimistic of beginnings for the family as, a couple of weeks before Christmas 1905, Hamsun, Bergljot and Victoria finally moved in.

Bergljot was neither practical nor domestic. In *Dreamers*, Hamsun describes the priest's attempts at turning his spouse into a proper housewife, trying to instil a sense of order and diligence in her, and it was much the same at Maurbakken. In all their previous apartments he had been more of a guest than an inhabitant, but this was different. This was a house of his creation, *his* house, and it was having to accommodate two other people. They may not have been complete strangers, but they were not how he wanted them to be.

Bergljot had become terrified of making mistakes, since Hamsun could work himself into a fury. It was not in her nature to retaliate. She accepted all the blame, apologising and promising to mend her ways. Hamsun's opinion was that he had been hard on himself for years and it had helped him; it would do Bergljot and Victoria no harm to learn to be orderly and frugal too. It was a timely bout of amnesia, considering the fortune he had frittered away. Hamsun had come back to his marriage with a bad conscience and was obsessed that things should be very different.

But this was not the life he longed for.

Hamsun began to write about the allure of nature; the desire to walk into the forest, to live alone in a turf hut again, as he had in Hamarøy five years previously. But what kind of life would that be? he asked himself in the book that would be called *The Last Joy*: 'You don't know what you're talking about. It's a life you know nothing of. Your home is in the city, and yes, you have furnished it with ornaments, pictures and books; but you have a wife and maid and hundreds of expenses. And asleep or awake, you are always on the run, never at peace. I have peace. Keep your highbrow aspirations, your books and art and newspapers, keep your cafés and your whisky that cause me nothing but grief.'[96]

The second book that Hamsun now began told the story of Benoni Hartvigsen, a fisherman and postman. It was set in Sirilund, where Glahn had unsuccessfully tried to capture the heart of Edvarda in *Pan*. Benoni agrees a lucrative fishing deal with Edvarda's all-powerful father, Mack, and with the proceeds purchases curtains for his windows and fine white shirts for church.[97]

In *The Last Joy*, an author dreams of escaping everything that was central to Hamsun's existence; in the other book, a character lives a life that bears a striking resemblance to the one Hamsun left behind in Nordland twenty years before. The crisis within Hamsun seemed to be playing itself out in his works.

Christmas was never an easy time for Hamsun, and this one was no exception. He managed to sell to a journal an extract of his novel about the man searching for himself in the forests, and to a newspaper the first three chapters of his other book, but his expenditure was out of control. His periods of sobriety grew shorter. He was drawn to the restaurants in the capital and was very rarely at home, and then only to see his daughter. Often unable to look Bergljot in the eye, he would lash out at her verbally. Alone, he cried in remorse and confusion. One day a fellow writer, Christian Gierløff, found him in a hotel room curled up in a foetal position. His sobs, according to Gierløff, sounded as though they were being wrenched from him. Gierløff had never seen either a child or an adult cry like this.

He made preparations for Hamsun to be admitted to a clinic.

On the first day of March 1906, Hamsun's own words filled almost the entire front page of one of Oslo's newspapers under the headline 'At the Clinic':[98]

I am lying here counting nails in the walls and listening to the harness bells outside, saying brrrr with every nerve – in brief, I have admitted myself. I am helpless, and will remain so for some days, thank heavens. It is utterly delightful not having to do anything for oneself, having nothing but doctors and nurses and kind people around me who want to do everything for me. I have never felt so good and warm inside, and I am certain this shan't be the last time I shall admit myself.

It happened last Monday, something snapped in me. I had been slogging at my craft for some time, and achieving a really good inner tremble and superb sleeplessness for days and nights. Then I got drawn to the highballs and the music in the cafés and lights and my friends – some days later my whole being ground to a halt.

What is the matter with you? said the doctor.

The problem is, I said, that I can't get full-cream milk here at the hotel. I want to leave, I'm not happy here.

Your hands are trembling.

You should see my insides! And I would so like this room to be only half the size and for it to be without a door, and for me not to hear a sound.

Your nerves are out of order, said the doctor.

Then I helped him hospitalise me.

The newspaper sold out instantly, and rumours spread.

Three days later Hamsun sent 'At the Clinic' to Albert Langen. Writing from a hotel room once again, he confided to his German publisher: 'I have built my lovely house now. But just as it was finished, my home and my family disintegrated. What a sad place the world is. Do you think Munich would be a good place for me to live?'[99]

Hamsun did not travel to Munich. Instead he relocated to a guesthouse just a few kilometres south-west of the capital.

The circle was complete. Almost ten years ago, he had met Bergljot in a place very similar to this; now in the spring of 1906, the papers were signed that would formally part them. Bergljot would be divorced for the second time. She was under no illusions about their ever coming together again.

Hamsun took over Maurbakken and the mortgage in order to sell it. He took the furniture he wanted for himself and left the rest for Bergljot. Their joint capital was transferred to her since she had brought it into the marriage. But dividing the child was harder. Bergljot would keep Victoria until she was eight, with Hamsun contributing monthly alimony payments, after which time Victoria would go to Hamsun. If either of the couple got married in the meantime, the other could demand immediate custody.[100]

Hamsun turned forty-seven in August and threw himself into his writing.

During September and October he worked day and night on a manuscript he had been tinkering with in Copenhagen. By the end of November *Under the Autumn Star* had been published. The working title had been 'Neuroses'. Having exorcised his demons, Hamsun returned in this book to a first-person narrative. It was a slender volume, no more than ten pages longer than *Victoria*, which had come into being during his final bachelor days in Valdres in 1898. He had broken his altar vows to love for better or worse.

Gone are the existential rebels of the first half of the 1890s. In *Under the Autumn Star*, Knut Pedersen, an ageing writer with a melancholy glint in his eye, is nursing his nerves in the countryside. In comparison with his predecessors, he poses no threat either to himself or others. He is more observer than active participant, more likely to argue things out in his own mind than to take action. He takes any woman he can: the priest's daughter Elisabeth, her mother and others. But it is the unreachable woman whom he tries most to impress. She is Louise Falkenberg, the wife of the captain, Pedersen's employer. Pedersen follows Louise to the city but falls short again: 'Then there was more wine, and then whisky. [. . .] And then a twenty-day binge when a curtain fell over my earthly consciousness.' Even love has lost its dangers. It is no longer a matter of life or death. It seems barely worth writing about.

Verdens Gang welcomed *Under the Autumn Star* ecstatically. Its critic could not express strongly enough how feeble and bloodless the vagabond figures portrayed in other books seemed beside Hamsun's wanderer, with his dexterity of mind and body. *Morgenbladet* was, true to form, scathing, declaring that this whisky-laced dirge proved Hamsun to be finished as an author. But despite its condemnation *Under the Autumn Star* had to be reprinted three times by Christmas. Hamsun had never experienced this rate of sales before.

Hamsun made a complaint about *Morgenbladet*'s persecution of him to the chairman of the Norwegian Writers' Union. It was a move carefully designed to coincide with the publication of a collected edition of his novels and short stories. As a counterbalance to the persistent negative reviews he had received over the years, particularly from the Right-wing press, Hamsun wanted to mobilise sympathetic literati into putting their names to a publicity article exalting his literary prowess. At least then his work might finally reach the readership of these hitherto dismissive newspapers. There was a great deal at stake now.

Ibsen had died in May of that year, but Hamsun still felt in the great man's shadow.

He felt Gyldendal could do more for him, at the very least give him terms equal to those of Ibsen and Bjørnson. He pointed out that

these two men are coming to the end of their output in these volumes, but I am at the height of my powers with a future ahead of me. [. . .] I am no novice, I have worked for 19 years, have published 19 works, and been translated into 16 languages, I get reprints again and again, especially in Germany and Russia (although in Russia I get not a penny's pay), and people send me letters of appreciation from every corner of the world as far as Australia and South America, but naturally most of all from the European countries. And here at home I still get the same print runs I had when I made my debut 19 years ago. I hope the wind will turn now.[101]

On the day he signed his new contract with Gyldendal he received a message that his father, aged eighty-two, had died.

Away from the City

Hamsun did not travel home to be with his mother for the funeral.

He frequently expressed a desire to revisit the landscape of his childhood, and yet now that the perfect opportunity arose, he declined to do so. Yet he had money enough, and since transport links to Nordland had greatly improved it would only have taken him a matter of days to make the journey. The trip would also no doubt have sparked more memories that would be useful for his current manuscript set in Nordland. He also had siblings there, among them a brother he had not seen for nearly thirty years. Not to mention his mother, a grieving seventy-seven-year-old widow who might have appreciated her famous son attending his father's funeral.

Instead Hamsun set to work on a lecture that tore to shreds the Bible's commandment to 'honour thy father and mother'. The old adage of contented childhood days, he declared, is a falsehood and an illusion. No adult suffers as boundlessly as an impressionable child. 'It is only fortunate that they forget more quickly, and overcome suffering more quickly – moving on to the next joy before falling upon new suffering. Childhood is man's most difficult time.'[102]

The fourth commandment, he claimed, was an outdated irrelevance that turned the truth shamelessly on its head. Procreation was an urge that gratified only the parents, the child having no part in it. The child had not asked to enter the world. An upbringing was not something a child had to be thankful for.

Hamsun gave the lecture six weeks later at the Norwegian Students' Union. A storm immediately broke out in the press.

In July 1907, he left Oslo with Victoria, who had her father on loan for a few summer weeks. He wanted to take her into the countryside, but not so far from town that it would be difficult to return by train. He booked them into a hotel in Kongsberg, a small inland town, founded on its silver mines.

Hamsun decided to stay on after summer was over, keeping the same room at the far end of a corridor on the first floor overlooking a quiet courtyard and garden. Along two entire walls and part of a third he put up shelves that he filled with books. The piles of newspapers and magazines grew on the coffee table. He threw nothing away and refused to allow the maid to dust anything.

As winter approached he even stored firewood in his room, stacking it high in crisscross fashion. He chopped the wood himself, carrying it up and laying it as his uncle had taught him. Thus, surrounded by the aroma of burning pine, he wrote, read and slept. Over his bed was a picture of Victoria, decorated with a sprig of lilac she had given him before leaving.

Hamsun was hardly ever seen in Oslo now. With his marriage over, he no longer needed to run from anything. He found peace, feeding the burner with pine logs, going for walks and playing cards with acquaintances, but not for money.

He abandoned his plans for a sequel to *Under the Autumn Star*. Knut Pedersen was a symptom of his need to escape Bergljot and the city. Now the break was made, he returned to the younger and more vital figure of Benoni Hartvigsen, about whom he had begun to write years earlier at Maurbakken. With the start of 1908, a fresh well of ideas and a host of new characters took form in his mind.

One figure after another sprang up around Benoni, characters that were drawn from people Hamsun had known or heard about in his youth. The lessons he had learned from Mark Twain after reading his books in America could now be put to use. Hamsun had begun to experiment with this different approach in *Dreamers*, but now he had the time to explore it fully. Caricature and a sense of farce were brought into play, poking gentle fun at his characters but maintaining warmth and generosity. He embraced the dialect he had cast off when he had left Nordland as an ambitious twenty-year old, bringing a new texture to his work. One beautifully drawn character after another steps forward from the crowd, distinguished and brought to life by their idiosyncratic speech, their blunders, their mispronunciations and malapropisms, their overly literal interpretations.

Hamsun now walks among his characters like an avuncular narrator. He reveals them, covers up for them, defends and explains them. In previous books he was largely in dialogue with himself, but in this novel, which he decided early on to call simply *Benoni*, he uses a host of techniques to speak more directly to his reader.

Aged forty-eight, Hamsun had finally succeeded in separating his self and his stories. It was necessary not only for his art but also for his psyche; he could not sustain the ruthless mining of his soul for material any longer. Now, as he trawled through his earlier books preparing them for republication in his *Collected Works*, he systematically toned down their more rapturous qualities. Observer and observed were increasingly distanced. His writing now quivered with sidelong glances and a sharp sense of irony.

Hamsun's customary grumbles about the misery of writing ceased. Being in Benoni's company did him good. The ambitious fisherboy was a movingly simple character, with nerves of steel when it mattered; hesitant in the presence of finer folk, yet a fiendishly good mimic. Benoni desires Rosa, the priest's daughter replete with a heaving bosom, ripe mouth, dazzling smile and heavenly light-brown hair. Benoni's rival, son of the sexton, is a law student, increasingly superficial, bone idle, ruined by city life. Reigning over the ensemble like a demigod is the tradesman Mack. His four-poster bed has silver angels at each corner but he is a devil with the girls between its sheets. He has his way with them in broad daylight too: the fleet-eyed Jakobine for one, whose dark ringlets are so tight she is nicknamed Bramaputra of the gunpowder hair; and, despite her jealous boyfriend, Ellen the maid. At the centre stands Benoni, continually rising in his own and others' esteem. He is a man to whom Hamsun suggested anything might happen.

As the author brought his book to its conclusion, he hinted at a sequel with the arrival of another woman. Benoni had succeeded in wooing Rosa, but Hamsun was not quite excited enough by her. He wanted a more dangerous woman, whom neither Benoni nor he could quite control.

Again it seemed that, through his writing, Hamsun caught a glimpse of what lay ahead in his own life.

Hamsun completed *Benoni* on 8 April 1908, and a week later checked into a hotel in the capital, intent on going on a drinking spree. It was a celebratory pause before reacquainting himself with Edvarda, the temptress responsible for Glahn's downfall in *Pan*, who would be central to the sequel Hamsun was now planning. She had, as the closing lines of *Benoni* had told Hamsun's readers, arrived with the spring. And it was now spring in Oslo too, a spring that seemed to infuse the world once more with invigorating, almost ecstatic energy. Perhaps it was no surprise that so many of Hamsun's own relationships with women flowered at this time of year.

Already on his first evening back in town, his friends were gathered. The very next afternoon, one of his drinking companions, the National Theatre director Vilhelm Krag, rang Hamsun, wondering if it would suit him to drop by the theatre. It concerned something they had discussed the night before. His long legs had to carry him no more than a few steps.

They were to change his life.

Part III

My Only Love on This Earth

Standing beside the stairs just inside the National Theatre was a twenty-six-year-old woman. She had been in Vilhelm Krag's office when he telephoned Hamsun to call by, and was now eagerly awaiting the writer's arrival.

She called herself Marie Lavik, a name she had taken to soften her mother's distress over the fact she was living in sin. She and Dore Lavik, a man eighteen years her senior, had been living with one another for five years, and together they had toured with a theatre company throughout Norway, Sweden and Denmark. Marie's performance as Elina in *At the Gates of the Kingdom* had been so impressive that the National Theatre had taken her on as a student. Now that the play was to be staged at the National, she was being considered again for the role. Krag wanted her to meet the great Hamsun himself, about whom she had heard many wonderful, but also some downright unpleasant, things said.

If she made a good impression she might get the role of her dreams. And Hamsun could help her play it as nobody had before.

As Hamsun ascended the steps a group of actors came out of rehearsal and flocked towards him. One of the older actresses cocked her head at him: 'Do you remember, Hamsun, you told me once I had a strong face?'

He smiled, and replied smartly: 'Oh really? No, I don't remember that, it must have been a very long time ago.'[1]

Hamsun pushed his way through to the stage-door office and asked for Marie Lavik. With that the giggling died away, and Marie stepped forward.

'Oh, but my goodness, how pretty you are, child!'

Nobody could have avoided overhearing him invite Marie to accompany him to the Theatercafeen. Descending the steps, he allowed her to lead the way from the stage door, across Stortingsgaten and into the restaurant.

Not even sixty steps, but far enough to change the fate of the woman at his side.

Hamsun removed his galoshes carefully and placed a heavy cane in the corner of his choice. Marie noticed he was slightly pigeon-toed, particularly when he swung one leg forward. She observed him closely. He was different from the way she had imagined him to be from looking at photographs and reading his books and plays. She searched for the refinement, the aesthetic sense in his bearing, but what struck her first and foremost was a kind of forcefulness.

Hamsun's eyes were not clouded with dreams; they were too light and slightly bloodshot, as though from too many tears, too many sleepless nights or too much alcohol perhaps. The chestnut-brown hair was beginning to grey. His profile was perfectly elegant, his moustache emphasising the sternness of his features which did not quite vanish when he smiled.

The waiter arrived with port and they raised their glasses. He grew merrier, she grew bolder.

When Marie told him she had decided to dedicate her life to the theatre she caught a glint of irony in his eye.

They sat there for some time, and then Hamsun escorted her back to the stage door, where he stood holding his hat in his hand, and watched her until she disappeared inside.

Early next morning a tall vase of red roses was delivered to the theatre. It stood in the doorman's office awaiting Marie's arrival. Trembling, she counted them: twenty-six, her age. There was no card.

Later that day she received an invitation to meet Hamsun at a hotel. He led her through closed doors into the restaurant where, around a table, he had assembled all of Norway's most prominent theatre critics.

'The Queen of Sheba!' he announced, throwing his arms open.

Marie was wearing the most beautiful dress she owned – moss green, and it flowed exquisitely. She was the only woman at the table that evening, and the following evening, and thereafter. She had been thrown into learning a demanding role exceedingly quickly. There were no rehearsals.

One evening Hamsun made her his. From that moment Marie's attention would be dedicated not to parts in plays but to her role in his reality. She was living her life in Hamsun's spotlight.

They had spent two wild weeks together and had only briefly been parted when Hamsun pencilled her a note, sending it by messenger from his hotel. They were his first written words to his new love: 'My Marie, I am yours, so wholeheartedly yours. I love you, I say that with my entire soul. And God bless you, that I met you in this life. Take things a little easy for now, and with time we might find a way. My Marie, my Marie, God, how beautiful you are. You have not the slightest notion that you are the loveliest being in the world. I see you coming towards me now – a princess. Not for a second do you leave my thoughts. Unfortunately I confessed to the waiter that I love only *one* woman, but I did not tell him her name. May God grant that things are not too awful for you at home, having to go back to the way things were before! If only I could take you and run away. Be calm, dearest, try to be calm, remember, whatever happens, I am yours.'[2]

The following day, now in Kongsberg, he wrote to her confessing the jealousy he had felt when they had sat in a café together, and how it gnawed at his soul that she might only be interested in him for the promise of the role of Elina. The next day he wrote asking when he could come to her.

He also wrote joyously to a friend: 'You can probably see from my handwriting that I have just returned from town, drunken and debauched – and listen to this! – in love. The devil take me, I've never been so smitten!'[3]

Three days later he received the reassurances from Marie that he needed: 'I love you, and mean that with all my heart. And absolutely not for any acting part, you must believe that.'[4]

He asked her to stand tall amid the good-for-nothings who surrounded her in the clowns' world of the theatre, who were only out to exploit and humiliate her. She told him that she thought about him all the time, with his mischievous look and ironic, haughty smile on his lips.

Marie read *Benoni* and told Hamsun how proud she felt when she saw all the excellent reviews. He thanked her on bended knee. 'Oh please bear with me for a long time, Marie, you can help me so marvellously if you want, you can make a prince of me; I shall overflow with writing and books in return.'[5]

Marie did not tell Lavik, who only made brief passing visits to Oslo, about this extraordinary man who wanted to steal her away from her present life.

Hamsun wanted to know every detail about Marie's life: how, when she was seven years old, her family had been forced to move away from their large house to a much smaller one, and how the local children had taunted them with cries of 'Bankrupt tramps!' And then, how another forced auction had consigned them to a dilapidated farmhouse. When she was sixteen Marie had pulled up roots again for Oslo, her father intent on his star-pupil daughter having the best teachers to help her make something of herself. She was sent to private school, and was one of three in her class to stay on into upper school, having won a scholarship. At nineteen she had been able to show her gratitude to her parents by passing her finals with flying colours.

Hamsun insisted on hearing how she and Dore Lavik had met: she had been teaching in a small town to earn money and prepare for university. Lavik had been performing in a play in the town, and had stayed at her lodgings. They had exchanged letters throughout the winter, and he had returned in the following spring. He was eighteen years her senior, bald-headed and divorced. But he could fulfil her secret dream to perform on the stage. She had auditioned for him, and contrary to her parents' wishes she had made her stage debut at the age of twenty-three.

Marie was curious as to why Hamsun, who knew so many great and famous people, could possibly want to know all about her small, ordinary life.

Had she not realised, Hamsun answered, that she was his only love on this earth?[6]

There Is No Such Thing as Harmony!

During the summer of 1908 Hamsun's feelings for Marie intensified, and with them jealousy that could cause him to make the most dreadful scenes. He started to demand she make ever greater sacrifices: she must make it clear to Lavik that her affair with him was over; she must break off certain friendships, and tell people not to greet her in the street; she should give up the stage and leave the city behind to live in the country with her new lover. They must, according to him, build their lives on stable ground. He knew all about such things; in his wallet he carried the insole of his daughter's shoe and a photograph of her, from which he had cut the image of his ex-wife.

Hamsun constantly trailed Marie, ringing her between rehearsals, demanding all her free time. Meanwhile Lavik continued to write passionate letters and telegrams to her from Bergen where he was on tour. During the day Marie rehearsed small parts, and in the evenings she performed the little she had been given. But around the clock she was hounded by two men who demanded she play the lead role in their lives. Unsurprisingly, her health began to suffer. Eventually, she was admitted to hospital and diagnosed with a kidney infection.

Dore Lavik was also suddenly hospitalised in Bergen, with acute pains. Marie wanted to visit him. Hamsun forbade it.

Lavik was operated on, but his recovery looked doubtful. Marie confided her fears to Hamsun, the one man she thought she could trust with her feelings of confusion: 'I believe that if he dies, the fault will all be mine. He's often said that when he no longer feels I love him, he'll die. And now I keep seeing his face in my mind, distorted with pain, and I hear him saying: "You don't love me, so I must die."'

That afternoon she received a message that Dore Lavik was dead. She asked somebody to telegraph Hamsun with the news. But instead of words of comfort from this man who had written so often about love, Marie received a blistering letter. Hamsun snarled that she had never loved him, that he had never been uppermost in her mind. She had not spared him the least intimacy about her life with the dead man, inflicting on him all her 'tender recollections of him [Lavik] and his "little soul": and the things he has said and done. And now when he has declared himself unable to live without your love, he goes and dies – of a distended colon! And I – his successor – have to receive telegrams, letters and tears of your deep grief – because he couldn't live without you – with his distended colon.'[7]

Marie should see that God had helped them, he explained, somewhat satisfied by events.

She found it impossible to view Lavik's death in this light. To Marie it seemed a punishment for her unfaithfulness to the man she had lived with for five years, for her failure to tell him the truth, and for not visiting him when he was sick. She had to atone for her sins. Marie would come to realise years later that this sense of self-reproach and shame led her stoically to endure more with Hamsun than she might otherwise have done.

Marie had to promise not to go to Lavik's funeral, never to visit his grave, and never to mention the dead man's name again. She must, Hamsun told her, avoid aggravating him, so he could master his feelings of jealousy. Marie voiced her fears that a harmonious relationship might never be possible.

'There is no such thing as harmony in love!' he told her.

'Do you mean that?' she asked, frightened.

'No,' he replied.[8]

Marie's devoutly religious mother tried to prevent her daughter giving up her career and position at the National Theatre for yet another divorced and older man.[9] And Marie did make a gallant attempt, when she applied for, and received, a position as a governess. But it was easy for Hamsun to curtail her efforts at freeing herself.

He now proposed marriage for the second time. Marie and he would be married the following spring. It was a decision that meant Hamsun would gain a wife but lose a daughter, since under the terms of his divorce settlement, his remarriage would mean that Victoria would no longer come to him on her eighth birthday as planned.

Hamsun started making plans for his future with Marie on a little farm, far away from anybody. She would look after the animals and their children; he would write books, and stay off the drink. But Marie would have to be put to the test in the capital first.

He moved her into a room in the centre of town, overlooking the delights and temptations of the city, and then forbade his fiancée to have any contact with anyone she knew from her theatre days. If she had an errand to run in town, she had to write him a note and explain afterwards how she had used her time. Meanwhile, Hamsun took an attic room close by. He would visit her at agreed times, although he would also turn up at others too, tapping on her door with his fingernails in a peculiar way. A sound that reminded Marie of gentle hail against a windowpane.

Hamsun's collection of books (mainly translations from other languages) covered an entire wall of Marie's room. She enquired if there were any he thought she should read, thinking that they might offer some insight into the man she was to marry. Hamsun's answer was immediate: Schopenhauer.[10]

Reading the works of this German philosopher, Marie learned that the will to live is the foundation of man's existence. It is a will that can never be satisfied except superficially and for fleeting moments. Life is a continuous and forever thwarted hunt for satisfaction. Man sets himself apart from other creatures, however, in possessing an intelligence that makes it possible for him to accept the desperation of this plight. This awareness is the means by which man tolerates the situation. We have to admit that we shall live and die fundamentally dissatisfied.

Marie was crestfallen. Why, she asked, had her fiancé suggested she read something so cynical about life, happiness and, implicitly, love?

It is better to expect too little than too much, he answered.[11]

Soon Marie and Hamsun stopped going out for their meals, and he rented a kitchen on the same floor as her lodgings. Marie borrowed a cookbook from her landlady, but Hamsun was soon issuing instructions on how to boil potatoes and how his food should be prepared and served. She must, he insisted, learn to be a good, self-reliant wife. At a nearby laundry she learned how to iron and starch his shirts. One day he placed a pair of scissors in her hand and asked her to cut his hair. She also kept accounts. She soon learned the necessity of tweaking the books a little to make them balance.

Marie often had to find discreet ways of dealing with Hamsun's irritability and tendency to irrationality. One morning, Hamsun lost an iron-supplement pill. The entire room was turned over in the hunt for it. The wood burner was the last place to be searched, and Hamsun dashed off to get the maid with the clear intention of having it dismantled. Meanwhile the pillbox was sitting on the table. When Hamsun returned with the maid, Marie was holding the pill aloft. She had found it, she declared, behind the burner just as he had thought. She was of course lying.[12]

Marie was alone every day and most nights in her flat, waiting for the tapping that signalled Hamsun's arrival. And all the time, right outside, her old theatre life glittered.

Nearing Christmas of 1908, *Rosa* was published. It was Hamsun's first book since he had met Marie. She scoured the pages for some trace of herself in the figure of Rosa. Coming from the theatre where an actor's life experiences inevitably affected the final performance, Marie naturally expected the central character of *Benoni* to have changed dramatically after all her creator, Knut Hamsun, had lived through that spring. Yet there was no change and no hint of their relationship. She was disappointed and hurt, particularly after Hamsun had declared that the thought of her infused his entire consciousness day and night, writing or not.[13]

It presumably never occurred to Marie that the character of Edvarda had anything to do with her at all.

Fourteen years ago in *Pan*, Hamsun had packed Edvarda off to Finland with a baron. Now, just as he had been entering his relationship with Marie, whom he found both threatening and alluring, he brought Edvarda back. In the novel *Rosa*, she retains that dangerous quality that had so fascinated Glahn in *Pan*: 'I believe in madness,' she says, 'in the power of its necessity, in the power of its own logic as a balancing force.'

But it is as if Hamsun wants to get revenge on Edvarda for not having chosen Glahn, and to punish her by displaying her misfortune to all. He even summons back the womanising Friar Vendt to force her to suffer the indignity of being utterly ignored by him. She comes to realise that she has never recovered from Glahn. This time Hamsun sends her off to England together with the drunken, although not unsympathetically portrayed, Sir Hugh. She enters a family stiff with rigid traditions and rituals: surely a punishment rather than a reward for the passionate Edvarda. It would be difficult to find a fate further removed from the grand, open seascapes of home. At the last minute, however, she does at least make the decision to take the children with her, and with them the chance of happiness.

Hamsun, it seems, was done with women like Edvarda: desperate, unpredictable and demanding. Women should be passionate, as Marie undoubtedly was. But they had primarily to serve a higher purpose. Children were the fulfilment of a woman's existence, and the greatest sorrow a couple could endure was the emptiness of a childless marriage. It was a theme he would explore in his next novel. But meanwhile, the idea for a new drama was growing rapidly.

Reality and fiction had always entwined themselves in unpredictable ways.

In early 1909, Hamsun began to look through some notes for another play. Marie tried to dissuade him, thinking that he was forcing himself to the task for her sake; long ago he had said that he would write a play for her, and despite his prohibition of her ever performing again, she thought he might still feel obliged to fulfil his promise. She now graciously released him from it. But once more she met with disappointment. The man who apparently despised the theatre informed his wife that he was working on a new drama not for her, but in the hope of a definitive success – both artistic and financial. He was determined finally to outshine Ibsen.

His new play would be about a former actress who betrays her much older husband.

Hamsun had recently given a glimpse of his working methods to Heinrich Goebel, a German who was planning to translate *The Wild Choir*: 'A great deal of what I have written has come in the night, when I have slept for a couple of hours and then woken up. I am clear-headed then, and acutely impressionable. I always have a pencil and paper by my bed, I do not use light, but start writing immediately in the dark if I feel something is streaming through me. It has become a habit and I have no difficulty in deciphering my writing in the morning.'[14]

He made no mention to Goebel of the fact that most of what he wrote made its way into the wastepaper basket. Neither did he tell him how overwrought and irascible he became. As Hamsun sat brooding, week after week, poring over his notes, it was Marie who had to take the brunt of his irritation and mood swings. They worsened when they were together. When one day Marie picked up a stray pea from the kitchen floor and threw it into the bin, Hamsun forced her to find it again, rinse it and put it in a box that he had painted and labelled 'PEAS'.

Increasingly Marie had a painful sense that her role in his life was neither as queen nor muse, but as a humble maid – despite her having more lines and time on stage. Or perhaps she was just a tool, one of the many Hamsun needed for his writing?

On Friday, 25 June 1909, Knut and Marie were married by a magistrate in Oslo. This time around Hamsun had approached a priest who was liberal-minded with regard to marrying divorcees, but he had been refused. He demanded his membership of the Norwegian state church cease immediately.

Marie's father was one witness, the other being the chief doctor in the hospital where she had been treated for her kidney infection.

After only a six-day honeymoon on a farm outside the capital, Hamsun deserted his bride. Leaving Marie at her sister's house, he headed off to the mountain valley of Østerdalen, close to the border with Sweden where he rented a room at a farmstead.

Victoria was to join him for a few weeks.

The two of them took walks and went rowing on the lake, and visited a farm so that Victoria could see the animals. Hamsun carried her high on his back, and she filled his room with flowers. Yet Hamsun's feelings for his daughter were changing. When she had been with him for little more than a week, he wrote to Marie: 'You are everything to me, I have even begun to grow somewhat distant from Victoria'.[15] Meanwhile Victoria asked him whether the newspaper reports of a second marriage were true. Hamsun tried to hold his tongue but forgot himself repeatedly and called his daughter by his wife's name. Again and again she asked whom he was writing to, and whether it might be Marie.[16] She was quite unaware of course of what her father had done, and that by marrying again, he had given up custodial rights.

Marie had not tried to disguise her sadness or jealousy at his leaving her so soon after their honeymoon. A note, which Marie enclosed with photographic portraits of herself that she sent to her husband for his fiftieth birthday, perfectly summed up their time together thus far: 'Nobody can make me so awfully miserable, nobody has made me so happy.'[17]

Arriving back in Oslo, Hamsun had gone on another drinking spree. Perhaps he was feeling tender after having asked his publisher for additional monies two days in a row, as well as borrowing another substantial sum. Hamsun replied to his wife's birthday greetings, on what he called the 'dismal 4th of August', in a somewhat cruel vein. He asked if she remembered as a child taking a bite out of a slice of cake to stop anybody else having it. When he grew too old for her, he would stop other men taking her by destroying her looks – perhaps, he suggested calmly, by throwing nitric acid in her face: 'But *then*, of course, I would sleep with you every single night and love you and be torn asunder because I had disfigured you for life. But I would probably have more peace of mind than now, having to live in eternal fear that some forester might cause you to blush with joy.'[18]

Three or four letters passed between the newlyweds every week during his absence, letters that often contained words to make the other sad or furious. Her past was like a crown of thorns on which they both continually pricked themselves.

She begged him to trust her, still unsure of the place she might find for herself in this autocrat's kingdom.

Let the Dirt of City Life Go

In the autumn of 1909, Hamsun was deeply involved in writing a new novel, *A Wanderer Plays on Muted Strings*.

Here he returns to the characters of *Under the Autumn Star* six years on. Knut Pedersen is Hamsun's observer now – almost his voyeur – reflecting particularly on the deepening estrangement between Captain Falkenberg and his wife, Louise. Idleness, indifference and childlessness have taken their toll, and infidelity has done the rest. Louise is seduced by a man of modern cast, the young engineer Lassen. Pedersen follows the couple from the Øvrebø country estate to the city, and there city life rapidly ruins Louise. She loses her sweetness and gentle gaze; her eyes, observes Pedersen, are like two flares at the entrance to a variety show. Showing no concern for her husband, the family farm or the children she might have had, Louise drowns, possibly a suicide, a lost cause. Only through contentment in motherhood and marriage, Hamsun thought, could a woman find salvation from collapse and catastrophe.

To this end, Hamsun impressed on his new wife the necessity of moving to the countryside: 'Let all the looseness and seduction and dirt and muck of city life go its own way. We shall live in the country. And there is another reason I want to be in the country: so that you shan't have as many opportunities to go astray if you tire of me some day. If you just paused on the street for a second in town, men would approach you. It is not quite so *easy* in the country.'[19]

In the novel, Pedersen watches the two former lovers as they stand on a bridge, staring coldly straight ahead. 'Heavens, love is such fleeting stuff! [. . .] Oh how special they once were to each other! But then they gorged on pleasure to excess, they turned love into a product measured by the metre. How foolish they were.'

In his own marriage Hamsun seemed to be doing his utmost to ensure love found no favourable conditions in the first place.

At the beginning of September 1909, Marie Hamsun packed up the possessions in her flat and Hamsun's attic. Almost thirty years since Hamsun's first arrival in Oslo, he and Marie were leaving the capital for good.

They rented rooms on a large mountain farm not far from the Swedish border. Hamsun organised for them to have a room each in the main building; Marie's was long and narrow with bare timber walls. Hamsun also took a writer's cottage across the yard, furnished sparsely with a chair, a small bed and a desk that he improvised, laying a tabletop across two trestles. Directly outside the window the river flowed over a small waterfall. Its sound would mean he was less likely to be disturbed by other noises.

Here Hamsun managed to settle down to some writing. He would hole himself up in his cottage early in the morning, and Marie would not see him again until suppertime. On some late summer evenings they played croquet with the other residents, and Marie soon discovered that he was incapable of losing gracefully; when they played on the same team he always blamed her when they lost.

Hamsun insisted that Marie keep her distance from the other residents. She was also instructed to limit her acquaintance with the widow who ran the house, since it was not proper for guests to be too intimate with their hosts.[20]

The days were interminable for Marie. She procured a sewing machine to occupy her time but, again, Hamsun could not resist taking over: the tailor's son cut her patterns, instructed her and corrected her.

In November 1909, Hamsun sent the last instalment of *A Wanderer Plays on Muted Strings* to his publisher.

Marie had begged to do the proofreading, only to find that the novel filled her with indignation on behalf of the female sex. Had all the women Hamsun met been so irresponsible, conceited and corruptible? Surely she was proving herself to be different. She told him she wanted him to stop using a first-person narrative in his books.[21]

Hamsun was particularly proud of the novel's postscript. His central character muses: 'There is no doubt it requires a certain degree of empty-headedness to go around constantly pleased with oneself and everything else. But we do all have moments of contentment. A prisoner sits on his cart on his way to his execution, a nail pokes into his backside, he moves and feels more comfortable. [. . .] The flesh suffers, one's hair turns grey, but a wanderer sends thanks to God for life, it was fun to live! [. . .] And that's the nub: the absolute mercy of being given life at all is ample prepayment for its miseries, each and every one.'

One plays with muted strings after the age of fifty, but there is still joy to be found. 'I am in no rush. It's the same to me, wherever I am,' Hamsun concludes in his book.

Marie, who had just reached her twenty-eighth birthday in November 1909, was not feeling quite the same way.

Hamsun reneged on his promise to look for a farm where he and Marie could settle. He needed to focus his whole attention on his work, returning to the play he had abandoned in Oslo, and so he moved out of the room adjacent to his wife's and into his little writing house.

But the moment he took his notes out, it was as though he was caught in a vice. He failed to make any progress at all with his drama, which would be about an actress, but neither could he let it go. He was ready to lash out at anyone and anything. At this point, it was the Russians.

In an effort to stop pirate editions of his books in Russia – about which Hamsun had even threatened to contact the king of Norway – he had reached an agreement in 1907 with the publishing house Znaniye in St Petersburg. He was to deliver his manuscripts to them two months in advance of all his other publishers, an arrangement that guaranteed him a handsome fixed sum of roubles each month. This did not prevent Hamsun now ranting against Znaniye's reluctance to pay him a big advance, as well as blaming his Russian translators for the miserable speed of the postal service between St Petersburg and Hamsun's own remote corner of Norway.[22]

Despite his bad-tempered griping, Russia was growing in importance to Hamsun. Theatres had begun to put on his plays. The well-known actress Mariya Nikolaevna Germanova played Elina in the Kareno trilogy of plays for the renowned Moscow Art Theatre. Hamsun had actually dined with this beautiful actress in an Oslo restaurant not long before his marriage to Marie, causing his fiancée not a little consternation.

Another Russian woman met a rather less courteous response. The translator Mariya Blagoveshchenskaya was obsessed with Hamsun, writing countless letters to him throughout the latter half of 1909. She swore she would die if they did not meet and tempted him with gifts: pictures of Dostoevsky, a doll for his daughter, sweets, a pipe, tobacco. Hamsun turned down Blagoveshchenskaya and all her baubles rather rudely, and received a reply to match. She demanded an apology, reminding him that his talent was a gift from nature that he could not take credit for: 'Poets are fickle people. But I will not tolerate your whims, and I shall not bend to your bombastic attacks with a friendly smile.'[23] She was, she declared, completely cured of her passion.

The reviews of *A Wanderer Plays on Muted Strings* were generally positive. The *Frankfurter Zeitung* bought the novel for serialisation. But even now, Hamsun failed to achieve significant sales, and blamed this on his publishers, whom he accused of not having advertised it well enough. He was in desperate need of money, particularly as he was increasingly determined to return to his Nordland roots. He wrote an article in which he extolled this fairytale land, describing the starry nights and northern lights, the miraculous summers and the stormy weather, and the unique character of its people. 'Nordland folk are good-hearted, patient [. . .] unlike the people in the south they do not claw their way through life in stingy greed; their unfettered lives as fishermen have naturally led them to be more tolerant by nature.'[24]

Marie was very keen now that they should settle. When Hamsun showed signs of changing his plans, which he did occasionally, she tried to convince him that she too desired a quiet and industrious life: 'I have wasted so many years of my life fluttering about and moving. Haven't you too, dear? Life is not so very long and we should establish something, I so want to have a home, a husband and child – I'll be twenty-nine soon. You always wanted this as well, but from your answer you seemed not to want it anymore. . . Last winter you drew the design for a house and I was so delighted. But in my silent prayers to you I begged for a house that grew smaller and smaller by the day. I am not asking for some Greek temple with a columned hall, I am asking, from the bottom of my heart, for a little place with two cows.'[25]

Bjørnson's Throne Is Vacant

Hamsun finished his play in the early summer of 1910. He had grappled with it through two stormy years of living with an ex-actress whom he constantly accused of wanting to return to her old decadent life. He had promised to write a play for Marie, but instead he had created a piece to settle a personal score with the city and its mores, especially those of theatre folk.

Juliane Gihle is a former variety singer married to a decrepit old man. She is unfaithful to him again and again, but each time she takes a new lover she has to lower her standards a little more. 'Do you know what my fate will be?

Things can only go downhill for someone like me, you know. You know I always say it will end with a negro? It really is true. And I'm not in the least bit ugly or old yet', she says in the first act of *In the Grip of Life*.

Hamsun proves her precisely right. In the final scene she gives herself to an eighteen-year-old black manservant brought back from Africa by the adventurer Per Bast. Juliane's passions eventually drive her to murder, when she kills Bast for desiring the younger Fanny rather than her.

All city dwellers, be they young or old, are corrupt, Hamsun warns his readers; but no milieu has a more damaging effect on the soul than the theatre.

He was pleased with its title, *In the Grip of Life*, and hoped it would be published and have Europe's major theatres fighting to premiere it, just as they had over Ibsen's plays – quite unjustifiably, in Hamsun's view.

But the Royal Theatre in Copenhagen signalled its interest. The director of the Moscow Art Theatre, Vladimir Nemirovich-Danchenko, eventually sent a message that the earliest he could produce it would be the New Year of 1911.

There were constant delays in the translation, being done by Peter Emmanuel Hansen and his Russian wife. Hamsun tried to reason with Nemirovich-Danchenko and his Russian publisher, Znaniye, and eventually discovered that the translators themselves were at the root of the problem. In 1908, Maxim Gorky, who also published with Znaniye, had condemned the couple's 'vulgar' translation of *Benoni*, and now Hamsun discovered that their work on this new play had satisfied neither theatre nor publisher.

Hamsun refused the couple's offer to visit him in Norway, and the relationship was broken off. He contacted Menartz Lewin, a Russian-born journalist living in Oslo with whom he had corresponded for the last two years. Lewin paired up with another Russian resident in Norway, Raissa Tiraspolska. Soon both Znaniye and the Moscow Art Theatre were making more positive noises. So too, in Germany, the Schauspielhaus in Düsseldorf drew up a contract for *In the Grip of Life*. And in Oslo, Vilhelm Krag decided to stage it at the National Theatre as part of its autumn season.

In the spring of 1910, Bjørnstjerne Bjørnson died. After denouncing him as a traitor to his country for accepting the Nobel Prize in 1903, Hamsun had tried to re-establish their relationship. Now he described Bjørnson in a new poem as one of the greatest men Norway had produced – as both poet and politician.

It was as though Hamsun believed that Bjørnson's mantle had been passed to him. His would now be the author's voice to guide the nation. He would be Norway's national bard.

With a deepened sense of duty, Hamsun involved himself in Norway's territorial conflict over Svalbard and Spitsbergen, accusing the polar explorer Fridtjof Nansen of being unpatriotic in his support of the Norwegian government's decision to invite Russia and Sweden to the negotiating table. Hamsun also wrote a furious article, which appeared in *Verdens Gang* in Oslo and *Politiken* in Copenhagen, about the effects of tourism in Norway. The country, Hamsun argued, was being turned into one colossal hotel. Foreigners filled the streets, the mountainsides, the river valleys, the farmsteads and mountain farms. To make it worse, Norwegians were welcoming them with open arms: father and son stood at the farm gates, bowing with cap in hand to catch the coppers thrown at them, while mother and daughter waited on their foreign masters up at the house. The British had reduced once-proud Norwegian farmers to monkeys. They no longer had time to till the soil, Hamsun lamented, when they were so busy entertaining the foreign guests. The newspapers gave more coverage to the prospects for tourism than the outlook for crops. 'We can get coffee now, and pay for it up front, we can hang curtains in our cabins, we can speak English to the drivers. But we have sacrificed our temperate natures, our calm, our small and quiet habits, our sense of industry, our inner selves are lost. [. . .] The Anglo-Saxon has imported his modern, warped view of existence, the Anglo-Saxon has derailed life.'[26]

In the summer of 1910, Hamsun was informed that the government wanted to make him a Knight of the Order of St Olav. A golden opportunity for the presentation would be the day that everybody believed to be his fiftieth birthday, 4 August 1910. Colleagues encouraged him to accept the honour on behalf of the whole of the writing profession. Hamsun declined the award.

He may have still felt bitterness towards the government after it had refused him a state stipend in 1899. Perhaps the derisive remarks he had made in the past about honour only being reserved for the old might make his acceptance awkward. Maybe he was concerned that such an honour would increase the weight of his legacy. Perhaps these were all contributing factors, but there was another still: the year he had trimmed off his age. He would not be fifty, but fifty-one.

Hamsun confided this fact to a Danish librarian and author, Carl Otto Dumreicher, who interviewed him in July. And since it was clearly the moment for revelations, the Norwegian told him a little about himself: that he devoured stories about hunting, books on nature, and histories, but had no time for literature. Although he enjoyed contributing opinion pieces to newspapers, the only writing he had really cared about for years was poetry – but since his income came largely from abroad, and poetry neither sold nor lent itself to translation, he had continued to write novels. Writing plays, he claimed, was most distasteful of all.[27]

Disagreeable as playwriting might have been to him, Hamsun cannot have felt anything but pride when *In the Grip of Life* opened at the National Theatre in Oslo in 1910; and the royalties of over 1,200 kroner were also welcome. In

Düsseldorf the play ran for nineteen performances and was declared a success. At the Moscow Art Theatre it was scheduled for their forthcoming spring season, to be directed (after the first director had been fired) by Nemirovich-Danchenko himself. A twelve-volume collection of Hamsun's works translated into Russian was also completed that year. In Germany, a translation of *A Wanderer Plays on Muted Strings* appeared and Albert Langen's publishing house finally brought out the second play in the Kareno trilogy, *The Game of Life*.

A large part of Hamsun's income that year, as in previous years, would come from Russia and Germany.

Hamsun and Marie rented a house in Elverum, the small inland town where Marie had grown up.

The fifty-one-year old was beginning to feel his age. His sciatica was bad and wasn't helped by massages. Influenza often confined him to bed. He was losing a lot of hair, and experimented with a stream of new, expensive wonder cures. He ordered an electric miracle belt, and immediately felt better, thanking its inventor in humorous vein.

To add to his newfound feeling of optimism, a letter arrived from Hamarøy from his childhood friend Georg Olsen, with wonderful news. A delightful farm, Skogheim, was up for sale close to Hamsun's childhood home. Hamsun knew it well. It had belonged to the sheriff.

Thirty-one years ago Hamsun had visited Bjørnson's farm, Aulestad. Now Hamsun wanted to live in the same style: with his feet fixed firmly on his own plot of land, his arm cradling a newborn child, and his gaze turned towards the seasonal changes so vital to a simple farmer's survival.

Putting Down Roots

In the spring of 1911, Hamsun made his way home to Nordland. This time he promised it would be for ever. He wanted to replant the roots he had torn up so determinedly all those years before. He had told Marie, from early in their relationship, how a life on the land would restore her health – and perform miracles on him.

Marie fell in love with the house the moment she set eyes on it in early March. It was a well-cared-for, modest building with old birch trees at the front. The main road ran above it, with a shop on the other side. The fields were on gently rolling slopes that faced the sun. Uncultivated deciduous wood-land stretched to a lake and the river Glimma, where Hamsun showed her the deceptive undercurrents.[28]

Marie wanted to move into Skogheim immediately but Hamsun was far from satisfied. He declared it would require extensive rebuilding, determined they should have a certain standard of living. Indeed, Hamsun even wrote to Oslo enquiring about the price of the red glazed tiles used on the roofs of *sorenskriver* houses, the grand residences of Norwegian government officials.[29] He occupied himself almost around the clock overseeing work inside and outside Skogheim and thinking over new plans.

They finally moved in later that summer. The bedrooms, and the room Hamsun planned to use as his study, were upstairs. Gone was the cosy farm-house decoration scheme. Every room had been wallpapered – red for the living room, green for the dining room – and it was now furnished Empire Style.

While the building work was in progress, Hamsun and Marie had often passed the parsonage grounds and the house where Hamsun had lived with his Uncle Hans as a boy. Hamsun's wife was naturally curious about her husband's childhood, and was made no less so by an interview that appeared in *Verdens Gang* upon their arrival in Hamarøy. Hamsun's mother, his brother Ole and a childhood friend had spoken about this famous returnee's previous life in the town. The friend had described how Hamsun's uncle had beaten the young boy until he bled. Marie asked Hamsun gently how he had ended up under the guardianship of such a cruel relative.

'He was the sub-postmaster, and I had such nice handwriting,' Hamsun answered.[30]

When she pressed him on the subject, he mumbled something about his uncle owning them all. But Marie found it hard to understand how his mother could send him back time after time when he returned home so badly beaten. He brushed it off. Marie had to understand they were poor, and his parents had sacrificed themselves for their children – especially his mother.

Six months after arriving, Marie had still not met her mother-in-law. Hamsun had visited her only once himself. He described the meeting with reluctance, telling Marie that she was a shadow of her former self, quite unlike the person she had been eleven years before. Hamsun was finding it hard to come to terms with her having grown old. Perhaps when he looked at her, he saw his future self staring back.

His father's death four years before had incited Hamsun's fierce attack on the fourth commandment to honour one's parents. Now his homecoming to Hamarøy and his elderly mother triggered another article entitled 'Honour Thy Young', which expanded on his incendiary lecture.

He describes the ugliness of old age in the blackest terms: 'The old person is nothing but the leftovers of a person, a distortion, a false vision.' Was it not true that Michelangelo refused to paint portraits of old people because they were so hideous? 'An old animal or an old horse, for example, is never disfigured to the extent that an old person is deformed. The old person walks clumsily, has a crooked back, is more or less bald and has unseeing eyes. Old people have ugly eating habits.' Old age was, in Hamsun's opinion, a time of disintegration; but society had elevated it. The old, Hamsun seethed, had been dead already for some time; they were simply not buried.[31]

One late autumn day, when Hamsun was away, Marie – who was four months pregnant – took a horse and cariole to visit her mother-in-law on her own. Tora Hamsun lived in a tiny shabby cottage with somebody who looked after her. She was eighty-one years old, terribly thin, almost completely deaf, totally blind in one eye and losing her sight in the other. She reminded her daughter-in-law of a mummy. Her voice was loud and harsh, and she still spoke the mountain-village dialect despite its being fifty years since she had arrived at the northern coastal village. Marie observed that she had made an effort to smarten herself up, and that even though she had a shoemaker for a son, she was wearing a pair of shop-made pointed shoes.[32]

At the beginning of March 1912, immediately before Marie was due to give birth, her husband disappeared again. He was going to write. He went far enough to ensure he would be unobtainable within the hour, or even within the day.

He escaped by the narrowest margin. Just two days later Marie telegraphed to tell him they had a son. Hamsun ordered a crate of blood oranges to be delivered to his wife and child, and from a travelling salesman he bought an enormous ostrich feather to complement the colossal hat he had bought for Marie. It was the most expensive he could find – 'you will never be able to pay me back for it, even if I get to sleep with you right through Lent', he wrote.[33]

Hamsun decided that the baby should be named Tore – the old woman of Hamsund must be honoured after all – and Marie arranged the christening. Still the new father did not return. Marie wrote to him describing how beautiful their little son was, how she was unable to take her eyes off him and lay awake at night. Hamsun reminded her to save some tender feelings for *him*.

Some two months later Hamsun returned. Marie had been contemplating what the poet's first words to his son might be. After standing for some time studying Tore's face, he declared: 'Goodness, what a big nose the boy's got!'[34]

But despite the bathetic jocularity, the birth heralded a new determination in Hamsun. He set about organising more building work and breaking new land. Skogheim should be a home that his first son and heir could be proud of, as well as a farm that would command respect in the neighbouring parishes. Never had writing been more important than now, since his words were serving a higher purpose: the author would ennoble the man of the soil. It was a scheme his fellow countrymen should follow, as his newspaper article 'A

Word for Us' made clear. Hamsun diagnosed a sickness in society and propounded work on and reconnection with the land as its medicine: 'We shall take our hands out of our pockets and begin work again. We will not be a mere nation of hoteliers and waiters. We will drain our marshes, plant new forests, colonise the mighty Nordland.'[35]

These were the very things Hamsun was doing himself. He also had to write.

Hamsun was more focused than ever on earning money for the family. His financial situation had improved dramatically thanks to the advances and royalties he was now receiving from several countries. Russia had developed into an important and incredibly lucrative market for him; he had negotiated a deal with a Russian publisher for his next book, *The Last Joy*, for which he received a sum of 5,000 roubles – enough to pay three or four manual labourers for a year. And Hamsun made good his promise to inhibit any Russian publishers and magazines from publishing his work without paying, engaging the assistance of the Norwegian legation in Moscow and the general consulate in St Petersburg to extract his royalties.

His raison d'être for writing plays had quite simply been financial reward. Now he could admit to himself that it had proved too great a challenge. Fiction would from now on be his main priority. One day Marie found him sitting in front of the wood burner feeding the flames with paper slips and entire sheets covered with his neat hand. It was four years since he had forced her to resign from the National Theatre, and now the playwright was handing in his own notice, page by page, into the flames.

Marie must have felt it as a victory.

Hamsun had originally planned to complete this play, now abandoned, as well as his novel before the end of the year. Getting the script that was to become *The Last Joy* finished was now a matter of some urgency. Throughout the summer of 1912 he sat in the main room of the house, while the women who worked in Skogheim went about on tiptoe, careful not to laugh, clatter the saucepans, talk too loudly or approach him before he signalled his availability.

Tore was quick to adapt to the new atmosphere too. He soon discovered that if he made the slightest noise, his father would pick him up and play with him, or instruct his mother to do so. That summer Victoria was allowed to visit Skogheim, but Hamsun found his daughter flighty and overly playful. After she had left he wrote to complain to her mother; Bergljot defended their daughter, who was, after all, only ten years old.[36]

Ever since his time in Valdres in the 1880s Hamsun had been convinced that the inland climate was good for his health. Now he travelled to Junkerdal, just 5 kilometres from the Swedish border, although he did not stop fretting about

Skogheim in his absence. Marie received long letters containing details of everything she was to remember. The frost mustn't be allowed to get the turnip leaves and potato plants; and were the men still turning the fields? Had the telephone been fixed? Had the blacksmith been asked to make a hood for the stove? Marie would do well to be nice to him. Perhaps he could also stop the wood burner in the living room making that incessant noise that irritated him? Had she and the maid finally stopped walking down the hallway to fetch water? Had she aired the cellar? The garden needed to be fertilised and well dug. He would have liked to add some more earth to the area of poor soil surrounding the servants' living quarters; it had to be spread evenly, not too thinly. There was no need to chop more firewood, since there was so much burnable material from the marshland being dug up.[37]

Now and again he partook of the joys the farm offered, such as the sixty barrels of potatoes they harvested, but joys were soon displaced by more worries: had the pig been housed in the barn? Had they made an opening in Rosmarin's stall so her calf could suckle? Had the two rocks that had broken the harvester been dug out of the field? The list was endless.

It was not unusual for women in fishing communities to be left to run the home, but none was as large as Skogheim. Marie was occupied from six in the morning until late at night, spending morning and evening at work in the cowshed, and preparing food all day, often in two rounds since they had so many employees. And there were all the other things that had to be done on the farm, the list of which continually grew as Hamsun set more plans for expansion in motion.

Marie was not happy about her husband leaving her in order to write. She felt it as a betrayal. After all, this was the life they had promised to create and to be content with: cultivating the soil, cultivating words, and cultivating a family – the holy trinity. But the reality was very different. Hamsun's writing took precedence over everything. In fact, he told Marie that the extra expenses would mean he would need to write even more. She tried to persuade him that the buildings at Skogheim did not have to be so big, fine or numerous, that the fields did not need enlarging, and that it would be more than enough for her to own and take care of three cows, a pig and some hens.

Hamsun's wife felt that her roots had at last been planted, roots that were as tough as weeds. But within her husband Marie saw a perpetual struggle between farmer and writer. There was little she could do to halt this. The thought of what would happen if the writer won out over the farmer kept Marie awake at night.[38]

Just Hysteria and Nerves

In the autumn of 1912, after only eighteen months in Hamarøy, Marie received a letter from Hamsun bearing the news she feared the most: 'No, it'll probably be impossible for us to keep the farm, it seems to consume me utterly, I turn to a jelly just thinking about everything back home, I hardly go any distance from it before I can work again and feel much healthier again too. Lord, what shall we do?'[39]

Hamsun wrote this while he was in the final stages of completing *The Last Joy*, which he had begun in 1906 before his final break with Bergljot. The unnamed narrator, an ageing writer, has left the city for the depths of the forest to seek inner peace and revivified creativity. The writing process is, he says, like the work of a smithy on a piece of iron, the rude ore of his inspiration: 'I have sought the forests to find solitude, and for the sake of the iron I bear within, a great iron that lies within me, ready to turn red. [. . .] I stand by my original vow to make this great iron glow within me, but I am nothing but laughable if I think it an easy task. And I cannot even be certain that I have any iron left in me, or that I am capable of forging it any longer, even if I have.'

The words were far from flippant. For years Hamsun had lectured and penned articles and letters warning of old age's erosion of a writer's prowess. Now *The Last Joy* had to be completed and delivered to the publishers in time for the Christmas season. He needed to be reassured of his capacities as a writer and, as always, he needed the money.

Modernity, the fall of woman and the decline of Norwegian society are Hamsun's abiding concerns in *The Last Joy*. Its location is a mountain farm that also takes in guests. The tourists' perverse idleness undermines the pride of the farmers and disrupts their rhythms of work. Hamsun's bitterness towards unthinking and exploitative visitors to his native land (first voiced in his article in 1910) is given full vent. His descriptions of the British, particularly two bustling, rude, ageing Englishmen who arrive at the guesthouse, are especially vitriolic. The narrator catches them performing an obscene act in the goatshed one night, and reflects:

Vice moves in loops, cycles, as does virtue, I have begun to think that nothing is new, everything returns and repeats itself. The Romans ruled the world once. Oh, how powerful they were, how unassailable, they permitted themselves a sin or two, they could afford to live at the arenas, they indulged themselves with young men and animals. Then, one day, their reckoning began to rain down on them; their grandchildren lost the odd battle, and their grandchildren again couldn't do more than sit and look back. The circle was closed; suddenly nobody had less power over the world than the Romans. The two Englishmen in the goatshed were of no concern to me; I was only a native, a Norwegian, I had better hold my tongue before these mighty tourists. But they belonged to the nation of sprinters, charioteers and degenerates that Germany's healthy destiny shall punish with death one day. [. . .] [I]f Germany had not kept them on their toes, they would have descended into pederasty in a couple of generations.

Hamsun was now wielding his literary pen to fight a bigger battle than that merely against the reviewers and critics. It was no longer possible, in Hamsun's work as in the wider world, to ignore the question of politics. Now even in his fiction Hamsun saw himself at the lectern. At the end of the book Hamsun makes a direct address to his public: 'To you, the new spirit of Norway! I have written this during a time of plague and because of a plague. I can do nothing to stop this plague; it is grown invincible, it wreaks its havoc with the approval and hoopla of our nation. It will presumably cease one day. But meantime I shall do what I can to oppose it. Even as you do the opposite.'

Hamsun warns his readers that he will not stop speaking out, and that he plans to write even more critically about society: 'I shall force even you to understand that I represent the truth.'

Some of Hamsun's harshest criticism is reserved for the modern woman. In *The Last Joy*, the beautiful schoolteacher Ingeborg Torsen leaves the mountain resort for the city and ruins herself, having affairs with a modern-day charmer (another man from the country now grown brazen and cynical) as well as an actor. She is saved by her marriage to a simple carpenter and farmer, and the narrator approves: 'Ah Lord, that young mother was so happy and so beautiful. Nothing could compare, her eyes were full of a mystical goodness she had never had before.' Ingeborg finds a meaning in life at last: children, perfect miracles. She wants many, standing one after the other like organ pipes.

Rejecting the banalities of the modern world, reconnecting with rural existence and making a fresh pact with life: this was the epitome of Hamsun's philosophy.

Gone are the existential characters, the loose cannons and vagabonds, the *Hunger* figure, Nagel, Glahn and Friar Vendt: old age has taken them and their successors. And Hamsun's female characters are no longer mere foils to the artist, whose purpose is to stimulate his work – by surrendering first to love's ecstasies, then a painful sexual game, and finally to eternal unobtainability (as exemplified in turn by Dagny in *Mysteries*, Edvarda in *Pan* and Teresita in *The Game of Life*). Hamsun had made a transition over the course of his novels. His authorial perspective had shifted from introspective participant to observer and voyeur. And as Hamsun began to hold his work at a further remove, the women in his books became increasingly maternal.

Through the failure of his first marriage and the advent of his second, Hamsun still nurtured wholeheartedly the notion of an ideal woman who would inspire him and his art. At the burgeoning of his relationship with Marie he had assured her that she would make him a literary prince. But, having won her, Hamsun immediately began to reshape her, moulding the woman he married into a farmer's wife and placing her in the landscape of his childhood.

Well before the Christmas rush, Hamsun was informed that *The Last Joy* would have a print run of five thousand copies, despite his never having previously reaped huge sales. 'It is so incredible that I scarcely understand it. Especially when my *Muted Strings* was so much better – since I was three or four years younger when I wrote it', he joked to his publisher in Copenhagen.[40]

Reviews were varied, but the positive ones were extremely good. Sven Lange set the tone in *Politiken*: 'The whole of Hamsun is in this book! Here we have the young nature-worshipper of *Pan*'s extraordinary prose; here the sharp and capricious polemics from *Shallow Soil* and the burgeoning eroticism of *The Game of Life*, and here too a touch of the stylistic magician and miracle worker of *Mysteries*.'[41] And best of all, according to Lange, was that the author was quashing his own theory about the impairment of ageing.

Success seemed to spill into other areas of life too. Just before Christmas Hamsun vulgarly boasted to an old acquaintance: 'He-hey, the springtime seems to have arrived in me already, I am using my woman like a boar, damn it, and eating better than I have for ages.'[42]

Of course, Hamsun bumped back down to earth, and Marie was not quite able to pretend that his threat to sell the farm had passed entirely without notice. Nevertheless, it was a better Christmas for the little family than their first had been at Skogheim, when Hamsun's neuroses had ruined the entire festive season for them all.

In January 1913, he again left the farm to go inland, taking a room at a coaching inn. Marie did not try to hide her sadness at his departure. She had tried to protect him from disturbances but it had made no difference.

Hamsun's writing progressed against the odds. He was now receiving a huge volume of correspondence which had to be dealt with – seventeen letters on one day, the third delivery in a week. His lodgings were also freezing cold; four very draughty windows did little to shut out the Norwegian winter, his thermometer dipping to $-39°C$ on one occasion. But the air was dry, and Hamsun sat well wrapped up with his back almost inside the wood burner.

As January rolled by, Hamsun's doubts about his new work receded, and he was buoyed by the prospect of success. At the end of February he wrote to Marie: 'It is going to be a huge book this time, but it will mean a great deal of work too, ought not to overdo it. Perhaps I have come far enough to be able to carry on at home.' But the bustle of Skogheim, he countered, made him fearful of losing his thread. 'If only I didn't hear Tore. It's not that he disturbs me, the poor little thing, but I get so terribly frightened that something might be the matter. I can't rest, I just sit there and listen. And then I just sit there and look at the clock, thinking how he ought to sleep, go for his walk, go to bed or have a bath, etc. [. . .] No, I am impossible, I am not a person any longer, but an instrument, just hysteria and nerves.'[43]

Hamsun's elucidation of his fraught sensibilities was entirely unnecessary. Marie had observed all her husband's neuroses at close quarters. But it must have been some relief that, yet again, he arrived at the diagnosis himself.

After two months Hamsun returned to Skogheim. It was financially imperative that he finish this next book as quickly as possible. The farm required significant investment. His income from Russia had fallen. Hamsun also remained heavily in debt to Gyldendal (totalling 18,255 kroner at the turn of 1912–13), and its monthly payments to him of 300 kroner meant the sum was growing steadily.

Hamsun also found himself embroiled in a legal battle with two of his German publishers. After Langen's death in 1909, Hamsun's relationship with Albert Langen Buch- und Kunstverlag had deteriorated. When it hesitated over publishing his *Collected Works* Hamsun signed a contract with another house in Munich, Georg Müller Verlag. Albert Langen's successor, Korfiz Holm, was furious. He demanded 100,000 marks to release the rights on all of Hamsun's works published over the last twenty years, from the time Langen and Hamsun had first met in Paris. The two publishers' ensuing battle became increasingly acrimonious. Hamsun had thought he could cultivate both houses, but quickly realised this was unrealistic, and that a return to his original publisher might be rewarded. When Georg Müller Verlag was slow in making his monthly payments, Hamsun saw his opportunity to jump, accusing the publisher of failing to fulfil their contract. The reply was instantaneous: a threat to sue and a demand for compensation from Hamsun for breach of contract. That summer the author was obliged to travel to Oslo to consult his solicitor.

At that time Marie was eager to show her first-born to her parents in Oslo, and reminded her husband of his acknowledgement that she suffered from too little suitable company. At the beginning of June 1913, Hamsun, Marie and Tore boarded the steamship that would take them south to Bodø; from there they would take the Hurtigruten ferry to Trondheim before boarding another train the following day. But Hamsun refused to allow his wife and child to accompany him any further; they were obliged to wait in Trondheim for his return, while he went on alone. Hamsun had made arrangements that did not involve them.

When his train arrived at Lillestrøm station, some 20 kilometres from the capital, Hamsun's daughter, Victoria, who was now almost eleven years old, was waiting for him on the platform – waiting merely to exchange a few words with him. Some days later she wrote to her father at the hotel in Oslo where he was staying, telling him that she still had not received a letter from him as he had promised: could he, she wondered, have sent it to the wrong address? If he wanted her to visit him in town, she reassured him that a maid at her aunt's house had promised to take her. 'Get better soon, then, dearest papa, if I do not meet you in Oslo, then you must tell me when you are travelling back, and I will come to the station to say hello to you, a hundred best wishes from your Victoria.'[44]

Writing back, Hamsun gave her permission to stand at the station once more when the train passed through Lillestrøm. This time, through the compartment window he handed her an envelope containing some money, which he stressed she should look after carefully. Victoria clutched it firmly in her right hand.

On his return to Skogheim, Hamsun wrote to his daughter to castigate her for offering him her left hand when they shook hands in farewell. Victoria wrote back, hurt and confused: 'I think it is very sad that you should think it was indifference that made me give you my left hand to say goodbye, I cannot remember whether I did, I do not understand why I would have, since I never use my left hand instead of my right; but perhaps I was holding the letter you gave me with the money that you said I had to take good care of in my right hand.' Forlornly, and slightly audaciously, Victoria berated her father: 'During the days when you were in Oslo I went around the whole time just wishing you would write and tell me I could come to see you and I was almost certain you would – and Ingrid had promised to take me to the hotel, so I think it was sad that I only got to see you for two minutes through the compartment window.'[45]

She also apologised for the fact that she had made him a birthday present for which he had no purpose: a little bag she had sewed for him to keep his watch in.

The View from the Hotel

Later in the summer of 1913, Hamsun left the farm, Marie and his one-year old son once more in order to write.

In a letter that her husband had recently asked her to make a fair copy of, Marie had read the words she most dreaded: Hamsun had described to his acquaintance how he longed for his city companions and for shared conversation. It was the world that he had taken Marie away from. She had put her hand in his, trusting that he would lead her to a good place. Now it felt as though he was letting go.[46]

Hamsun was in deep conflict with himself. At the bottom of an otherwise businesslike letter to his publisher in Copenhagen, Hamsun confided: 'I am living in such a deep depression here that I am heading for my own demise, and such a tremendous amount of work awaits me. No, I really should never have bought myself a farm, the unreasonable demands of the servants leave me so dreadfully agitated. I should have just had a cottage. I should have been lounging under a palm tree and been a Buddhist with a notebook in hand; instead I am constantly torn from my work and from myself to organise the maintenance of the farm. If only I could get rid of the farm again.'[47]

That summer Hamsun exchanged correspondence on the possible purchase of other properties: a large townhouse in Drammen, not far from Oslo, or a mansion in an upland valley. Anywhere but Skogheim.

Hamsun had come back to his own people. But in truth he wanted as little to do with them as possible. An array of Hamarøy's inhabitants tried to meet him, to force themselves upon this famous writer. He wanted none of it. Any intrusion on his carefully guarded privacy was intolerable.

Neither were Nordland folk as he had idealised them. They were no better or worse than people anywhere else: here too people had a growing lack of respect for their betters, were less willing to work than he remembered, and were just as avaricious and materialistic. They too were turning their backs on the land and sea, and taking work in the cities. They were children of the new times, children who had lost their way.

Hamsun, the grand man of literature, no longer belonged in their world – life had separated him from the populace. He wrote an article expressing his outrage at all those who tried to make him their equal, who could not perceive his difference.

Indeed, the whole pyramid of Norwegian society was in the process of being toppled, in his view. The old ruling classes were becoming increasingly isolated, while the ordinary man's sense of his own importance swelled with his increasingly impertinent demands for wages, free time and equality. The general populace advanced the grotesque idea that they should be regarded as equals to the doctor, the sheriff, the businessman – and himself.

The old times meeting the new: this was the subject of his next novel, *Children of the Age*.

After staying only a few days at Skogheim, Hamsun travelled on further to Bodø, where he continued working on *Children of the Age* in the tower room of a hotel.

Nobody, not even Marie, could conceive of the superhuman effort it took to grasp his imaginary universe in its entirety, a universe constantly under threat of disruption from noise, something catching his eye, people coming too close to him on the stairs or in the street, being stared at in the dining room, or letters, telegrams, telephone calls that required him to put his work down. Everything could fall to pieces, sometimes so utterly that he would have to start all over again. He was Atlas, carrying an entire world.

Hamsun's creative process always began in the same way. Using any scrap of paper he could find – calendar pages or the backs of other notes, or whatever was to hand – he would scribble down ideas as soon as they seized hold of him. He would arrange these notes in little piles of paper slips spread out over his table, like a game of patience. It was Hamsun's task to see which slips would slot together, making a greater whole or blending with each other, to come to life. Chance was master in this phase of his work. Later he would play God.

Often, when he was brought back to reality by a noise or a light going out, or lack of paper, he would look in astonishment at what he had produced: an exchange of dialogue, the outline of a character's fate, elements of a plot, a striking description. He chased these flashes of inspired grace more frantically than ever now. As he got older, Hamsun no longer slept so deeply at night, and he could slip into a half-doze for large parts of the day; his ideas, if he could catch them, compensated for his lack of energy. Hamsun was an increasingly nervous and hungry predator, scouring for signs of possible prey, always prepared for the chase.

This was his method: waiting watchfully for these charmed moments. Let there be life, he said, spreading these little scraps of paper across the table. And there was life, so much life that the characters defied their creator, escaping his grasp before he finally reined them in again.

Humour had always played its part in Hamsun's novels, but now touches of irony, things that made him chuckle or occasionally laugh outright, became increasingly important to him. His writing progressed a little more easily after-wards. His mood could also be lifted – and his conscience lightened – when he sent gifts home, although the mood at Skogheim now was dark indeed. Marie was pregnant again and suffering from sickness and dizziness, just as she had with Tore. After the couple had spoken on the telephone one day, Hamsun thought she sounded like someone about to die.[48]

Christmas, the most lucrative season for the book business, was fast approaching. Hamsun did not know how much longer he dared wait before submitting the manuscript to his publisher. He must have it published in time for the book-buying frenzy. Gyldendal's management telegraphed him with a hugely flattering answer; a book by Knut Hamsun could be released any time he wanted, and his script would be in production within hours of the last page being received.[49]

On 25 October 1913, the first 150 pages went off to Gyldendal. Hamsun's relief, coupled with the knowledge that the absolute deadline was approaching, released a sudden burst of creativity. He told Marie proudly: 'Did not sleep until five in the morning and I am pretty beat, but heavens I am as happy as a champion, since I managed to write more yesterday and last night than I have in all these months. I worked for ten hours yesterday. I am shaking badly today. The end of the book is in sight, but with so many characters, there are a great many threads to pull together, so it takes longer than I thought. Just these few words today, my love, coming as soon as is possible. It helps me when you are happy.'[50]

Christmas Eve delivered the gift that Hamsun had longed for, more than any other, over the years: a decisive sales success. *Children of the Age* outstripped his publisher's expectations. The demand in Norway and Denmark in the run-up to Christmas was such that Gyldendal had to extend the print run to fourteen thousand copies. Coupled with this, Hamsun was being paid more per copy than before. Sales of his previous book, *The Last Joy*, had now reached six thousand, and it was ready to be sent out to Germany as well as Russia, where it was to be translated by Mariya Blagoveshchenskaya, the lady who had sworn never to have anything to do with him again. *Benoni* had also been reprinted that year, and *Pan* achieved twenty thousand copies in a new edition.

Hamsun had lived through a huge change in Norwegian peasant culture. He had witnessed, and indeed joined, the vast exodus of people to the great continent in the west and to the fairyland of the north. In his fifty years, he had commented with increasing bitterness on modern life: industrialisation, urbanisation, democratisation and the class struggle. The Norwegian people had been lured away from their existence tied to the land: 'The small fields they owned, the uncultivated lands to which they had access, the toil of getting winter firewood home from the wild forest – the whole crofter's existence was no longer worth living; why, one could buy one's flour ready-milled at the harbour now', he wrote in *Children of the Age*.

Willatz Holmsen is a lieutenant and third-generation squire in Segelfoss, northern Norway. His wife, Adelheid, is a descendant of the ancient Hanoverians. They are rich in tradition if not in capital, and have the respect of the ordinary folk. Tobias Holmengrå, a local fisherman's son, returns to the village like a king with a fortune made in South America. Purchasing land from Holmsen, he erects factories and tempts men to leave the plough and the boat. The villagers are transformed into a new breed of demanding and obstinate factory workers, some even going on to become conceited 'learned men' and government officials. Holmengrå is an upstart, with the talent to seize opportunities and topple the traditional divisions of class. He breaks the ancient relationship between the gentry and the common man. Holmsen is certainly not blind to the consequences of selling his land to this newcomer. 'He seems to have tasted his own destruction', Hamsun ruminates in the book.

Twenty-five years before, Hamsun's characters allowed themselves to be driven by impulse – sometimes with catastrophic results. Here, Holmsen has steadfastly honed his own nature to conquer every impulse. He is strong-willed to the point of destructiveness, rigidly obsessed with upholding his name and reputation. Thus, he watches the family and locals attached to Segelfoss Manor become the citizens of Segelfoss Town. The community slides into industrialised urban misery. He loses property, wife and son. Nobody challenges the squire's power directly, but he is gradually rendered powerless, and Tobias Holmengrå, the boy of humble origins, becomes the true master of the manor.

The modern world turns every sphere of life into an arena of conflict. Society breaks down in *Children of the Age* because of the incompatibility of new and old; since Willatz and Adelhaid are unable to reach out to one another, the Holmsens' marriage breaks down too. While Hamsun's descriptions of societal trends were becoming less nuanced, his portrayal of marriage employed an increasingly broad and subtle palette. Adelheid drowns, with the implication that it was partly intentional, just like Louise Falkenberg in *A Wanderer Plays on Muted Strings*. Marriage defeats both these women, but with one fundamental difference: Adelheid is a mother, and through her children she finds redemption. At the close of the novel, Willatz and Adelheid's son returns; Tobias Holmengrå's daughter, Mariane, awaits him.

Between Christmas and New Year, Hamsun started hinting that he would have to go away again to write the sequel. Marie, who was now six months pregnant, tried to hold him back but it was useless. A few weeks into 1914, she stood on the steps of Skogheim and, together with Tore, waved him goodbye. Marie knew that each time the writer within Hamsun won out over the farmer, it became more likely that he would decide to sell the farm.[51]

Hamsun booked himself into a hotel in Bodø, renting three rooms on the top floor: one in which to sleep, one to ensure there would be no neighbours to disturb him, and a third with a view towards the courtyard, in which he would write.

Hamsun's finances had improved considerably. Four printings of *Children of the Age* had brought him 9,000 kroner and reprints of older books over 3,000 kroner. He also earned between 3,000 and 4,000 kroner from Germany and elsewhere in 1913. Most of this had gone towards paying his debt to his publisher; he had managed to pay half of it back, with 10,000 kroner outstanding. He had almost 8,000 kroner in his bank account. A first officer of a ship might earn up to 2,000 kroner per annum, so Hamsun could count himself relatively wealthy, particularly when the money from Russia came in at the beginning of March. The Moscow Art Theatre paid him 5,000 kroner and expressed interest in a further play, bringing the total monies he had received from that country to almost 30,000 kroner. He would soon also receive payment from the Deutsches Theatre in Munich which, under the directorship of Max Reinhardt, was to stage a production of *In the Grip of Life*.[52]

But Hamsun did have to face one financial disappointment. The 'Goya' he had bought on his gambling spree in Belgium had hung on his wall for ten years, during which time it had been derided several times as a worthless Rubens imitation. This was now confirmed by a man whose judgement Hamsun trusted. The painting was worthless after all.

Hamsun travelled back to Hamarøy at the end of March. He had sat in Bodø shuffling his precious slips of paper, but had failed to make any of them tessellate. Neither did he manage anything more significant at Skogheim.

On 3 May 1914, Hamsun became a father for the third time. His new son was given the name Arild. The two-year-old Tore was forced from his mother's lap, just as his father had been at the same age. During the months that followed, Hamsun spent a great deal of time with Tore. Marie found this most touching.

Victoria, who very much wanted to visit her father, was sent word that it would be inconvenient.

War and Murder

In the summer of 1914, Hamsun purchased some new maps of Europe. Early that autumn the Great War that would threaten its very contours broke out.

When war was declared, Hamsun wrote immediately to his German publisher, Langen Verlag, with a message of support: 'You know my old sympathies lie with your country rather than with England. So long as Germany remains the master of Europe, Norway and Sweden will be saved once again.'[53]

His sentiments were expressed even more strongly in the German periodical *Simplicissimus*: 'I am convinced Germany will be victorious over England one day. It is the natural order. England is a country that finds itself in steady decline; it still retains some long, tough roots, but no blossoms, no crown. Germany, in comparison, is brimming with strength and youth.' He was utterly convinced that Germany would rule England one day. 'And I *hope* that Germany is victorious this time. A hope guided by my old, unshakeable sympathies for Germany, and also by the love I have for my own fatherland, which can only gain from a German victory.'[54]

In the same issue of the journal, Langen Verlag ran an advertisement for *The Last Joy* featuring a quotation from the novel prophesying the fate of the degenerate English, the 'nation of sprinters, charioteers and degenerates that Germany's healthy destiny shall punish with death one day'. It caught the attention of Georg Brandes, who launched an attack on Hamsun in *Politiken*. Brandes argued that he was profiting from the war; the connection between his pro-German stance, which Hamsun touted in numerous articles and letters, and the marketing of his books to the German public was obvious and rather unseemly.

Hamsun sent the article to Langen Verlag and requested that the author be boycotted. Brandes's outburst was, according to Hamsun, a hate-filled rejoinder to Hamsun's recent suggestion that the ageing Dane seek a devoted public amongst people of his own age, which was now around seventy-five.[55]

Meanwhile Hamsun turned his ire on a professor of European Literature at the University of Oslo who had criticised him in *Tides Tegn* for his anti-English outpourings. He scorned the scholar for having read so many books about England and for still believing it to be a powerful nation. '[You ask] why it is nothing less than the natural order that Germany will be victorious over England? The Germans, being the blossoming and healthy nation they are, have a very high birth rate. Germany needs colonies, England and France have more colonies than they need.' He reminded the professor that the population of Germany had grown by thirty million in forty years. 'Surely this is a force of nature? And is England capable of crushing it? Explain how it could be done! Not even the invincible Armada can halt the population growth of Germany. Some day, perhaps not while England is getting help from half the world against Germany, perhaps not for a long time – but *some day* Germany will punish England with death, because it is the only natural outcome.'[56]

Hamsun's article 'The Child' dealt with a very different, but equally contentious subject, which triggered a debate that would smoulder for years. Hamsun was enraged that a young woman who had murdered her newborn baby had only received an eight-month prison sentence. The natural order of things, he declared, had been turned upside down. The relationship between parent and child – the theme of his lecture attacking the fourth commandment – was in disarray. Orphanages were forced to go cap in hand while society erected palaces for the crippled, blind and old, and let off a child-murderer with just eight months behind bars. Hamsun demanded the death penalty: 'Hang both parents, be cleansed of them! Hang the first hundred of them, they are beyond hope.'[57]

Numerous people spoke out against him, questioning whether he under-stood the social structures from which such tragedies arose. Among these voices was a young writer who would later win the Nobel Prize: Sigrid Undset. Since her debut in 1907, her novels, exploring the lives of young women, had attracted huge attention. Undset and others pointed out that women who were guilty of infanticide almost always proved to be good people after serving their sentences.

Hamsun spat back that a woman's natural purpose was not primarily to be a good person: 'When she has given birth, her purpose as a woman is to be a mother.'[58]

When Hamsun wrote these words in March 1915, Marie had just told him that she was expecting their third child.

Myriads of Characters

Striving to write a sequel to *Children of the Age*, Hamsun travelled to the small northern town of Harstad at the end of January 1915. After little more than a week he told Marie how desperately miserable he felt: 'Things have never been as bad as they are now. It is not even that I am empty, but I cannot get started. I have a myriad of characters left over from my last book, I have copious working notes, stacks of sketches and dialogue for every character.'

With ideas already in such abundance it was unthinkable to start a completely new book, but Hamsun felt almost desperate enough to do just that. 'The material is of such enormity that it overwhelms me and I can't get properly started. I sit here each day, struggling. But now I pray to God I shall find some sort of solution.'[59] A month later nothing had improved. He tried night and day, but made no progress, and felt utterly dejected. 'I shall never write a *sequel* again, this is what is breaking me. After all, I already have twenty-nine major and smaller characters from *Children of the Age*, and now I am setting out with that number again. But I had such a mass of preparatory work that I was reluctant to scrap it.'[60]

In March, he informed Marie that he would try to write at home. Worried she would be unable to clear the way of disturbances, Marie warned him: 'A move will be a colossal change, I am terrified you might come to a standstill.'[61]

By August, he had completed half his manuscript, but grumbled to Christian Kønig (now director of Gyldendal's operations in Oslo) that he could not promise to have the novel finished for Christmas. He told the Dane that he was desperate to be rid of the farm, and wondered if his publisher might help him out by buying it.[62] He did not receive a response.

In September, he sent the first half of the manuscript to Oslo, and by October he was at the finishing stages, with just fifteen more pages to complete. His nerves were like jelly, but he was pleased. At the end of the month he telegraphed the title, *Segelfoss Town*, and delivered the final section, written on the back of some proofread pages, by the first week of November. He complained angrily to his publishers that he had received an envelope addressed anonymously 'To the Author'. Had Gyldendal found it necessary, he asked sarcastically, to address envelopes to Ibsen and Bjørnson in a similarly impersonal way? 'Not that I am comparing myself with them – although I have done things these gentlemen have done standing on my head.'[63]

Hamsun bemoaned his wretched health. In a letter to an editor in the capital he described how he had to have his paper held steady with a clip so that he could write with one hand and hold an electrode to his head with the other. He had advanced from electric belts to instruments that produced static electricity: 'This is how I have had to work for two years, my nerves are pretty bad.'[64]

But in truth his capacity for work was enormous.

As a leading social commentator, Hamsun had written numerous articles in the Norwegian and Danish newspapers, and started two debates that aroused widespread interest.

As a writer of letters, he had produced almost two hundred, some of them long and all of them drafted in rough beforehand. He continually returned to the same themes relating to the international political scene: that England represented a danger to Norway and every other small nation, and that Germany must bring England to its knees.

As a son of the now eighty-five-year-old Tora, he spent a considerable amount of time corresponding with a childhood friend whom he entrusted with organising various practicalities for her – the recurring theme in these letters being his surprise at the amount of money she got through.

As a farmer, he initiated the building of a mill and dairy at Hamarøy, and under the motto 'No detail of the farm is too small to attend to' he oversaw what had become a considerable project.

As an art lover, he had hunted through several towns for an attractive calendar to hang in Skogheim's dining room; when he couldn't find anything suitable he made one himself, painting a frame for it on his return home. He also found time to write to his artist friends, and to buy and commission paintings and sculptures. He enjoyed setting them impossible tasks. Axel Ebbe could apparently draw anything one could think of: Hamsun asked for a scream in the desert.[65]

And as a family man, he brought provisions back with him or filled crates with food to send home when he was away. He bought his sons wind-up cars and toys of all sorts, and procured all kinds of new gifts for little Ellinor, who had come into the world in October 1915.

In addition to all this, over the course of 1915 he had written *Segelfoss Town*, his longest book so far, which was released in two volumes. He was pushing himself, claimed Hamsun, in order to support eight people across three households. Every one of them was reliant on his books. 'I am writing with blood in my ink – until ink runs in my blood', he lamented.[66]

Hamsun convinced his publisher to sell the two volumes of *Segelfoss Town* at a reduced price in order to increase sales. It was a smart move. The original print run was eight thousand copies, but the publisher was immediately obliged to order several thousand more from the printers, as well as a third batch in the run-up to Christmas. When the Danish editor of *Politiken*, Henrik Cavling, telegraphed to say that *Segelfoss Town* had almost been torn from the shelves of the book warehouses in Copenhagen, Hamsun quipped: 'I'm selling cheap this year. Stock clearance!'[67]

The reviews, almost without exception, were ecstatic. Critics praised the way Hamsun had developed the plot and depicted the changes in the little town of Segelfoss since *Children of the Age*. Tobias Holmengrå and Theodor på Bua now reign supreme in the town, but both lack the noble nature that would emanate from the old squire of tradition. Their manners are a pretence, albeit a pretty one: 'Everything of worth that hangs in the air between educated folk, including their manner of speech, he had made his very own – well done, Mr Holmengrå, superbly well done! But he was two centuries younger than the inhabitants of Segelfoss Manor; he had learned to raise his hat, but did so like a slave.'

The spirit of the age is a gigantic fearsome mould that grabs and recasts people's natures. The characters are entranced by the desire for authority and money. Tobias and Theodor are challenged from every quarter by people who demand power and seize it for themselves. The lowliest folk dare to debase them, since fear of punishment has been democratised into nonexistence. Hamsun pours scorn on the ordinary folk, the fishermen and farmers, lured by affluence which they have neither the good sense nor the character to handle: 'Their desires are of the proletariat,' he writes in *Segelfoss Town*, 'and their perpetual dissatisfaction differs from that of any animal, since their gaping mouths are always open for more, more.' The small middle class comprising the doctor, lawyer, newspaper editor and a few others incessantly seek alliances from above and below. These are the characters Hamsun draws with the least humanity, making clear his derision of their self-seeking cunning.

At the heart of this novel are the secret dreams nursed by the industrialist Tobias and the businessman Theodor, and their consequences for the community.

Tobias longs to be respected and invents new ways to maintain his mystique; Theodor worships Tobias's daughter, Mariane, from afar. As figures of power, these two men are weak in comparison to the patriarchs like Mack and Willatz Holmsen who dominate Hamsun's earlier works. Tobias has neither Mack's ruthless and possessive relationship to women, nor Holmsen's rigid hold over his own desire, but Hamsun is fascinated by him; Holmengrå exits the story on a southern course, as mysteriously as he entered it. The archetypal businessman of the new generation, Theodor is drawn with great sympathy. He is the son of Per på Bua, a demonic figure closely resembling Hamsun's Uncle Hans. Theodor's sad longing for Mariane allows him to grow in strength, the miraculous power of love transforming him into a better man.

Aftenposten's exalting review of the book was typical of the critical reaction to *Segelfoss Town*: 'There has never been anything better written in the Norwegian language – a novel of this kind cannot be bettered. [. . .] It is a book to return to, it grips one over and over again. And it will keep coming back to mind, as everything does that sheds meaning on life.'[68]

Hamsun awaited the reviews from certain critics more impatiently than others. One of these was the Dane Sven Lange, who often traced developmental lines through Hamsun's oeuvre when reviewing his newest tome. His article in *Politiken* reached Hamsun just before the New Year of 1916.

It could not have come at a better time.

Full Control – But at What Price?

The close of 1915 saw Hamsun deeply immersed in his own work, this time not writing but reading – namely, his entire literary output since the autumn of 1888.

Gyldendal had finally agreed to his idea to publish another *Collected Works*, containing not only his novels and short stories but also his plays and poetry. Immediately after sending off *Segelfoss Town* in November, Hamsun started sifting through all his earlier books. Again he set about a process of revision. He wanted to rework parts of his verse drama *Friar Vendt*, as well as his poetry collection *The Wild Choir*, and to make some small improvements to other works. After having read half of *Hunger*, he grumbled to Kønig: 'By God I can't bear it, you must do with me as you please. [. . .] The problem is: I am so embarrassed that I'd like to scrap the whole lot and rewrite everything.'[69]

Hamsun now had before him Sven Lange's review of *Segelfoss Town*, in which the reviewer also looked at the entire sweep of Hamsun's literary output. In Lange's view, Hamsun's work had begun with a certain capriciousness, exemplified by *Mysteries* which, like this latest novel, was set in a small town. His style had peaked in the early years with *Pan*, taken a tumble in the empty effects of *Queen Tamara*, livened up in his travel writings, lost its way again in his attempt at gilding the youthful fantasy world of *Rosa*, and had vanished altogether in the hopeless play *In the Grip of Life*. But then, according to Lange, a miracle had taken place. Around Hamsun's fiftieth birthday, when according to his own assertions he should have shut up or died, he had blossomed into full literary maturity. *The Last Joy*, with its central question 'Can I, an old man, achieve anything any more?', was an extraordinary piece of self-evaluation. Hamsun had derided himself for growing old, yet listened in wonder to the voices that came to him. And he had brought a wealth of new characters into literature's eternal light: fishermen, craftsmen, tradesmen, peasants, workers and the thin layer of the upper classes who belonged to this small coastal community in the north.

Such a host of characters was made to dance about like dolls strung up on the author's fingertips; Lange was hugely impressed by the way Hamsun could bring them all to life in the reader's mind.[70]

The fifty-six-year-old author sat crowned in glory, on his own farm close to his childhood home, rereading his first novels. It was a confrontation he found embarrassing.

Only in that autumn of 1888 had Hamsun first succeeded in writing the way he had dreamed of doing for over a decade. He learned to capture the distorted images he glimpsed of himself and the workings of his mind. But the strain in writing *Hunger* and then *Mysteries* had been terrible. Over the years he had pushed too hard, torn at his own defences, inflicted permanent damage on himself. It was impossible to carry on in that way. After *Mysteries*, in books like *Dreamers*, *Benoni* and *Rosa*, he began to weave the rich fabric of northern Norway into his work. The artistry was in his portrayal of characters bedecked in this fine fabric, using the rich dialect, the peculiar names, the unique scenery and the stories he had heard in his youth. With each book the distance between narrator and narrated had widened and become safer.

His main challenge was to keep tabs on this burgeoning cast of characters. Hamsun was in full control now.

There are two artists in *Segelfoss Town*. The first, Bårdsen, is a failed playwright who works as a telegraph operator; he starves himself to death. The second, Willatz Holmsen Jnr, is a musician and composer, but within him two different natures collide: the artistry and imagination inherited from his mother Adelheid, who was a singer, musician and diarist; and the intractability of his father the squire. Perhaps something of Hamsun's own contradictory nature is contained in this character. Certainly the evocations of Holmsen's inspirational surges echo Hamsun's descriptions in *Bjørger*, written in his late teens, and *Hunger*, when he was nearly thirty: 'It flows and flows out of a mind overfilled, and continues to flow; he sits like a blind man in receipt from above, writing in light. Writing and writing. Occasionally he brings his hand thudding down onto the grand piano, writes again, whimpers in harmony, feels nauseous and spits, writes on. This goes on, the hours pass, oh the hours riding on this wave!'

Hamsun was in great need of such a surge.

At the end of the book, Holmsen journeys southwards, just like Tobias Holmengrå. Neither the adventurer nor the artist can flourish on the coast of northern Norway.

And what of Hamsun himself?

Time after time in his books, Hamsun had depicted the unhappiness of those whose roots had been ripped up, who had come adrift, separated from the soil. In 'A Word for Us', an article Hamsun wrote in 1910, he had warned: 'We have some roots in our soil, we cannot cut them, they are what make us stand upright.'[71]

I Must Be Rid of This Farm

Four and a half years earlier, Hamsun had returned to the land of his childhood to replant his roots in the freshly ploughed earth. But however long the farmer spent digging his fields, the poet-vagabond in him continually interrupted him in his labours. The tiller of words whispered beguiling promises to the tiller of the soil. Each new book kept the writer away from the farm for months on end. And each time the writer roamed, the farmer's disdain for him grew.

At the beginning of 1916, Hamsun sought a resolution to his dilemma in the slips of paper that he pondered over. His new novel would be about a man of the soil. Meanwhile, he put Skogheim up for sale in the newspapers – without informing Marie. She rallied the local sheriff, priest and doctor to talk him out of it, and they succeeded in halting proceedings. The planting was late that year.

Hamsun had already made detailed notes for his new book, soon to be known worldwide as *The Growth of the Soil*. It was alive with evocations of the idyllic, rustic life that Hamsun had simultaneously sought and denied himself: 'For hundreds of years his forefathers had sown the grain, an act of reverence on a mild, windless evening, preferably in a blessed, fine rain, and preferably as soon as possible on the return of the grey geese.'

Hamsun sowed his own fields as he wrote about his latest character, Isak, doing the same. However, the writer told people that he never wanted to farm again. He must leave Skogheim. He had only given Marie a temporary reprieve.

But the solid peasant feet that Marie had inherited from her mother's family were now firmly planted in the spring earth of Skogheim. She reminded him of all the promises he had made, the dreams they had shared and together brought to fruition. She was thirty-four and had three small children, and unlike him she had left everything behind from her old world.[72] He had simply brought everything with him and carried on as before.

Marie was angry and she was frightened. She was fighting for her role in life, a role she had been initially hesitant in taking on, but that she had mastered with increasing assurance, a role that she had expanded steadily with determination and wisdom, so that it could no longer be construed as secondary to his. She had become more than just the author's housewife.

Hamsun, however, was finished with Nordland. When the rest of the family had gone to bed that New Year's Eve he wrote to a friend: 'Listen to me. I must be rid of the farm now. I cannot go on working with it any longer, my health is failing entirely.'[73]

Hamsun began 1917 with his mind made up. He had to escape the peasant life if he was to continue writing. Marie and the children would have to give way.

He contacted a man who was well connected among the wealthier echelons of Oslo society. Thirty-five years after the editor of *Aftenposten* had given column space to the works of the young Knut Hamsun, his successor came to Hamsun's aid. Together with fourteen other wealthy men from the capital, he declared himself willing to buy the writer out of the farm. If things came to the worst the group could survive some financial loss; after all, they were securing a cultural treasure for the nation.

The city men received news at the beginning of February that ownership must be transferred swiftly. Hamsun could not manage another spring: 'I want to delve into a great forest where nothing can disturb me. I have a great work in hand – if my health could improve just a little!'[74]

He was working on *The Growth of the Soil*, about the pioneering farmer Isak and his wife, Inger, with her good, strong hands. And about their two sons, Eleseus and Sivert, and the short stub of a pencil that Eleseus steals from a visiting engineer which will determine his entire future – a future in the city, free of their farm at Sellanrå.

Despite Marie's protests, Hamsun tore the family away from Hamarøy in the beginning of April 1917. They were to return south. The author, who was in the midst of writing a book in which he glorified peasant life as the only natural form of existence, rendered himself landless. He sold his farm, animals and equipment, and moved his family to a pharmacist's villa in Larvik, a small town by the Oslo Fjord, some four hours' boat ride from the capital.

Hamsun had in fact spent many happy moments as a farmer during the past six years. He drew on these in *The Growth of the Soil*, reliving the sheer joyousness of cultivating the land: 'And day after day was taken up by his working with the soil; he cleared new land of roots and stones, he ploughed, harrowed and fertilised his field, worked with the pick and shovel, broke lumps of earth and crushed them in his hands and under his heels; a farmer through and through, he turned his fields into velvet carpets.' Sowing was the most sacred of a farmer's activities: 'Isak walked bareheaded, in Jesus's name, sowing the seeds, resembling a tree stump with hands, but inside he was like a child. He took care over each throw, he was kindly and resigned. Look, these minute grains will surely sprout, and turn to ears and more grain; and so it is over the whole earth when the grain is sown. In Palestine, America, in the Gudbrands Valley – the world is so vast, and this tiny patch that Isak went and sowed was at the centre of it all.'

For the peasant farmer within Hamsun, the farm had often felt this way: Skogheim was the epicentre of the world. But the author rebelled against this sensibility. A love for the soil had been ingrained in Hamsun since his childhood in Hamarøy, but as with Isak's book-corrupted son Eleseus, he had discovered the enchanted world into which a pencil stub might lead its owner. It was an irony, yet a necessity, that he began work on his peasants' gospel at the same time as he laid plans to escape this world which he held most dear.

I Am Not Happy in the City

Marie Hamsun was eight months pregnant when they arrived in Larvik in April 1917. She was not pleased with their new home, a self-important two-storey villa with high garden steps, situated in the middle of one of the smartest areas of town. It was, it seemed to her, merely a reflection of her husband's desire to be accepted into high society. Marie had adapted well to running the farm in Nordland, and had found contentment in their joint vision of a simple country life. When Hamsun was absent she had reigned supreme over her Nordland kingdom. What could she be now, apart from a mother to her children? And there were so many other people here who clamoured for her husband's attention.

In the early hours of 13 May, Hamsun became a father for the fifth time. Marie brought the child into the world while her husband slept uninterrupted, under the same roof. Even that morning, Hamsun's edict that he must not on any account be disturbed before breakfast was followed to the letter. Marie and the children kept out of sight, waiting for him to leave the house, and the maid who served him alone in the dining room did not utter a word to him, since she had not been addressed. It was only when Hamsun caught sight of a strange woman leaving the house that he realised it was the midwife.

The excitement of seeing the new baby was irresistible. Hamsun decided her name should be Cecilia. It was, he said, as though silk glided through the name.

The beautiful Swedish woman at the town's baths and spa was also called Cecilia.

Towards the beginning of November 1917, Hamsun was bringing *The Growth of the Soil* to completion. For six years he had lived the life that he prescribed for others, but could not finally live himself. As he sat in his back yard in Larvik, he started to write about Isak and Inger's existence in increasingly idealised terms – necessarily so, if he was to carry on believing his own message.

The mysterious Geissler, one of Hamsun's vagabond figures, is given an increasingly central role. He is tricksy, expelled from somewhere, utterly dependent on inspiration. Like other such characters in Hamsun's work he is a good helper, from a fairytale turned inside out since it is not the dream of winning the princess and half the kingdom that drives him: he is free of illusions about himself, and his own life tends towards catastrophe. He will, however, find a way to use himself for the good of others and waves a magic wand over Isak and Inger's little family.

Geissler bridges the cultivated and uncultivated worlds, standing between Isak's peasant culture and modern society. Hamsun could not allow the contemporary world with its demands for orderly paperwork to swallow Isak, any more than he could allow Inger, who kills her newborn child out of compassion because she has inherited her harelip, to be engulfed by its demand for retribution; Hamsun's earlier concerns about infanticide are debated with a greater level of complexity in this book than in his newspaper articles. In *The Growth of the Soil*, Hamsun showed that he had understood what some other social commentators refused to take into account: that escape to a traditional farming life completely free of the modern goods-and-services economy was an impossibility. Geissler conveyed the message that civil law was as important as the law of nature.

The Growth of the Soil thus represents a compromise, an acknowledgement that nature and culture must enter an alliance.

When he was working at his best, perhaps Hamsun saw his mission as a writer as being to create characters that made it seem possible to live a fulfilled life. Until this point, his characters had all suffered some form of internal conflict. He now required a figure cast in the same reliably solid mould throughout: a man who becomes one with the soil through his sacred labours.

The final page of *The Growth of the Soil*, written at the beginning of November 1917, is a homage to such a man: 'Farewell, farewell . . . There goes Isak sowing; a troll of a man, a tree stump. He wears homemade clothes, their wool spun from his own sheep, boots from the hide of his own cows and calves. And he walks religiously bareheaded as he sows. [. . .] He knew what was needed. A man of the fields in body and soul, and a farmer without self-pity. A ghost from the past who points the way to the future.'

After portraying the collapse of the old patriarchal peasant society and its consequences in *Children of the Age* and *Segelfoss Town*, Hamsun now shows the way forward. Breaking new land is the challenge for the young today.

A month after he completed his manuscript, Hamsun confided to an acquaintance in Nordland: 'The curious thing is that I have rid myself of the farm, but my health has not improved, and I feel so utterly miserable no longer being a farm owner. [. . .] I have an ineradicable desire for the soil.'[75] Nine days later he reiterated this strong desire for the land. He felt a 'longing for fields again. There is nothing strange about that, it is merely my destiny. I have my roots in the country. The first thing I read every morning are the farmers' magazines.'[76] And soon after the new year he confessed: 'I loathe it in town. And my children can't stand on their heads here in our garden, which is full of black earth. If I were in slightly better health now, I would have bought myself a little farm again and had fields, meadows and animals and forest.'[77]

The Growth of the Soil was a book written to serve a worthy cause, he explained, and he had even thought to subtitle it 'A Book to My Contemporary Norwegians'. But it was also a book that he had needed for himself, to enable him to walk away from Skogheim. This had not after all proved straightforward, and he was now keeping himself informed about farms coming up for sale. Life in the pharmacist's villa in the little town had failed to bring him happiness after all.

The Growth of the Soil transformed Hamsun's fortunes. Eighteen thousand copies had to be printed before Christmas. The Norwegian and Danish edition alone earned him 27,000 kroner. Publishers in many other countries also wanted to print it. Hamsun had now been translated into twenty-three languages.

The first printing of eight thousand sets of his *Collected Works* was also almost sold out. A further printing secured him an income of 76,800 kroner, equal to the combined yearly salaries of more than twenty-five teachers. Bergljot received 25,000 kroner in payment for the gambling debts Hamsun had accrued in 1901. All his other private debts were also cleared. In Germany, his books continued to come out in new editions. In addition, Langen Verlag began publishing the *Collected Works*. He wrote to Herman Hesse to thank him for praising his writings so highly.[78]

Hamsun had just turned fifty-nine. Twenty years before, when he was approaching forty, he had given disdainful lectures about Ibsen and other writers who had grown old, describing how they scraped their books together with trembling hands and wrote from a state of emptiness. As he reached the end of his forties, he had given another lecture postulating the terrible consequences of ageing. Originally he had set the age for the cessation of development at fifty, though he later conveniently suggested that this could vary by a decade: 'In his fiftieth year, he slipped into life's after-dinner stage, from now on he entered the stage of decline, where he would remain until death. He got habits and routines, took particular walks along particular routes, nothing happened in his life after ten in the evening, it became increasingly rare for him to expose himself to anything unfamiliar, he restricted his travels, gave up many of his previous pleasures because of ill-health or impotence, enjoyed stillness, occupied himself with pouring scorn on the opinions he had held as a young man, and getting offended when people acted without due deference for this activity. Such is the life of the old.'[79]

Of course, anyone who had even a slight knowledge of Hamsun's crusade against Henrik Ibsen knew exactly at whom this tirade had been aimed.

Hamsun had written twenty-six books in the twenty-eight years since *Hunger* appeared in 1890, and he was making notes for his twenty-seventh. Harry Fett, Norway's director of Cultural Heritage, a man entitled to propose candidates to the Swedish Academy, informed Hamsun that he had nominated him for the Nobel Prize.

He may have been fifty-nine but Hamsun fully intended to produce many more books. He was realising that, despite all his previous protestations, he did, after all, need the strength that came to him from working the land. Perhaps in that sense, *The Growth of the Soil* was one of the most truthful books he had written, since it proved to be a book about himself.

In the early summer of 1918, Hamsun had spotted an old farm, Nørholm, further down the south coast of Norway and not too far from Lillesand where he had written parts of *Mysteries* in 1890. The place appealed to him tremendously, and feelers were put out about its purchase. A new season in his life was about to begin.

A Paradise on Earth

Hamsun bought the somewhat run-down farm on the south coast between the small towns of Grimstad and Lillesand. The transaction was hard on Hamsun's pocket, if not on his soul.

The vendor of the property was a practised speculator, a man who had spent a lifetime haggling over anything and everything tradable. And he took full advantage of the purchaser, who suffered from the erratic attitude of the nouveaux riches towards money; Hamsun had always swung between excessive generosity, feigned indifference, cautiousness and stinginess. The owner of the farm held fast to his asking price, despite his having already sold off the animal stock, farm equipment and timber in situ, all for a handsome sum. In fact, spying the hunger in Hamsun's eyes, he upped the price, and then raised it still further. Hamsun finally gave him 220,000 kroner for Nørholm – enough to pay a year's salary to all the fifty-eight teachers in the five surrounding villages.

Hamsun was determined to show how the owner of a farm with as rich a tradition as Nørholm should meet the challenges of the modern world.

In his recent books, he had depicted how landless country folk could fashion their own new-ploughed paradise through their labours. He needed Marie to be positive and capable in the way that Inger in *The Growth of the Soil* was, not unhappy like Adelheid in his Segelfoss books.

Hamsun demanded Marie's enthusiasm but she was unable to muster any excitement for their new home when she first visited it in the autumn. She saw the leafy deciduous forest rising like flames against the grey mountains, and sky and sea that met in the narrowing bay beyond. But beautiful as the lines of the landscape and buildings of Nørholm were, it all seemed hemmed in. Marie clambered up onto a hillock and glimpsed the ocean, but she was still unmoved. She saw nothing of what she was searching for. Nothing here reminded her of her childhood's boundless forests. This was a country for giants, where massive rocks rose from the earth, so enormous no human could ever shift them.

Arriving at Nørholm with all their possessions one cold November day, the couple discovered a serious flaw in their plans: the main building had neither electricity nor water, as they had known as, but all the same they had failed to pack a single paraffin lamp. They lit numerous candles, but all the candles in the county could not have lit that rambling old house.[80]

Soon Hamsun had a total of eleven people working inside and out. The cost of buying the house itself, and now the mounting wages and bills, was all to be paid with money yet to be earned. The rebuilding project he now embarked upon would last for the next twenty-two years, and would include renovating all existing buildings and erecting new ones, making alterations to the barns and animal enclosures, experimenting with new plants, ploughing up new fields and planting forest land, putting more fences up, and establishing a garden with several kilometres of paths, numerous bridges and a jetty.

The locals and those employed at Nørholm soon formed a good opinion of Mrs Hamsun as a kindly, down-to-earth woman. About Mr Hamsun, however, they may have been a little more reticent. He could be friendly one moment and explode over something trivial the next, storming off, only to return a moment later as though nothing had happened. He was pedantic about timesheets – woe betide anybody who tried to sneak themselves an extra hour's pay, or failed to record an absence – but at times he would generously top up the weekly wage packets.

People soon learned it was risky to come bustling up to Hamsun directly; it was far safer to approach him through his wife or one of the housekeepers. He made no effort to hide the fact that he liked some people better than others. But his preferences and antipathies were not always easy to understand. In some situations he could appear almost naïve, while at other times he revealed a fiendishly sharp insight into unexpected issues. He seemed hard of hearing, though some implied it was only a pretence, employed when it suited him. If something needed lifting he had ample strength to do it, but was generally otherwise occupied. The few who dared to ask about how and when he wrote received vague answers. Several had seen him stand at a distance, take pencil and paper from his pocket, and make notes.

The womenfolk sighed over Hamsun's beautiful children.

The eldest, six-year-old Tore, soon found friends on the local farms and with great ingenuity set about giving his little brother, Arild, the slip. Tore had picked up some rather juicy expressions from both the north and east of Norway, while the younger boy was quick to grasp the local Eide dialect. With no big brother in sight, Arild attached himself to the local labourers, energetic and talkative as he was.

Ellinor, aged three, and eighteen-month-old Cecilia stayed with their mother and the maids.

After only one month, Hamsun found that his building costs already totalled 10,346 kroner and 56 øre.[81] Never had the mutual dependency of bankbooks and Hamsun's own books been clearer to him as Christmas 1918 approached. If he had remained in Nordland or Larvik, Hamsun could have lived well on the income from his previous works without the need to write more. Now it was impossible. The fifty-nine-year-old author could not allow himself to slow down.

As 1918 turned to 1919, Hamsun continued fashioning his paradise while the victors of the Great War, Britain and France, began to reshape Europe.

There had been some sympathy in Norway for Germany at the outbreak of war, but it had soon been ripped apart when German submarines attacked Norwegian trading ships sailing under a neutral flag. One Norwegian, however, had remained loyal. Hamsun told friends that he wept over the idiocy of his fellow countrymen who were celebrating Britain's renewed rule of the seas. They were, he snorted, like foolish children.[82]

Hamsun had lost his first war.

Six days into 1919, Hamsun received the news of his mother's death. She was eighty-nine.

Tora Hamsun had given her famous son life and shaped his personality in fundamental ways. But her life had barely been touched by his. Hamsun's fame and fortune gave him the power to transform his parents' existence completely, but they would never have wanted that. Instead he provided them with little luxuries they could not have otherwise afforded: better coffee, shop-bought bread, a tablecloth, a silk shawl, a brooch for special occasions. His parents' desires had been far from lavish. The most valuable thing he had been able to offer them was the knowledge that they would never be dependent on the parish.

A message was sent north from Nørholm that none of them would be attending the funeral.

On the day Hamsun was told of his mother's death, he took out a wooden toy that had belonged to him as a child in Hamarøy. It was a driver on a horse-drawn cart, seated atop a large pile of timber, steering with the reins. With the help of a clever arrangement of cords, the driver and horse could be made to move. But it was now broken. He packed it up carefully and sent it, along with some money and a letter to the man who had made the toy, asking him, with some urgency, to fix it. Hamsun would paint it himself when it was returned. It would be as good as new.[83]

In Versailles, a conference intended to restore world order began. Great Britain and France held the reins firmly, and were determined to cow Germany into obedience. On the same day as the talks began, Hamsun received a letter from Langen Verlag, his publishers in Munich. Despite Germany's defeat, its own internal crisis and national feelings of hostility towards a 'neutral' Norway, the German public had not turned their backs on Hamsun; his *Collected Works* was attracting enormous interest in the country.

Langen Verlag asked whether he wanted to receive his monies straight away, but with the exchange rate being so poor Hamsun felt it better to wait, adding that he had every confidence in Germany's future. And he soon received heart-warming news: several German theatres were interested in putting on his plays, and interest was being shown in the film rights for *Victoria*.[84]

Hamsun carefully kept track of everything written about Germany in the Norwegian newspapers as well as in the Danish newspaper *Politiken*. The German elections were won by the Left-wing Liberals and the Catholic Centre Party. Germany's politicians gathered in Frankfurt to establish a new constitution.

In Norway, the fragile spirit of cross-party cooperation engendered when the union with Sweden was dissolved had long since evaporated. The Norwegian Labour Party was increasing in popularity and gaining political influence. It was also moving steadily towards a closer affiliation with the international communist movement, eventually to result in its becoming part of the Communist International. The other parties were trying to ensure that the socialists were kept out of the corridors of power.

Hunched over the newspaper headlines Hamsun regularly burst forth angrily that the world was facing ruin, and Norway with it.

But at least he was sure of one thing: he had bought himself a paradise.

Master of Nørholm

By the end of January 1919, Hamsun had installed himself in a hotel in Lillesand. Once more he shuffled his little notes and laid them out like a game of patience, trying to get some of them to correspond, to combine into something more than loose ideas on leaves of paper.

He was only there for a few days, returning to Nørholm feeling unwell. Marie, who had watched the pattern of her husband's health over the last decade, had foreseen a reaction of this sort after he suffered the news of his mother's death and the defeat of Germany. The frequent occasions when Hamsun consigned himself to bed often had little to do with illness; he had an unfortunate tendency to be unwell when life's events were unpalatable.

Having been painstakingly nursed at home for a week, he wobbled out of bed and allowed himself to be driven the 9 kilometres back to Lillesand by taxi. From there he continued, as always, to demand that he be kept fully informed about everything that was happening on the farm, including all the building works and children's activities. Simultaneously he stressed the importance of his not being distracted. Marie managed somehow to fulfil this impossibly contradictory task by offering her husband rose-tinted versions of the truth.

Hamsun took daily walks in the little town of Lillesand. He sat at the table in his hotel room with his slips of paper spread before him. He stood at his window which faced the bridge and market square, watching. But

Hamsun's writing was not confined to the precise depiction of that world. He was no journalist. He was a writer who developed multiple exposures of his impressions of the multitude of places he visited.

Hamsun held out for four weeks, though he was finding it difficult to focus properly. Then back to Nørholm he went, brandishing things once more for all his children and birthday presents for Tore, who turned seven on 6 March 1919. Hamsun took the birthday boy into the large upstairs living room and told him to stand next to the doorframe with his back straight. He marked his son's height on the doorframe with a pencil. At the age of seven, Tore's father explained to him, it was possible to predict the height a child would reach in adulthood. By his estimation, Hamsun said proudly, Tore would be taller than him.

Taller than his father! When Tore stood close to Hamsun now, he almost had to break his neck to look up at him.[85]

In the evenings, Hamsun would sometimes sit at the big table in the middle of the living room upstairs and read to the children. Hamsun and Marie did not always agree about what constituted suitable reading, since the ages of their brood spanned five and a half years. Hamsun would pick books that Marie had set aside for the two older boys, or even books that had never entered the children's room. He would tell them about curious things that their mother would never have spoken of, though the children also knew that he would become angry more quickly than her when they argued, talked at once or interrupted.

It was not unusual for him to gripe about a particular author's style. But his young audience had no objections; if the book was so below par that their father threw it aside and told them stories from his own childhood, so much the better.

Before turning out the lights, he would remind them of how proud they should be to come from such a wonderful place as Nørholm, an estate with one of the longest and most distinguished histories in the region.

Having done a great deal of work on the farmhouse itself, Hamsun now turned his attention to the outhouse, which contained both the animal stalls and the barn. He had plans for a rather grander purpose-built cowshed. The cows might be destined for the slaughterhouse one day, but they might still appreciate having come from a decent home.

Work had progressed well by the late spring of 1919, when it occurred to Hamsun that the dung cellar under the cowshed might need enlarging to house all the manure he expected his future prize cows to produce. With the shed almost complete, the options were either carefully to support the structure and dig underneath, or alternatively to blast it out.

Estate owner and master builder agreed on dynamite. They concurred about the need for precise measurement and careful positioning of the explosive to prevent accidental damage. Where they disagreed, however, was on how the measurements and positioning should be applied. The tremendous explosion did not blast inwards or enlarge the cellar: it lifted upwards, ripping through the solidly built barn and scattering it skywards. Nails, bricks, stones, planks and manure flew around the ears of the two explosives experts.

Far away in neighbouring counties, people rolled about with laughter. Hamsun took no notice.

Harder to ignore was the desperately slow progress of his next novel. He had promised that he would have it ready in time for Christmas.

His mood was certainly not improved by what he read in the newspapers that summer. On 28 June 1919, Germany was forced to sign the Treaty of Versailles. It seemed to Hamsun that the host nation and its allies were plundering the country shamelessly: Germany had to give away 13 per cent of its territories, renounce its colonies, accept French occupation of the Rhine's west bank and the confiscation of its gold reserves and investments abroad, as well as surrender its entire navy and large parts of its merchant fleet, and reduce its industrial output. Still the Allied victors were not satisfied. A separate conference in London would settle the amount of compensation to be paid. Across Germany businesses rushed to call in outstanding debts, fearful that the steadily swelling inflation would slash their value. Hamsun did not pursue his monies from Germany. He had significant amounts of cash coming in from elsewhere; Gyldendal's Norwegian branch alone paid him royalties amounting to over 90,000 kroner in 1918, equivalent to the yearly salaries of more than twelve county court judges. Yet Hamsun's expenditure was outstripping his fortune. He now borrowed more money from his publisher against a book he had barely begun.

Once more, Hamsun attempted to release the flow of ideas by going away. But it occurred to him now that he no longer needed to travel so far. Two empty cottar's cottages had come with the purchase of the estate, and he established himself in one of them, delightfully named Hasseldalen – 'Hazel Valley'. It was little more than a quarter of an hour's walk from home.

But Hamsun still found it hard to surrender himself to the world of his characters, and block out everything and everybody on the farm.

How We All Struggle

The approach of summer 1919 brought Hamsun's sixtieth birthday ever closer. Gyldendal was keen to mark the occasion with a special illustrated edition of *Pan* on the twenty-fifth anniversary of its first publication.

Ever since Hamsun had decided, when he was twenty-nine, to declare himself to be one year younger than he actually was, the subject of his age had been a bomb waiting to detonate. Gyldendal's Oslo offices were abuzz with nervous speculation. There was no denying that there had only been nine years since the celebration of Hamsun's fiftieth birthday, and the Norwegian press would be merciless in its treatment of this Danish publishing house if it appeared to be unable even to keep track of its Norwegian authors' birthdays.

Christian König had no alternative but to ask Hamsun himself. It caused a fluster at Nørholm. Hamsun's solution was that Marie would have to carry the can. On an old envelope he carefully wrote the message she should telegraph immediately in her name: 'Gyldendal, Oslo. Hamsun sixty years on 4 August this year. Mrs Hamsun.'

The hacks were still unable to resist flapping over the extraordinary fact that the decade separating the fiftieth and sixtieth birthdays of Norway's best-known writer was a year short. Others got the blame. It never occurred to anybody that Hamsun himself might be at the heart of the confusion.[86]

While Nørholm was besieged by the national press, Hamsun secreted himself in a nearby town and Marie directed the troops on the estate. Norway's major newspapers devoted numerous pages over several days to Hamsun. The minor ones allowed special correspondents to write long articles, and their editors dedicated space to him in their columns. Hamsun's birthday also received extensive press attention in Denmark, Sweden and Germany.

Helge Rode of the *Berlingske Tidende* in Copenhagen set the tone: 'He is the great literary magician of the North. [. . .] He plays with his readers, like a cat with a mouse, and what a pleasure it is to be the mouse.' In Sweden, Anders Österling wrote in *Svenska Dagbladet* that Hamsun had, in his most recent works, forged himself a place in the consciousness of the Norwegian people as guide and interpreter; this was a man of the people, yet of true aristocratic nature. Österling was, as Hamsun was fully aware, a member of the Swedish Academy that selected the Nobel laureate.

But there were some dissenting voices to be found, primarily among the Left-wing press, who disliked Hamsun's reactionary ideas, noting that he put himself 'at odds with the course of progress'.[87]

Hamsun found himself brooding on the subject of death a great deal. Marie tried to raise his spirits by describing the children to him in a letter. She was hardly encouraged by his answer: 'Yes, how they strive, how we all struggle and strive – and then in a few years we are dead! All we have are the children we leave behind. Good God, the little ones! [. . .] How bloody miserable life is. But we probably come back, we are not finished when we die. Although sadly I don't believe we meet again or recognise our little ones on the other side. How wonderful it would be to rejoice at what splendid people they turned out.'[88]

He was toying with just such ideas in his present work, *The Women at the Pump*, in which a postmaster presents a forceful argument for reincarnation: 'Essentially we all stand on an equal footing and have the same opportunities, some use them, others misuse them. [. . .] But the important thing is that we do not come back to the same state each time, we have it in our power to improve our circumstances for our next life.'

Hamsun was very much engaged in the betterment of his earthly existence too.

He kept himself updated with the efforts of his Swedish friend Albert Engström, who was putting him forward for the Nobel Prize. An announcement was made in the Swedish newspapers, swiftly followed by the Norwegian magazines, that Hamsun was in the running.

Engström had recently written eloquently about Hamsun in a Danish magazine, alongside contributions by other Scandinavian cultural personalities. One of these was the Swedish novelist Selma Lagerlöf, although she herself was conspicuously careful to restrict her praise to his latest novel, *The Growth of the Soil*. As a past Nobel Prize winner and member of the Swedish Academy, she had enormous influence over who should receive this honour.

In 1919, Hamsun was nominated for the Nobel Prize for the second year running. His position as one of the Nordic world's foremost writers was indisputable when viewed from Oslo or Copenhagen, and even from Russia, Germany, Poland, Holland or Italy. But Stockholm's opinion was harder to judge. Norwegians had always struggled for recognition in Sweden.

But there may have been other reasons for doubting the suitability of his nomination; issues that certain members of the Swedish Academy felt unable to ignore so soon after the Great War. Although the country from which the candidate hailed was neutral, the same could not be said of the man himself. Hamsun had repeatedly and vehemently proclaimed an unshakeable conviction that Germany ought to bring England to its knees.

Hamsun had preached the gospel not only of the soil, but also of war. Could the members of an institution whose criteria for selection were founded upon a recognition of the futility of war isolate Hamsun's writings so completely from his politics? Academy member Per Hallström was charged with the task of evaluating the Norwegian author and the opinions expressed in his works.

In twenty-eight handwritten folio pages, Hallström declared Hamsun to be one of Norway's foremost writers, but not a suitable candidate for the Nobel Prize. In his opinion, *Mysteries* was a hotchpotch work characterised by 'unusual crudeness'. Hamsun's vagabond romances were 'boorish'. His latest novel, *The Growth of the Soil*, was, Hallström admitted, ground-breaking, but a single book of quality was not sufficient to merit the Nobel Prize. Besides which, concluded Hallström, Hamsun seemed more than anything to be 'an anarchic force, who fails even to recognise the legitimacy of the ideals which the Nobel Prize seeks to reward'.[89]

The report triggered a debate among the committee's members about the very principles of the prize itself, and about how Alfred Nobel's requirements should be interpreted almost twenty years after their original formulation. The discussions were secret, but over the summer some details were leaked: *Stockholms-Tidningen* reported on 13 August that the next Nobel Prize winner might be Hamsun – but not necessarily in that year. Indeed, the newspaper revealed that the Swedish Academy, the Royal Swedish Academy of Sciences, the Karolinska Institute and the Norwegian Nobel Committee might not award their respective prizes that autumn at all. This was partially correct. Only three of the five prizes were awarded that year, with no prize for chemistry or literature.

When this was made public, Hamsun rushed to reassure his promoters that he was not disconsolate, although he was disappointed, he told Engström, on behalf of his children, who presently stood to inherit such enormous debts. As for himself, he wanted for nothing except perhaps a new coat; his current one, which had once had a silk lining, was now twelve years old.[90]

The prize money would have come as a welcome relief to Hamsun, who was increasingly worried about how long he could expect new editions of old books to subsidise the business of running and improving Nørholm. Work on his next novel went smoothly only for short periods, then dried up completely. Initially he had indicated to Kønig that the book would be ready in the new year for publication in the spring. He had never let more than two years pass between each book. Now approaching sixty, he was having to slow his pace.

The news that he would not receive the Nobel Prize, despite so much speculation in the press and letters of advance congratulation from far afield, came in at the same time as his first harvests at Nørholm. There were mounds of superb potatoes and turnips, an excellent harvest of grain, the new barn was filled with hay, and the prize cows that were now housed in the cowshed provided 519 litres of milk for the dairy that September.

But the accounts showed that, despite the bumper harvest, and discounting any investments, the farm was in deficit. Hamsun confessed to several people that he was hiring too much help at too high a price (he now had a staff of six), and that he lacked a true farmer's shrewdness in selling the fruits of their labours.

The German public continued to buy vast numbers of Hamsun's novels and the *Collected Works*, but the tight economic restrictions enforced by the Allies prevented Hamsun bringing his money home. Kønig advised him to move the money that the Germans owed him into shares in industry, but Hamsun answered that he had no understanding of such things. If he lost a few marks he was not going to grieve. 'In my view Germany fought a battle against the world, but on behalf of the whole world and against the infinite vileness of the English – I shall not be alone in these opinions in the future.'[91]

More Germans seemed to perceive Hamsun as a writer of almost prophet-like proportion. One man, Christian Lassen, took it upon himself to promote among the future German elite what he believed was character-building liter-ature. He had recently bought a thousand copies of books by Thomas Mann, Ernst Bertram and Martin Havenstein for distribution in German universities and, around Christmas, Hamsun's *Children of the Age* and *Segelfoss Town* were also circulated. Lassen felt sure, he told Hamsun, that the students would understand 'the kernel of these books: what Nietzsche calls *Die Genialität des Herzens*, which sums up everything you, my dear Mr Hamsun, have written! The entire problem of humanity's rise and fall in three to four generations, which must be viewed without moralising, but only with love, comes across with such vitality in your books.'[92]

The author thanked the letter-writer with a photograph of himself on which he wrote in bold letters: 'Long live Germany! Knut Hamsun. 20 November 1919.'

At the beginning of 1920 Hamsun cleared his debt with his publisher; he received 24,000 kroner in royalties from a reprint of more than ten thousand copies of *The Growth of the Soil*; and a further 10,000 kroner from Stockholm as a first instalment of his advance from Svenska Andelsförlaget. Meanwhile, after enjoying substantial success with *Hunger*, his publisher in Hungary was eager to translate several more books. His publisher in Holland was also keen to publish more of his works, and in France interest was being shown in *Benoni*, *Rosa* and *Mysteries*.

The script that Hamsun was currently engaged on was, by early 1920, progressing better than he had dared hope, but bringing it to a close was proving difficult: 'I'm not dead in other respects, it's just that I can't seem to finish this novel. Oh, this blasted novel that drains me of enjoyment and strength and time and health and peace of mind! This will be my last. If in the name of our blessed Lord I ever finish this huge book then perhaps I will not be so raw inside.' He had never felt quite so old and feeble as he did now, when he insisted and repeated his vow: 'This shall be the last of this trash – trash!'[93]

Marie had lived with Hamsun for far too long to believe him. She was the mother of four of his children, the working wife of his second farm and also his secretary. He had sworn when they met to make her a queen if she promised to love him, though it had soon become obvious to her that love might be central to his books, but not to his life. The major role he had assigned to Marie twelve years before, and which he continued to expect her to fulfil, was for her to help him write. He reminded her of this one day after she visited him at his hotel: 'You were so *happy* with things. And then that makes things easier for me.'[94]

One thing had lightened Marie's burden. Closer to him than anybody, she had been pleased to note that over the course of a quarter of a century, with each book, her husband took a further step outside himself, and away from potentially uncomfortable disclosures. Hamsun had transformed himself from self-revelatory writer to observer. Increasingly distant – and increasingly omnipotent – Hamsun could now steer his characters exactly as he pleased. His own persona no longer stood in their path. Gone was the masking and unmasking, the introspective search that had filled him with such self-loathing.

With *Children of the Age* and *Segelfoss Town* Hamsun had written two books about the fall from power of the great Norwegian landowners: men like Willatz Holmsen, who founder when they encounter the modern world and its new masters, the chieftains of industry. Men whose downfall was largely due to their being too proud to fight the changing times. In *The Growth of the Soil* Hamsun had gone on to depict the once-landless Isak who conquered the wilderness, transforming it into fertile fields and meadows, Isak who resolutely turned his back on the times and never allowed himself to be tempted to sell his land. Yet Isak's first-born, Eleseus, was nonetheless ensnared by modernity and seduced by the bright lights of the city.

It is in the city that the corrosive spirit of the contemporary world is engendered, and it is from the city that it spreads.

Hell Is the City

Norway was undergoing a period of extraordinary social change. Rural settlements, once self-sufficient, had in the final decades of the last century become increasingly dependent on trade and the world economy. Almost half the population of Norway now lived in towns, which had doubled in size since Hamsun had made his debut with *Hunger*. The urban hell would be the subject of *The Women at the Pump*.

Hamsun drew on impressions that he had formed in a small town along the Oslo Fjord, to which he had retreated immediately after delivering the final proof corrections for *The Growth of the Soil*. A drama had unfolded on his window ledge. The dungflies were consuming the houseflies, and when they had eaten them all, they began eating each other. It was a potent metaphor for the people in the cities who were so far removed from their origins, from the soil and the seas, that they had turned on each other. Hamsun called an article, published in *Aftenposten* in the summer of 1920, 'The Neighbouring Town', underlining how disturbingly commonplace this phenomenon was in modern-day Norway.[95]

Hamsun was writing much more fluently, with up to three good writing sessions daily, and that summer *The Women at the Pump* approached completion. The beginning and the end of any novel were always the most challenging. His father, a tailor by trade, had always impressed upon his son how important the first few stitches were, and how disastrous it could be to a garment's final appearance if it was hurried at the finish.

In July, Hamsun read the edited script of all the chapters he had delivered so far. He did not trust the typesetters. Among other sins, they had neglected to follow his instructions to use spaced type instead of italics. 'Italics are a leprosy and a mange', he told Kønig in July, his vitriol obviously having deepened during the four years since he described italics as a mere skin rash.[96]

He invited Kønig to Nørholm. After the kindhearted publisher had finished spoiling the children with Danish sweets, Hamsun showed him proudly around his paradise. The publisher also had some important matters to discuss. Gyldendal was in the process of reviewing Hamsun's position in Britain which, like that of many international writers, was very unsatisfactory. Various books had been tried out and publishers contacted without success. Gyldendal was intending to make a fresh attempt at winning British readers over with a translation of *Pan*. To help things along, Hegel and his board of directors were even considering setting up new branches of Gyldendal in London and Chicago.

In America at least, negotiations with Alfred Knopf's large publishing house for the rights to some of Hamsun's novels, carried out through the agent Curtis Brown, had come a long way. H.G. Wells had agreed to give a commentary on *The Growth of the Soil*, and offered a ringing endorsement: it was one of the greatest books he had ever read, exquisite from start to finish, infused with wisdom, humour and tenderness.[97] Kønig promised to make it clear to the directors in Gyldendal's Copenhagen offices how impatient Hamsun was with the Americans, and how dissatisfied with the British.

Knopf's offer to Hamsun was a good one, but there was one suggestion from the publisher that had to be swiftly dropped: Hamsun dismissed any proposition that the plays and poems be omitted from his *Collected Works* because of the steep rise in paper and printing costs.

That autumn, Hamsun finished his darkest book to date. His disgust for everything modern, for the liberal urban life, democratisation, industrialisation and consumerism, all of which he saw stemming from the victors of the war, makes parts of *The Women at the Pump* gloomy in the extreme. Hamsun's mischievous smile seems to have been replaced with a grimace.

The Segelfoss books had shown that nobody escaped the effects of societal change. In *The Growth of the Soil* Hamsun held up a vision of the ideal life that could be achieved if only people fled the towns. Nearly thirty years before in *Mysteries*, Nagel had perished in the stuffy atmosphere of petit-bourgeois society; Minutten, the cripple who mastered the art of self-delusion, had been allowed to survive. In *The Women at the Pump*, the cripple took centre stage.

Oliver Andersen is one of Hamsun's most loathsome creations. He barely resembles a human being, 'incomplete, even as an animal, as a four-legged creature. And not only is he a cripple, he is a hollowed-out cripple, empty. Once he was a man.' He is so content with his reptilian existence that he is unable even to feel self-loathing. A man without genitals, who is nonetheless convinced that he is the father of his wife's four children, as well as of a child whose mother he has scarcely met: in urban culture, self-delusion lies at the heart of survival.

In this book, the cripple is a symbol of modern urban man who, by dint of his parasitic nature, will always survive. Men and women of finer natures might fail, but the scoundrel, Hamsun writes in his book, 'was made of tougher stuff, less refined and sensitive, more uncaring, and thus made of the right human stuff to withstand life. Who had descended lower than him? But with a bit of luck, a little pilfering, the odd successful crime, he was a happy man again.'

Once more, it is as if the spirit of the age has ripped everybody up by the roots; but here Hamsun's depiction is scathing, even dogmatic. The factory owner, master of the modern age, lured

> youth away from their natural place in life, and exploited their strength for his own financial advantage. That's what he did. He established a fourth class in a world that had too many classes already, a whole class of industrial labourers, the most superfluous of all workers. And then we see what a contortion of a human being such a worker becomes after he's learned the tricks of the upper classes: he abandons his boat, he abandons the land, he abandons his home, parents, brothers and sisters, abandons the animals, trees, flowers, the sea, God's skies – and instead he gets the Tivoli, the Working Men's Club, the public house, bread and circuses. These are the benefits for which he chooses the proletarian life. And then he bellows: 'We workers'.[98]

The novel's message was strident, but Hamsun had exhausted himself in completing it, finally submitting the manuscript just a week after his deadline. It was hardly surprising Hamsun was tired, said his publisher; during the course of the last seven years he had written over 1,500 book pages. A magnificent output, Kønig added encouragingly.

The Women at the Pump was to be published simultaneously in Oslo, Copenhagen and Stockholm on 10 November. The cover price was 19 kroner. Booksellers had already shown considerable interest; Hamsun's publishers decided on a run of fourteen thousand copies for the first edition. And the critics were no less curious; their first verdicts appeared on Thursday, 11 November.

A funny but biting book, concluded *Aftenposten* in its predominantly favourable review. The Swedish critic, psychologist and literary scholar John Landquist, who had a book out on Hamsun, was extremely direct: he saw a strong connection between Hamsun's compulsion to imbue his earlier vagabond-heroes with sadomasochistic traits and his present preoccupation with the psychology of the cripple. Many critics disliked this theme and tendency in his writing, while others hinted that Hamsun's work had perhaps lost its fire.[99]

If Hamsun had shown the way to the promised land in his previous novel, in *The Women at the Pump* he assumes the mantle of doomsday preacher, warning his readers not to take the path offered by the false prophets of modernity. Hamsun was not alone in his opinions. In Norway and indeed all over post-war Europe, people were fighting the forces of change with increasing resolve. Like Hamsun, they were drawn into the struggle between irreconcilable opposites: peasant fatalism versus modern man's desire for control over nature; mystery versus science; biology versus intellect; farmer versus industrial worker and citizen; patriarchal order versus emancipation and democracy; agriculture versus the artificiality of industry and the consumer economy. They added their voices to a movement that promised to bring back the best of the past.

Hamsun's disdain for elected politicians also continued to deepen during these years, as people exercised their newly gained right to vote. The party system had become an arena for careerists, mediocrity and political chicanery, he ranted. He was angered because universal suffrage did not, in his opinion, result in the election of the highest achievers. They chose other paths – in business, art and learning. He had observed this in America and now he saw the same in Norway.

Neither did ordinary country people escape Hamsun's ire; many of them, he thought, had also been corrupted by the times, which turned them into pleasure-seeking consumers and intolerable upstarts.

Life must return to more natural ways. He was waiting for somebody with an unshakeable strength who would take it upon himself to put the world back on track.

Hamsun had held out enormous hopes for the war. But after more than four years of fighting, the English were victorious, both on the battlefield and in the salons where Europe's future was being decided. His Anglophobia was never more relentlessly expressed than in *The Women at the Pump*. 'I wonder perhaps whether the English have their own God, an English God, just as they have their own currency. Can there be another explanation for their incessant drive to conquer more of the globe, and their belief that when they are victorious they have done a good and noble thing?' asks one of his characters.

A growing number of Europeans had started to single out the Jews as the agents of society's ills. Hamsun probably viewed the British in much the same vein. Yet in the political arena there was a general demand for a more humanitarian approach; ideals of democratisation and equality were winning through in country after country. The most famous living writer in the Nordic region was finding himself increasingly out of step with these developments; his sympathies lay with the authoritarian and anti-parliamentarian forces that, at the same time, were gathering across Europe.

Friends and Enemies in Stockholm

In the late summer of 1920, as Hamsun was completing *The Women at the Pump*, the members of the Swedish Academy debated who should be awarded the Nobel Prize for Literature.

Hamsun had been nominated a third time. Many people were working actively on his behalf, in particular the Swedish poet Erik Axel Karlfeldt, a literary heavyweight and the leading authority in the Academy. In 1918, its members had wanted the prize to go to Karlfeldt himself, but as secretary to the Academy he naturally turned the offer down.

When in the previous year Per Hallström had presented his report pointing to the lack of appropriate ideals in Hamsun's work, Karlfeldt decided to investigate the validity of this interpretation – spurred on no doubt by his own fascination for Hamsun's prose.

But Karlfeldt also had other overriding motives. From the prize's inception, the requirement for 'idealism' in literature had as frequently been cited in disputes revolving around political opinion as it had in ones about literary quality. Karlfeldt felt this had prevented some distinguished Swedish authors and literary figures from being elected to the Academy, and that candidates for the Prize – including Ibsen, Strindberg, Zola, Tolstoy, Twain, Conrad and Gorky – had been argued against, and sometimes even disqualified, on political grounds.

As the Academy's secretary, Karlfeldt felt it was essential to define the aesthetic principles upon which the awarding of the Nobel Prize rested, instead of ceaselessly disputing breaches of quite subjective and contemporary political considerations. Karlfeldt himself had nominated Hamsun for that year's Nobel Prize.

A preliminary working committee ranked the most likely candidates before the main discussions of the Academy took place. Hamsun won three out of five votes: Selma Lagerlöf and Henrik Schück found themselves unable to 'acquit' Hamsun of what one of them termed 'Hamsun's Norwegian brutality'. They felt the prize should go to Georg Brandes.

While Karlfeldt argued for Hamsun's literary value, Harald Hjärne, chairman of the committee and ally of the cause, made a surprise move. Thus far, the prize had been awarded for the entire body of an author's work, or on rare occasions with a particular focus on certain aspects of their oeuvre. Now Hjärne, a history professor, drew the Academy's attention to a point in the statutes that had largely been overlooked, which stated that the prizewinner should be selected from those who had been of the greatest benefit to mankind in the preceding year. Hjärne's conclusion was that the rules did not prohibit them from awarding the prize to an author for a single work; they even encouraged them to do so. Although it was almost three years since the publication of *Growth of the Soil*, it was Hamsun's last book and, Hjärne argued, a novel that satisfied the criteria.[100]

Was the author who had scorned the scholarly and pedantic study of texts to win the Nobel Prize thanks to an academic's meticulous rereading of a will?

Hamsun had himself reneged on another of his favourite grumbles when, in September 1920, he had instructed his publishers to leak the title of his new book to the newspapers. Hamsun had frequently poured scorn on Ibsen for engineering the release of information to the press about new works, so as to make himself appear more mysterious and interesting. Now he had done the same.

The Swedish newspaper *Dagens Nyheter* printed an article which was picked up instantly by papers across Europe and Scandinavia, including Norway's *Aftenposten* and Denmark's *Politiken*, largely because it fuelled speculation of a more important nature. 'This year's Nobel Prize to Knut Hamsun?' speculated *Dagens Nyheter*, insisting that a reliable source had confirmed the Norwegian would be this year's winner.[101]

On Friday, 12 November, the speculation was confirmed. Hamsun made the front page of all major Scandinavian and German papers. He had won the Nobel Prize for Literature.

The first person to telephone the newspaper-free Nørholm on that Friday morning was the editor of Grimstad's local paper. Marie answered and he congratulated her on Hamsun's triumph, enquiring if the prizewinner might be available for comment.

Marie was clearly taken by surprise. The Hamsuns, it seemed, had not been informed directly from Sweden.

Marie agreed that the editor could call back later.

As always when he was at home, Hamsun sat alone before a beautifully laid breakfast table in the dining room.

Marie had performed the maid's role in countless plays in which the dramatists had always given precise directions for her to enter stage left or right, speak her line and then exit again. Now she forgot everything she had ever learned. She was overjoyed.

'The prize changes nothing for us now,' he said, without looking up from his food.

Marie did not leave. 'But the honour, Knut!'

Finally looking up, he snapped darkly: 'So you don't think I've had honours enough?'[102]

The pile of telegrams and letters grew rapidly. So too did Hamsun's bank account. Kønig immediately began planning a third edition of the *Collected Works* in twelve volumes, the royalties for which would come to 140,000 kroner. Hamsun would receive approximately the same sum again in Stockholm on 10 December, meaning he would be free of debt before the year was up. According to his most complimentary commentators, however, two generations of readers across the entire civilised world owed Hamsun something that could not be measured in money, and for which they could never sufficiently repay him.

The Swedish Academy's choice this time did not provoke discord. There may have been contemptuous mutterings in countries like Britain and France where Hamsun was largely unheard of, but where his books were known the applause was enthusiastic – in Germany and the Nordic countries, overwhelmingly so.

To Stockholm with a New Dress

Hamsun felt mounting dread at the idea of travelling to Stockholm.

It was probably the inescapable confrontation with his own past opinions that caused him the greatest trepidation. Was the man who had so decried the worship of writers going to allow a medal to be pinned on his starched shirt? Was he going to be living testimony to the vileness of venerating the old, the dying and the undeserving? And prove by his very presence what old age does to even the truest and strongest, when the lure of money and glory are great enough?

What on earth should he say? The man who had always insisted that writers were vagabond souls, more closely related to organ grinders and disenfranchised vagrants than tax-paying homeowners who peddle their talent for money. Should he dress up in shirt and tails, and bow left and right? – The man who had objected that such grandiose gestures and passionate veneration contaminated youth's healthy powers of judgement?

The years had long since stolen his youth. But wait . . . the years had also given him new youth. What if he were to bring his eighteen-year-old daughter with him to Stockholm?

Victoria declined his invitation.

The ceremony took place in the Music Academy's auditorium. Prince Carl, who was distributing the medals, sat at the front of the podium together with Princesses Ingeborg and Märtha. The prizewinners were seated behind the rostrum on a raised stage. Marie and the other wives sat in the front row of the audience. When the chairman of the committee, Harald Hjärne, took to the podium to give his speech outlining the reasons for the Academy's selection, Marie watched her husband's fragile, poker-like expression with some concern.

Hamsun descended to receive his medal and cheque, bowed, and to resounding applause returned to his seat. Marie began to fret about the banquet and his acceptance speech.

She was not reassured when she saw whom he had been seated next to.

Marie knew her husband's deep aversion to the unmarried and childless Selma Lagerlöf. At such a strained occasion, with his acceptance speech looming and alcohol to hand, a misjudged word could be enough to spark an explosion. But the two guests shared an apparently friction-free exchange. Hamsun was doubtless unaware that his dining companion had voted against him on the committee.

A toast, conversation and speeches. Soon the floor was given to the winner of the Nobel Prize for Literature. Hamsun rose to thunderous applause. There was not the slightest hint of nervousness in the man who so regularly bemoaned his tattered nerves. He took a sheet of paper from his inside pocket, but began by speaking from his heart.

Marie could see he intended to lay himself bare, something he rarely did these days, either in his life or his writing. The audience was enthralled, and very moved. His voice, his presence, the setting, the words – after just a few sentences she watched people reaching for their handkerchiefs. The Swedish diplomat to her right was wiping tears away. Marie could breathe again, assured of what deep down she had never doubted: that Knut Hamsun would be triumphant once more, conquering himself yet again.

He mused about how he should respond to the warm generosity of his audience, which lifted him so high he almost lost his footing: 'It is not easy to be me at this moment. I have been laden with such honours and riches tonight, but this last tribute came as a wave, and has left me reeling.'[103]

He would, he said, refrain from giving wise speeches to such an audience, especially since the scientific world had already taken the floor. But he thanked the Academy and Sweden on behalf of his country. He was proud that the Swedish Academy had thought his shoulders strong enough to bear the weight of this honour.

He had written his books in his own humble fashion, he told them, but had learned from so many others, not least from the last generation of Swedish poets. But he felt neither qualified, nor indeed young enough, to talk about literature in these terms: 'I haven't the strength. What I would rather do at this moment, in all this light, and in this excellent company – is to walk up to each of you with flowers and gifts. To be young and to ride this wave. That is what I would have liked to do on such a grand occasion, for one last time. But I no longer dare, I could never rescue my image from caricature.' He lacked the most important thing of all, and that was youth. He finished by raising his glass to the youth of Sweden, and to all that was young!

For this climactic moment to be truly affecting, he had thought, his eighteen-year-old daughter should have been at his side.

Hamsun spent the next few hours clinking glasses. Everybody wanted to make his acquaintance: royalty, men of state and church, businessmen and men of letters – as well as the few vagabond souls in the hall. He was the centre of the festivities, just as he had been the social hub of the wild carousing in Copenhagen at the turn of the century. Beautiful women flocked to him. The waiters had to top up his glass repeatedly – indeed, he seemed to have several on the go. Marie tried to restrict his drinking, reminding him of the next day's heavy schedule, and how evenings like this could leave him ill and completely exhausted. She suggested that they retire to their room at a sensible hour.

He brushed her off.

Increasingly concerned, she sought the assistance of Albert Engström and Axel Karlfeldt, at first verbally and then in the form of a little note: 'I have gone back to my room, number 317. *Perhaps* you and Engström could tempt my husband to follow me! For the sake of tomorrow and everything.'[104]

It was a neat attempt, but it had absolutely no effect. Nobody wanted to lose the increasingly ebullient prizewinner, and he had no intention of missing out on anything or anybody.

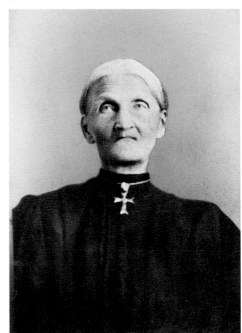

1 and 2 Knut's parents, Peder and Tora Pedersen.

3 and 4 Hans Olsen, with whom Knut and his sister Sophie Marie (right) lived. The young Knut despised and battled against his uncle.

5 An already self-conscious fifteen-year-old Knut around the time of his confirmation in Lom.

6 The new shop assistant (far right) and a group at Nicolai Walsøe's house in Tranøy, 1875. Walsøe's daughter Laura, Hamsun's first love, is serving the coffee.

7 Drude Janson – a woman with deep and fervent longings.

8 Hamsun, aged twenty-four.

9 Slaying his literary forebears in his lectures and articles, Hamsun rapidly caught the eye of the caricaturists. Here, surrounded by swooning women, he stands atop the decapitated heads of the leading literary figures of the day – Ibsen is wedged under his left foot.

10 Albert Langen launched his own publishing house shortly after meeting Knut Hamsun – and thus the writer's conquest of Germany began.

11 Anna Munch was obsessed with the idea that she and Hamsun were meant to be together.

12 Bergljot and baby Victoria. They became accustomed to Hamsun's absences.

13 Maurbakken, 'Ant Hill', 'a house in which to grow old and wise'. Hamsun stands in the centre, pipe in mouth and papers in hand, giving detailed instructions to his labourers.

14 Marie, at this time still living with Dore Lavik, who became Hamsun's 'only love upon this earth'.

15 On 25 June 1909, Knut and Marie were married in Oslo. She was twenty-seven years old, and he was forty-nine.

16 Growing ever more confident that Germany would bring England to its knees, Hamsun's attacks on the British and their supporters increased in number and intensity after the outbreak of the Great War.

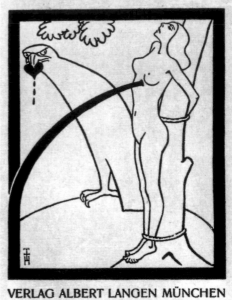

17 Whether at war or peace, the German public devoured Hamsun's distinctively-designed books.

18 One of Tore's many portraits of his father, this one inked when the budding artist was only ten years old.

19 Victoria Hamsun, just before she left for France on her father's orders – a journey which would lead to her directly defying his will.

20 Johan Irgens Strømme, the psychoanalyst who released a 'new spring' in Hamsun.

21 The family at Nørholm, a place that Hamsun felt his children should be proud of calling their home.

22 Marie and her daughters in the cherished Cadillac.

23 The Hamsun children growing up: Cecilia and Tore standing, Arild and Ellinor in the foreground.

24, 25 and 26 Hamsun, at the height of his literary career, invested a considerable amount of his fortune in improving Nørholm – but some of the exquisite rooms were seldom used.

27 Knut and Marie Hamsun,
August 1930.

28 Harald Grieg took over from
Christian Kønig as Hamsun's publisher
at the end of 1927. Here he is shown in
jovial mood with his author.

29 Despite his advancing age, Hamsun chopped his own firewood and carried the logs up to his room until he suffered his second stroke in 1945.

30 Hamsun, pictured here on his farmland, railed against modernity and all its contraptions.

31 Knut and Tore Hamsun meeting Terboven at Skaugum in 1941, an occasion which the Reichskommissar twisted to his own propandist ends.

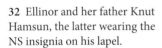

32 Ellinor and her father Knut Hamsun, the latter wearing the NS insignia on his lapel.

33 Knut Hamsun approaching Berghof and his appointment with Hitler, 1943. To the left of Hamsun is the Führer's press chief Otto Dietrich, to his right are Egil Holmboe and, just behind, Hitler's interpreter Ernst Züchner.

34 Terboven greets Hamsun at Fornebu airport after his return from Germany. It was another convenient propaganda opportunity.

35 Gabriel Langfeldt, chief psychiatrist of the Vindern psychiatric clinic, who analysed – and aggravated – Knut Hamsun.

36 Christian Gierløff was a great source of
help to Hamsun after the war, but even so he
incurred the writer's disfavour.

37 Sigrid Stray, who defended Knut and Marie
Hamsun during the 'traitor trials' of 1947.

38 Hamsun during his court trial in Grimstad, December 1947.

39, 40 and 41 Marie comes with the spring, Nørholm 1950.

Marie was probably right to be a little concerned. Later that night, meeting the Academician Henrik Schück, Hamsun gave him a hearty slap on the back, and told him he was basically a jolly nice Jew.

He was in somewhat wittier form the next morning. Extremely hung-over and still in full party regalia, he disarmed a bristling Marie who berated him for only having managed to remove his bow tie before passing out on the bed, after having been dragged to his room by Engström and one of the waiters.

'Darling, you mean I've slept all night without my bow tie?'

The party was over.

Svenska Dagbladet had held back its review of *The Women at the Pump*. That Friday, 11 December 1920, an extremely grim critique glared from the page at a very hung-over Nobel Prize winner. But for once it simply washed over him. Hamsun was bent on enjoying the celebrations. They had three more days in Stockholm, and Marie could at last shine at his side.

But she was not to shine too brightly. Before they came to Stockholm, Hamsun's jealousy had raised its head once again. Marie had bought a dress for the occasion in Silkehuset, an exclusive shop in Oslo. It was a rococo design with a tight bodice spangled with anthracite beads, the most beautiful dress she had seen in all her thirty-nine years – and it cost more than a worker's yearly salary. On her return to Nørholm with her purchase, the tailor's son had nodded his appreciation of the quality of the materials and had not been the least concerned about the expense. It was not every day he could show the Swedish nobility what a beautiful wife he had found for himself.

Thrilled, Marie had tried it on, the skirt a froth of taffeta as she twirled towards her husband, glowing with excitement. Then she noticed the anger in his face. Did she really intend to parade herself in Stockholm wearing such a low-cut dress? Marie tried to explain that it was a *modelkjole*, a uniquely elegant design – and only a little décolleté. But why should it be a little décolleté, a little shameless? he had asked in a dangerous tone.[105]

He had demanded she go to Grimstad to buy some black tulle so that the dress might be altered. The tailor's son had gathered the additional material and, with a shaking hand, had inserted it at her bosom, covering the decorative pink rose. The day after the party in their suite at Stockholm's Grand Royal Hotel, Marie Hamsun packed it away.

She had felt ridiculous in it, but had worn it nevertheless – perhaps as much from stubborn pride as cowed obedience.

Shortly after the new year in 1921, Marie received a snide little memento from Albert Engström: a sketch of a troubled man brooding over a tiny shot glass. Bearing down over him was a portly ball-and-chain of a wife.

Come, Death!

Just before Christmas 1920, Hamsun returned to Nørholm and his daily writing routine.

He had sworn to Marie that *The Women at the Pump* would be his last book, but his conviction was momentary. It was wholly impossible to stop writing now. If his output were to dry up just after he had received the Nobel Prize, he would be living proof that to honour the old is to genuflect before death. He had to go on.

As a younger author he had ridiculed old age, and as the years passed he had made light about his own ageing. In *Segelfoss Town*, he had depicted old age in all its ugliness, as had scarcely been done before. Now the sixty-one-year old set out to write a novel in which he would defend death's right to take its dues. Meanwhile, he planned to prolong his own life.

For some years, Hamsun had been growing increasingly interested in the work of Dr Eugene Steinach. This Austrian doctor had been investigating the influence of sex hormones on the ageing process, and claimed to have found a method of slowing and, in some cases, even reversing it. In various articles which he had asked Kønig and others to send him, Hamsun read that it was possible to undergo a small, completely safe and almost pain-free operation, closing the spermatic duct and causing the production of male hormones to rise. The treatment would leave him sterile, but according to Steinach these hormones would now be released into the blood rather than going to waste.

For Hamsun, sterility was a relief. He had enough children, and Marie had given birth four times in less than six years.

Added to which, the trembling in his right hand had worsened, and it seemed that this too might be improved by the operation. From a young age, Hamsun had blamed this problem on having overstrained his hand. He had written too much, and so hellishly fast when he was inspired; and, having used a pencil all his life, he had pressed down too hard. Over time he had developed a technique of supporting his right hand with his left, contriving ways of holding the paper steady while both hands were occupied with writing. He had also attached a piece of metal to the shaft of his pencil to make it heavier, but continued to guide his right hand with his left, shunting both hands back and forth, line after line, as he wrote.

He had largely overcome the shaking of his hand, but not the fear that it might be a symptom of his having inherited the same disease that had afflicted his Uncle Hans. The consequence of this disabling ailment would surely have been too dreadful for Hamsun to contemplate: a life without writing.

At the end of January 1921, Hamsun booked himself into a hotel in Oslo under a false name. He asked everyone he corresponded with to burn his letters and keep his stay in the capital a secret, blaming this unusual request on his being ill and unable to cope with more public attention.

In truth, he was terrified that news of what he had recently done might be discovered.

At the start of the month he had travelled to Oslo and from there to Denmark. The operation was supposed to have been performed in Dr Steinach's clinic in Vienna, but nervous of the long journey Hamsun had decided to stay in Copenhagen, where a student of the Austrian doctor was practising. On 18 January, he was admitted into the Kommunehospitalet, and the following day they operated.[106]

Only days later he took the boat back to Oslo, where he was now convalescing in a hotel.

Attempting to slow the ageing process was tiring.

As 1921 got under way, Hamsun drew up the most pleasing end-of-year accounts of his life.

The fact that *The Women at the Pump* had received such lukewarm reviews had done nothing to dent sales. Less than two weeks after the book had come out in November, the print run had reached 24,000. Hamsun's income from book sales throughout the year in Norway alone exceeded 110,000 kroner.

The publisher Alfred A. Knopf in New York informed Hamsun that *The Growth of the Soil* had awakened so much interest that Knopf was now interested in publishing most of his other books. Publishers from all over the world were sending new translations to Nørholm. A message came from Stockholm that the Nobel Prize money had been exchanged into 179,000 Norwegian kroner.

Confirmations of the German public's addiction to his books continued to flow in from Munich. It was as though one of their own writers had been honoured with the Nobel Prize. In Darmstadt and Brünn, performances of *Queen Tamara* had been received positively, and new performances were being planned. Langen Verlag was preparing a new fourteen-volume edition of his *Collected Works* which was due out in the spring. This was, Hamsun wrote appreciatively, extraordinary at a time when 'the Allies are doing everything they can to destroy the life and values of your country'.[107]

He would soon discover the total amount that the Allied victors of the Great War were demanding of Germany: 132 billion gold marks in war reparations, yearly interest payments of 2 billion, and a 26 per cent levy to be charged on all German exports. Yet the greatest cause of bitterness among the German people was article 231 of the peace agreement, which without any qualification stated that Germany – and only Germany – had been responsible for the war.

Hamsun was furious on behalf of the German nation.

Success and Anxiety

Making headway with his next novel was Hamsun's main priority throughout the spring and early summer of 1921. He shuffled back and forth with his bundles of paper between his cottar's cottage up in Nørholm's forest and various hotel rooms in nearby towns. His characters were proving difficult to steer, although they were easier to handle than the people in his life.

He upset himself one day after having snapped at his youngest son, Arild, for not shutting the door behind him when he came into the dining room. 'I shouldn't be so irritable with all of you', he apologised to Marie.[108] But his regret did not penetrate very profoundly; he instructed her to prevent such episodes in future, and to tell the seven-year old not to be so fidgety with his hands and feet.

That autumn Arild was to start school. His father's scepticism about book learning had deepened during the two years that Tore had been trotting off to school. He would write angrily on the subject of school education in his next book, *Chapter the Last*, with the suicidal Leonhard Magnus as his mouthpiece. Life is too short for such trivialities; the only form of true schooling 'is a mother's daily instruction and a father's daily teaching, school is something that's just been thought up, an institution that complicates life on purpose, making it more troublesome to live from our sixth year until death'.

Hamsun was also at odds with the neighbouring farms about the price of transporting his milk from Nørholm to the dairy in the nearest village, Grimstad. No longer willing to kowtow to them, he resolved to transport it himself – in his own automobile. The idea of owning a car had fascinated him for some time, and now he finally had an excuse. Eagerly he wrote to car dealerships, studying advertisements and brochures, finding out about various models, prices and the finer technical details. 'Naturally, I must have a car, there are not many people these days who get by without one when they live in the countryside, nearly 10 kilometres from the nearest village.'[109] Hamsun was not comparing himself with just anybody, of course – there were probably no more than five thousand cars in the whole country – but he was one of the few who could afford one. It called for another building project and he ordered work to be started immediately: cars could not be left outdoors any more than horses.

There was no need to bow to his neighbours' demands, or anyone else's. Not even to his American publisher, Alfred Knopf, who was travelling to Europe and was keen to meet the author in whom he had invested so much. Hamsun sent his apologies, citing the state of his nerves. He was immediately able to sleep more soundly. Nothing calmed him more than being able to say 'no' to powerful men who were unused to rejection.

His growing children exacerbated Hamsun's problem with his nerves more and more often. Three of them celebrated birthdays in the spring of 1922: Tore turned ten, Arild eight and Cecilia five. Ellinor would be seven in the autumn.

Hamsun had left his first child, Victoria, when she was still a toddler. The previous spring he had sent her to France, giving her an education that he had never received himself. Hamsun had plans for his eldest daughter. Victoria had grown up to be a very beautiful young woman. She had a good portion of her mother's naïveté and mild nature, but also a considerable amount of her father's tenacity. It was a quality she had already needed.

Having spent her childhood being overprotected by a worried mother, and instructed from afar by a father who was seldom satisfied with her, it was perhaps not hard to predict that Victoria would go one of two ways when she went to France: either go completely wild or develop a strong attachment. She took the latter course.

Despite his renowned insight into the workings of the heart, her father did not immediately realise what was happening. Victoria did not dare tell him. It was not until she began repeatedly making excuses for not travelling from the coastal town of Honfleur to Paris that it dawned on him. Hamsun was determined to steer her away from her attachment towards the right kind of circles in Paris, and later New York, where he boasted that many influential men were eager to do favours for him. Hamsun intended to elevate his daughter so she could escape all the humiliation he had once suffered. He wanted only one thing in return: utter obedience.

At midsummer 1922, Victoria sent a letter to her father that he took to be a capitulation, promising to proceed to Paris. He rewarded her obedience with 2,000 francs, unaware that a second letter was already on its way to him.

She was engaged to be married. Her all-powerful father's permission had not been asked.

In her letter Victoria described his future son-in-law. Dederick Charlesson was the twenty-seven-year-old son of a British consul, and had served as a British officer during the war. Enclosing a photograph of her fiancé wearing a British uniform, she hoped her father would not feel anything against their engagement. It appears she had absolutely no idea of Hamsun's vehement dislike of her fiancé's nation. Some days later Victoria received her father's ruthless response, in which he refused to have anything more to do with her: Victoria's duplicity made it impossible. As far as he was concerned, she had already chosen her new in-laws over him.

Over the next weeks, months and years, Victoria wrote numerous letters to him.

He never answered.[110]

After the publication of *The Women at the Pump*, Hamsun had been determined, as a demonstration of his strength, not to allow more than two years to pass before the completion of his next book. But by the summer of 1922 he had been forced to relinquish his plan. The operation that was meant to have increased the production of invigorating hormones had not fulfilled its promise.

Marie was twenty-three years Hamsun's junior. That spring she had made her own literary debut. Inspired by her life with the children, she had written a book of poetry, published under the title *Small Poems*. One of Norway's leading critics was very impressed: 'She has brought no shame on her name', he concluded.[111]

Her husband had encouraged her and guided her towards the final draft. After the collection was submitted he also took charge of its publication, instructing Christian Kønig in Gyldendal's Oslo offices to launch a strong publicity campaign, and then lower the cover price immediately while also ensuring every bookshop in the country was overflowing with Marie's book. Copies for review were also sent to the newspapers in Denmark, buttressed by advertisements.[112]

Marie benefited from the kind of launch few debutant poets could dream of. Soon publisher, author and husband realised with satisfaction that the book with the most unassuming title for years would need to be reprinted.

The author couple celebrated with a trip to the capital. On the boat trip back, they brought with them a magnificent present for themselves: a little-used Cadillac, purchased for 12,000 kroner. It was entirely impractical for the transportation of milk churns, of course, and when the local military authorities wanted to borrow it for a mobilisation exercise Hamsun sent them packing. This was not a car for some idle army recruit to drive. It was nothing less than a stylish lounge on wheels.

The adept Marie took driving lessons, while the owner – who had watched many a taxi driver steering, pressing down pedals and pulling levers – was sure he could master it by himself if he studied the brochure closely. He tried, just once, in the courtyard. It was only thanks to Marie's quick-witted intervention that an accident was prevented.

That summer, brimming with pride, Hamsun fetched his old Valdres friend Erik Frydenlund from the steamship in the Cadillac (chauffeured by the lady of the house). Hamsun thought it time to blow away the cobwebs on the old friendship of his youth. 'The days have a sad tendency to kick dust into our lives, until we are completely buried in dirt and misery, and no longer what we should be for old, deserving friends.'[113]

They had not met since the summer of 1898, when Hamsun had been working on *Victoria* in the mountain valley. The reunion went splendidly.

Nonetheless, Hamsun's daily writing regime was strict. After breakfast he would go straight to his writing room – the cottar's cottage, now re-erected just beyond the courtyard – and there he would stay until precisely four o'clock. One of the maids brought lunch to him.

During a trip to Arendal in the summer of 1922 – combining some necessary dental work with more writing – Hamsun confided to Marie that he was struggling with severe anxiety, feeling increasingly in need of a nanny or nurse. He sat behind locked doors for almost the entire day, terrified of everything and everybody. He felt he was an absolute idiot, and was concerned that the outlook seemed pretty grim for her, being a whole generation younger than him. 'I could give up, but I think you'd prefer me to get the book finished at least – oh God, there is so much left to do.'[114]

Work on the manuscript drove him on from place to place. In one fear-filled hotel room he succinctly appraised his situation: 'Well, now we shall see what I am destined for, life, death or decay.' Five days later he howled: 'Father in Heaven knows whether I haven't turned into an utter idiot, Marie.'[115]

Ten-year-old Tore was warned of the dangers of life as an author: 'You've got to understand I can no longer write books quickly, since I am sixty-three now, and lots of people die when they're that old.'[116] Hastening to comfort both himself and his soon-to-be-fatherless son, he informed Tore that he might, after all, live until he was ninety. He reassured the boy that he thought of him and his brother and sisters every day, but explained that he was made anxious both by being away from them and by being with them.

The Tightrope Walker

One Friday evening in early February 1923, Hamsun began writing an unusually optimistic letter to Marie. Everything was going extremely well; he wrote a little every day, and the eczema on his nose had improved since he had stopped using the cream. Now he was considering removing the false teeth he had got for himself in Arendal; perhaps his own would grow back.

He was in such a good mood that it worried him. 'I have often thought that something catastrophic might happen, we have probably had too much good fortune for it all to end well', he predicted.[117]

If only Marie could stop bothering him with upsetting news from home, he could see a real hope of adding yet another book to the others; after receiving the Nobel Prize, he confided, he had been hugely doubtful of this possibility.

Marie had not harboured any such doubts. She knew his changing moods all too well. And she also knew what lay in store now that his demands for peace had grown so uncompromising. Nothing must irritate him, agitate him, make him uneasy or upset him, or even make him too happy. She had an impossible task.

Hamsun regularly asked her to visit him in the hotel rooms he rented in the nearby villages. After all, if his operation was to have any effect, he had to keep his levels of hormone production up.

In the spring he decided to attempt writing at Nørholm. He would, he informed her, emphasising the gravity of the situation, need to be treated as warily as though he were a rotten egg. She hardly needed telling.

Soon after his return home, Hamsun's nerves claimed their first victim. Mornings were always the most critical time of the day. If Marie could get him safely ensconced in his writer's den after a breakfast taken in solitary majesty, then trouble might be averted. On a daily basis she inspected the 300-metre walk out to his cottar's cottage, clearing the path of anything that might cause irritation. It was a danger-filled stretch where he had to expose himself to the hazards of reality before playing God once more at his writing desk.

The front door had hardly closed behind Hamsun one spring morning when Marie heard an appalling commotion in the courtyard. Looking out of the window, she perceived the reason for her husband's yells and some terrified squawks. One of their Italian hens, doubtless convinced she was fighting for her life, was flapping desperately to escape the man chasing her with his walking stick. The young hen was quick, but her pursuer was cunning. He predicted her wish to return whence she had been chased, opened the garden gate, placed himself partially out of sight, and then struck at her with fatally perfect timing.[118]

Hamsun continued to work in his cottage for a couple of months, before moving to another hotel room in the early summer of 1923. His stay had an ominous start, so dreadful that he could scarcely wait for daybreak to write to Marie.

At two o'clock in the morning he had awoken from a nightmare, his heart pounding. His dream had begun with a gypsy taking one of Marie's rings and then breaking a precious crystal bowl. Marie seemed unperturbed, and permitted the gypsy to eat with them, first once and then several times. Hamsun was offended. He went out and returned to warn them that the cows had escaped from the shed. They did not react. He went back out and found all the hens gone too. Again he returned, but the gypsy and Marie were interested only in each other. Then all three were outside the house. He found the behaviour of the intruder and Marie so offensive that he went back into the house and, watching through the window, he saw the scoundrel put his arm around Marie and wander across the courtyard with her. 'You said nothing, you didn't scream. You let yourself be led away. I saw it through the window. I did nothing either, but stood and watched. But I planned what I would do when you came back home.'[119]

The mother of four might have felt a secret thrill that her husband still thought she could be attractive to a virile young man, even if it was only in a dream. After all, with all the months he spent away from home in hotels and guesthouses, it was she who had grounds to be jealous. What woman could resist flirting with the great Knut Hamsun?

Whenever Marie voiced such worries he would brush them off, reminding her that she knew the reality of his existence only too well. His oversensitivity meant he could not bear people to come too close. Shyness of strangers manifested itself increasingly in anxiety. He ate his meals outside the hours designated by the hotels so as to avoid the gaze and attempted approaches of his fellow guests. He rarely permitted the maids access to clean his room. His note-covered scraps of paper and his manuscript demanded all his time and energy.

Marie was aware of all this. But she also knew the other side of him; how he could suddenly switch, grow sociable, lean across a table and gaze at a woman with that dangerous sidelong look, and formulate a few choice phrases that would make any female imagine she had entered a Hamsun novel that would never end.

She dreaded it when he packed up his belongings, and she dreaded it when he sent word of his impending return. When he was at home, his presence filled every room in the house and even the grounds of Nørholm. When he left the pressure would ease, just as after a long spell of rain. But then came the thought of what he could do when she was not around. Marie was a tightrope walker of some adroitness, but her jealousy often threatened to topple her from the wire.

Hamsun displayed no such balancing skills, particularly when it came to family matters. He had banished his daughter Victoria to lifelong exile for marrying an Englishman. Now he was taking his youngest brother, Thorvald, and his nephew Almar to court to stop them using the name of Hamsun which he had conceived and adopted throughout his writing life.

He had already started proceedings against them two years before in an attempt to prevent what he described as the cheapening of his name. He had been infuriated on reading about the filming of *The Growth of the Soil*, parts of which were being shot in Nordland, to discover that he was not the only one in the credits to bear the name of Hamsun: his dissolute nephew Almar was to play the role of Isak's son Eleseus.

Hamsun threatened to reveal compromising information about them related to some semi-illegal activities, and attempted to buy them off; Almar demanded 8,000 kroner, four times as much as Hamsun offered. As so often, his sense of having been wronged knew no bounds. He wanted the prime minister to intervene in this matter, just as he had solicited both his and the Speaker of Parliament's attention when he was plagued by poison-pen letters at the turn of the century. Again the attempt was unsuccessful.

The question of whether the great writer himself had sought permission to use the name Hamsun was raised. 'Surely it would be surprising if I, whose name is known in twenty-five foreign countries and languages, among my own nation, in my own country, should apply to the department for permission to continue using the name Knut Hamsun', he sneered.[120]

The judicial authorities worked slowly, and attempts were made from various quarters to reach an amicable agreement. But Hamsun was determined to take his brother to court.

The vigour of his rancour in these matters belied the fact that he was getting old. His hearing was now deteriorating, and the trembling in his right hand continued to worsen too. Marie offered to help him by making his fair copies, but they both knew Hamsun needed to do this work himself, since he sometimes made substantial changes before delivering a final manuscript. Dictation was out of the question. Instead Marie assisted him with his extensive correspondence. He would often give her a rough outline of a letter and entrust the rest to his faithful secretary. Marie was soon adept at forging his signature.

This involvement offered her a deeper insight into his world. She understood more, but also came to know more, and this reassured and disturbed her in equal measure.

The tightrope walker found herself in an extremely demanding position.

The Wizard's Cold Artistry

Chapter the Last, which Hamsun completed in the autumn of 1923, reflected facets of its author's family life.

Two boys of Tore and Arild's age are disciplined by their academic father, who is the butt of the author's scorn. Hamsun advocates the need of these boys for an untamed world, free from adult interference. It was an ideal Hamsun could not live up to himself, since he was constantly correcting his own children.

Julie d'Espard, the central character, is the product of a Norwegian-French relationship – and the French side has certainly done her no favours: 'She knows nothing in particular, she speaks the bland Norwegian of the middle classes, she sings no better than anybody else, has never learned to run a house, is unable to do a day's work or make herself a blouse, but she can tap on a typewriter and she has learned French. Poor Julie d'Espard!' This was most likely a sigh directed at his eldest daughter, who in his eyes had been ruined in France.

As the twentieth century rolled on, so too did the Europe-wide exodus from the countryside to the cities. But a new fashion was emerging for sanatoriums and health resorts in the countryside, offering a pseudo-peasant life for a weekend, a week or a month. It was a phenomenon Hamsun had touched on more than ten years before in *The Last Joy*. In *Chapter the Last*, he launched a furious attack on it. His message was clear: city folk did not make themselves healthier in either body or soul by such visits. There was only one way to be saved, and that was to turn one's back on city life altogether, and till the earth.

Just as he had done himself.

To emphasise the proximity between sickness and health, the action unfolds in a sanatorium and mountain farm directly adjacent to each other. Two characters, the spoiled city girl Julie d'Espard and Mr Flemming, a farmer's heir ruined by city life, are staying at the health resort. Flemming has checked into the sanatorium suffering from a pulmonary infection, which worsens as none of the promises advertised is fulfilled. Almost accidentally, Flemming finds himself staying at the small mountain farm, the home of Daniel, a true heir to Hamsun's Isak. Lying wrapped in Daniel's animal skins, Flemming is brought back to health on a diet of simple peasant food, sour cream, flatbread and dried meats: 'it tasted of childhood and simple origins [. . .] oh God only knows how weak and feeble he is! But there is healing in the very air of this room, bacteria of a wholesome sort, lodged perhaps in the old walls, God knows, a sleeping potion, a yeast, red blood cells, health, life.'

If Flemming is healed in body, he is not cured of the city's corruption of the mind; he fails to change his ways and his life takes a very bad turn. By contrast, Hamsun puts up a tremendous fight for Julie d'Espard's salvation. This sassy city girl has all the negative characteristics of his previous female figures and more, but she is rescued in the end. And this despite Hamsun not sparing many human lives in *Chapter the Last*: no fewer than seven characters die before the final scene, which is nothing short of a massacre.

Did his tale of the city girl and peasant boy Daniel have to end happily, so Hamsun could continue to believe in his own utopia? Julie's deliverance is proof that there is hope for those who have sunk deepest. In the history of European literature, the peasant romance had never been more powerfully presented. And there was no misinterpreting the message of this novel: salvation lies in abandoning city living for a healthy peasant existence.

Chapter the Last appeared simultaneously in Oslo, Copenhagen and Stockholm. Just two weeks later the publishers had to order another printing. The critics were divided. Some had had their fill of what they termed Hamsun's reactionary obsessions, but quelled their irritation because of the book's literary quality. Others were wholly negative, including Hamsun's old foe *Morgenbladet*: 'This is nothing more than a book in which people are killed – casually, meaninglessly – and without artistic merit.'

Leading Norwegian critic and writer Sigurd Hoel was scathing: 'Hamsun is a wizard. He plays and the people dance. But this time his notes offer no warmth. It seems he can no longer be bothered to warm us.'[121]

A Giant Buys Himself

Hamsun's cultural and economic status had grown formidably. It was to drag him, early in 1924, into a contest of national consequence.

For over a hundred years Norwegian publishers had fought a battle, both cultural and economic, for the country's authors to publish their books with Norwegian rather than Danish publishing houses. Gyldendal had established its office in Oslo in 1904 to serve its stable of Norwegian writers, and most importantly Knut Hamsun, more effectively. This had been perceived by many Norwegians, however, as a provocative move. The history of foreign rule still rankled; the term 'four-hundred-year night' is still used to refer to the period 1380–1814 when Norway lived under Danish rule. Thus, the Oslo branch of the Danish publisher was perceived as the last bastion of Danish imperialism in Norway.

The fact that no open conflict had erupted was largely due to the prudence of Christian Kønig, who directed the office, but in the spring of 1921 a young twenty-six-year-old Norwegian, Harald Grieg, had joined Kønig as co-director. Grieg, a graduate in philology who had been a journalist with *Tidens Tegn*, soon threatened to destabilise the status quo.

Anti-Danish feelings came to a head when an over-eager Grieg and a more cautious Kønig attempted to sell Gyldendal's books through outlets other than bookshops. There was huge support among the Norwegian public for the traditional bookshops, and some began to boycott books published by Gyldendal. It was a move that threatened the Danish publisher's position in Norway. Nobody saw this more clearly than one of the leading Norwegian publishers, William Nygaard.

Nygaard had sounded out the possibilities of a merger between his publishing house, Aschehoug, and Gyldendal's Norwegian section just before Christmas 1923. The reactions of the two Gyldendal co-directors were almost diametrically opposed. Kønig saw Nygaard's enquiry as the beginning of the end, since as far as he was concerned an eventual Danish-Norwegian separation was inevitable. Added to which the sale or merger of the two publishers would provide a welcome excuse for him to leave Oslo and return to Denmark permanently. Grieg, however, hatched a rather more sophisticated plan. He wanted to get Norwegian investors on board to buy the Oslo branch of Gyldendal from under the nose of his competitor, William Nygaard.

During a stay in Oslo in February 1924, Hamsun, who was Gyldendal's leading author by a large margin, was given an insight into the game that was unfolding. On his return home to Nørholm, he prepared himself for the ensuing book war. He carefully totted up all his assets on a slip of paper. Gyldendal's Oslo office owed him 167,000 kroner, an amount equal to the publisher's profits for the entirety of 1922. Additionally he had 53,000 kroner in Gyldendal's central account in Copenhagen, and shares amounting to 19,000 kroner. There were several thousand kroner in various bank accounts. In total, he had 311,000 kroner and, according to payment plans for his *Collected Works*, he would receive a further 100,000 kroner from Gyldendal in April.[122]

In Copenhagen, Gyldendal's director, Frederik Hegel, and his board remained undecided as to the best course of action: continue as they were, negotiate a merger with Aschehoug, or trust to Grieg's ability to raise enough capital to buy the Norwegian end of the business. The positive noises coming from Hamsun no doubt contributed to Hegel giving Grieg's bid a chance. Eventually the board decided to offer Grieg and his supporters the opportunity to buy, but at a cost of 2.35 million kroner for the authors' rights, the back catalogue and the Oslo premises. A formidable challenge for Grieg & Co.

The timing of this could not have been more unfortunate. The economic boom that had begun during the war was long over, and investment capital was scarce. Grieg and his team soon realised that it would be impossible to raise the entire sum as capital; half the money required would have to be borrowed. Furthermore, not one Norwegian bank was willing to lend the money to bring this slice of Norwegian heritage home to Norway.

Kønig and Grieg needed to find strong public personalities to spearhead the campaign for a separate Norwegian house, and they needed to secure the backing of willing shareholders. Grieg travelled optimistically to his home town of Bergen to court Christian Michelsen, a shipping magnate and ex-prime minister – generally considered a hero for his stand against Sweden in the struggle for Norwegian independence in 1905. Michelsen, however, refused point-blank to spend a single penny on securing the Norwegian authors. Meanwhile, Kønig called on Hamsun at the beginning of June 1924 in the hope of whetting his interest. The Dane told Hamsun that he expected the returns on any investment to equal the banks' standard interest rate. He expressed irritation at the Norwegian banks' failure to recognise the sizeable value of the rights to the authors' works. Hamsun of course saw the absurdity of this oversight, and nothing would have pleased him more than to prove the financiers wrong.

But he also had a more personal motive for backing the purchase. Hamsun did not want William Nygaard as his publisher. Several times in the past when Hamsun had considered transferring to a new publishing house, Nygaard had turned him down.

Initially Hamsun offered Kønig and the 'home-buying' team a large loan. But Kønig had set his sights on obtaining Hamsun's shareholder signature on as large a portfolio as possible. Eventually Hamsun agreed, and since he was effectively buying himself back, he could hardly quibble at the price. He offered to buy an impressive 200,000 shares, bringing his total shareholdings in line with the amount he had paid for Nørholm four years previously.

A delighted Kønig accepted gratefully. When he heard what Hamsun wanted in exchange, however, much of his joy evaporated: Hamsun stipulated that Kønig must continue to work with the new publishing house. It was an enormous sacrifice for Kønig, putting paid to his hopes of returning to Copenhagen, but there was no choice. The master of Nørholm was not an unreasonable man on the whole – so long as he got his way. Kønig agreed to run the company with Grieg until his sixtieth birthday, at the end of 1927. The most difficult part would be telling his wife and children.

Before the publisher left Nørholm, Hamsun told him another novel was in the pipeline. He had begun toying with some ideas after he had delivered *Chapter the Last* the previous autumn, but he had been too tired and his nerves had been too frayed. Now he planned to begin work again towards the end of summer, and hinted that the book might be ready for publication by Christmas 1925.[123]

Kønig had two pieces of good news to take back with him to Oslo.

There was a determined campaign to win support from a long list of possible investors in the capital and elsewhere in Norway. Surely they would want to invest in bringing home national treasures to Norway, under Norwegian ownership. But the campaigners met with a lukewarm response. The fact that Hamsun, with all his literary and financial weight, was prepared to stand as guarantor failed to make any real impression on other potential investors.

It did, however, make an impact on Hegel and his people in Copenhagen. They relaxed their conditions, turning 1 million kroner of the buying price into a loan to be repaid in ten annual instalments, and reducing the total price by 150,000 kroner.

The campaign to buy Gyldendal for Norway was gathering momentum. That autumn, the Norwegian newspapers added their voices to the campaign, publishing leading articles on what was seen as a potentially historic move by Grieg and his team – the 'buying back' of Norwegian authors for Norway. Back in Copenhagen, Hegel tried to maintain the appearance that nothing had been decided, and that operations might continue as before. Knowing that Hamsun read the Danish newspapers every day, however, he sent him regular updates reassuring him that the sale would indeed go ahead.[124]

Despite the Norwegian newspapers' bullish support, share sales were still sluggish. By the end of October, only half of the required 1.2 million kroner had been raised. At the beginning of November, Grieg and forty signatories – including the chairman of the Norwegian Writers' Union, Arnulf Øverland, several prominent politicians and, of course, the most famous of all contemporary Norwegian writers, Knut Hamsun – went to the major newspapers with a public invitation. But this further beating of drums had little effect.

'It seems, unfortunately, that patriotism is more in the Norwegian man's talk than in his heart', snarled Hamsun, who was especially angered by the booksellers.[125] An increasingly desperate Grieg now had a sales brochure made under the heading 'Back Home to Norway' which listed all the important Norwegian writers who would be brought back to their home country. Hamsun's name took pride of place at the top, followed by those of Bjørnson and Ibsen, Kielland and Lie, Amalie Skram and Ivar Aasen in pairs further down. It was distributed in huge numbers and brought in a further 150,000 kroner.

By Christmas, they were still short of a quarter of a million kroner. Grieg went to Copenhagen just before the new year, hoping desperately that Hegel and Gyldendal might cut their selling price even further. On 30 December, he came back empty-handed. But a number of hesitant new buyers had now come forward, and before midday on the very last day of 1924, Grieg sent a telegraph to Hegel: they had raised the necessary share capital of 1.2 million kroner.

Hamsun had contributed a sixth of the total.

The journalist and author Nordahl Grieg congratulated his brother that same day. 'The things that have been added to our cultural wealth with this purchase are of great significance. [...] They are books that sit in the bookshop windows of the world's major cities, as well as in civilisation's outposts in Africa and Asia – from today they will be sent out under the Norwegian flag – a fully Norwegian flag.'[126]

Nordahl was aware of the more complex truth behind this bonanza. Just a year earlier, Harald Grieg had been floundering, desperately attempting to save his publishing career. His leaky boat had been given a solid keel when, six months later, Hamsun decided to contribute the larger part of his capital and to use his influence with Hegel. Without Hamsun, Harald Grieg and his supporters would have sunk in the Skagerrak.

The preening Harald Grieg had never met Hamsun personally. Now he pressed his co-director to organise a personal introduction to the man most responsible for his formidable rise to director of the publishing house that had brought Norway's literary heritage home.

Eternal Conflict

Hamsun's financial position was stronger than ever: at the beginning of 1925 the Tax Office conservatively estimated his fortune at 419,000 kroner.

But there were significant outgoings. The farm at Nørholm was being subsidised heavily, and there were numerous new projects: building work, laying new roads and improving old ones, digging ditches, draining marshes and planting trees. Hamsun put all the monthly accounts, together with his managers' records, into huge envelopes large enough to hold the papers for an entire year. The man who usually added everything up so meticulously never jotted down a single figure on these envelopes, nor indeed anywhere else. It was as though he did not want to look reality in the face.

After all, in his novels farming never operated at a loss.

The Nobel Prize had opened the doors to several more publishers in new countries, and his readership was widening steadily. Sales in America also rose steeply: in the space of just six months, *The Growth of the Soil* sold 18,010 copies, *Hunger* 14,693, *Pan* 8,966, *Dreamers* 4,696, and *Shallow Soil* 3,086. After taxes and fees, his royalties amounted to 84,000 kroner.

But still neither the Nobel Prize nor world fame seemed to make the slightest impression on the British readership. Whereas sales in America at the beginning of the 1920s brought in 130,000 kroner in royalties, they brought in a paltry 2,000 kroner from the whole of the British Empire; across eighteen months, nearly 30,000 copies of *The Growth of the Soil* were sold in America while only 2,000 were sold across the Empire. *Pan* was bought by only a few hundred British readers. When the pathetic figures in pounds, shillings and pence arrived, it was all Hamsun could do to try and ignore this insult. He had sold more books in Holland than in Great Britain and all its colonies put together. In September 1925, he received a cheque for no less than 108,933 kroner from sales abroad, only 2,000 of which were royalties from British book-buyers.[127]

The British did not have a taste for Knut Hamsun. The Germans, on the other hand, could not get enough of him. Ever increasing sales figures were reported from Germany: *The Growth of the Soil* 23,000, *Hunger* and *Pan* 21,000, *Victoria* 18,000, *Mysteries* and *The Women at the Pump* 15,000. Both *Rosa* and *Under the Autumn Star* had gone into their sixth printings, and his *Collected Works* was selling well. The German theatres were also producing his plays. And 1,200 new gold marks were being transferred regularly to one of his Norwegian accounts, a good sign of the recovery of the whole of German society.

The German nation that was getting back on its feet was neither cowed nor begging, but it was deeply divided. Still, politicians touting extremist ideas were meeting with more antipathy than in the past; in the Reichstag elections in the autumn of 1924, the ultra-nationalist parties won only 3 per cent of the vote. The foreign minister Gustav Stresemann's conciliatory approach to the victors and the Dawes Plan's injection of dollars into the German economy were starting to pay dividends. Government fears of both Left- and Right-wing extremists faded.

On 20 December 1924, the courts decided that one of Germany's better-known political prisoners, Adolf Hitler, should be released. As a twenty-nine-year-old corporal, he had been seriously wounded towards the end of the war in 1918. His doctors had freed him of his fears of going blind, and he had freed himself of his youthful dreams of becoming a painter or architect. Instead he left hospital filled with a conviction that fate had chosen him for a much greater purpose. His task, as he saw it, was to heal the entire German nation. In Munich, he had become heavily involved with groups that were strongly hostile to the Republic, to democracy, to the Jews and to Left-wing radicalism. Earlier in 1924, he and other coup plotters had been brought before the judges accused of high treason. Hitler was sentenced to five years in the Landsberg Prison in Munich. Inspired by a laurel wreath hanging on the wall of the common room, he had there begun writing his political manifesto, *Mein Kampf.*

Hitler had been released after less than a year. The Bavarian regional interior minister was convinced Hitler would run out of steam. Others thought the beast was tamed. Hitler, however, vowed to carry his revolution through to its conclusion by legal means. He had understood that democracy had to be voted to its knees, defeated by a Trojan horse sent into its centre: an explosive mixture of terror, promises, fear and hope.

He was not going to satisfy himself with the restoration of pre-war borders. 'We take up where we broke off six hundred years ago. We stop the endless German movement to the south and west, and turn our gaze toward the land in the east. At long last we break off the colonial and commercial policy of the pre-War period and shift to the soil policy of the future', he had written in *Mein Kampf.*[128]

They were the very sentiments Knut Hamsun had expressed throughout the war, when writing about the German people. The sacred longing for the soil was something Hamsun understood, just as his parents had; a longing that made it possible to hold out and to sacrifice whatever was needed.

In Locarno, Switzerland, a treaty was signed by Germany, Britain, France, Belgium and Italy agreeing to respect Germany's new borders to the west. Germany also agreed to the demilitarisation of the Rhineland, as well as to refrain from the use of force to extend its borders eastwards.

From his head office in Munich, Hitler was reaching ever larger sections of the nation with his hard-hitting slogans: 'Germany is starving on Democracy'; 'We won't let Germany be crucified.'

Technological and economic changes were moving faster in Germany than in the rest of Europe. Many Germans felt a deep repugnance for the modern world that gave so little place to any romantic ideal. Hamsun's novels were increasingly clear in their expression of this discomfort and their longing for times past. His books were distributed by his Munich publisher across the whole of Germany, Austria and the German-speaking regions of Switzerland and elsewhere. For many Germans, the Norwegian author who stood in such bold opposition to the changes of the modern world was growing in status as a prophetic figure.

Meanwhile, at Nørholm, Hamsun the farmer and author blasted his way ever deeper into the forest. He had become something of a dynamite enthusiast, since his path seemed eternally blocked by rocks rising out of the ground.

He ordered roads to be laid and bridges to be built to the very edges of his kingdom. Wide roads were required for the heavy machinery brought in by horse, tractor and lorry, and large loads had to be carried out of Nørholm quickly. Wetlands were drained, ploughed, sowed and harvested. Thousands of trees were planted. Outhouses were built. Stone walls were constructed and barbed wire set up around the outlying fields. The inner courtyard was made impenetrable by means of a 2-metre-high iron fence with four locked gates. Hamsun carried the keys to three of these gates with him. The fourth hung in the hallway that led to the kitchen, and woe betide anybody who opened Nørholm's gates to the wrong people.

Thus Hamsun extended his realm, driven by his unyielding longing for the soil. The destiny that had befallen the estate owner Willatz Holmsen was not inevitable after all; the industrialists of the modern world would not necessarily defeat the farm owners as they had in *Children of the Age* or *Segelfoss Town*. In tilling the soil himself, Hamsun had triumphed over the pessimism of his own works – but he had not found a way to overcome the mental rigidity that was preventing him from writing.

Part IV

A New Spring?

In his early, wild years Hamsun had believed that his ability to write would never fade.

At the time he had bragged about the delicacy and sensitivity of his nerves: how he had bound a scarf around his left hand for six weeks while he wrote because he could not even bear to feel his own breath on the surface of his skin. That he had not been able to withstand the flare of a match being lit, and had had to strike it under the table.[1]

Hamsun was impatient and ruthless with himself, and constantly strove to hasten the arrival of the wave of inspiration. Just how merciless he could be he had described in *Hunger*. But by the time he was writing *Mysteries* and *Pan*, the cost of this struggle could no longer be disguised.

Hamsun had always reassured himself, and others, that his attacks of nerves would pass. He had tried alcohol, electric currents, massages, pills, potions, creams and dozens of other miracle cures.

He had thought that working with the soil in the countryside of his childhood would help him develop nerves of steel like his creation Willatz Holmsen; but his condition had only worsened, and he had been forced to leave. He had lain on the operating table and had his nether regions sliced into, in the hope of slowing the steady decline of age.

Nothing had helped.

In the previous year Marie, twenty-three years Hamsun's junior, had brought out her second book. The children in her stories perhaps resembled Marie and her siblings thirty years previously, as well as her own children now. She gave the adult characters certain traits from her own mother and father, and herself. Conspicuously absent from her work, however, was the father of her four children.

Nobody knew better than Marie the reasons why Hamsun had no place in a book describing children in a harmonious adult world. She had called her new work *Village Children: At Home and on the Farm*. It described the rural idyll that her husband had dedicated himself to since 1912, and that Marie now also allied herself to.

Now, in the new year of 1925, Marie was in full swing writing a sequel to this. She required no wave of inspiration, simply a few hours to herself after the children had gone to bed.

Hamsun had also stopped waiting for great waves of creativity to wash over him, settling instead for incremental progress, step by step, word by word. Large sections of *The Women at the Pump* and *Chapter the Last* had been written in this way, but they still required huge concentration. He might still be remarkably supple in body – he was indeed capable of making impressive physical leaps – but his once-agile mind appeared to be stiffening. It was something that he attributed at least in part to his anxiety attacks, which now led him to barricade himself behind closed doors.

The year began badly. The Oslo County Court rejected Hamsun's claim that he should have sole use of his surname, ruling in favour of his younger brother Thorvald and nephew Almar. Thorvald had proved to the court that he had enlisted with the Field Artillery on 2 October 1890 under the name Pedersen Hamsun; and since Knut had been a relatively obscure and disreputable writer at the time it seemed unlikely that the name would have gained Thorvald any advantage. Five years later he had also married under the name of Hamsun, and three years after that his first child had been baptised Thorof Oskar Almar Hamsun.[2]

Knut Hamsun was devastated. It seemed his very name was under threat of being taken from him, since for him the idea of sharing it was as good as losing it.

He blamed his lawyers for losing the case, rebuking them for not having shown him the opposition's arguments as he had asked, leaving him unable to challenge the points that had been made. He declared his intention to appeal to the High Court.

Such words were easy. Others were increasingly elusive.

Hamsun was no longer in a fit state to write. He searched for the invigorating effects of his operation, which he had been promised would release a wild play of hormones, producing new surges of energy and inspiration upon which to ride – not as wild perhaps as in his youth, but enough to carry him into the heart of his next book.

Unable to progress with his own writing, Hamsun trawled the newspapers for signs of positive developments in Germany. He had never abandoned his belief that the young nation would fulfil its natural destiny: that of defeating the degenerate English. He felt sure it was only a matter of time. But Germany would have to get back on its feet again first.

As the autumn of 1925 progressed, Hamsun still failed to make headway with his next novel. He expressed his fears about this in a letter to the writer Hjalmar Pettersen on 11 October, writing mournfully: 'Not much will come of my writing from now on.' On 4 November, he told his publisher Kønig: 'Writing books draws further and further away from me.'[3] The title of his previous book, *Chapter the Last*, seemed to be proving unnervingly prophetic.

But could he imagine a life without being able to write? His wife certainly could. Marie dreamed of him relinquishing his writing and releasing her from the impossible balancing act of her present life. She and the children were always having to play second fiddle to the great lord and master of the house. If he gave up his books, everything would be different.

Hamsun always kept a miracle or two up his sleeve for his characters – when they deserved it. Dr Steinach's operation seemed not to have been the miracle cure he had hoped for, but perhaps he had not quite given up hope when in November 1925 he came across an article in *Aftenposten* about a newly published book, *Nervøsitet*.

Hamsun bought the book, devoured it and immediately wrote to its author, Dr Johan Irgens Strømme. He soon received a reply, and after an exchange of letters, Hamsun decided to undergo treatment with the doctor.

Strømme had completed his medical degree at the University of Oslo and then gone on to study psychoanalysis at the Bürgholz University Psychiatric Clinic in Zurich. He had worked in two of Norway's major hospitals for the treatment of mental illness, and had run a private practice in the capital since 1916. Despite his credentials, however, Strømme was one of Norway's most controversial doctors: psychoanalysis was still largely unrecognised on the fringes of Europe, and he had been declared a charlatan by his medical colleagues.

For Hamsun, reading the introduction of Strømme's book had been like revisiting his own thoughts when, as a young man, he had written *Hunger* and *Mysteries*. According to the doctor, people who suffered with nerves counted among society's finest human beings. And something else caught Hamsun's eye: Strømme repeatedly insisted on the significance of a wife in a man's life. Strømme proclaimed that in his fifteen years as a psychoanalyst, he had seen too many wives fall short. They ignited discord within the marital relationship, which caused their husbands problems at work and aggravated their nerves. Men's neuroses, said Strømme, could often be traced back to wives who either were, or pretended to be, frigid; if they had given more of themselves to please their partners, their wounded husbands would be healed.[4]

The growing distance between himself and Marie, his nervous anxiety, his writer's block – Hamsun felt as he did when one of his games of patience resolved itself. He may well have made the decision, there and then, that Marie also should undergo treatment with Strømme one day.

On Sunday, 3 January 1926, Hamsun boarded the coastal ship for Oslo. He was as desperate about the lack of progress in his writing as he had been when boarding another ship, bound for America, forty years ago. Surely it was time for all this to end.

The couple had been quarrelling about this very matter, as Hamsun left Nørholm that winter's day. Later, in his cabin, he began writing a letter to his wife, complaining that she had not even bothered to wish him luck on his journey.[5]

After his arrival in Oslo on Monday morning, he proceeded to Strømme's consulting rooms in Oscars Gate, north-east of Slottsparken, or the Royal Palace gardens. Climbing two flights of stairs in a house resembling a grand hunting lodge, Hamsun searched among the nameplates and rang the bell.

After a short introductory conversation, the psychoanalyst asked Hamsun to make himself comfortable and relax, and to tell him about any dreams he might have had lately – perhaps last night.

Hamsun began to describe a dream. The patterns of his speech struck the psychiatrist for their remarkable similarity to the style and rhythms of his writing.

'Somebody was carrying a child but, as far as I could see, they were not carrying it as they should. It was swaddled so tightly that the child was unable to bend. I said: Bind the child so it can bend! Children should be able to bend, the best thing would be for it not to be swaddled at all. But this child was tied up like a parcel and carried under arm. The child should have been loosened so it could bend. One gets no peace from the masses. I think I am too tightly bound. Too rigid. And now that I have started treatment with Dr Strømme, I hope passionately that I might loosen my inhibitions and become more able to bend.'[6]

To bend. To yield. This from the man who forty years ago had growled at God that he would never do either.

Strømme promised Hamsun a new spring – his exact words – and the author was to come to his apartment once a day, sometimes twice. Hamsun was one of Norway's most famous men. It was hard to keep a low profile in the capital, but he tried. He walked between his hotel and Strømme's rooms rather than taking the tram, thus avoiding having people in close proximity. He also stayed away from the cafés and restaurants. Several acquaintances who had heard he was in town invited him out; he turned them all down. But he did persuade Marie to visit him.

He met her off the boat one cold January morning. Hamsun prattled endlessly about the treatment which, among other things, was based on loosening up the unconscious and allowing it to flow. Strømme had been quite sure Hamsun would soon be back working at his best again. Hamsun wanted Marie to start treatment with Strømme as well.

Marie remonstrated that she needed no such thing, but Hamsun was insistent that it would help *him*. The doctor had been sure of it.[7]

Hamsun tried a softer approach when he wrote to Marie on her return home. He told her that he had bought two enormous reels of shoemaker's thread with which to sew on some buttons, and imagined how she might think of him sitting there, his right hand trembling as he threaded his needle, tacked, knotted and sewed: 'So now we have enough shoemaker's thread to last until you and I move into our dear little cottage in the forest, when we shall go out into the night and look at the weather and scratch our heads.'[8]

Way up in the forest where Marie often walked there was a lake, beside which Hamsun had once said they would build a little house, if Marie wanted. He had even searched out a plot and on a little rise paced it out. This was where they would retire to when their children took over the running of the farm. Now he repeated his promise, although things would have to improve between them so he could write again.[9]

Strømme was pleased with Hamsun's progress. His subconscious was active, giving the writer strange dreams and powerful imaginings. One night he dreamed of a heavily pregnant girl. Somebody said in the dream that it was not her belly that was growing fuller, but her soul. Could it be that he had grown fertile and had begun to open up, he wondered during his session with Strømme.[10]

One afternoon on the way back to his hotel, a blindingly simple thought struck him: just why had he always been so afraid of other people? It seemed absurd. He pledged from now on to hold on to that idea as hard as he could.[11] Indeed, that evening he invited the head waiter from his hotel to accompany him to the cinema.

Hamsun shared this new insight with Strømme the next day. The doctor was pleased. He told Hamsun about another patient who had begun her treatment on the same day as him, a woman in her thirties who was fearful of growing old, going mad and dying. She had had two children by her husband, but was, according to the doctor, frigid. Strømme told Hamsun that he had sent her home that very day.

'Were you unable to tackle her problems?' the author asked.

'She is cured!'

'And she'll stay that way?'

'In my fourteen or sixteen years, none of my patients has ever had a relapse.'[12]

That evening Hamsun presented all these miracles in a letter to his wife. He insisted she read Dr Strømme's book *Nervøsitet*.

I Shall Write Like a Young Man Again

Hamsun was regaining his sociability, spending more time in the hotel dining room, leaving the hotel more frequently and using public transport, revisiting the old streets he had known so well twenty, thirty, forty, now almost fifty years ago. Memories from his *Hunger* times were reawakened. One night he dreamed about one of the editors who had helped him in those difficult times.[13]

After two months his treatment was taking effect. 'The doctor is certain that a spring will well up inside me, and I shall write like a young man again. [. . .] There is no doubt I walk a little taller with the thought of this spring which is going to well up inside me, and as I stand on the tram surrounded by people I feel that I don't hide away as much as before,' he confided to Marie.[14]

He even spent several evenings playing poker with old acquaintances.

Strømme asked Hamsun to conjure up his first childhood memories. The earliest he could bring to mind was the smell of the fruit trees and a particular flower in the garden of his home in the mountains, when he was not yet three years old. His next memory was from the family's journey northwards by steamship along the coast to Nordland; he remembered screaming, and his mother scooping him up in her arms and showing him the ship's engine room. The sight of the great shiny pistons plunging up and down had calmed him.[15]

Security and rupture, nature and technology: it was from the tension between these poles that much of his work sprang.

The doctor asked him to talk about his childhood. His father had come to him in a dream, and Hamsun had fallen into an abyss, screamed three times and woken up. He had often dreamed he was falling. Strømme asked him what he associated with this image.

Hamsun answered that if he were truly to recover, his fear of falling might return.[16]

One night during his third month of treatment, ideas again started to flow. Hamsun reached out immediately for pencil and paper, and in the darkness he began to write. He felt enormous exhilaration as he tapped into experiences from his youth over forty years before, when he had first cut himself adrift and become a wanderer.

He allowed memories to surge forth, and he added to them, honed them down, merged and twisted them, collecting them once more into little piles of notes. Impressions of Hamsund and the parsonage grounds at Hamarøy, Walsøe's trading post on Tranøy, his two years spent as an assistant teacher and as sheriff's assistant in Vesterålen, his visit to Zahl on Kjerringøy. Memories of roaming free as a pedlar and market stallholder on the Nordland coast. And of his fellow traveller who, being ten years his senior, had seemed to have such boundless life experience, and who had been master of the art of mixing truth and lies with wide-eyed innocence.

Hamsun wondered if the novel that was now emerging might be called *Wayfarers*. One thing was certain: the story would centre on two wanderers, August and Edevart.[17]

With the approach of spring, ideas bubbled up inside him. The piles of notes were steadily rising. Once again he laid them out on his worktable to commence his literary game of patience. The sixty-six-year-old could no longer write as he had in his youth, but young people would be at the heart of his next narrative.

Some days before midsummer 1926, Hamsun was back at Nørholm. He liked nothing better than receiving the welcome that greeted a long-awaited traveller. There was huge excitement as he unpacked all the presents for the children. He had been in Oslo for over five months, his longest absence. It had brought its rewards, however. The pocket of his suitcase bulged with his notes and sheets of writing.

But before he attended to his literary work, he had to see to his farm.

The inhabitants of Eide and its neighbouring regions were much more interested in gossiping about Hamsun's farming activities than they were in discussing his books. Many a weather-beaten farmer shook his head at the 'squire' of Nørholm. All were in agreement that Hamsun thought big – but few thought he showed good judgement. And those who had read his works were left even more perplexed. The writer lauded the lack of pretension in humble farming folk, and ridiculed those who thought they could buy everything; but the moment he put down his pencil and turned his attention to his own estate, it seemed all this was forgotten. Hamsun could have upwards of ten men working for him, as well as two or three girls working indoors and in the cowshed.

The creator of Isak Sellanrå had a vision for Nørholm: to transform it into a great arable farm. He was not to be dissuaded, despite his neighbours' strenuous warnings against draining the wetlands and planting them with grain.

His fellow villagers also found his use of forest land rather unorthodox. Among other things, Hamsun opposed the thinning down of trees in order to give new plants more light, or removing shrubbery around young trees just as they began to grow straight. As far as Hamsun was concerned, the forests were there . . . to be walked in, not to be chopped down.

Locals were also surprised at the size of his herd, which Hamsun was planning to increase still further, to keep as many as forty cows. When he had taken over Nørholm in 1919 there had been no more than eight stalls in the cowshed. This was really all the farm could support.[18]

Plans for Hamsun and Marie's little lakeside cottage, in which they were to live in their dotage, went unmentioned throughout the summer and autumn of 1926. As soon as Hamsun had reassured himself that the expansion of the farm was going to plan, he disappeared into his writer's cottage.

By the end of July, Hamsun was already so confident that a new novel was taking shape that he informed his German publisher Müller-Langen Verlag, though it was unlikely to be a lengthy manuscript. He was, after all, coming up to his sixty-seventh birthday. But less than four months later, he sent another message indicating that the book was probably going to be much longer, although it was unlikely to be complete until the following summer. He assured his publisher that it would be an exceptional work requiring a large print run.[19]

Hamsun tried to convince his wife that Dr Strømme was to thank for the renewal of his talent. He was determined they should both go for treatment that winter.

Marie had her own opinion. Surely the well of creativity, as Hamsun saw it, had always gushed open when it had been clogged up for long enough? A natural law had been at work, like a pregnancy carried to full term. Hamsun had certainly never kept his labour pains to himself, but now his complaints were worse than ever. Marie felt sure that whatever Hamsun was in the process of creating, it was truly significant.[20]

Hamsun left for Oslo in November 1926, again without Marie's blessing. She had tried her utmost to resist his desire for her to undergo analysis with Strømme, but Hamsun was determined. He constantly used Marie as his excuse for any problems he might have: she had to be cured so that he might be whole again.

Hamsun's contemporaries had either put down their pens or passed away, but Marie's sixty-seven-year-old husband was rambling on about writing like a young man a third of his age. He had discussed his latest work with her a little, outlining its theme: the misery experienced by those whose roots are ripped up. But was he not in the process of doing the very same to his own family? His children were to be taken away from their home – and all for the sake of his writing.

Hamsun organised a place in Oslo to house seven people, in addition to himself: Marie and the four children, a reliable maid and, since nobody was sure how long they would be away, a tutor. In mid-November, they moved into a villa on the Bygdøy peninsula on the outskirts of Oslo.

He had also found a small servant's cottage in the vicinity where he could write.

In early December 1926, Marie ascended the same flight of stairs that her husband had first taken eleven months earlier. One of the first things that struck her about Strømme was how softly spoken he was. Growing a little deaf, her husband had begun to raise his voice when he talked to people he found it difficult to hear. It now dawned on Marie that many of their marital secrets must have passed through these walls. Her ears burned.[21]

Marie had skimmed through Strømme's book *Nervøsitet*. She had found it distasteful, objecting to the close association the doctor made between sexuality and neuroses, as well as his descriptions of women, which were often insensitive and derogatory in the extreme: 'These women, who are dead, impotent, who only get wrapped up in their lack of desire and cultivate it – they are fundamentally pitiful creatures. Instead of rejoicing aloud from joy during intercourse, they lie there and spread their legs and let their minds wander on all kinds of nonsense between heaven and earth – and the husband, who married a living person once, now holds an ice block in his arms.'

During his first session with Marie, Strømme remarked how wonderful it must be to live with a man like Knut Hamsun. She answered that it was not always so and that in fact it was often dreadful.

'Oh?'

'Yes, it's like driving a car; you never know what might be around the next corner.'

'Hmm. A car, you say? That's interesting.'

'In what way, doctor?'

'The car is a sexual symbol.'[22]

And there it was again. Strømme was obsessed with the intimate details of people's lives. Marie found psychoanalysis as a science rather far-fetched and, on the whole, closed her ears to the doctor's advice. After all, she was not in his consulting room of her own free will: her 'treatment' was being delivered under duress.

Sometimes the couple would cross paths as they left and arrived for their appointments. They were not allowed to discuss what happened in the doctor's office – but how could they avoid it?

When he was not with his psychoanalyst, Hamsun sat in his cottage working on his novel. By the beginning of April 1927, he had delivered the first part to Christian Kønig at Gyldendal. Now, with his permission, Marie finally returned to Nørholm with the children as well as the maid and tutor. More than ever she felt the need to make him understand that this was where she and the children belonged.

Hamsun stayed on for a month longer, to complete both his analysis and his book.

The children had grated on his nerves dreadfully in Oslo. He had never managed to tolerate them in close proximity for long stretches of time. At Nørholm there was more space to keep children and adults separate, but even this did not prevent the tension between Hamsun and his children increasing after his return home that spring.

Tore was now fifteen, and he and his brother, Arild, two years his junior, were locked in competition with each other, while Ellinor, who was twelve, and her younger sister, Cecilia, constantly bemoaned the pranks their brothers played on them. Hamsun's hearing may have worsened, but his ability to pick up the slightest noise from the children, even at a distance, seemed to have intensified.

Marie tried to explain to her husband that the children could only tiptoe around him for a little while. They were simply being children, and there was no wicked intent in their making a commotion. He brushed all vindications aside: it was a question of upbringing. When the children were small, Marie had been able to deal with this irritation by keeping them out of his way. Now that was impossible.

After Tore, his eldest, had been confirmed, Hamsun sent him away to Valdres, the mountain valley of which he held such fond memories. Tore struggled at school, did not participate in any boisterous games, and preferred contemplation to practical, outdoor activities. His father, in generous mood, consoled him: 'You would prefer to dream and meditate than join in with healthy play and boys' activities. Listen, this is neither laziness nor sluggishness, it is just the way you are. And it may well turn out that your persistent dreaminess and introspection could benefit you one day. If I had not had the same tendency, then I probably would not have done the work I have. But that is the point, we do <u>also</u> have to work.'[23]

Some days later Hamsun confided to his brother Hans that he did not want Tore to inherit the farm. Arild would be much more suitable. He explained: 'Tore has no interest in the estate, he only wants to read and draw and such nonsense. [. . .] Arild on the other hand is a smart lad in that he wants to work the soil and go fishing and do everything he can with his hands. He has to be the one to take over the estate as soon as he is old enough. I cannot run the estate, I have had tenant farmers here for eight years and am only waiting for Arild to be old enough.'[24]

Hamsun was writing again almost as he had done in his youth. Now he expelled the first of his own children, some fifty years after he himself had been driven from his childhood home.

Old Man's Prattle?

In the autumn of 1927, some four years after the appearance of his last book, Hamsun completed *Wayfarers*. It was the longest hiatus between publications of his career. He was worried, he told Kønig, that it might be nothing more than the prattle of a boring old man.[25]

The chilly response to *Chapter the Last* had doubtless contributed to the crisis that had driven him to the psychoanalyst's couch. Sigurd Hoel had been one of those to deliver an unfavourable response to his last novel, and Hamsun must have been particularly eager to know if he would be reviewing *Wayfarers*. He did – but this time he was full of praise. 'This is as richly animated as the masterpiece of his prime, *Segelfoss Town*, and is as tranquil in its style as *The Growth of the Soil*, but is far more alive', Hoel declared. '*Wayfarers* shines with as much lustre as Hamsun's best books, created by the consummate master', added *Verdens Gang*.

The Danish critic Tom Kristensen concluded that Hamsun was the only literary prophet in the North who could, by dint of his greatness as an artist, hold whatever opinions he liked.[26]

This time there were no mutterings that Hamsun's scathing critique of society had detracted from the warmth of his characterisation. It may well be that this was at least partly owing to the psychoanalysis he had undergone.

From the first dream that Hamsun had described to Strømme – the child so tightly bound it had been unable to move – the doctor had helped him to understand that he was seeing himself. Psychoanalyst and patient had discussed Hamsun's need to achieve greater flexibility. Strømme had encouraged Hamsun to explore another dream too.

Hamsun was in a house when some gypsies arrived. One of them knocked on the windowpane, asking to be allowed in. 'He had not come to beg, he had something important to explain. When the gypsy came into the room, I drove a drawing pin into his chin, mostly to see how much he could endure,' Hamsun told the doctor. But the gypsy hadn't flinched. Another man, whom Hamsun held in high esteem, promised to help chase the gypsies off. The two men each picked up a large pole. Then, to Hamsun's dismay, his ally began doing business with the gypsies. The drawing pin scratched Hamsun's leg, and he suddenly found that it had worked its way under his skin. He tried to dig it out but couldn't, and gave up. Then the pin slid out of its own accord.[27]

It was a goldmine of a dream for a psychoanalyst, and proved also to be a revelation for the patient, exposing his innermost conflicts: eternal vagabond versus propertied man; order versus disorder; poet versus farmer; fantasy versus rationality; literature versus politics.

The psychoanalyst had helped him understand that he had to allow these contradictory aspects of his personality to live side by side, as allies. His dream showed him that the gypsy whom he had tried to reject, and even hurt, had something important to tell him. The tightly swaddled child, the gypsy and the pin that came gliding out of his leg – these were all images of himself.

Hamsun's sessions with the psychoanalyst had an immense influence on the ageing writer – as much as his encounter, nearly forty years before, with Copenhagen's literary milieu and its interest in the new psychology. Had it not been for the developments in this field in the latter part of the nineteenth century, it is unlikely that Hamsun would ever have written *Hunger*, *Mysteries* and *Pan*, and joined the ranks of internationally acclaimed writers. And without the introduction of psychoanalysis at the beginning of the twentieth century, to which Strømme had given him such a personal introduction, *Chapter the Last* might well have been his final book.

Through Strømme's insistence that his patient return repeatedly to his childhood and to his relationship with his own children, Hamsun had been able to access two of his most important resources as a writer: his own emotional life and his memories of Nordland. And with the help of his dreams, Strømme showed him the most important thing of all: the best of his work had been born of the colossal tensions between the poles of his personality. In shutting one side of himself out, he no longer had the same level of conflict within his mind – the crucible of his writing. Existence is a battle, and a poet's work requires these multiple selves to be brought into close combat.

From its very inception *Wayfarers* seems to have been inspired by the memories of what he had said in a lecture many years before: that writers were not educators or reformers of society, they occupy themselves not with morals but with emotions. Writers were neither thinkers nor social commentators, but rather they were fantasists, storytellers, wandering minstrels and vagabond souls.[28]

This was the stuff of his most recent novel.

From the very beginning the tone is set: two men come lumbering northwards, their faces swarthy, one of them carrying a barrel organ on his back, and they cheat everybody in a little fishing settlement. The young Edevart is a failure at school, but nevertheless he exposes the rogues. Edevart is one of the hubs of the book; his counterpart is August, a vagabond and an orphan set adrift in his childhood just as Hamsun had been. 'He comforted himself with lies, which he believed himself perhaps', Hamsun writes. August is bursting with talent and potential. Like many of Hamsun's previous vagabond figures, he has a compulsion to make himself separate and to stand out from the crowd. Thus, he constantly exaggerates, sometimes with success, sometimes resulting in a fiasco. The esteem of others is important to August, making him helpful and practical, and generous to the point of self-destruction. Like his literary predecessors, he is unhappy in love, yet here he is not affected greatly – something quite new in Hamsun's work.

August is one of those characters who litter Hamsun's books, who embody tenets about the very creation of art – about the writer and the act of writing itself – that Hamsun propounded. The narrator of *Hunger* acted as a symbol of the artist's creative force. Nagel in *Mysteries* stood for the true artist's lack of compromise. Johannes in *Victoria* represented the creative man's encounter with passionate love. And Knut Pedersen in *Under the Autumn Star* and *A Wanderer Plays on Muted Strings* was the artist who analysed society.

August, by contrast, is the idea: imagination in all its wonderful and dreadful manifestations, a concoction of good and bad. At the end of *Wayfarers*, Joachim, Edevart's brother (and polar opposite) and the mouthpiece of the author, sums up: 'From the day this voyager of the seas appeared from the depths and darkness, he affected every soul in the village and surrounding area, he was the source.'

Hamsun was now clear that his writing had always been born of his own inner contradictions. He was both the fantasist who can never stay in one place for long, and the steadfast, strongly rooted farmer. Hamsun might show disapproval of August's lack of conscience, his modernity and disorderliness, but he seems enchanted by him too.

Just before the novel went to print, Hamsun celebrated his sixty-eighth birthday. Gyldendal's directors were convinced the Norwegian public would relish the old man's prattle. They ordered fifteen thousand copies of the first edition for the launch, an unprecedented number for any author.

Five days before Christmas 1927, the eighth printing of *Wayfarers* was being distributed to bookshops that had already sold out. Thirty thousand copies had now been printed. Sales had broken all records in Norway.

The rapturous directors of Gyldendal persuaded their star author to answer a questionnaire for their 1927 Christmas catalogue. The final question was 'What is the worst thing you can imagine?' Hamsun answered: 'To die. I would happily skip it, if it weren't an obligation!' Hamsun was certainly feeling his age, and in a letter to Kønig bemoaned the agonies of growing old: 'I'm bedridden again – I was working outdoors, and as usual I overdid it and ended up soaked to the skin. Getting old is a lousy business!'[29]

But how much longer could Hamsun go on for? For a considerable time when he was writing *Wayfarers* he had been sure it would be his shortest book; in the end it was his longest, over six hundred pages. But he still had dozens of unused notes and a fair number of completed pages. What was more, he had hinted to his readers at the end of *Wayfarers* that there was more to come: 'He did not return – for many years.' He had laid an obligation upon himself.

All the critics commented on this promise of a sequel, and delighted readers in many countries waited in anticipation. But there was one person who was not happy with the prospect of his writing another book.

A certain bitterness towards Hamsun's writing was gnawing at Marie. His work had come between them, and had cost her and the children a great deal over the years. He could not, or would not, acknowledge the great debt he owed them. In the eighteen months when he had not been able to write, however, he had repeatedly told his wife that he needed her.

Marie had known that behind this affirmation lay a desperate plea for her to help him write again. She had smoothed the path for him once more. Now she was growing increasingly impatient for some form of recognition, a reward for her contribution. First from her husband – and then from the public. She knew this would not happen until he had laid down his pencil permanently. Only then would she be able to find compensation as the great writer's wife and, eventually, widow.

As the decade neared its close, Hamsun contemplated his own mortality. He thought about his eldest daughter and the sort of inheritance she had a right to. He contacted her mother in an attempt to arrange things. Victoria refused his offer. He was furious. She had defied him again.

A Literary Emperor

Around Christmas 1927, Hamsun lost someone of great importance to him: Christian Kønig, who had served as his trusted publisher in Oslo for so long, was going back home to Copenhagen. He was awarded both the Norwegian St Olav Medal (his name having been put forward by Hamsun) and the Dannebrog from Denmark. The Nobel Prize winner's presence at the leaving party was a third honour. His falling asleep over the dining table with his head half in his soup bowl, after he had shown the youngsters how to drink whisky instead of 'lady's drinks', was seen as an additional compliment.[30]

Harald Grieg now took over as Hamsun's publisher, proving himself to be extremely effective in securing favourable contracts with foreign publishing houses. Hamsun was soon sending the majority of the foreign-rights enquiries to him rather than to Jakob Hegel in Copenhagen, who had handled them for many years.

The challenges were various: difficult negotiations in Sweden, publications in Russia, agreements with translators in the Ukraine, enquiries from foreign film directors, extracts of *Shallow Soil* for an American textbook, interest from a French publishing house in *Benoni*, *Rosa* and *Pan*. Grieg often succeeded in negotiating large advances, as well as closing several agreements for new translations and hunting out pirate editions, particularly in South America. His influence was extensive.

A very satisfied Hamsun grunted his approval and told his dynamic young publisher that he no longer required detailed updates. Two months into 1928 came the ultimate vote of confidence: Gyldendal's director was free to carry out business and make as many agreements with foreign publishers on his behalf as he saw fit. He had Hamsun's complete trust.

'I shall seek to do everything to the best of my ability', promised the publisher.[31] It was a promise Grieg would stand by for many years to come.

In 1928 Hamsun was seldom in his writer's cottage, where he kept his notes for his sequel to *Wayfarers*, although he assured a Russian language professor with whom he was in correspondence that he was far from finished with his character August. But the expansion of his earthly kingdom could not wait if his time was soon to run out. Arrangements had to be made for Arild to take over a model farm. This was how Hamsun wanted to be honoured by his heirs. His literary legacy, on the other hand, would belong to the nation, Europe and the world.

He was receiving constant proof that he would one day belong to that pantheon.

When Maxim Gorky reached his sixtieth birthday, Hamsun was invited to pay tribute. He obliged, insisting that no other modern writer had had such a powerful impact on him – clearly forgetting a note he had scribbled in the back of one of Gorky's books, complaining that it was boring and that its characters lacked variation. The Russian returned his compliments: *The Growth of the Soil*, *The Women at the Pump* and *Chapter the Last* were works of genius. Hamsun, Gorky declared, was the greatest artist in all Europe. There was no one to equal him, anywhere.[32]

A book was also being planned in honour of Mark Twain, and his family asked Hamsun for a contribution. He wrote an apposite salute: 'Just the mention of Mark Twain's name makes me feel like smiling, because his humorous spirit was overwhelming. But he was not only a humorist, his humor had weight, he was a teacher and educationalist. He offered people the deeper and worthier truths in the form of wit.'[33]

The committee for the centenary celebrations of Tolstoy's birth also approached Hamsun. In a telegraph he told them: 'I honour Tolstoy's memory highly.'[34]

Standing on Hamsun's bookshelves were eight books that had been written about him, works of varying length which he insisted, quite disingenuously, he had never read. Two new biographies were being compiled for the forthcoming celebrations planned for the autumn of 1929, to mark his seventieth birthday.

Walter Berendsohn, a German-Swedish professor of literature at the university in Hamburg, had been approached by Müller-Langen Verlag to write a biography of Hamsun. Berendsohn wrote to him in the spring of 1928 to clarify some biographical details and to request an overview of all the articles he had written. Hamsun answered that he had forgotten everything, and kept nothing. However, it must have occurred to him that Berendsohn's book presented the perfect opportunity to remind the German readership of his loyalty to their country. He became more forthcoming in the letter: 'I do recall, now I think of it, writing some articles during the war, but I don't remember whether that was in 1917 or otherwise, but they were political articles. I was quite alone here at home standing on the German side, where I remain to this day – all of Norway took the other side.'[35]

Three days later he wrote to Korfiz Holm, now the director of Müller-Langen Verlag, declaring that he wanted nothing to do with the biography. He could not cope with the attention, he told Holm; he already refused to meet the press and fled strangers on the street when they gawped at him as if he were some exotic creature. Besides, enough had already been written about him. Yet, despite going to great lengths to explain how unobtainable he was, he concluded that he would make an exception for Berendsohn, the publisher and Germany. The literary researcher could visit Nørholm after all. Marie would receive him.[36]

Shortly afterwards Hamsun received renewed confirmation of how much the German public valued him. *Chapter the Last*, which Norwegian critics had generally panned, was to be printed in Germany in an edition of 105,000 copies. Hamsun warned his publisher to think twice about selling the books off cheap, as though they belonged to a dead man's estate: 'I am not quite dead yet!' His snarling retort was perhaps just as much a rejoinder to himself, written as it was on his sixty-ninth birthday.[37]

His collaboration with Berendsohn went sour as soon as the biographer began poking about in Hamsun's past. When Berendsohn suggested that Felix Holländer's accusations of plagiarism in the early 1890s had caused him deep hurt, Hamsun flatly denied it. And at the mention of his difficulties in Paris he conceded only that he had been concerned by his inability to speak French. Berendsohn's claim that Hamsun had met and been influenced by Thomas Mann was also repudiated; he had not even read the German's work until quite recently, he told Berendsohn, although he did think *Buddenbrooks* was 'one of the world's monumental masterpieces'.[38] There were, however, three authors that he admitted were of particular importance to him: Dostoevsky, Nietzsche and Strindberg.

Hamsun also kept a wary distance from his Norwegian biographer, Einar Skavlan, editor of *Dagbladet* and former artistic director of the Norwegian National Theatre.

In October, the efforts of Hamsun and others to secure the Nobel Prize for the Norwegian poet Olaf Bull came to naught. It went instead to Sigrid Undset.

Hamsun comforted himself with a comment in the *New York Times Book Review* which declared that *The Women at the Pump* was proof that Hamsun's own Nobel Prize was well deserved.[39] And further encouragement came from Harald Grieg; if he pulled off his latest deal to translate *Victoria* into Esperanto, Hamsun would be represented in twenty-seven languages. Before Christmas, Hamsun's substantial article on America and the spirit of the age, 'Festina lente', was published in all the major Nordic newspapers, and later in several American newspapers. It was further proof of Hamsun's international literary reputation, but also a salutary reminder of the role he saw for himself as Bjørnson's heir and Norway's national bard, responsible for leading his people.

Marie herself was further augmenting the literary name of Hamsun. By her forty-seventh birthday in October 1928, *Ola in the City*, her fifth book in six years, sat on the bookshelves at Nørholm. At the end of November her contented husband wrote to her: 'I see from an advertisement that you have been printed in 5,000 copies, a fabulous number for a book of this kind, a children's or young people's book. I languished with a print run of 3,000 for 22 years. Not until we moved to Nordland did I reach more [with *The Last Joy*].'[40]

The critics were also delighted with Marie's latest book. But it was with a certain melancholy that she registered her success. The story of these children and their growing into maturity had reached its natural conclusion. She did not know what to do next. Hamsun forbade her to write novels for adults, so she wrestled poetry from herself when the inspiration caught her, which seemed to happen with increasing frequency these days, particularly as she spent more and more time alone.

In the late autumn of 1928, Arild was sent to Valdres to join his older brother, Tore; the two girls lived in rented rooms with a family in Grimstad, where they attended school.

Marie was left with a house emptied of children, and with more time on her hands than she knew how to fill. Hamsun, on the other hand, complained that the days were never long enough.

Greatness, What Is That?

An increasingly embittered Marie watched as her husband threw himself into the plans for his seventieth birthday on 4 August 1929. This was now the sole focus of their existence and had been for a long time, although Hamsun would not admit it. Henrik Lund painted his portrait for the tenth time, and a photographer came to Nørholm with a car full of equipment to immortalise everything: the extended cowshed, the fence around the goose pond, the garden, the roads through the forest up to the marshes, as well as the interior and exterior of the main house.

Extensive attention had been paid to the aesthetics. At the beginning of June all the houses on the estate were painted white, while the barns and stables, the equipment shed and garage were painted a traditional red-brown. Several extensions had been made to the main house, and the addition of a balcony over the entrance supported by elegant colonnades gave the desired effect of a grand country estate. Inside the house, almost a century old now, staircases had been moved and walls knocked down to make space for Hamsun's pride and joy: the salon. He declared that he wanted to honour the young, and to this end had constructed and decorated a room so that the young people could dance. If one came from a proper home, he said, one should have space to dance the polonaise without having to move the furniture around. In his books Hamsun rarely devoted a sentence to the description of interiors, and when he did it was usually to emphasise a character's vanity; yet he seemed intent on turning his own home into a mausoleum.

He never seemed to have time to talk with Marie about the little cottage up by Langtjernet Lake, the one he had promised to build for the two of them.

Resentful and indignant, Marie would probably have found the contents of a parcel delivered before Hamsun's birthday extremely illuminating. It might even have caused her to reassess her scepticism about psychoanalysis. A young colleague of Strømme's had taken it upon himself to read all of Hamsun's books and, through them, to make his own analysis of the author's personality.

Dr Trygve Braatøy included a note with the parcel asking whether, with the approach of his jubilee, Hamsun might consider recommending the publication of this script; Gyldendal had already refused out of regard for their author. Some time later Hamsun returned the parcel with the following message written on the envelope: 'You could have spared yourself the trouble of sending me this manuscript, I never read anything written about me.'

Braatøy was heartily amused: the packet containing the manuscript had clearly been opened.[41]

Like Strømme, Braatøy had studied Sigmund Freud's theories on the unconscious, and had made a study of Hamsun's books to try to identify the inner
powers that drove this author. His observations might well have rung true with
Marie. Looking at *Hunger*, Braatøy closed in on the narrator's meeting with
the elusive young woman Ylajali: 'In a moment my thoughts by some capricious notion take a strange direction, I feel myself gripped by a peculiar desire
to frighten this woman; to follow her and cause her some hurt.' Braatøy
pointed out that the character's need to subjugate those who move him
becomes a recurring theme in book after book.

Strong conflicts and colossal mood swings mark all of Hamsun's characters,
he continued; they have the soul of the rejected, the scars of the dejected. Such
people need constant and tangible evidence of their success; their low self-
esteem demands the subjugation of others in order to demonstrate their
own strength. Hamsun's characters live in constant insecurity about their own
situation.

Braatøy was fascinated by how many of Hamsun's male protagonists follow
a fixed pattern in their romantic relationships. Again and again his characters
fall for women who are not free. Again and again their husbands and lovers are
left cuckolded. The psychoanalyst pointed to the author's childhood, in particular to the fact that during his formative adolescent years, when his relationship to his mother should have had a chance to mature naturally, he was
denied access to his childhood home and kept under the control of his uncle.
As a result, Braatøy said, Hamsun idealised his mother while simultaneously
suspecting her of being instrumental in the arrangements with his uncle. This
had caused a painful split in his perception of his mother and the women who
would take her place. In his earliest books Hamsun resolved this conflict by
having his mother-figures die. The more skilful his writing grows, Braatøy
suggested, the more intricate the expression of this rift in his psyche becomes.

Braatøy drew a comparison between Hamsun and Maxim Gorky. Both had
struggled long and hard before they succeeded. Might one not expect them to
feel a shared empathy for those who struggled for their own betterment, and
that of their families? But the Norwegian would never stoop to be one of the
proletariat. He remains a romantic, drawn increasingly back to the past, and
thus never breaks free.[42] The manuscript was aptly titled 'Life's Circle'.

No doubt against the wishes of the notoriously private Hamsun, Trygve
Braatøy's book was eventually published around the time of his seventieth
birthday. Gyldendal, meanwhile, published Einar Skavlan's biography, *Knut
Hamsun*. Skavlan's main focus was on Hamsun's literary output, and, in
contrast to Braatøy, he did not delve into any connections between life and art.
In his final sentence Skavlan wrote: 'Growing old also suits Knut Hamsun.'
They were words that would be overtaken by future events, words that Skavlan
would one day regret writing.

Well ahead of the birthday celebrations, the Hamsuns had laid plans for their customary cat-and-mouse game with the press. Hamsun bought a new car, a Buick. He was so concerned about being recognised by journalists and intrusive members of the public that he even considered shaving off his distinctive moustache. Tore suggested that he might have read too many crime novels.[43]

An enormous pile of letters, telegrams and cards awaited Hamsun at Nørholm – 657 in all. Congratulations came from all four corners of the world: the writers' and journalists' union in Munich, and admirers in Helsingfors, St Gallen, India, Greece, Poland, Hungary, Romania, New York, Holland, Leningrad and Johannesburg. The headmaster and students of a school in Czechoslovakia sent their good wishes and thanks. Two German universities wanted to bestow honorary doctorates on him, and Aleksandra Kollontay, the Soviet Union's representative in Norway, extended an honorary membership of the Moscow Academy of Science and Art to him. Others solicited his support for various causes, including an organisation gathering intellectuals to oppose war. A German offered an idea for a novel Hamsun might use, for a small payment. A Swede sent word of his latest invention, the Salvator fire-escape rope. Oskar Pollak from Prague thanked him again for the signed and dedicated copy of *Victoria* that Hamsun had sent thirty years ago. A Danish consul general in Tunisia reminded him of his time in Paris. From Illinois some distant relatives told him they had seen his picture in the American newspapers and were very proud. An acquaintance wrote from Calvados telling him that a French magazine had described him as the greatest novelist of all time.

In the *Festschrift* one international literary heavyweight after another confirmed Knut Hamsun's unique qualities. The Spaniard Jacinto Benavente expressed huge admiration for him. John Galsworthy hoped the flame of his genius would burn for years to come. André Gide covered almost two pages and Maxim Gorky required six. Gerhart Hauptmann described Hamsun as master of the portrayal of the human soul. Tom Kristiansen paid homage to a dangerous hero of a generation of Danish writers – dangerous because he had spoken to their subconscious. The brothers Heinrich and Thomas Mann both wrote eloquently about him, as did T.G. Masaryk, Ludmilla Pitoëff, Hjalmar Söderberg, Jacob Wassermann, H.G. Wells and Stefan Zweig.

Never before had a Norwegian received such accolades from so many prominent figures outside Norway; three of Hamsun's admirers were already Nobel Prize winners, and two more would go on to receive the world's foremost literary accolade.

Five contributors to the *Festschrift* came from the German-speaking regions, and others made reference to his unique position in Germany. The German newspapers confirmed this, almost outdoing the Norwegian press in dedicated page space and superlatives. Across the whole of Germany, editors and literary columnists seemed to vie with each other over who could be most zealous in the praises they heaped upon the seventy-year old.

And of course greetings from German readers made up a large part of the pile of post that was heaped up at Nørholm. They had been admirers of Hamsun's works for forty years. Max Reinhardt staged *In the Grip of Life* in Berlin in November; the public's excitement was so great that it continued in repertory for a total of seventy-four performances. German publishers had been the first to translate him. Now over 500,000 copies of *Hunger* had been printed in Germany, a figure exceeding the total sales of the book elsewhere across the globe. The same was also true of almost all his other major works. More than 100,000 copies of *Pan* had been sold, and his popularity was continuing to grow; nearly 70,000 copies of *Wayfarers* had already sailed out of the bookshops.

It was as if there was a need in Germany to hear Hamsun's strident message: never yield in adversity, defy everybody and everything. He was a prophet preaching a gospel of vitality in steadfastness. His novels, articles and plays were continually reconfirming his stature. Here was a man who made a stand against the changing times. After his seventieth birthday celebrations, this cult of Hamsun grew even stronger.

In October 1929, the German foreign minister Gustav Stresemann died. Since 1923 he had been instrumental in his government's attempts to minimise the destructive effects on Germany of the Treaty of Versailles, and he had shared the Nobel Peace Prize in 1926 with the politicians who negotiated the Treaty of Locarno. His vision was to ease relations with the countries Germany had been at war with, thus establishing a favourable climate for trade and clearing the way for a swift recovery of the economy. In the process he would keep extremism, from both Left and Right, in check.

Stresemann's approach had succeeded. At one point the exchange rate had hit 4.2 trillion marks to the dollar, but reform of the currency put the country back on track. Foreign money was being invested in Germany again, and the numerous restrictions placed on the nation after its defeat were being relaxed. Even that most painful boil of all – war reparations and the repayment schedule – had been lanced thanks to the seemingly indefatigable Stresemann.

Hamsun could see that Germany was standing tall again, in the eyes of its citizens and the world, and everything was in place for its steady progress to continue.

But in the same month that the father of reconciliation politics passed away, the New York Stock Exchange crashed. Within weeks the shock waves had spread through the world's markets. The crisis hit Germany particularly badly. Foreign investors pulled out, causing production to fall dramatically and tens of thousands of factories to close. During the course of just a few months, foreign trade had fallen by half. Mass unemployment and economic depression meant that the German people could scarcely get hold of the necessities for survival.

Germany was caught in a downward spiral that would only worsen.

From his various places of residence, Hamsun followed the newspaper coverage of developments in Germany closely. There were regular articles about Hitler, who continued to bombard the German people with his fiery rhetoric. He denounced Stresemann, Herman Müller and other leading politicians as traitors to the homeland. But when the electorate had gone to the ballot box in the 1928 election they had rewarded the Social Democrats and the Centre politicians for the recent economic growth, although twelve members of Hitler's party, the NSDAP, won seats in the Reichstag. One of these was Joseph Goebbels, a philologist with literary aspirations and a great admirer of Hamsun. Another was Hermann Göring, the pilot who had returned from Sweden after marrying a wealthy woman. Only a week after the election Göring had expressed his disdain for democracy: 'What do we care about the Reichstag? [. . .] [A] dungheap, there is no need to use euphemisms like "state".'[44]

The Norwegian newspapers reported Hitler and his party's attempts that autumn to reverse the agreement that Stresemann had negotiated immediately before his death. It was a move that made Hitler popular with the German business community, the majority of whom had supported conciliatory politics but had opposed the war damages agreement, which assumed Germany would be paying the Allied victors until 1988.

Hitler challenged the German people to stand up against this 'slavery', and he won a vote in the Reichstag to hold a referendum. With businesses lending their financial support, Hitler was turning his talent for political agitation and organisation into a propaganda machine the likes of which Germany had never seen before. But the majority of the German nation still voted for the politicians they knew best; less than 14 per cent voted to reject the agreement on war reparations.

When every fourth family in Germany found itself hit by unemployment, feelings began to change. Many more became weary of appeals for level-headedness, maturity and modesty from their so-called responsible politicians. They had lived through war, defeat, shame, years of hardship, a short flash of optimism – and now a new crash, which threatened to drive them into an abyss. Perhaps these new politicians who called the old ones traitors were right after all.

On 2 February 1930, Hitler reassured his followers that 'in two and a half, three years at most [. . .] our movement will be victorious'.[45]

A Red Streak

At the beginning of 1930, Hamsun travelled to the mountain valley of Valdres with his sons, Arild and Tore, where they were still attending school. Occupying a corner room with a balcony from which he could observe the comings and goings in the little town of Aurdal, Hamsun was intent on finishing another novel.

Before they boarded the coastal ship for Oslo, Hamsun had stocked up on writing equipment. His bill came to 12 kroner and 74 øre. There wasn't a business in all of Norway that could show such high returns on each krone invested. The cost in human terms, however, was much higher, and it was Marie who kept the accounts for those. Hamsun had managed to write a certain amount after his seventieth birthday celebrations. Through the autumn and towards Christmas, when it had grown too cold in his writer's cottage, he had moved into the room next to hers. She had heard him holding lengthy conversations with August and his other characters. And the more his hearing deteriorated, the louder he spoke.

Now Hamsun sat out on his balcony in Valdres for several hours each day, dressed in Eskimo-like attire, enjoying the combination of fresh air and work. He had returned to the place where he had been happiest in his youth, driven by a desperate hope of unleashing a fresh wave of inspiration. By Easter, he was able to send more than half of his next novel, *August*, to Harald Grieg, who immediately replied with news that publishers in Germany, the USA, Sweden, the Soviet Union, Holland, Czechoslovakia, Poland and Finland were all waiting impatiently for the rest so they could begin work on translations.

Hamsun, while living in the same town as them, had the chance to observe his boys. They had very different personalities. The youngest was 'rather slovenly, doesn't wash properly and constantly wears a yellow kerchief round his neck, even though he has plenty of smart shirts with collars to match. But hell, he's a fine lad, big, a grown man almost, and broad to match. Tore, tall and slender, prefers to wear the very best clothes the whole time, with good shoes, collar and tie. A gentleman.'[46]

But in those early summer months, everything revolved around the completion of *August*. Hamsun was determined to give it his all – and a little more besides.

On 17 May, Norwegian Constitution Day, Grieg informed Gyldendal's largest shareholder that the returns had gone up from 5 to 7 per cent. Repayment of the enormous debt to Gyldendal in Copenhagen was well ahead of schedule. It was an opportune time for Grieg to suggest a substantial pay rise for himself, bringing his salary to 30,000 kroner a year; he now earned more than Norway's prime minister, and twice as much as Oslo's police chief.

A man with such a high salary must surely be able to do him a favour, thought Hamsun. The manager of a hotel had drawn his attention to the fact that a unique china service from his establishment was soon to be put up for auction. Grieg received his instructions: 'I have been interested in this service for half a lifetime. [. . .] Do not let it go, stay in there to the last krone. Don't care how much it costs – must have it!'[47]

Never one to pass up an opportunity to throw a party, Grieg now had three reasons to celebrate: the profits of his publishing house, the knowledge that this year would bring a new Hamsun novel and his success in securing the antique china service which Hamsun had so set his heart on. Hamsun allowed himself to be persuaded to attend the merrymaking in Oslo. Champagne fizzed and Hamsun offered the orchestra greater and greater sums of money to play 'La Paloma'.

His dinner partner, the Swedish author Marika Stiernstedt, enchanted him. 'Everything was wonderful as long as it lasted, and I would have followed Marika Stiernstedt for many, many miles had I been forty years younger', he confessed to Grieg.[48]

The beautiful author sent him a letter and gift. After a week back at Nørholm, Hamsun packed wife and daughters off to Valdres to attend the boys' end-of-term celebrations. The following day he wrote to the woman who had made such an impression on him: 'My dearest – God bless you, fair lady, it is enough to crush me. I opened it on the train from Valdres to Oslo, and I shrank with humility. With inferiority. With agedness – yes, agedness. What in the world could I offer you? My Nobel Prize medal? But you would only return it. I could come to Stockholm, to thank you, and travel back again. But I am forty years too decrepit. I can only offer you – not so much special reserve – but the poor remnants of myself. But you shall have my sons, they are young like you. Oh heavens, how delightful you are. I remember seeing it, feeling it. [. . .] They say that old age has its joys, but it is not true. One can be busy with one's children, but joys – ? No. You sent a red streak through me. It has been years since the last time. [. . .] It was sweet as long as it lasted, there was a red streak in that evening.'[49]

It had been a long time since he had written anything like this, perhaps as long ago as when he had described the love between Johannes and Victoria. Then as now, the woman to whom he was married could no longer inspire the fever, the streak, that this new encounter had kindled in him.

Hamsun had worked hard to finalise yet another novel for proofreading. By autumn, *August* would be appearing in countries across Europe. Three and a half years ago, Strømme had promised him a new spring. And despite

Hamsun's melancholy, the doctor's promise had been fulfilled and exceeded: Hamsun was already considering the idea of writing a third book in his series about August, this time about an old man who regains his youth through a woman lighting up a red streak inside him.

It was midsummer 1930. Hamsun would soon be seventy-one years old.

A Convalescent in Search of Reconciliation

For several years Hamsun had suffered from urinary problems. In the early autumn of 1930, Arendal Hospital diagnosed prostate hypertrophy. He needed surgery. Whether he had cancer or not could only be confirmed during the operation.

He wrote to Bergljot's sister, Alette Gross in Hamburg, and asked her to inform his first wife about the operation and his decision to put his financial affairs in order, in case of his death.

When his daughter Victoria heard about the forthcoming operation via her aunt and mother, she decided to send him a letter that she had written three weeks previously but had not had the courage to post: 'I have not written to you for many years, because sadly I knew that you preferred it that way, but the punishment you have dealt me is too *harsh*, Papa. I dare to appeal to you once more. God grant that you might understand and forgive me whatever wrong I may have done you. I hold you dear with all my heart, if you have the smallest grain left over for me, then do not damn me any more, it is too awful. You would not believe how it has weighed me down through the years.'[50]

Victoria searched for a reason for the gulf between them. 'We know each other so little, and perhaps that is where a good deal of the unhappiness lies.' She described how she treasured the memories of the few summers when she had been allowed to visit him as a child. 'I can remember all the way back to Nordstrand, how you took me to the general store and bought little rings that tarnished and from which the stone fell out after only two minutes, so I had to have a new one. And you played cards with me and called me scallywag when I won; or you helped me find shiny stones and pick campions along a disused railway line in Kongsberg.'

She went on: 'But then so many years passed, from when I was ten until I was sixteen, during which you never asked to see me, even though we lived quite close in those last years. Do not misunderstand: I have no right to reproach you for anything; you may well have had your reasons of which I am unaware; I just want to show you that circumstances have turned us into strangers, and that I have had little opportunity to show my affection. If you think it has been absent, despite all this, then you are very much mistaken.'

Victoria had not visited Norway since the summer of 1923 when she had come to Nørholm; Hamsun had stood in the doorway looking at her, refusing to talk, and had finally turned his back and left. Now she suggested she come again, this time with her two children. 'Erik and little Dederick Knut; just imagine if they could see their grandfather, whom they will hear about throughout their lives, and whose books they will read. You once said that only weak characters forgave, but I see things differently. I know that it will go very much against the grain for you to stretch out a hand to *me*; I will understand its worth, and be grateful to you for the rest of my life.'

Hamsun finally broke his nine-year silence. He wanted to tell her something in case he should die on the operating table. 'Whatever I might have had to forgive is long ago forgiven, I have much too much else to deal with here to go around concerned by the past. [. . .] On my side, you must excuse whatever I have said and done at the frustration of things not going according to my plans.'[51]

In the margin of the letter he also explained why he had behaved so dismissively when Victoria had tried to visit him seven years ago: 'I didn't receive you on that occasion because I was struggling with the last line of a new book.' But she was still not welcome at Nørholm.

Hamsun asked her to accept an inheritance settlement now, bearing in mind that the value of his estate would decrease in years to come. But it was perhaps already too late. In nine days he would go under the knife, 'and if I die the doctor told me it will happen fast. Personally, I am not a jot concerned about how things go for me, we all go that way, yes all of us, I shall die old anyhow, I'm already seventy-one.'

Victoria reassured her father that she wanted only a reconciliation with him, not money, though this was not quite true. As Hamsun prepared to go into hospital, his daughter and her lawyer calculated his worth. Marie armed herself for a battle over her own children's inheritance.

Marie drove Hamsun to Arendal Hospital on Monday, 15 September 1930. When he had checked in, Hamsun's consultant, Peter Nicolaysen, followed Marie out. He wanted a word with her alone.

'I have to alert you to the fact that this operation does not come without risk. And that it might be cancer.'

'Does my husband know?' she asked.[52] Only now did she realise that the man who had always fussed over the slightest discomfort had kept the real fear that he might be dying to himself for a whole month.

Some cheering news was delivered by the consultant the next day. The operation Hamsun had undergone in Copenhagen ten years before which was supposed to revitalise him, and which in truth had had little to no effect, now at least delivered some concrete benefit. Hamsun would need one procedure less.

Hamsun passed the time reading detective novels by Edgar Wallace and various books about great historical figures, as well as writing a number of letters.

He was taken into theatre on 2 October. Later that day the telephone rang at Nørholm. The consultant spoke to Marie, informing her that the operation had gone well, with no serious complications. The question that was foremost in her mind was answered in the negative: it was not malignant. Indeed, Hamsun was as fit as a fiddle and the consultant was finished with him.[53]

The lawyers, however, were not.

Hamsun's lawyer calculated that the inheritance settlement of 50,000 kroner that he had offered to Victoria was far too much: 38,000 kroner would be a fairer figure. After conferring with his still bedridden client, they agreed on 45,000 kroner. When Victoria's adviser described this as a generous offer, a satisfied Hamsun made a note on the outside of the envelope in large letters: 'Generous!'[54]

This harrowing situation had finally been brought to a satisfactory conclusion, and his relationship with his daughter into a much better climate. At least, that was what Hamsun believed. But now Victoria and her adviser played their trump card. They assumed this figure related only to his present fortune, and Victoria wanted her share of his future earnings and royalties on an equal footing with Hamsun's other children. He refused this request point blank.

The last time father and daughter had conversed properly had been on the Christmas weekend of 1917. A month before Christmas 1930 they were to meet again, formally this time, in Oslo. Marie accompanied Hamsun to lend her assistance. He nursed a hope of soothing the antagonism between these two women.

Victoria demanded 100,000 kroner. Her father offered half that amount. Negotiations disintegrated into a slanging match between the forty-nine-year-old Marie and Victoria, twenty-one years her junior. Victoria's lawyer suggested that father and daughter continue the discussion in a separate room.

Now it was Hamsun's turn to get sentimental, while Victoria hardened. He reminded her that they had asked each other's forgiveness. He was old, and would soon die. Could they not be reconciled at last? She had to believe that he wished her only well, but it was impossible for him to give her everything she demanded since that would be unfair to his other children.[55]

Perhaps that is what Victoria sought: to be given proof that for just once in her life she had been put first, favoured above his four other children.

When they parted, the rift between father and daughter was far greater than could ever be measured in kroner and øre.

Hamsun wrote reminding her that she would not be able to count on his integrity, or indeed his lack of it, once he was dead. It would be too late. Six months passed before Victoria wrote again, asking her father's forgiveness for not having taken his offer to pay her out of the estate, and soliciting her inheritance to be paid to her now. She had read with concern the newspaper reports of Hamsun threatening to sell all his rights and give the money to charity: 200,000 kroner in all. Needless to say, wife and children in Nørholm were not thrilled with these munificent promises. Hamsun had appeased them by doubling his life insurance policy for the four children.

After some negotiation, Victoria received a little less than the sum Hamsun had originally offered her. At last the troublesome daughter was out of all their lives – or so they thought.

A Romantic

There was enormous interest in Hamsun's sequel to *Wayfarers*. Two days before *August* was released to the public on 1 October 1930, Gyldendal had already had to print a further five thousand copies; the first edition of twelve thousand had not been enough to fulfil even the initial orders from the bookshops.

Only a few reviews expressed any reservations about the book. One of these appeared in *Aftenposten*, which praised parts of the novel but generally found it to be a pale repetition of *Wayfarers*. Surprisingly, the normally hostile *Morgenbladet* was extremely enthusiastic, praising the narrative perfection of *August* and declaring it to be incomparable and consummate in every detail. The Danish critic Tom Kristensen, who had impressed Hamsun with his own novel *Hærverk*, was equally unwavering: 'A book for which Knut Hamsun should have won the Nobel Prize a second time.'[56]

Sigurd Hoel had positive things to say about Hamsun, although he had strong objections to his moral message: 'Hamsun is a reactionary, in the true sense of the word, he mistrusts the direction in which the times are moving, he regards these [times] as ill-fated, he feels progress should be turned back [. . .] to the patriarchal, idyllic, romantic era before industry and trade unions and collectivism and restlessness entered the world.'[57] The romantic Hamsun was, according to Hoel, incapable of seeing the impossibility of this dream.

At the opening of *August* twenty years have passed since the end of *Wayfarers*. Edevart and Lovise Magrete Doppen have left for America. August has gone to sea, leaving the people of Polden with a hunger for modernity.

Two people, however, are unaffected by the departures. Pauline has managed her brother Edevart's assets splendidly, and is now applying herself cool-headedly to the running of the general store, café, lodging house, post office and more besides. Joachim, the third of the siblings, is now mayor, having built his farm up to be the largest in the small town.

The three characters who have torn up their roots have, it transpires upon their reappearance in Polden, fared less well. Lovise Magrete's sweetness, motherliness and temperance, which had once been so beguiling to Edevart, have mutated into vulgarity, cynicism and extravagance. Edevart has lost his spark and, worst of all, he is unrecognisable to himself. August has lost his gold-capped teeth and has brought some unspeakable disease upon himself. He still brims with ideas and energy, but is more dangerous. His travels have left him in thrall to the delights of the modern world. No longer content simply to offer the people of Polden telephones, electric lights, a herring meal factory, bank, hotel, white curtains, decorative plants and gardens, he tempts them to give up their old way of life, their farms and the fishing that have fed them. When times grow harder, the factory stands empty of machinery and there are no fish to feed the townspeople, hunger brings the worst out in them. August has to flee from Polden.

Hamsun had called August an agent of the age, and in this sequel he persisted in his condemnation of almost everything August set in motion. Yet Hamsun still seems unwilling to let him leave, fail or die. His protagonist weathers humiliation, defeat and ruin, and, often against all odds, triumphs. Hamsun had considered naming the book 'Pauline', but had abandoned the idea. The book's eponymous character would not be the woman of reason, but August the fantasist, dreamer and wanderer.

Perhaps Hamsun's extraordinary love–hate relationship to August was born of an increased self-awareness gained from his treatment with Dr Strømme. In both *Wayfarers* and *August* he seems to recognise that he himself might have ended up like either Edevart or August. But unlike August, Hamsun had a fruitful outlet for his imagination in his writing. Added to which, his farming had helped him to put down roots, giving his life even greater meaning than writing could alone – or indeed the pursuit of love which would be Edevart's path.

'Willkommen, Knut Hamsun!'

For many years Hamsun had longed to return to Germany.

With the exception of their visit to Stockholm to attend the Nobel Prize ceremony, Hamsun and Marie had never travelled abroad together. In mid-January 1931, however, they embarked on a train journey from Oslo that would take them through six countries. Berlin was their first stop, Nice their second. They intended to cheat the winter and greet the spring.

Travelling with them was Tore, who was recovering from a throat operation, accompanied – since he would be away for two months – by his young tutor who would ensure the young man's notorious laziness was kept in check. Hamsun was undecided as to how long he and Marie would remain travelling.

The group had only just entered Germany when they discovered that news of their trip had spread. The press had announced that Knut Hamsun was visiting Germany for the first time since his stay in Munich in 1896. 'Willkommen, Knut Hamsun!' announced the front pages of many of the capital's newspapers, eager to salute the reclusive author who had emerged from his chilly northern lair. Journalists, photographers and admirers all gathered in Berlin to catch a glimpse of the celebrity. When the small Norwegian party arrived at the Central Hotel in Friedrichstrasse, there was a crowd of people all wanting autographs and, if possible, to talk to the author whose works they knew so well and about whom they had heard so much.

The family had wanted to do some sightseeing in Berlin, but Hamsun barely left the hotel. His room rapidly filled with flowers, letters and gifts from determined admirers and newspaper hacks. The press was so persistent that Hamsun instructed Tore and his tutor to take shifts standing guard at the hotel entrance, before the staff took charge. Nonetheless, an American correspondent managed to slip past the security, penetrating all the way to Hamsun's room before being discovered and swiftly ejected.

After two days they continued their journey.

Tore was sent down to hail a taxi and check no journalists or photographers were hiding in the lobby or street outside. Having been given the all-clear, Hamsun hurried out of the hotel and into the car. Just as he was closing the door, a fragile-looking young woman ran forward with a bunch of roses.

'Ich danke Ihnen für Victoria,' she said, catching her breath.

'What is she saying?' he asked Marie, who translated.[58] Hamsun took the girl's hand in his and held it for a long time without uttering a word. Tore noticed how his father blushed as she looked at him intently.

The next day they travelled through southern Germany. Hamsun was in excellent spirits; he hummed to himself and spent the journey alternately studying the landscape and reading Sherwood Anderson's *Dark Laughter*. Tore read his father's notes on the last page: 'Almost any sentence of this book can be placed in almost any part of the book without the least ill-effect.'[59]

Hamsun hung the bouquet of roses on the wall of the carriage. They were wilting, he commented rather wistfully, to Marie's obvious irritation.

Twenty-four hours after leaving Berlin, the train chugged into Milan. They were to eat supper at the station restaurant. Hamsun's high spirits had dissipated. At the table he put his glasses on and began straightening the prongs on the forks. He then started on the knives and spoons. Marie and Tore's embarrassment grew, particularly as his inspection and repairs were accompanied by a loud commentary. Hamsun then insisted on deciphering the microscopic inscription engraved on the cutlery. He could read the word *Solingen,* but grew irritated that he could not make out the rest. Neither could the others.

'And I don't suppose there's any information to be had!' he shouted angrily, turning his plate upside down.[60]

Much to everybody's despair he insisted on the mystery being solved, greatly delaying the arrival of their meal. Still Hamsun refused to be rushed. Not until five minutes after the train had been due to leave were they finally standing on the platform. Fortunately the train was delayed too.

Upon reaching the Italian-French border at Ventimiglia the next morning, their suitcases were searched by a customs official. An increasingly irate Hamsun told Marie to make it categorically clear to the Frenchman how disrespectful this behaviour was. The customs official carried on rummaging. It did not make the slightest difference when Marie informed him of Hamsun's celebrity; as far as the official could see, he was simply a cantankerous old Norwegian. This ignorance inflamed all Hamsun's antipathies towards the French. When the official asked if he had any tobacco, Hamsun puffed on his lit pipe and refused to answer. The question was repeated, and Hamsun slapped two packets of Tidemand's Blend down on the table. The official took them and vanished.

Tore ventured to inform his father that he would have to pay duty on the tobacco. Hamsun snorted that he had travelled through Sweden, Denmark, Germany, Switzerland and Italy without paying duty, and he was not about to start now. The official returned waving a slip of paper on which he had written '20 francs', demonstratively spreading his ten fingers twice in the air.

'What the hell! Am I meant to pay 20 francs for so little! I'd rather throw the tobacco away!' Hamsun bellowed, tearing the packs of tobacco out of the Frenchman's hand and opening the compartment window.[61]

The official had dealt with difficult passengers before. He grabbed the modest contraband and disappeared along the corridor, promptly returning with reinforcements. Three officials now explained to Hamsun that if he did not pay 20 francs he would be arrested immediately. Tore's tutor gazed with increasing disbelief at the writer's provocative behaviour. Marie and Tore knew only too well that Hamsun would never give in. They dreaded the prospect of staying in a French border town while the jailed Hamsun called upon the aid of every ambassador and minister he could think of – and then wasted their remaining time abroad initiating imaginative retaliations.

Tore was well practised at defusing tensions between his mother and father, and he now hit upon a solution. He beckoned the three uniformed men out into the corridor and offered them some Norwegian stamps from his suitcase that the official had shown considerable interest in. The agreeable young man won a smile and a handshake, and the Frenchmen moved on to the next compartment.

More than a little pleased with himself, Tore returned to the family's compartment with the two packs of tobacco. His father growled that he ought not to have interfered. Tore was rewarded by his mother's appreciative glance.

A couple of hours later they arrived in Nice. The changes in the landscape as they journeyed southwards had pacified the leader of their little party once more. Hamsun had already booked the family into one of the town's better establishments, Hotel Carabacel. The efficient porters duly trotted off with their suitcases. Hamsun did not notice them, and began searching desperately for his luggage. When he found out that everything was already in their rooms, he was livid: they had not asked his permission. He refused to tip the porters and shooed them away, growling in Norwegian that they might get a little something on his departure.

Hamsun did not part with a single extra sou during their entire stay. As a result, the service that the family received was hardly of the best, despite Tore and Marie slipping staff the occasional tip.

As they departed from the hotel two days later, they were unexpectedly treated like royalty. Hamsun had left a princely sum over and above the total of their bill.

They took a taxi to the final destination of their trip, the small town of Beaulieu-sur-Mer just outside Nice. The couple went for long walks along the shore and up into the hills. Hamsun murmured his appreciation of the local farming methods as he watched the peasants rolling reed mats over the carnation fields to protect them against the cold nights. He wanted to be there when they rolled them back. The couple never forgot the concentrated scent of carnations.

The invigorating effect of the first signs of spring in this Mediterranean town convinced Hamsun that winter must soon release its grip on the south coast of Norway too. Only two weeks after having left Oslo, Hamsun and Marie packed to travel north again while Tore and his young teacher remained.

On the way back, the couple spent a day in Hamburg, staying the night at the fashionable Hotel zum Kronprinzen. Marie was going to meet some important people in this old Hanseatic city.

She had already been instrumental in establishing links between Knut Hamsun and Germany. When she had come to Germany three years before to represent her husband at the Heidelberg Festival, Marie had attracted the attention of the Nordische Gesellschaft, an organisation dedicated to strengthening the ties between Germany and the Nordic countries. Knut Hamsun's contribution to the forging of cultural links had, of course, been staggering, but they could not expect this retiring and now elderly man to make many personal appearances. Marie was the perfect solution. She knew his writing better than anybody, was an author in her own right (her children's books were rapidly gaining popularity in Germany), had a good command of German, and with her experience on the stage, was sure to be a hit on any podium. Some of the organisation's associates had made approaches.

Now, at the end of the family's journey, new links were established between Hamburg and the Hamsuns.

Every tourist makes comparisons between conditions at home and those in the countries they visit, and the Hamsuns were no exception.

In Norway, the Labour Party, which was presently in opposition, had decided on a policy of disarmament during its annual conference. The government had again made large cuts in defence spending. On several occasions Hamsun had warned against any pacifist thinking. War, he postulated, was not unnatural: the battle for survival was simply a part of life. Only recently Hamsun had warmly thanked a Norwegian officer who had praised the heroism of the German soldiers on the Western Front.[62]

Thus Hamsun registered with satisfaction the growing demands for rearmament in Germany. Hitler was instrumental in this. From his headquarters in Munich he had expanded his party so that it was now the second largest in the country, after the Social Democrats. In the Reichstag election six months previously, 6.4 million Germans had voted for his National Socialist Party. Seemingly indefatigable, Hitler attacked the Treaty of Versailles and peace treaties in general, declaring that they were all strangling Germany. The National Socialists vowed to fight them, on behalf of future generations, with all the means at their disposal. They would not let Germany be poisoned by the pacifist spirit.

To disarm a country is to give up your right to a home, Hamsun reasoned. Hitler proclaimed the same. The German people must be equipped with both the gun and the plough. Hitler's relentless attacks on the treaties that shackled Germany, on incompetent and treacherous politicians, on the modern age and on the Bolsheviks' corrosive impact on society resonated with many – Knut and Marie Hamsun included.

When the Author Opens Up

In the first half of 1931, Hamsun began work on his third novel centring on the character August. There was still material left over from his two previous books, and endless little piles of notes.

The fact that he was writing again, and that Marie was not, came between man and wife.

Hamsun tried to apply a salve to the wound. He suggested that Grieg bring out new editions of Marie's books – two collections of poetry and three children's novels – boasting that she was unequalled in Norway both in prose (for children, naturally) and verse. He also fought her corner when the Norwegian Writers' Union failed to offer her membership, threatening to withdraw his own; she was promptly accepted.[63]

The children remained a bone of contention, however. Marie felt he was driving them away from their home far too soon. One by one they were leaving, first Tore and Arild for Valdres, and now Ellinor for a convent school in Germany, to which Hamsun was determined Cecilia would soon follow.

That summer Hamsun considered rekindling his contact with Johan Irgens Strømme. The psychoanalyst had helped him to write again, but his relationship with Marie had deteriorated. And he had not yet recovered from the operation he had undergone nine months previously. The doctors had warned him that it might take several years, and that some things would probably never be normal again. The majority of those who had prostate surgery were rendered impotent.

Hamsun probably felt the need to discuss this sensitive topic. But he did not go to Strømme, choosing instead to consult another psychoanalyst. The meeting must have been less than uplifting; Tore received a letter from Hamsun afterwards saying that his father would 'soon be superfluous both at home and in life'.[64]

Instead, as so often in the past, Hamsun translated the anguish of his own life into his work.

When the children returned to Nørholm with their friends for the summer of 1932, Hamsun decided to leave. With the side pockets of his suitcase stuffed with notes, he asked Marie to take him in the Buick to find a suitable place to work. She drove him around south-west Norway for two days. On the homeward journey they spent the night in a hotel in Egersund, a few kilometres west of Stavanger. The next day Marie drove home without him.

Lodging with a quiet couple, who left the author in peace in his shaded room, Hamsun's creative block finally loosened that July. Less than two weeks later he had completed more than twenty pages of his next novel – always the most difficult part of any book for him.

At the beginning of this new book, which would become *The Road Leads On*, Hamsun brings August ashore at the location of his 1915 novel *Segelfoss Town*, where he settles for good. Segelfoss has grown, transforming itself into the kind of small town that August had dreamed the fishing community of Polden might become. The people of Polden had let the ambitious August down; or perhaps it was the other way around.

August is still a staunch believer in progress, but his enormous appetite for work now has a practical outlet. With his quick mind and capable hands, he makes himself indispensable to Segelfoss's most important man, Gordon Tidemand, who has taken over from his businessman father Theodor. Gordon received an excellent grounding in business abroad, bringing back furnishings and knick-knacks requested by his father each time he returned home. The numerous rooms in the palatial home stand sadly empty save for the mirrors, chairs, tables, sofas, carpets, wall hangings and paintings, vases, chandeliers, ornamental beds and gilded angels. A scornful Hamsun reveals the upstart's efforts to surpass the mansion's former grandeur. Hamsun had himself indulged in the same excesses at Nørholm.

August has grown old along with several other characters and, not least, their creator. For the first time Hamsun describes old age with a more profound understanding, and decisively not with the disgust and contempt he had displayed in *Rosa*.

In early books such as *Mysteries* and *Pan*, Hamsun had captured his characters' subconscious lives by delineating their direct experience of love. Now he revealed the subconscious of the ageing August through actions driven by an old man's longing for love, not its satisfaction.

The beautiful Swedish authoress Marika Stiernstedt had caused a red streak to glow in Hamsun once more, perhaps for the last time. Hamsun would allow August the same small ecstasy.

The little piles of paper were being spread and shuffled again. Hamsun took great care over these slips, since each and every one could prove useful. They were swapped and switched as Hamsun searched for ideas that would lock into each other, or characters who could interact – an arrangement that might fire him off in new directions.

Hamsun was writing again at last, although his characters, he felt, were resisting his intentions; he would try to rein them in but the most wilful of them, including August, seemed almost beyond his control. But Hamsun also recognised this as a creative necessity. He could let himself go in his writing in a way he never could in the real world. He was presiding over all these voices, but he could also move among his characters, become one of them, talk with them and then withdraw again to the position of observer, narrator, commentator. Talking out loud with his characters, he would put words into their mouths. Hamsun remained in continual dialogue with himself in this act of creation, open in a way that he never was for anybody in life. And it took a Herculean effort to keep this universe of his creation intact.

Early in 1933, an author in Norway shuffled little squares of paper so that they might form a greater whole. In Germany, a politician contemplated the cards that fate had dealt him. The decisive game between democracy and dictatorship was about to be played out.

The World Has Come to the End of the Road

Across Europe in the late 1920s and into the 1930s, political opinion became increasingly polarised; at one extreme was Stalin's communist Soviet Union, and at the other, Mussolini's fascist Italy. After a Conservative victory in Norway's 1930 elections, Hamsun had urged Parliament and government that the seditious activities of the communists and socialists should be stopped – if necessary by force. During the summer of 1932, he renewed these demands. In a preface to a book, he launched an attack on the dangers presented by the Labour and Communist parties: 'What is happening in our country? Violence, law-breaking, and revolution, taken to the extremes only barbarism and disorder can reach. This is not just a momentary flash of anger – the aim is to create long-term fear and chaos among the people. It is a plot, and its goal is the destruction of life, law and justice. In one place the police are attacked, society's guardians of order – elsewhere gangs prevent people from working. In one place they use knives, in another guns. Violence, lawlessness, revolution. I put today's newspapers aside and await new outrages tomorrow. Am I living in Norway?'[65] Hamsun named a man whom he believed could be Norway's salvation: Vidkun Quisling. The former military captain had worked alongside Fridtjof Nansen on humanitarian campaigns in the Soviet Union and had, for a brief time, been Norway's defence minister. Having come into conflict with his colleagues, Quisling had established his own party, Nasjonal Samling, the NS Party, strongly inspired by Italism fascism and the National Socialists of Germany. Now, like a modern-day John the Baptist, Hamsun identified Norway's saviour.

In Germany an increasing number of people saw Adolf Hitler as their redeemer. He vowed to rescue the nation from the misgovernment of professional politicians, from the Bolsheviks' coup plans, and the continued attempts by the Allied victors to destroy Germany. In two sets of elections during the spring of 1932, Hitler stood for president against the patriarchal Paul von Hindenburg, winning an impressive 36.7 per cent of the vote. Hitler was building support with breathtaking speed and effectiveness, making use of all the new technology available: radio, gramophone recordings, film, aircraft. Over the course of two weeks he held fifty public meetings across the country.

In the elections of July 1932, 37.4 per cent of the German people voted for the Nazi Party. The Social Democrats won 21.5 per cent and the Communists 14.3 per cent of the votes. In November's parliamentary election the Nazis fell back from 230 representatives to 196, but this did not impede the fall of Franz von Papen's Conservative government ten days later. General Kurt von Schleicher became the new Reichskanzler or Chancellor. His attempts to split the Nazis failed; Hitler's grip on his party was too strong. The recently deposed von Papen allied himself with Hitler, and it took the two men less than three months to outmanoeuvre von Schleicher.

On 30 January 1933, Hitler was sworn in as Reichskanzler for a government in which Franz von Papen's Right-wing party held a majority. Hundreds of thousands joined a torch-lit procession through the Brandenburg Gate to celebrate Hindenburg and Hitler, and over the next days and weeks unprecedented numbers of politicians – national, federal and local – switched allegiance. They sensed the new chancellor's colossal will to power. It was a quality about which one of Hitler's former campaigners, General Erich von Ludendorff, had warned Hindenburg: 'By appointing Hitler Chancellor, you have delivered the country to one of the greatest demagogues of all time. I solemnly prophesy to you, this damnable man will plunge our Reich into the abyss and will bring inconceivable misery down upon our nation. Coming generations will curse you in your grave for this action.'[66]

Attitudes in the Norwegian press were even more polarised than they had been previously. Left-wing newspapers railed against the fascism that was sweeping across and threatening to swallow up so much of Europe. Norway's conservative press welcomed Hitler as a man of action, capable of stemming the chaos caused by the chattering democrats and driving back the threat of Bolshevism. Momentous events in Germany were being reported almost daily.

After only four weeks as chancellor, Hitler had suspended basic legal rights and habeas corpus. Blaming the Bolsheviks for starting the fire that gutted the Reichstag building on 27 February, Hitler criminalised the Communist Party and prohibited all political activity by other parties. Flags bearing the Nazi Party's swastika were raised on all public buildings. Over the next few days the Sturm Abteilung (SA) forced a number of federal governments to resign.

The new Reichstag was opened on 21 March. Over the next days the Third Reich was born in the consciousness of the German people and the rest of the watching world. Newspapers competed to carry the most gripping coverage of these heavily symbolic ceremonies.

On 24 March, Hamsun would have read the sensational news from Germany. In the first session of the Reichstag on the previous day, Hitler had mounted the podium and in effect demanded that absolute power be handed to his government and himself, securing the two-thirds majority that he required. He did not attempt to disguise the true nature of his intentions: 'We are ruthless. I have no bourgeois scruples! They think I am uncultured, a barbarian. Yes, we are barbarians! We want to be. That is an honourable epithet. We are the ones who will rejuvenate the world. This old world is done for.'[67]

Hamsun heartily approved of what was happening in Germany. And there was another man who had fought his way to absolute power for whom Hamsun had also recently expressed his high regard: 'Mussolini is a man to whom I would happily offer my deep felt admiration and respect – mercy upon us, what a man in the midst of these confused times.'[68]

Hamsun had never been a supporter of democracy. The writer craved a dictator. Power was not to be shared.

Neither, Hamsun felt, was his name – a name that had gained respect and admiration of its own kind. Hamsun had lost the case against his brother and nephew in the local courts, but now took his appeal to the High Court. When it became evident that he would suffer a second defeat, he bought the name from his relatives.

But that year Hamsun instigated another set of proceedings, this time against the family that had owned Nørholm for more than a hundred years. He was determined that their right to use the estate's name, in keeping with Norwegian tradition, should be removed. Astonishingly enough, Hamsun won, although the decision was so questionable that sixty years later the Norwegian prime minister himself became embroiled in restoring the name of Nørholm to its historic holders.[69]

Hidden Romance

On 10 June 1933, Hamsun sent the first part of *The Road Leads On* to Harald Grieg. As always, he was haunted by thoughts of disaster: 'I have no copy, so I am worried and nervous that my gold nuggets might be lost through theft or fire.'[70] On his seventy-fourth birthday he delivered the second section, and ten days later a delighted Grieg received the remainder, accompanied by the author's own recommendation: 'Some good stuff and some garbage, just as in every book.'[71]

It was published on 5 October in a first edition of fifteen thousand copies. Once more the critics were filled with admiration for Hamsun's capacity to engage readers with his characters. It was a long time since he had written a book containing so little social critique or so few dramatic events. Reviewers devoted little space to the easily explainable plot and concentrated instead on the rich gallery of characters: Theodor's widow, known as Old Ma; her lover, the gypsy Otto Alexander, Tidemand's father; the postmaster and the doctor with their dissatisfied wives; the chirpy young pharmacist; the hotel owner, 'a man with much of the woman about him'; the road builders who work under August's leadership; the Sami woman, Åse, who practises her dangerous magic arts; and several young characters, including the peasant Karel and the charming Cornelia.

It is a book that reflects Hamsun's own complex notion of existence; pessimistic in its unflinching portrayal of life as worth little in the grander scheme of things; resigned in its assertion that life must nonetheless be gone through with; hopeful in its belief that life's possibilities are never quite exhausted until it is finally over. The lucky throw has no age limit.

Hamsun was seventy-four himself when this tightly woven homily about old age and eroticism appeared. Until this point Hamsun had only depicted the hideousness of the old at the table and in bed. Now he allowed an old man to run riot through a whole novel.

Knut Hamsun had rediscovered the vagabond in himself.

Like the host of other wanderers created by Hamsun before him, August is also made wretched by love, embarking on the same sorts of abortive erotic exploits and committing the same follies as *Hunger's* narrator, as well as Nagel and Glahn. However, August does not share the sadistic misogynistic streak of these earlier characters.

Again Hamsun offers a bitter portrayal of how sex, power and money (or lack of it) are closely bound together. August's infatuation with a young girl is laughable, almost onanistic. He attempts, as Mack does in *Pan*, *Benoni* and *Rosa*, to buy a woman's affections. But he lacks Mack's will to power. August is a dreamer, not a tyrant, 'an old man turned into a juvenile, who bragged about what he had and denied any shortcomings'. The author, after his operation, may have felt the same way.

Old Ma offers August love, tenderness, care and desire – fulfilling all the requirements described by Dr Strømme in his book *Nervøsitet* for an ideal wife and healthy woman. However, Hamsun was finding life with his own Old Ma back at Nørholm increasingly unsustainable.

In the late autumn of 1933, Marie broke down. Her youngest child had just left home. Once more she totted up the emotional accounts, and again found Hamsun in arrears – to the children and to her. When would she be in a position to call this debt in?

The departure of the children had begun five years earlier when Hamsun sent Tore to Valdres. Most recently her husband had insisted on Cecilia going to Germany. This was the worst blow. Marie was sent to a psychoanalyst in Denmark, and from there she travelled to Germany to spend some time with her daughters. Hamsun left for Cannes to bring Arild and Ellinor home. They had ignored his orders to stop squandering his money so recklessly.

His youngest daughter, Cecilia, was causing Hamsun the greatest concern. She criticised the new Germany, writing letters to her friends and the maids on the farm describing the despicable behaviour of the Nazis that she was witnessing. Her father had no desire to hear this. 'Cecilia, you are living in a great country now, you can be sure it is a great and wonderful country. You mustn't go writing to the maids about this or that person committing suicide, they will think it is awful in Germany. Write about the things Hitler and his government are achieving, despite the whole world's hatred and hostility. You and I and everybody will thank and bless Germany. It is the country of the future.'[72]

The sixteen-year-old Cecilia was naturally deeply upset by the Nazi's terrorisation and persecution of alternative thinkers, Jews and other groups. Her father, however, had made it clear that she was expected to close her eyes to this brutality and injustice. Only positive impressions ought to be communicated. Her mother backed him up.

The couple at Nørholm had never previously been united upon any matter so much as they were on the new Germany. They experienced the power of standing shoulder to shoulder, of having a subject they could discuss without fear of sparking disagreement. He followed events in his newspapers, magazines and books. She visited Germany more and more frequently.

Prostrate before the Incarnation of Power

In the summer of 1934, after an alleged coup attempt, Adolf Hitler executed seventy-six prominent members of his party without trial. One of the victims was the previous chancellor, General Kurt von Schleicher. One does not shoot generals, an indignant Hamsun told Tore, before sending him off to Germany and Munich.[73]

Some days after these murders Hitler gave his people and the wider world a lesson in the grim justice of the Third Reich: 'I gave the order to shoot the ring leaders in this treason, and I further gave the order to cauterize down to the raw flesh of this poisoning of the wells in our domestic life. Let the Nation know that its existence – which depends on its internal order and security –

cannot be threatened with impunity by anyone! And let it be known for all time to come that if anyone raises his hand to strike the state, then certain death is his lot.'[74]

The Führer had sanctioned mass murder in the service of the common good.

The SS, which had been one of several military wings of the party, under the leadership of Heinrich Himmler was now made into the guardian of the National Socialist ideology. Mere brute force would no longer be the primary means of change and enforcement. The modern revolutionary was an administrator who executed the duties laid down for him by the SS state, loyally, dispassionately, and without questioning the legitimacy or objective of these duties.

Hamsun made a public statement in *Aftenposten* defending the pervasive terror that Hitler had, with such appalling efficiency, introduced in little over a year. Hamsun's anger had been aroused by Johan Fredrik Paasche, a professor of European literature, who had warned Norwegians sympathetic to Vidkun Quisling and the NS Party to take note of events in Germany and to learn from them. The dictatorship had crushed all freedom of expression, he stated. Nearly 100,000 Germans who had opposed the Nazis already sat in concentration camps. Children were being encouraged to betray their own parents. Nazification was penetrating the private sphere.

Hamsun argued that this was the price one had to pay to build a new society. What the professor and his fellow critics of the Nazis had failed to understand was 'that this involves the re-education of a society of 66 million people, *from the roots*, and that Germany has struggled with this for fifteen months, has tried new approaches, has made mistakes, has tried again – and all this, while subjected to the <u>entire world's economic, political and moral animosity</u>. [. . .] What if Mr Paasche had just the slightest inkling that there might be some basis for this bloody drama in Germany.' Hamsun continued sarcastically: 'No, let's bring back the old Germany, the Republic, when the communists, Jews and Brüning ruled over this essentially Nordic country.'[75]

As early as the summer of 1934, it was clear that Hamsun comprehended better than most the explosive power that lay at the heart of Nazism, and he defended its detonation. Hamsun went public with his loyalty to Hitler's Germany, and the more he was criticised for these opinions over the coming years, the more sacred they seemed to become to him.

Marie herself published a fervently pro-Hitler article in the Norwegian newspaper *Nationen*. She had visited Germany again and was carefully grooming her husband's and her own extensive German contacts. The couple gave their wholehearted backing to the newly established Hitler-friendly

Norwegian-German Society. As a further indication of support, Hamsun declared he was sending all his children to Germany to learn from the country's exemplary people; it was an opportunity that Hamsun thought should be made available to many more Norwegian youngsters.[76]

The Hamsuns in turn received regular confirmation that their affection for Germany was reciprocated. The Nazi leadership in Frankfurt wanted to honour Hamsun with the Goethe Prize. He refused to take the prize money; it seemed clear to him that under the present circumstances Germany needed every mark it had. On the same day as he wrote expressing his deep concern for the poverty and unemployment suffered by the German people, he demonstrated total lack of concern for the plight of Germans imprisoned for their opposition to Hitler: the organisation War Resisters International received short shrift from him when they asked him for his support in pressurising the Nazi regime to free political prisoners and reinstate some basic civil rights. 'If the [German] government have gone so far as to set up concentration camps,' he told them, 'then you and the world have to understand it must be for good reason.'

He received a stinging reply: 'Dear Herr Knut Hamsun, it is extraordinary to see you lying prostrate before the incarnation of power.'[77]

It was a reaction that undoubtedly reflected the disappointment felt by many Norwegians concerning the politics of their beloved author. Not only was Hamsun still the grand old man of letters, renowned and idolised internationally; his articles and increasingly the political commentary in his novels about the future of Norway had seemed to confirm him as the rightful heir to Bjørnson – the next towering national bard for which this young nation continued to feel such a need.

But there was an increasing feeling that Hamsun was trampling roughshod over the unstated foundations of such a role, namely a sense of solidarity with the oppressed against the oppressor.

Hamsun argued that the Nazi dictatorship's heavy-handed actions were defensible since they were done for the common good. The rebuilding of the German nation, as he saw it, demanded enormous sacrifice. Besides, he argued, did anyone have the moral right to criticise Hitler's Germany? Concentration camps had been invented by the English during the Boer War, along with a host of other monstrous methods used to subjugate the world to the military, economic and political dominance of the Empire. How could the new Germany be criticised for being a little harsh with those who sabotaged its progress? Fascism was far preferable to the iron grip in which the Soviet Union held its people. 'At some time or other, in some form or other, fascism will trickle through to Norway too. Only the blind cannot see the difference between the world and politics before and after the [Great] War', Hamsun had stated in a newspaper article six months earlier.[78]

That summer, Hamsun seriously contemplated seeking an audience with Haakon VII, Europe's only elected king.[79] He probably felt driven as national bard and moral guide to his nation to talk face to face with the king about the need for Norway to strengthen its ties with the Third Reich. The political beliefs he had formed in the last war had not altered: only a strong Germany could protect Norway from the British Empire. If a quasi-neutral Norway turned its back on Germany again, it would play straight into the Englishmen's greedy claws.

Nothing came of Hamsun's desire for an audience with the king. He had to find other opportunities to present Hitler's case publicly.

Father and Son in Goebbels's Clasp

In Berlin, Hamsun's public expressions of support were soon picked up by Joseph Goebbels's Ministry of Propaganda. The Nazis now had complete control of the press, theatre, broadcasting, publishing, visual arts, music, film and universities in Germany. The political credentials of artists, academics and intellectuals were evaluated by the Reich Chamber of Culture. Those who failed to make the grade were either arrested, forbidden to work or merely sidelined. Thousands left the country and were subsequently stripped of their citizenship, among them Thomas and Heinrich Mann and Albert Einstein.

But the vast majority stayed behind to contribute, more or less actively, to the Third Reich's cultural and scientific output. Fear and opportunism were not the only driving forces. Many people found Nazism's anti-intellectualism very appealing.

One such was the writer Gottfried Benn, who explained his confidence in Hitler's regime to his exiled colleague Klaus Mann, Thomas Mann's son: 'And since I grew up in the countryside, and among farm animals, I also still remember what native grounds stand for. Big cities, industrialism, intellectualism – these are all shadows that the age has cast upon my thoughts, all powers of the century, which I have confronted in my writing. There are moments in which this whole tormented life falls away and nothing exists but the plains, expanses, seasons, soil, simple words.'[80]

For years Hamsun had been expressing precisely these sentiments in a host of articles and books. He had been honoured with the Nobel Prize for *The Growth of the Soil*, a novel that stood firm against the modern era and the dominance of reason. He blazed the trail for those who dared to break from the stranglehold of contemporary civilisation and search for answers in the ancient world and the tilling of the soil.

Hamsun's unique status in Germany was largely ascribable to his work chiming so closely with a tradition that had begun in Germany with Neo-Romanticism. This movement argued that the modern world's so-called 'progress' actually represented a serious decline, that the human soul had degenerated and the natural order was in disarray. Successive generations of German authors had taken up the theme, but few had achieved the poetic and penetrative power of Hamsun. In book after book, this prophet from the unspoiled North had worked his way ever deeper into the hearts of his German brethren. He was a Nordic Wagner; both men had succeeded in arousing antipathy towards the ideals and values of modernity, as well as a yearning for a return to the earth and a natural way of life, the dream of a golden age, a paradise.

It was almost as though these two artists had been created to serve the Nazi ideal. And they were certainly put to use. The composer was dead and could not protest, even if he had disapproved. Hamsun's pen, on the other hand, had been active on behalf of the dictator from the beginning.

Adolf Hitler, Joseph Goebbels, Alfred Rosenberg and other Third Reich ideologues skilfully exploited and manipulated people's distaste for the modern age, their anxieties about the future and the lure of nostalgia. They promised to heal society, to give every citizen's life a deeper meaning. The people, party and state would be served by all as one single organism, and the SS would help them attain this goal.

Tore arrived in Munich late that summer to study painting, but after only a few weeks he applied to join the SS. The Nazi Party naturally recognised the value of cultivating a relationship with the great Knut Hamsun's eldest son.

Hamsun meanwhile continued to set aside moral and legal tenets in his quest to defend the expansion of Hitler's Germany. He expressed his delight when, in January 1935, Hitler held a referendum to reunite the Saar (which had been put under international administration under the Treaty of Versailles) with Germany, and won a decisive majority vote in its favour. It had been a predictable outcome, but Hitler used it as evidence of the inherent injustice of the agreement drawn up in Versailles. In Norway, Hamsun was jubilant. The following day he congratulated a German: 'I wish you, and all Germans, good fortune today with the Saar.' In the Nordische Gesellschaft's journal he cautioned all those trying to halt Germany's expansion: 'When the German region of the Saar is completely reunited with its motherland, the tension among these people will be smoothed. There will be new tension if French policy – with England's backing – tries once more to shackle Germany in continued degradation.'[81]

The countries that had established a new order in Europe and a set of treaties built on new principles of international law were incapable of defending their creation. The bulwarks fell. In March 1935, Hitler publicly repudiated the Versailles Treaty, and announced Germany's expansion of its air force and the reintroduction of compulsory conscription. In June, Britain signed an agreement with Germany allowing it to increase its naval strength; it was, in the view of the enraged Churchill, suicide. The vision of eternal peace in Europe had lasted barely fifteen years. The build-up of military force had begun in earnest.

From that summer onwards, there seemed little difference for Hamsun between understanding, explaining and defending Hitler's Germany. He seemed increasingly impervious to any evidence or reasoning that might sway the opinions he had held for so long, and around which he had constructed an entire political belief system. He saw the rivalry between Germany and England as a consequence of the laws of nature. Germany had a need, and thereby a right, to conquer new lands. All good Norwegians should define themselves as Germanic, since ancient blood bonds and centuries of trade and cultural exchange united the two peoples. Norwegians who loved their country must turn to Germany to seek protection from England.

But there was another motivation: Adolf Hitler.

More than most, Hamsun had an intuitive understanding of Hitler's tremendous drive. He was not just Germany's Führer; he was a future leader for Europe, a reformer of the highest order, a warrior for all humanity.[82]

In November 1935, Hamsun launched an attack on the German pacifist and journalist Carl von Ossietzky.

Ossietzky was forty-six, as was Hitler. The two men's lives had, in some respects, run on a strange parallel; both had served as corporals in the Great War, returning home stripped of all illusions and wanting to create a new Germany. But where Hitler had advocated militarisation and expansion, Ossietzky had thrown himself into peace activism and condemnation of his alter ego.

Ossietzky's political work and revelation of Germany's secret military build-up had already resulted in a prison sentence for espionage in 1931. When Hitler gained his majority in the Reichstag immediately prior to the Nazi takeover of power, Ossietzky wrote despairingly of his fellow countrymen: 'The National Socialist Party has finally given fifteen million Germans the party they have always longed for. [. . .] Economic collapse has unveiled the middle classes' inner coarseness, their crude antipathy to culture, their brutal craving for power – traits they had previously attempted to disguise, or reserved for their private lives. Only once before has nationalistic blood thirst and political ineptitude celebrated such unfettered triumph. That was at the outbreak of the war.'[83]

Unsurprisingly, Ossietzky was near the top of the list of people the Nazis wished to arrest. He was sent to a concentration camp where after some time an international delegation visited him. When asked if there was something in particular he needed, Ossietzky requested books on methods of punishment in the Middle Ages, thereby conveying everything the outside world needed to know about the Third Reich's treatment of prisoners. He became a figurehead for various groups across Europe fighting against Hitler's Germany. Albert Einstein, Thomas Mann and the prominent theologian Karl Barth, all Germans in exile, were among those campaigning for Ossietzky to receive the Nobel Peace Prize.

The five Norwegians tasked with finding the worthiest candidate for that honour failed to select anyone in the winter of 1935, drawing speculation that Ossietzky was too inflammatory a choice for the Nobel committee, who generally moved cautiously in troubled international waters. But it was clear that Hamsun wanted to eliminate Ossietzky once and for all from the Norwegian Nobel committee's discussions. He was incensed that Ossietzky, and those of a similar mindset, could threaten his vision of an ever closer relationship between Norway and Germany. He saw them as part of a plot from Moscow. Norway's destiny stood in the balance.

In an article published in two of Norway's major newspapers, Hamsun launched a vitriolic attack on Ossietzky: 'What if Herr Ossietzky helped by being a little positive in these turbulent times, during which the entire world is baring its teeth at the authorities of the great nation to which he belongs? What does he want – is it German military build-up he wishes to demonstrate against, as a man of peace? Would this German prefer his country to remain crushed and humiliated among nations, thrown on the mercy of France and England?'[84]

There was a fierce response to Hamsun's outpourings. Thirty-three Norwegian authors put their names to a joint expression of regret that their literary colleague had trampled on a defenceless prisoner for no other reason than that he had had the courage to stand up for his convictions, and had risked his life in so doing. Hamsun's attack on Ossietzky was commented on in newspapers around Europe; Heinrich Mann criticised him strongly, and the German author Erich Kuttner sent a letter to Hamsun from exile saying that his cynicism revealed a serious flaw in his character.[85]

Conservative newspapers both inside and outside Norway, however, wrote in support of Knut Hamsun, as they had done so often before.

At the Gates of the Kingdom

On the first day of August 1936, Adolf Hitler opened the eleventh Olympic Games in Berlin. 'I call upon the world's youth', intoned the Führer as the olive branch was handed to him. Germany would show the world that claims of terror, oppression, anti-Semitism and rearmament were false, simply scare tactics created by the enemies of the Third Reich.

As soon as this gigantic public-relations stunt masquerading as a sporting contest was over, Hitler announced his extension of conscription to two years. Two weeks later, the dominant theme at the eighth Nazi Party Congress was rearmament. Hermann Göring's phrase – 'Guns before butter' – would be the new directive for the already hard-pressed German people.

At around this time, Hamsun was notified by his German publisher Müller-Langen Verlag that 73,000 copies of *Wayfarers* had been printed. Germany's population seemed to be in his thrall too.

The seventy-four-year-old Hamsun published another novel late that autumn, to which he gave the heavily symbolic title *The Ring is Closed*.

In the three years he had spent writing this book Hamsun had thoroughly absorbed Joseph Goebbels's 1933 call to artists: 'The artist undeniably has the right to call himself non-political in a period when politics consists of nothing but shouting matches between parliamentary parties. But at this moment, when politics is writing a national drama, when a world is being overthrown – in such a moment the artist cannot say: "That doesn't concern me." It concerns him a great deal.'[86]

It was a known fact across the world that Hamsun was using his pen to defend Hitler's Germany. The question for many was the extent to which the artist supped from the same cup as the politicians.

Jørgen Bukdahl, a prominent Danish critic, writer and expert on Hamsun, presented the problem in the Copenhagen newspaper *Politiken*: '[Hamsun] is an admirer of Nazism, with its blood and soil and procreation, and its entire religious "Heimat" culture. And Germany admires him in return as the magnificent, racially pure, blond Teuton. How naïve one can be, when reason leaves and blood enters. The spirit of his work is carried by the exact opposite of Nazism; it is born of a revolutionary individualism and anarchism and is a striking protest against [. . .] the intrusiveness and psychological constraints which go by the names of both communism and Nazism.'[87] The Hamsun who supported Hitler and Nazism was entirely separate from the Hamsun who was capable of writing *The Ring is Closed*. According to Bukdahl, these two figures were deeply at variance with each other.

It was a complete acquittal. Other critics in Norway and elsewhere felt the same. The only person of real standing in Norwegian public life to condemn Hamsun outright was the anthroposophist Alf Larsen. After reading *The Ring is Closed*, Larsen was left in no doubt about Hamsun's political affiliations: 'Hamsun is Nazism before it arrived.' Larsen would not countenance the division between Hamsun's politics and the imaginative content of his works that other critics insisted on: 'He should have created great works for us that could have lifted our hearts and minds and directed our gaze upwards; now he has accustomed us to looking down and only seeing everything that is paltry and twisted and banal: man as an animal. And it is true, it cannot be denied, people have *become* almost like animals, but that is not because they are that way by nature, but because great thinkers like Knut Hamsun have seen them that way, and taught them to see themselves that way.'[88]

In *The Ring is Closed* Hamsun returns to the southern village depicted in *The Women at the Pump*. Abel is the only child of a miserly lighthouse-keeper and an alcoholic mother. As a young boy his heart is stolen by the pharmacist's daughter, Olga. He in turn steals a jewel from a statue of Christ in the church in an attempt to win her love, but she rejects him. She becomes engaged to, and then marries, another man. Abel travels to America and meets Angele, whom he shoots after she discards him, framing her lover and his friend for the crime. The murderer-thief, much older, returns to Norway and confesses his dark secret. Olga is so aroused by the thought of his committing this irrevocable act that she surrenders herself to Abel. Nobody captures her interest in the way that he does. She tries in vain to push him forward in life, but Abel's lack of initiative borders on the pathological.

Abel does not, like so many of Hamsun's earlier characters, hope for a stroke of luck. His only ambition is to stay alive on the barest necessities of life, living in a shack and surviving on other people's leftovers. Here we have echoes of Hamsun's debut novel, in which his narrator explores the physical and psychological effects of hunger and craving. But, by contrast, Abel in *The Ring is Closed* has eradicated any desire he might have. He puts what scant concentration he has into letting any opportunities for another life slip from him: qualifications, inheritance, employment, enduring relationships. Hamsun offers his readers a literary figure that any self-respecting Nazi would find deeply troubling.

Hamsun suggests the same reasons for Abel's flaws and weaknesses as he does for Edevart's in *Wayfarers* and *August*: his roots have been wrenched from the soil, and his dreams of love have been broken. Incapable of living up to any of his own expectations, he represses them and neglects the needs of others. Sexually potent, Abel is existentially impotent.

In Lili, Axel's wife whom Abel seduces, Hamsun had conjured a new image of female sexual perfection: 'The mild Lili had been awakened after all these years of faithful marriage, only now was she awakened to truly erotic experience. Previously it had been nothing more than tolerant duty, sterile duty and compliance, now instead she was more than a little desperate. She made love often and wonderfully, and she did not hide the fact that she was almost crazy for it.'

In the privacy of his writer's cottage, Hamsun could dream up this paragon. He and Marie, whom he had once described as his only love on earth, had for many years been entangling themselves in each other's vicious circles. Hamsun had watched the dream of romantic love turn into a nightmare.

His career as author – and politician – continued to soar to new heights.

On 2 October 1936, the curtain rose on *At the Gates of the Kingdom* in Berlin's Stadttheater. It was a tremendous success. The audiences revered Ivar Kareno: the man who refused to yield, who championed obstinacy, vengeance and hatred as moral ideals, the man who saw war as a preferable option to setting aside his pride, the man who put his trust in the 'natural despot' and the 'great terrorist'.

Kareno, dreamt up by Hamsun forty years before, reviled the English, democracy and pacifism. His words now rang with a prophetic, almost mythical significance in the Third Reich's capital, where expectations were growing for the gates to be flung open, letting the Führer's troops loose to conquer new lands.

One November evening the audience streamed into the Stadttheater unaware that one of their fellow countrymen had been awarded Europe's most prestigious prize earlier that day. The German authorities had not yet released the news about Norway's humiliation of mighty Germany; selected by a Norwegian committee, the 1935 Nobel Peace Prize had been awarded retrospectively to Carl von Ossietzky.

The higher echelons of the Nazi Party had been worried that this might happen, since it presented them with a dilemma. Ossietzky could not simply disappear. If he died in the concentration camp, the world would need some convincing that he had not been murdered; if he survived until the awards ceremony, his presence might prove even more awkward for the Nazi leadership.

Göring ordered Ossietzky to be brought to the Gestapo's headquarters. The prisoner was extremely weak from being tortured and suffering the camp's appalling conditions. He was offered a deal. He would be freed immediately and given a lifelong yearly state pension of 6,000 marks if he agreed to refrain from any contact with peace organisations outside the Third Reich, and to inform the Peace Prize committee in Oslo that he did not wish to be a candidate for the prize.

Ossietzky refused.

News of the Nobel Peace Prize was announced on 23 November, a dark day in the Third Reich's three-year existence. On the following day, Propaganda Minister Goebbels issued a communiqué: 'The awarding of the Nobel Peace

Prize to a notorious traitor is an outrageous challenge and insult to the new Germany, and will be given an appropriate and unequivocal answer.'[89] The Führer himself prepared a decree forbidding German citizens to accept any Nobel Prizes; Germany would establish its own national prize for the arts and sciences worth 100,000 marks.

Hamsun was far from alone in expressing his disquiet and regret at the Nobel committee's decision. *Aftenposten* declared in its editorial that 'the Norwegian people have had no part in the giving of this award. The Peace Prize has been used as a challenge and rapier thrust against those who think differently. It will raise no more than a smile, the only appropriate response for a superior nation.' Heinrich Mann, on the other hand, felt that this was one of the few good pieces of news he had heard for years.[90] The Paris newspaper *L'Air nouvelle* suggested that this particular Nobel award would hold a prominent place in the history of twentieth-century civilisation.

The 1936 prizewinner was Carlos Saavedra Lamas, the Argentinian president of the League of Nations. He arrived in Norway to collect his prize on 12 December. The German authorities, however, had refused to give Carl von Ossietzky permission to attend. It was a sad reflection on the international political situation: the leader of an impotent assembly was present with his entourage, while the citizen of a country that had withdrawn from every world organisation, broken every peace treaty and violated every human rights agreement was incarcerated in a Berlin hospital.

There was another conspicuously empty seat in the Oslo University auditorium: King Haakon VII was absent from the ceremony. The palace gave no explanation.

Germany's plans for expansion were now undeniable. German troops reentered the Rhineland, currently under French jurisdiction. Having thus protected his back against the Western powers, Hitler set his sights on the East, just as he had promised his people he would. Germany and Italy had signed a treaty proclaiming the Berlin–Rome Axis on 25 October, and a month later Germany and Japan agreed the Anti-Comintern Pact directed against their shared enemy, the Soviet Union. Italy would join the agreement the following year.

On 30 January 1937, the Reichstag renewed Hitler's extended powers for a further four years. Goebbels hailed the first four as the greatest political miracle of the twentieth century. Delegations travelled to Berlin from across the world and elsewhere in Germany to admire the Nazi showcase: large-scale building projects including roads, parks, kindergartens and sports facilities; the eradication of unemployment in a nation that, only a few years previously, had had more than four million unemployed; subsidised housing and workers' canteens – the list of successes went on.

In Norway, Vidkun Quisling was one of a growing number of politicians who commented positively on developments in Germany. Hamsun encouraged all who were sympathetic to Quisling's cause to help him raise money.

Hamsun's own financial capacities were formidable.

After regretting selling the rights to his books, he had bought them back from Gyldendal. Hundreds of thousands of marks were streaming into his bank account. In January 1937, *Friar Vendt* premiered at the Stadttheater in Göttingen. *Victoria* was broadcast on German radio. In March, the Stadttheater in Essen produced *Queen Tamara*, which would soon move to Danzig. In May, Hamsun was informed that forty thousand copies of *The Ring is Closed* had already been printed. The theatre in Lucerne staged *The Game of Life*. In the early summer filming began for a German version of *Pan*. In June, *The Growth of the Soil* reached 126,000 and *Victoria* 115,000 copies printed, while *Pan* and a German special edition of short stories had both had print runs of 50,000.

The statements he received from sales in Great Britain were still insultingly derisory in comparison. From 1934 to 1936, his royalties from Britain and the Empire totalled less than 400 kroner.

The build-up of military force in Germany continued. It was no longer a question of if but when Hitler would storm the gates of the British Empire.

I Feel Sympathy for the Jew Too

In the period preceding Christmas 1937, Hamsun decided to travel abroad. Marie would not be accompanying him. The acrimony between the couple had been increasing, and Hamsun wanted to get away, far away from Nørholm and Marie.

In the final pages of *The Ring is Closed* he had sent Abel back to America, and now fifty years after Hamsun had last travelled there, he toyed with the idea of returning himself. He had received several invitations; he might even write his next sequel there. He had discussed with Tore his desire to get away somewhere to write, and one country that had come up in the conversation had been Palestine; Hamsun wanted to see the plantations.[91]

He had read accounts of Jews leaving Europe, the Soviet Union and America to farm land that the Arabs had left uncultivated for hundreds of years. Waves of immigrants were now flooding into Palestine; tensions were running high between native Palestinians and Jews. Increasingly restrictive immigration laws had been introduced across Europe, making it virtually impossible for Jews or gypsies to settle anywhere permanently. The Nazis were swift to exploit this in their propaganda; if Chamberlain and other state leaders were so concerned about the Jewish population, why were they so reluctant to ease their own border controls?

As early as April 1933, Hitler had invoked the first boycotts against Jews, and these had steadily increased. With each tightening of the screw, tens of thousands of Jews were forced to flee. Hitler had revealed his ultimate goal: the rebirth of the nation, the deliberate creation of a new kind of human being. 'Anyone who understands National Socialism only as a political movement knows virtually nothing about it. It is even more than religion; it is the will to the creation of man.'[92]

Some Jewish emigrants hoped to find refuge in Norway. One such found his way to Nørholm in the autumn of 1933. Hamsun called on Harald Grieg for help, and Grieg notified the police. Since the man had no work permit he was put in prison. Hamsun wrote to Grieg to tell him that he felt 'sorry for the Jew too, without land, undoubtedly crazy and without a stone to rest his head on'.[93] If the man wrote to him, Hamsun would slip him a banknote.

Hamsun had no reason to be anti-Semitic. He had come into contact with countless Jews during his lifetime, from the watchmaker in Nordland in his youth to many members of the literary circles of Denmark and Norway. The Brandes brothers were Jewish, as was Christian Kønig. As far back as 1926, Hamsun had published an article in which he gave a broad account of his attitude. In his opinion the Jews were a very talented people. He drew the line, though, at 'the most unsympathetic ones, those who have intermarried with the native population, and in particular their offspring who are so ambitious for advancement in art, politics and literature, the impudent ones, the presumptuous ones, whose talents are often shallow, merely learned by rote'.[94] Taken out of context, these ramblings would be perfect for the Nazi propaganda that came later, but Hamsun went on: 'overall the Jewish people are of high intellectual prowess. Where do we find the equal of their old poetry, their prophets, their songs? And consider how extraordinarily musical these people are, certainly the most musical people on earth.'

The Jewish people should, in his opinion, be brought together in their own land. His reasoning was that this would allow the Jewish people to 'use their best qualities to benefit the entire world' while at the same time ensuring that 'the exclusive white race need not endure any further mixing of blood'. The obstacle to this solution lay, as he saw it, in the two nations he loathed the most: 'In these times, when second- and third-rank nations like France and England persist in acquiring colonies they do not need, there is little chance that they will apportion some of the earth for a sufficiently large Jewish land. But as long as this fails to happen, the Jews have no home other than the homes of others. They must continue to live and work in foreign societies, to the detriment of both parties.'

Two years later his liberal attitude appeared to have hardened. Hamsun's endorsement of a Swedish anti-Semitic book, *Kreuger kommer tillbaka* (Kreuger Returns) caused consternation among those concerned with the plight of the Jews. 'I am completely overwhelmed by your book', he telegraphed the author Gustaf Ericsson, giving him permission to print his praises on the jacket.[95]

At the beginning of February 1938, Hamsun was given an opportunity to see at first hand the consequences of Nazi policy for the Jews.

Arriving at the Stettiner railway station in Berlin, he was met by Tore and Ellinor and the three of them headed to Ellinor's flat. She mentioned casually that she was a member of the Kameradschaft der Deutschen Künstler, an exclusive club of the Third Reich for artists, visited occasionally by Adolf Hitler – and she informed her father that she had indeed met the Führer although she did not tell him all the details of the meeting: Ellinor had been at the club one evening, and had just lit a cigarette when Hitler approached her table. Her companion desperately tried to alert Ellinor in time for her to stub it out, since everyone was aware how fanatically Hitler hated smoking. But he must have been in an unusually good mood, or otherwise determined to leave a good impression on Knut Hamsun's daughter. While the whole room held their breath, Hitler flung his arms open gallantly and exclaimed: 'But, of course, Fraulein Hamsun may smoke her cigarette!'[96]

The Führer's reaction might have been very different had he known that the daughter of Germany's great friend was living alongside Jews. Outside the block of flats where Ellinor rented accommodation stood two benches with large yellow lettering stipulating that these were for the use of Jews only. Hamsun wanted a rest before the three of them went inside. Tore drew his attention to the writing on the bench. Ridiculous nonsense! Hamsun burst out.

Tore, soon to turn twenty-six, had many Jewish friends. One of these was Max Tau, a publisher whose dream was to get a Norwegian resident's permit. Tau and Tore had agreed that Tore's father would be the man to arrange this. In exchange, Tau had organised some illustration work with publishers for the young painter.

Tore planned the meeting between his father and Tau with great care. He took his sister and father to Die Traube, a restaurant that he knew his father would like: spacious and light, with white tablecloths and smartly dressed waiters. Another reason for the choice was that Jews were still permitted entrance here. Tau soon arrived.

Suddenly, in the middle of their meal, all the diners in the restaurant rose and, gazing up at a balcony, began to clap. An elderly man stood there, arm raised high in a Nazi salute as he relished his applause. One of the waiters explained that he was a well-known war hero, Field Marshal von Mackensen.

Max Tau looked down, troubled by what such adulation and warmongering might lead to and what it would mean for his people. Hamsun's reaction went unnoted.

After dinner Tore set to work on his father, giving him a thorough insight into the ruthless consistency with which Hitler's Germany was persecuting its Jewish population. Hamsun was not altogether receptive. He had sympathy for the Jews, of course: Tau seemed a good man, and he was a friend of his son and daughter. But he received so many requests for help from Jews and others who wanted to use his name. If he helped one, it would lead to a stream of other hopefuls making appeals and he would be unable to oblige them all.

While Hamsun was in Berlin, Hitler entered his final confrontation with the country's sceptical military leaders. The purge and complete restructuring of Germany's Foreign Office begun three months earlier was now complete. In a four-hour, uninterrupted speech Hitler explained how Germany would start its push into new territories. In what would be the last government meeting in the Third Reich on 4 February 1938, Hitler ensured that all power was now concentrated in his hands. The dictator was ready to continue with the war that had temporarily been halted by the treacherous treaty of 1919.

On 11 March 1938, the German war machine crossed the Austrian border, the army trailed by SS units prepared to implement an instantaneous crackdown on any opposition and on the Jewish population. Prominent Jews such as Sigmund Freud and Stefan Zweig managed to escape. Many others were killed or arrested. Some took their own lives: one of these was the sixty-year-old Jewish writer Egon Friedell, who jumped from the window of his flat in Vienna as the SS stormed the building.

Friedell had compared Hamsun to Homer in his book *The Cultural History of Our Time*. When Friedell had been told that his *A Cultural History of Antiquity* was to be published in Norway, he had asked Hamsun's permission to dedicate the work to him. Hamsun had been happy to accept.

Neither Hamsun nor Tore was in Berlin when German troops entered Austria. By then, father and son had travelled to Dubrovnik in Yugoslavia, via Bari in Italy. Their original plan to go on from Italy to the Middle East had been abandoned, and they descended instead on this old Croatian town, a favourite destination for wealthy Northern Europeans.

Radio and newspaper reports informed them of Germany's unification with Austria and Hitler's march into Vienna. Hamsun was thrilled. But his delight was stopped short when Tore spotted news of Egon Friedell's suicide in one of the German-language newspapers. Hamsun burst out spontaneously: 'He should have come to me.'[97]

Hamsun was being pressured from various quarters now to voice some disapproval of Germany's actions. He refused, and received yet more letters full of disdain and condemnation. Yet during that spring and summer, he requested that Friedell's *A Cultural History of Antiquity* be sent directly to him by Aschehoug in Oslo as each instalment was published. Hamsun aired his thoughts about Friedell's sad fate to his Norwegian translator: 'I cannot help but think that there must also have been a <u>personal</u> motive for Friedell's suicide. It must still be possible to find out what!'[98] Hamsun's considerable need to justify himself in his own eyes and the eyes of others appeared now to have allied itself with an ardent defence of Hitler's Germany.

Tore did, however, persuade Hamsun to put in a good word for Max Tau. As a result, the publisher was given permission to travel to Norway.

I Feel I Am Decaying

Hamsun failed to make any headway with his writing in Dubrovnik in the spring of 1938. The slips of paper refused to connect. It was as though he had dealt too many awkward cards in *The Ring is Closed*.

At the beginning of May, Tore left Dubrovnik for Norway, first making a short visit to Berlin where Ossietzky was now on his deathbed.

The pacifist had received no visitors for a long time, but that Easter a Norwegian couple had traced him to the poor quarter of Pankow. They were surprised at how well informed he was about political developments in Germany and across Europe. He was convinced Nazi Germany was preparing for imminent war. Conscious of the nationality they shared with Hamsun, who had written so scathingly about the pacifist, the Norwegians apologised for his insults and pro-Nazi involvement. Ossietzky brushed it all aside: 'I do not know him as a person, only as an extraordinary writer.'[99]

He had praised Hamsun in print and had read all his books, apart from *The Ring is Closed*, which had only recently appeared in German. The Norwegians promised to send him a copy as soon as possible, and if they ever met Hamsun to pass on his regards.

On 4 May 1938, just as Tore entered Berlin, a German news agency reported that Ossietzky was dead. Spring, it seemed, had had a detrimental effect on the patient.

Like so many visitors from northern climes, Hamsun had an unrealistic notion about the warmth of the spring in southern Europe. It was not until mid-May that he removed his winter coat – indoors. 'But I'm so stiff with the cold, I'll never thaw again. I don't do any work, don't even attempt to start, don't go out of the house, I sit here being nothing', he moaned to Tore. He reminisced about the times when he could sit and write solidly for long stretches. 'I remember I sat in Paris – to my own enormous surprise, by the way – for sixteen hours at a time without eating, doing nothing but writing. Yes, that was then, now I am good for nothing, even though my brain seems to have improved a little with the warmth.' At the beginning of June he reported, not without some pride, that he had managed to write a poem, and to make some notes for another novel.[100]

At the end of June, he packed up the little he had managed to write during his stay in Dubrovnik. He may well have given up on a sequel to *The Ring is Closed*. He travelled back to Berlin by train and, for the second time in 1938, had an opportunity to taste life in the capital of the Third Reich.

Tore was no longer in Berlin, as he was currently pursuing the affections of a Norwegian pianist, but Ellinor remained – to the detriment of Hamsun's bank balance. He had given his daughter 12,000 kroner during the course of the previous year – four years' salary for an office worker – yet when she visited her Berlin dentist she had asked for the bill to be forwarded to her father.

A third member of the Hamsun family was also in the city: Marie had accepted an invitation earlier in June from the Nordische Gesellschaft, to participate in a Nordic Day in Lübeck at the end of the month.

She examined the guest list, noting the people she already knew as well those whose acquaintance she was keen to make. The crowd with whom she mingled included some of the most significant figures in the Third Reich: Heinrich Himmler, Reich leader Alfred Rosenberg, officials from the Interior and Reich ministries, the leader of the Nordische Gesellschaft and several regional leaders, senior members of the Berlin police, the lord mayor of Lübeck, the chief of the air force training school in Dresden, the chief of staff of the SA and others.[101] Hermann Göring was not present, but Marie had met him in 1936 when she attended a party at his Berlin home. Indeed, Marie, Ellinor and Tore Hamsun had all been courted by some of Nazi Germany's most important men.

Marie had been a star attraction.

After his return to Norway, Hamsun burned many of the notes that he had hoped to transform into another book. As autumn turned to winter he was on the verge of giving up. On 7 January 1939, he wrote to an acquaintance: 'I feel I am decaying, absolutely incapable of work. [...] I shall never "write" again.'[102] His close friends and correspondents were used to his laments over his struggles to write, but there was a different ring to his words this time.

Hamsun would be eighty in a few months' time. In Norway, Germany and elsewhere, publishers began to prepare their jubilee editions. Harald Grieg informed Gyldendal that 1.5 million Hamsun books had been sold in Norway to date, and that he had a trick up his sleeve to reignite interest in Hamsun – an assertion perhaps based more on wishful thinking than on reality.

The new campaign that Grieg had designed was intended to contextualise Hamsun's maverick politics. He printed a selection of Hamsun's old articles in a new volume, hoping to prove that Hamsun had always held strong, controversial views. This, he hoped, would make the author more palatable, in both the short and the long term, to an increasingly politicised readership.

Despite Grieg's best efforts to make his author more marketable in time for his eightieth birthday celebrations, interest in his books – apart from in Germany – was waning. Barely half the Norwegians who had bought *The Road Leads On* three years ago purchased *The Ring is Closed*. Foreign sales were also disheartening.

It was clear that the Nobel Prize winner had knocked a considerable amount off his own value by his public support for Hitler and Nazism. This came to the fore when Hamsun once again offered to sell his book rights to Gyldendal; Grieg wriggled out of discussing this idea in any real depth, blaming turbulent times. Indeed, he was no longer as keen to engage closely with Hamsun, either in writing or in person.

The German government stood at the front of the more modest queue of well-wishers that formed on 4 August 1939.

Adolf Hitler sent congratulations to the octogenarian, as did Hermann Göring, Joseph Goebbels, Baldur von Schirach, Joachim von Ribbentrop and Alfred Rosenberg. The latter described Hamsun as 'the great creator of Nordic characters, and a stalwart friend of the new Germany', continuing: 'Just as you created your characters for the world out of an indestructible will, you have released many similar feelings in the German people and given German literature life-giving impulses.'[103]

The German newspapers marked the occasion with equal enthusiasm. The letters from well-wishers in Germany outstripped those from Norway. Twenty-three German artists and significant figures celebrated him in a separate publication through Goebbels's National Chamber of Literature and the Nordische Gesellschaft. They noted both his contribution to the strengthening of German-Nordic cooperation, and his huge spiritual importance for the new Germany – its artists in particular and its people in general. The greatest names, however, were markedly absent; the Mann brothers and others who had honoured Hamsun on his seventieth birthday had already fled the country and were living as refugees.

To Win or Perish

Three weeks later, in August 1939, the war Hamsun had been waiting for broke out. He had always supported Germany's politics of aggression.

Time after time, the Führer had exposed Britain's and France's lack of determination in defending the borders they had established in the Treaty of Versailles and the League of Nations. Now German forces took significant swathes of Czechoslovakia, and encroached upon the Baltic under the pretence of protecting the oppressed descendants of Germany in Lithuania. Hitler wanted to establish a deployment area for the war he planned against the Bolsheviks, forcing back the Soviet Union's western border and creating a new *Lebensraum* for Germany on the fertile steppes stretching from the countries east of Germany far into the Soviet Union. To this end he wanted to unite Germany with East Prussia, demanding the return of the Free City of Danzig on the Baltic Sea and permission to construct transport lines across the Polish Corridor.

But the Poles refused to give way on both counts. Representatives of the German government contacted Hamsun in connection with his jubilee celebrations, requesting him to write a foreword to a publication justifying Germany's historical territorial claims. It was a task he fulfilled as soon as he returned to Nørholm.

The Poles had to understand that they could not prevent the return of this old German city. Hamsun thought that Poland had started to come to terms with it, but when 'England began to prowl around Germany again from habit, the Poles became obedient once more and handed their country over to be a link in the English chain. [. . .] They trusted the tatters that remained of the Versailles Treaty', he quipped. 'No power on earth can prevent Danzig being taken from them.'[104] Hamsun urged the ethnically German population of Danzig to hold out because 'you are good enough, you are Prussians and belong to the great German nation'.

For more than twenty years, Hamsun had maintained that a repeat confrontation between the young Germany and the old powers of Great Britain and France was inevitable. He had been right. A pact of non-aggression between Germany and the Soviet Union had been signed by Ribbentrop and Molotov late on the evening of 23 August; the two powers had also secretly agreed to divide Poland between themselves, and had set out designs to share the rest of Eastern Europe. But even after this agreement became known, prime ministers Neville Chamberlain and Édouard Daladier had still attempted to put pressure on the Polish, British and French authorities to negotiate with Germany. It seemed to Hamsun that the British and the French were willing to bend to any degree – naturally, at the expense of other nations – to avoid another great war.

The Polish prime minister, Josef Beck, held out, rejecting all attempts at a compromise.

For more than six years, Hitler had been using political pressure to extend his territories at the expense of his neighbours. Now he invaded Poland, and for the first time met with military resistance. On 3 September, Britain and France declared war on Germany.

The Poles had scant defences against Europe's most modern army. Troops on horseback were mowed down by German tanks. On 17 September, the Red Army also invaded. Two days later the occupying forces met in Brest-Litovsk. The world had never seen a war machine able to advance with such speed as the German army. The notion of *Blitzkrieg* – lightning war – was suddenly a bloody reality. The British and French promises to Poland now seemed very hollow; instead of sending military assistance, they set about strengthening their own defence lines towards the western borders of Germany.

Norway declared itself neutral, but from as early as 5 September the British had started to apply pressure on the Norwegian government.

They demanded that Norway stop exporting a number of goods essential to Germany and its war plans. The second demand, which of course undermined Norway's neutrality, was that it should offer large parts of its merchant fleet to the Western powers. The demand was rejected, but it was impossible for little Norway to refuse further negotiations. Britain and Germany were at war, and Norway found itself involved once more.

So far Hamsun's political analysis had proved sharply astute.

I Bring Greetings from Hamsun

A couple of weeks into the war Ellinor Hamsun married Richard Schneider-Edenkoben, who was more than twenty years her senior. He had been given leave from the German campaign in Poland. The couple had met in Berlin; he was the writer and director of a film in which Ellinor, an aspiring actress, had been given a part.

Marie travelled to Berlin for her daughter's wedding, together with Tore, Arild and Cecilia. Rumours spread before and after the wedding that the marriage brought Ellinor and the Hamsun family into close contact with important Nazi circles. Members of the Schneider-Edenkoben family occupied high positions in Nazi Germany; the cousin of Ellinor's new husband had recently been appointed Reich minister of Poland.

Few Norwegians were aware of just how close contacts already were between the Hamsuns and the higher echelons of German society. In 1936, Marie had twice met Goebbels in his office, and Ellinor had accompanied her on one of those occasions. Ellinor had also attended a private function at his home, while Marie had been a guest at a similar party given by Göring.

It was then that Marie had seen Hitler for the first time. The Führer had given a speech in the Deutschlandhalle, Germany's grand new venue. Tickets had sold out weeks beforehand despite the hall having a capacity of twenty thousand – Marie's contacts had nevertheless managed to get her a VIP ticket.

Two years later, in the summer of 1938, in Lübeck, Marie had been invited to lecture on Germany's friend and prophet Knut Hamsun.

The desire to stand on a stage had never deserted her. Neither had the need to communicate a message in which she fervently believed, and to engage in something greater than her marriage. At the same time, this would be a good opportunity for her to bind herself to her husband's works, reinforcing the link between their life together and his books, and negotiating the place she had planned for herself when Hamsun finally stopped writing.

She arrived home from her daughter's wedding on the day of Poland's surrender, 6 October 1939. If international developments did not frustrate her plans, she would return to Germany in five weeks to begin her lecture tour. She could not be prised from the radio, so intent was she on following events in Europe; many other Norwegians were doing the same, although few would have felt as directly involved as the family at Nørholm.

At 8.15pm on Monday, 13 November 1939, precisely to plan, Marie Hamsun mounted the podium to applause in Hanover's town hall. She had tried on numerous outfits before settling on a dark silk dress and a plain bolero jacket supplemented with a solid gold necklace, a gift from her husband.

The hall was decorated with Nazi standards, Norwegian flags and flowers. Few seats were empty. There were many uniformed men in the audience. Germany was at war.

Marie, who would turn fifty-eight in less than a week, was well prepared. She had spent a great deal of time deciding on the opening line of her performance.

'I bring greetings, from Norway, from Knut Hamsun.'[105]

She would repeat it in town after town. It worked like magic.

These words instantly cast her as the bearer of a sacred message. Having read the eightieth birthday messages to Hamsun from Alfred Rosenberg and other prominent Nazis, she knew his works had found a place deep in the hearts of the German people.

After these opening words Marie could steer her speeches in almost any direction. She might focus on her husband's writings, or elaborate on his message in them, conveying his thoughts on the current political situation. Or she might play on her audience's sentiments, describing how Hamsun stood waiting impatiently on the road outside Nørholm for the postman to bring the papers, or quote his political outrage at the despicable conduct of the Western powers and the cowardliness of the Norwegian government which grovelled before the British, or impart his joy at Germany's military triumphs and the Führer's extraordinary will to victory.

By seven o'clock the next morning she was already aboard a train, and at three o'clock in the afternoon she stood on a platform in Dortmund: 'I bring greetings, from Norway, from Knut Hamsun.'

And so on to Bonn, Cologne, Aachen, Rheinhausen, Rheydt, Düsseldorf, Kaiserslautern, Würzburg, Stuttgart. She used the little free time she had to write an article for a Norwegian newspaper and a letter to her husband. 'Morale here is high, those hoping for unrest will be disappointed. [. . .] I have an overwhelming impression of consensus, willingness to sacrifice and trust in Hitler', she assured him. And she had news that must have excited Hamsun greatly, news that was still to take the world by surprise: the Germans had not yet put their newest weapon to use. 'The feeling is that England will soon tire, they have never had to endure war on their own turf, and this will happen now. No German doubts that England must and shall lose! I have been to the front and talked with the soldiers, they were like children, so certain, in excellent humour in the knowledge that the Führer knows what he is doing and how to succeed.'[106]

The following day Marie delivered parts of her lecture programme on German National Radio. That evening she stood on the stage in Nuremberg. Newspaper coverage about her was increasing and her lecture venues were never large enough. Erlangen was her next stop. From there Munich, Vienna, Villach, Breslau, Gablonz, Apolda, Arnstadt, Dresden, Chemnitz. She had planned to take Sunday, 10 December off, but was asked to appear at the Reichsführerinnenschule in Potsdam. It was a prestigious invitation. She needed little persuasion.

Marie Hamsun rounded off her tour in Berlin, where a room had been reserved at the Hotel Kaiserhof. Plans were already under way for another series. During those five halcyon weeks in November and December 1939, Marie must have felt that her time had come at last.

Part V

Nothing but Reality

While Marie was away in Germany in the lead-up to Christmas 1939, Knut Hamsun took over the large room on the second floor. He positioned the enormous table, around which the children had done their homework, so that maximum daylight fell on it. This was where the eighty-year old would now spend his days, reading much and writing a little, mainly letters. He had hung an enormous world map on the wall, which he studied painstakingly as he read the newspapers, marking locations with drawing pins as they were reported on by the war correspondents.

The land of his imagination, of which he had been a tireless explorer for so long, had closed its borders to him. For the first time in his life he had almost nothing but reality to cling to. Perhaps his planned sequel failed to materialise not only because it was too demanding for an elderly man, but because Hamsun found himself so deeply involved in the contemporary drama.

In *On the Cultural Life of Modern America*, written over forty years before, Hamsun had expressed his dismay at American democracy after experiencing it at first hand. It engendered in him a longing for what he described as 'the dazzling chess moves, the massive revolts by individuals, which in a single stroke can propel humanity forward for generations to come'.

He had at last found an individual whom he believed capable of such brilliant leadership: Adolf Hitler. Even if the writer had felt able to apply himself to his novel-writing, it is by no means certain that he would have done so at this point. He would use the power of words for quite a different purpose.

There was a broad political consensus in Norway that the country should stay out of the war, as it had in 1914. In a joint meeting before Christmas 1939, all the Nordic state leaders declared their neutrality. In the eyes of Knut and Marie Hamsun, and other passionate supporters of Hitler's regime, this was mere window-dressing. They were in no doubt that the pro-British Norwegian authorities would try to play the same double game as they had in the last war, assisting the Allies in various ways, including with the provision of important supplies. Under the cloak of neutrality, Norway would work against Germany.

The first four months of the war demonstrated how difficult it would be to resist being dragged into the conflict. The war was moving closer; in December alone, three ships sailing on behalf of the Allies were sunk by German U-boats in Norwegian waters. Purely by dint of geography, Norway rubbed up against all the major players; it shared a border in the north with the Soviet Union, its closest neighbour to the west was Britain, and to the south lay Denmark and Germany. Norway also had Europe's longest coastline, which stretched for 35,793 kilometres; domination of vast areas of the North Atlantic was thus a tangible prize for whoever controlled this little northern country.

Furthermore, Norway was crucial to Germany's supply of iron ore. The Third Reich consumed 11 million tonnes of it annually, almost all of which came from northern Sweden. But for nearly six months of the year the Swedish port of Luleå was frozen over; a railway line had been laid to the Norwegian town of Narvik, whose harbour was ice-free all year. Churchill, First Lord of the Admiralty after the outbreak of war, suggested military intervention and the laying of mines in the northern regions, although these plans were blocked.

Chamberlain, Hitler and Stalin were all fully aware of the frailty of Norway's capacity to defend its neutrality.

As leader of Norway's Nazi-sympathising NS Party, Vidkun Quisling travelled to Berlin for a meeting with Hitler shortly before Christmas. Quisling's sense of his own importance was very inflated given the standing of his party which was the smallest in Norway. He made it clear that he intended to seize power by means of a coup. He purported to have information about a secret agreement between the Norwegian and British governments that Norway's 'neutrality' would be biased towards the Allied forces. After the meeting, Hitler ordered the Supreme Command to investigate how Germany might occupy Norway.

On the day of this meeting, Hamsun wrote a letter to Johan Mellbye, a former Norwegian politician, rebuking him for having terminated his hitherto close relationship with Germany. Mellbye had criticised Hitler's alliance with Stalin, the break-up of Poland and the Soviet Union's attack on Finland. Hamsun again passionately excused Germany's sins: 'We should not scratch at Germany's fresh wounds for the moment. [. . .] Don't you think that Germany itself is ashamed? Surely you must realise that Germany had to act like this, in order not to be strangled by external constraints?' According to Hamsun, the Soviet Union was a puppet and the British were pulling the strings 'to squeeze the life out of what is today a shackled Germany. Our disapproval should not be directed towards Germany. The day Germany has gained breathing space on the Western Front, it will turn round and throw the Russians out of the Baltic Sea and the Nordic countries again. Germany is waiting. We too must wait.'[1]

A British attack on a German ship anchored in Norwegian waters – which had several hundred British prisoners of war on board – sharpened focus in Berlin on the necessity of invading Norway. On 20 March, Nicolaus von Falkenhorst reported that the plans were ready. All that remained was for the Führer to order the attack.

On 1 April, Hamsun published a newspaper article urging Germany to protect Norway from the British: 'The thought of our present situation – and what might lie ahead of us – paralyses us with feelings of impending doom. We have no strength, the Bear from the East and Bulldog from the West are watching us, we are their prey. So many ordinary people in the street are hoping that Germany will protect us – not today, sadly – but when the time is ripe. We want to remain where we are, as we are. We do not want to become part of an alien power. Many of us rest our hopes on Germany.'[2]

Hamsun's prayers were answered. In the early hours of 9 April, Germany invaded Norway and Denmark. Norwegian soldiers put up greater resistance than Hitler's troops had expected. On the fifth day of fighting on Norwegian soil, Hamsun made the final corrections to an appeal he had written to the Norwegian people; he called the article 'A Word for Us'.

The circle was complete. When he had first moved to Nørholm in November 1918, Hamsun had just lost his first war. He had wept bitter tears then over the foolishness of his countrymen who allowed themselves to be deceived by pro-British politicians and the press. Now he watched events repeating themselves. The Norwegian royal family's escape to London, and the propaganda that surrounded their relocation, confirmed in the public's consciousness that Norway's true defender was Britain and its aggressor was Germany. Indeed, all across southern Norway, desperately inadequately armed men fought to halt the progress of the lethal German war machine, sacrificing their lives in the attempt.

Yet Hamsun insisted again and again in his appeal that Norway was not at war. Goebbels himself could not have formulated it better:

But are we at war with Germany? No?

Germany has taken over our defence. We are neutral.

We hear from various quarters that Germany is meeting Norwegian resistance. Some are saying that Norway is expecting help from England. Have we still learned nothing about England's promises and guarantees of help?

The Norwegian people must come to their senses, while there is still time – and before England brings the war to our country.[3]

After trumpeting his views so loudly during those first weeks of the occupation, Hamsun received a great many letters in response. Some praised him, but most expressed anger and, surprisingly perhaps, Hamsun filed away a selection of the vitriolic missives. 'Now that you have shown the Norwegian people what kind of Norwegian you really are, we are burning your books, and after the speech of 2 May the creator of these books deserves the same fate.'[4]

The speech that the anonymous letter-writer referred to was an article that several newspapers had printed, and that had also been read on state radio. In it, Hamsun called on Norway's resistance fighters to lay down their arms: 'It is no use everybody grabbing guns, and standing there, mouths frothing at the Germans; tomorrow or some other day you will be bombed. England is in no position to come to your aid, in your little groups, rambling about the valleys, begging for food. Norwegians: throw down your guns and return to your homes. The Germans are fighting on behalf of us all, and breaking England's tyranny against all neutral countries like our own.'[5]

Some Norwegians saw the occupation as an advantageous opportunity: in the upheaval, certain issues might be brought back onto the political agenda. One of these was a lawyer, still aggrieved at Norway's failure to reclaim Greenland from Denmark in 1933 at the International Tribunal in The Hague. He approached Hamsun for help, since he clearly had considerable faith in his powers of influence: 'He is the Norwegian with the biggest name in Germany. If he puts Norway's case forward, it will be hard for the Germans to ignore him.'[6] The lawyer asked Hamsun to contact Hitler's right-hand man in Norway, Reichskommissar Josef Terboven, about the issue.

A successful Nazi Party man, Terboven had arrived in Norway on 26 April 1940, two days after his appointment, with orders to establish calm, order and security in the occupied territories. He was given absolute power in his pursuit of these goals. In his first public speech in Norway, Terboven reassured the country: 'The German people hold an open hand out to the Norwegian people, in honesty and sincerity, ready to engage in brotherly cooperation founded on mutual respect.'[7]

Hamsun certainly took the new Norwegian ruler's words of friendly cooperation at face value. Not long afterwards he wrote to him, broaching the subject of Greenland. He was, Hamsun said, fully aware that Germany had more on its mind than a little island in the North Sea stolen from Norway by the Danes in 1814. But Hamsun informed Terboven that Denmark now intended to sell Greenland. 'Allow me, Herr Reichskommissar, to lay my prayers before you: that the sale of Greenland must at least be postponed. This is all Norway's prayer.'[8]

In a draft of the letter, which Hamsun sent to the lawyer, he added a note asking if he should also write to the German foreign minister, Joachim von Ribbentrop: 'If you feel I ought to contact Ribbentrop in German, I shall do that too. He has been well disposed towards me.' Hamsun clearly felt he could influence the German authorities over this pressing issue. Ribbentrop who was the high protector of the Nordische Gesellschaft, had met Marie on her recent trip to Germany and had sent the prestigious author his warmest regards. Close contacts were already well established between Nørholm and Berlin.[9]

When the Danish critic Tom Kristensen heard that Hamsun had come out in support of Germany, even after Hitler's invasion of Norway and Denmark, he burst into tears: 'To think that Nazism had at its disposal a magic flute with such a wondrous tone, so wondrous that we couldn't afford to cast it from us.'[10]

Yes or no, Herr Reichskommissar?

Reichskommissar Josef Terboven had, of course, been thoroughly briefed on the special relationship between the Hamsun family and the new Germany. Terboven was uniquely positioned to assess their usefulness and exploit the ties.

He immediately sent an assurance to Hamsun that his enquiry about Greenland would be given the utmost priority, both in the Reichskommissariat and in Berlin. He promptly sent three of his men down to Nørholm. Their visit bolstered all Hamsun's positive impressions of Germany: the swiftness of the Reichskommissar's reply, their general thoroughness, the assurance of good will towards the Norwegian people. The main topic of conversation was Greenland, but Norway's future rule was also discussed. Hamsun was keen for a new government to be put in place, peopled by Norwegians and led by Vidkun Quisling as prime minister. 'Quisling is a man of quality [. . .] more than simply a politician, he is a thinker, a constructive spirit.'[11]

Quisling made several visits to Hitler during the summer and autumn of 1940, as did Terboven. The Reichskommissar and the NS Party leader were adversaries from the outset. Each attempted futilely to oust the other. On 25 September, Terboven announced that the Norwegian government and Parliament, as well as the royal family, were now permanently abolished. A National Council would be put in place, of which nine out of the thirteen cabinet members would be selected from the NS Party. Responsibility for overseeing that this council fulfilled its duties according to the directives of the occupying force went not to Quisling but to Terboven's National Commissariat.

Three days later Hamsun wrote a newspaper article arguing that Quisling was the right man to lead the country.

Norway's other recent Nobel Prize winner, Sigrid Undset, had given a press conference in New York in which she had warned America and other free nations to guard against traitors. She lamented that Norway had viewed these people as nothing more than eccentric fools. The two men she had most in mind were not difficult to identify: Knut Hamsun and Vidkun Quisling.

Later that year the exiled Thomas Mann, another winner of the Nobel Prize, discussed the deplorable situation in Norway, expressing sadness at the fact that Norwegian writers had, with the exception of Knut Hamsun, been silenced. He described Hamsun as 'a man who has given us magnificent books which I admire greatly. His misfortune is greater than ours'.[12]

Until the occupation and well into the summer of 1940, politics had become one of the few topics that Marie and Knut Hamsun could discuss without acrimony, but this too became tainted now. Conflicts rarely stemmed from a difference of opinion; it was more often a question of the balance of power between them.

Marie set off for Germany via Denmark. She was to visit her daughter Cecilia who was studying art at the academy in Copenhagen, and then to travel on to Germany to see Ellinor and to plan another tour. Meanwhile, Hamsun was on a political mission to Berlin.

Plans were afoot for three pro-German Scandinavians – former president of Finland Eivind Svinhufvud, Swedish explorer Sven Hedin and Knut Hamsun – to seek an audience with Hitler to strengthen links between Finland and Germany, thus easing pressure from Stalin. Hamsun had another reason for wanting this meeting: presenting the Greenland issue to Foreign Minister Ribbentrop in person. Arild would accompany him on the journey.

However, the planned meeting with Hitler failed to materialise; neither did the hard-pressed Ribbentrop find time to meet Hamsun. But Hamsun did taste the terror of war at first hand. On 7 October, the British carried out the most extensive retaliatory bombing of Berlin to date; Hamsun and Arild would have been in the city by that point, as would Marie. Ellinor and her husband lived in Berlin, but also owned a farm in Wefelsfleth in Holstein, where the family sought refuge. From here, Hamsun, Marie and Arild travelled back to Norway, where an invitation was waiting for Hamsun.

Goebbels was to visit Norway in late November 1940, and naturally Hamsun was on the guest list for his grand reception. He declined the invitation, most likely because he was hoping for an exclusive meeting with Goebbels. A second invitation arrived, inviting Hamsun to meet the propaganda minister in Berlin on 20 January.

Before Christmas, however, it would be Marie who headed back to Germany. Her new lecture tour was to extend even further than her last, when she had visited a not inconsiderable thirty towns and cities. This time Marie was to cover every corner of the country in the course of three months.

The combination of Marie and Knut Hamsun was irresistible to the German public, and she always spoke to packed houses. The various German editions of *The Growth of the Soil* totalled sales of close to half a million copies while *Victoria* had sold out in an edition of 270,000 copies, with a second edition of a further 110,000. As an author in her own right Marie was also enjoying substantial success with over 100,000 copies of her children's books in print.

After nine months of German occupation, thousands of Norwegians had been arrested. Hamsun was largely indifferent to their plight. They had got themselves into this futile and unnecessary position, he thought; it was foolhardy and politically misguided to oppose the occupying forces. At the start of January, he recorded a radio interview saying as much. 'We have to reconcile ourselves with the way things are today. This is not only wise, it is Norway's only salvation.'[13]

But Hamsun could not quite push aside thoughts of his countrymen's tragic plight. When Harald Grieg wrote to him to 10 January 1941 asking for his help in obtaining the release of Ronald Fangen, the chairman of the Norwegian Writers' Union, Hamsun consented. Fangen was the first author to be arrested by the Germans in Norway.

Grieg suggested he contact the Gestapo but Hamsun, as was his wont, went to the very top. And Reichskommissar Terboven was certainly keen to meet the man who was soon to enjoy Goebbels's undivided personal attention in Berlin.

In the middle of January, Norway's occupying ruler received Hamsun at his residence, Skaugum, previously the Norwegian crown prince's abode. Tore accompanied his father to act as interpreter.

Terboven had made an excellent career for himself in the Nazi Party; Hitler had been his best man in 1936. He had a quick mind, and his ability to handle himself in the face of political wrangling was even more impressive. He had a capacity to focus utterly on his goal, which at present was achieving complete control in Norway. But one of his most useful attributes perhaps was his complete lack of conscience.

The German also had an absolute grasp of the importance of propaganda. There was good reason for him choosing to meet the author in this particularly symbolic location. As soon as Hamsun had got a good light on his cigar, an *Aftenposten* photographer arranged by Terboven burst into the room and fired a flash. As it went off for a second time, Hamsun almost managed to turn away. He did not disguise his fury. Terboven immediately waved the photographer away, but he had captured what had been requested: the perfect picture of Knut Hamsun engaged in pleasant conversation with the Reichskommissar.

In reality the conversation was anything but pleasant.

Hamsun was still boiling over from the intrusion, and Terboven's manner made things worse; Tore knew all too well that this pent-up rage would soon find an outlet.[14] The rumours about Terboven's rigidity and his uncompromising opinions were, it became clear, well founded. Hamsun petitioned the German's sympathy, mentioning Fangen's poor health; he told him that the arrest had drawn enormous negative attention, and thus a release might have a favourable effect on public opinion. But Terboven was not to be swayed. He began leafing demonstratively and laboriously through the reports of Fangen's trial, reading an endless stream of quotations from the interrogation records, intent on proving that Fangen was anti-German. Finally, Hamsun exploded, demanding a straight answer: yes or no. There was no need for Tore to translate the answer.

The meeting was over.

Even If Hitler Himself Invited Me

The Reichskommissar and the author parted with diminished respect for each other on that January day.

Terboven had expected, from reading Hamsun's articles and Goebbels's own reports on the Norwegian, that Hamsun would be strong and uncompromising in his stance towards all of Germany's enemies. The man Terboven had met was, in his opinion, a sentimental, rambling and confused old fool. Hamsun, meanwhile, had expected to find a polite, welcoming and respectful Reichskommissar, a wise 'nobleman' who would understand that his distinguished guest would not bother him with a trivial matter, but that this was something in the interests of their respective countries. Instead the meeting had been a carefully planned propaganda coup.

The following day a prominent article appeared in *Aftenposten* accompanied by the compromising photograph, describing how thoroughly Hamsun had enjoyed his delightful visit to the Reichskommissar's residence the previous afternoon. The article also reported that Terboven had invited Hamsun to accompany him by plane to Germany; in fact he had, but Hamsun had not exactly accepted with pleasure, as the newspaper claimed. There was no mention of Hamsun's appeal for the release of Fangen, the reason for the visit in the first place.

No doubt Hamsun dreaded taking that flight with Terboven to Berlin. But his spirits would have been lifted by what awaited him at the other end: talks with Goebbels about Norwegian-German affairs, which he expected to be conducted in a rather different atmosphere of mutual trust and respect.

It was to be a very short flight. The wheels had barely left the ground before the plane bumped back down to earth again. When the passengers got out they realised the plane had come to a halt at the top of a slope leading down to the sea. A prickly Terboven ordered schnapps to be served in the waiting hall before they went their separate ways. Hamsun and Tore were informed that another flight would be aranged. Day after day they were told they would have to continue to wait owing to poor flying conditions. On the eleventh day, flying conditions were much improved, but Goebbels and his entire family were now bedridden with influenza. Hamsun's visit to the propaganda minister was postponed indefinitely.

On 30 January Hamsun returned to Nørholm, disappointed but with no intention of reneging on his participation in the future of Norway. In a newspaper article he set out the basis for a German-Norwegian partnership, calling again on the commonality he saw: 'Just as our two countries have in earlier times been closely bound in trade, learning, travel and the basics of life, so a rich cultural period will flourish again in Norway and the North, which is founded on German philosophies. The conditions are all in place. This is not a prophecy, it is based on solid knowledge and historical intuition. It is a deep consciousness of both the known and the unknown, rooted in kinship and blood. We are all Germans.'[15]

In spring 1941, Reichskommissar Terboven's men contacted Hamsun again to ask whether he would now care to visit the influenza-free Goebbels. The short and swift reply delivered through Tore was: 'I shall not travel to Germany, I cannot speak German, I am deaf and I am eighty-two years old, so I am not some attraction to be carted around and shown off. [. . .] Everything taken into account, I wouldn't drag myself to Germany, even if Hitler himself invited me.'[16]

Hamsun had decided to sidestep the Reichskommissar. What the grand old man of literature wanted now was to talk with the dictator himself.

Hamsun continued to propound his message for Norway. In a further article, which was published in numerous newspapers, he wrote: 'Germany has given us its word that it will respect our national freedom and independence entirely. This is as good as an oath. But our obligation is to ensure that we deserve this promise: as a united Norway we will join in union with the other European states under German National Socialist leadership. This is our task.' Hamsun seemed to have a new ruthlessness about him. No mercy would be shown to those who resisted: 'Any opposition will be crushed.'

Hamsun's vision for Europe had been thirty years in the making, and now it would finally be realised: 'Hitler has not hidden it from us: Germany will rule us and Europe! We are finished with England. We have glimpsed our salvation and refuse to be exploited and used by the long-in-the-tooth British in the future. We have changed direction, and are venturing into a new era and a new world.' In conclusion, he gave his oath of allegiance: 'So much has been written by so many about our future. But of them all, Hitler has spoken to my heart.'[17]

Hamsun was well aware that this declaration of allegiance would be registered by men who had the Führer's ear. On 1 December 1941, he completed his longest wartime article, written specifically for the extremely influential German magazine *Berlin–Rom–Tokio*. Like an Old Testament prophet he condemned the unjust – Churchill, Stalin and Roosevelt – and held up the righteous: Hitler.[18]

The Bolsheviks had, he argued, destroyed the Russian soul: 'The Russians had their unique character, something was still left of their origins, but now after twenty-four years of Bolshevism it has vanished in a daily routine of iron, blood and cement. [. . .] There is no compassion, no mercy today, only blood.' The English, on the other hand, were the most cowardly people in Europe, the world's most educated nation of butchers, a country prepared to make a pact with the devil if the opportunity arose – witness the secret alliance of Churchill and Stalin.

It had been a worldwide conspiracy to break Germany once and for all, set in motion years earlier. 'When the English joined forces with the Bolsheviks, a third partner was already waiting in the wings: America. They needed to equip themselves with men and weapons, because a big war lay ahead of them. The Bolsheviks wanted to rescue their world revolution, and the English their empire. Germany had to be destroyed, even if that meant all of Europe went down. It did not weigh heavily in the scales of these two partners, nor the third, that by doing this they would sacrifice millions of soldiers' lives, that they would erase the whole of European cultural life, and drive its countries back to barbarism.'

The evil trio had come together to plot how they might 'finish Hitlerism off and break Germany's spine. But victory was not to be had so easily, since the greater part of Europe was standing behind the much-hated Germany now. [. . .] He's an enterprising fellow, that President Roosevelt. He can delay England's ultimate fate, or push it forward, but he cannot prevent it. He can send money to China and weapons to the Soviet Union, but he cannot alter the joyous fact that the Bolsheviks' time in Europe is coming to an end. He may be able to prolong the war, but in the meantime the new order in Europe is fast advancing, since all nations are cooperating politically, financially and culturally with the Axis Powers.'

Hamsun's article caught the attention of Goebbels. 'Hamsun has written an enormously witty, and also exceptionally insightful article. [. . .] Hamsun is one of modern Europe's foremost intellectuals, who has always remained true to the banner of the new order',[19] he trilled.

In 1940, Hamsun had called on young Norwegians to throw down their guns and not waste their lives in resistance against German forces. Just six months later he was urging them to volunteer for the Eastern Front.

In the summer of 1941, a legion of Norwegian volunteers was incorporated into the SS to fight alongside their German brethren against the Russians. They needed the manpower: the gruelling winter, colossal distances and relentless military resistance had stopped the advance of the German campaign towards Moscow. Hamsun's twenty-nine-year-old son Arild joined up with numerous other volunteers from many countries.

The majority of Norway's young men, however, did not follow the old writer's fiery call to arms. Quite the opposite, in fact: they concocted various ways of resisting the occupying forces and those who served them. In the course of the next four years, twenty thousand Norwegians would be interned in Grini, the principal prison camp in Norway used for political prisoners. Many of them were remarkably young.

Hamsun had frequently written about the problems caused when the old are out of step with the young. It did not seem to occur to the elderly author that this might now be applicable to him.

In the early hours of 26 November 1942, the deportation of Norwegian Jews began: 582 were put aboard the *Donau* after being rounded up by the Norwegian police. Very few people had yet realised the scale and ferocity of this monster that Hitler had unleashed. Out of an eventual total of 762 Norwegian Jews sent to German concentration camps, fewer than thirty would survive.

After Germany's invasion of the Soviet Union, the aggressiveness of the occupying forces had increased not only to Jews, but anybody who showed the least sign of opposition to them or the NS Party. Resistance was classified as an attack on Germany, carried out by saboteurs working in tandem with the British. Norway was the deployment zone for Germany's campaign against the Bolsheviks, and was thus of great importance to the Nazi forces. Ports along the entire length of Norway's coast were used by German U-boats and warships as bases for attacks on Allied convoys transporting weapons and equipment to the Soviet Union. Hitler was increasingly convinced that the Allies would try to liberate Norway, and as a result continually strengthened security there. The German military presence was impacting deeply on the lives of ordinary Norwegians.

As the years of occupation passed, the regime grew more brutal in its treatment of prisoners. The threshold for crimes punishable by death was continually being lowered. During the first year only a few Norwegians had been condemned to die, and all but two of the sentences had been commuted to imprisonment. By 1942, however, the death toll had risen to 121. Despairing relatives turned increasingly to Nørholm, begging for the help of the influential couple in securing the release of detainees or in saving those condemned to death. Knut and Marie Hamsun tried to sway the authorities, but only rarely did their appeals bring results.

Hamsun was sure of one thing: that Terboven's rule of terror was crushing any vision of Norway playing a prominent part in the future of a Greater Germany. Strings were being pulled behind the scenes for Hamsun to be given an audience with Hitler.

The Web of Destiny

Despite his best efforts, Terboven failed to remove Quisling from the Norwegian political scene. As the leader of the NS Party, Quisling had a great deal of influence over the government established in October 1940, despite his not being included in it. In February 1942 he was appointed as minister president with, on paper at least, the powers that had been held by the king and parliament.

Quisling had written to and periodically had meetings with Hitler throughout the occupation. His objectives were to agree a peace settlement between Norway and Germany, as well as a constitution giving Norway home rule and a treaty ensuring a leading position for Norway as part of a Greater Germany – goals that were largely confluent with the feelings of Knut Hamsun.

Before the end of 1942, Quisling estimated that no more than one in a thousand Norwegians supported the occupying German regime headed by Terboven. As the new year wore on, it seemed to him that support was dwindling even further. This was one of the driving factors for his requesting another meeting with the Führer in early 1943.

On 19 April, Quisling met Hitler in Klessheim Castle close to Berghof, the Führer's summer residence. Terboven was present, and watched gleefully as Hitler bombarded his visitor, as so often, with an endless stream of monologues. Hitler was unable to make Quisling any promises about Norway's future or the new European order under a Greater Germany. The war, Quisling was emphatically told, had to be won first.

The minister president was undeterred, however. He was determined that the Norwegian position should be put forward. Hamsun, indisputably the most well-known and respected Norwegian in Germany, was the perfect man for the task. Final preparations for Hamsun to visit Germany were put in place.

Hamsun was soon to be eighty-four years old. He had avoided making any appearances at large gatherings for years, irrespective of who made the request, but this time he made an exception. That June in Vienna, five hundred writers from forty countries would gather, including an assembly of the most outstanding representatives of literature from Germany.

Edwin Dwinger, a German writer, eulogised their guest of honour:

> How many authors that Germany has brought to the world have abandoned us during the war – always abandoned us? How many have forgotten, not only that we made them known to the world, but also that we loved them? – But they have allowed their hearts to be confused by cheap hatred. Hamsun stands alone at our side – in a storm from every side, and so we thank him, not just for his art, which has enriched our people beyond words – but we thank him also for his unshakeable position which gives us as much strength now as his work did for a generation. For, can we think of anything more encouraging than the knowledge that the greatest living writer in our time stands on our side?[20]

Hamsun could not be tempted by money or prestige, but the old man could not resist that other most desirable object: power. It was the possibility of gaining the power to influence the fate of his country – steering Norway to take a leading role in a future Greater Germany – that had now seduced him. It was with this in mind that he had agreed to attend the Vienna Congress in June, expecting that if he did so, his greatest wish would be fulfilled: an audience with the Third Reich's Führer himself.

Marie later described her husband's preparations for the event:

> It hit him like a bolt of lightning that if he could go, the opportunity might present itself to have Terboven removed. He grew utterly obsessed with the idea, although any politician could have told him it was a poet's dream and no more. For weeks he sat with his head filled with thoughts, playing patience and mumbling and learning by heart, sometimes I could hear him through the walls and floor, just as when he wrangled with August in his room. [...] Every day [it was as though] he stood face to face with Hitler, going over the same phrases again and again, the best he could come up with. And then Hitler would perhaps answer this or that, and then Knut Hamsun would think up another response ... Day after day he sat writing, crossing things out, building, tearing down. He used to get up restlessly and tiptoe round the room in the same nervous way as he did when he was working on a manuscript. He was as anxiously protective of his writing table as a broody bird over its nest. If anybody wanted to come in, he would always meet them at the crack in the door.[21]

It is, of course, perfectly reasonable that the prospect of meeting Hitler threw Hamsun's fraught nerves into such disarray. But it is unlikely that the possibility of coming face to face with the Führer struck Hamsun only now. He had probably been preparing for a direct dialogue with Hitler ever since his first distressing meeting with Terboven in January 1941, and repeated invitations from Goebbels would only have strengthened his conviction that such a meeting might eventually be possible. When Goebbels extended another invitation to Hamsun, the elderly writer accepted.

A visit to Goebbels would mean Hamsun making two flights to Germany in the space of a month, but he was fully determined to meet both the minister and ultimately the Führer.

Around mid-May 1943, Hamsun's eldest daughter, Ellinor, who suffered increasingly from mental illness, anorexia and alcoholism, was to be brought home from a clinic in Baden-Baden. The plan had been for Marie to travel alone to fetch her, but Hamsun now accompanied her to Berlin.

On 19 May 1943, Magda and Joseph Goebbels entertained Hamsun and Marie in their mansion in Hermann-Göring Strasse. The couples spent two hours together.[22]

The talented Goebbels had risen up the ranks, and was now the third most powerful man in the Nazi hierarchy. His latest directive was to whip up the masses in Germany and its occupied territories into such a great psychotic frenzy that they would sacrifice and endure anything in the name of the Third Reich. Goebbels was a master of propaganda, a political genius who could elevate lies to such an extent that they metamorphosed into truth. Recently he had turned his attention to the necessity of 'Total War'.

Although Marie had previously met Goebbels, this was her husband's first encounter with him. Minister and writer made a huge impression on each other. Goebbels mentioned in his diary that when they stood face to face, Hamsun was so moved that tears came to his eyes and he had to turn away.

Goebbels struggled to communicate with the increasingly deaf author. Marie had to holler translations into her husband's ear, but the comments she passed on were all complimentary: Goebbels declared Hamsun to be one of the world's greatest writers. During their conversation it was mentioned that his *Collected Works* were no longer read in the Nordic countries. Goebbels burst out that this was a disgrace, and decided there and then that the *Collected Works* should be reprinted in an edition of 100,000 copies. The writer declined gracefully, pointing to Germany's dreadful paper shortage.

The two men also discussed politics. Goebbels made a note of the fact that Hamsun expressed disdain for the British, and that his belief in a German victory was unshakeable.

On his return to Nørholm, Hamsun resumed work on the speech he planned to give in Vienna, and even more importantly on what he intended to say to the Führer about Terboven's brutal regime and his hopes for Norway's future. He also racked his brain to think of a suitable way of thanking Goebbels. On 17 June, he hit upon a solution. Some years previously Selma Lagerlöf had called upon writers to sell their medals to raise funds to help Finland; now Hamsun would sacrifice his Nobel medal for Germany's cause. He sent his gift to the minister with a note: 'Nobel established his prize for the previous year's most "idealistic" writing. I know of nobody, Herr Reichsminister, who has unstintingly, year after year, written and spoken on Europe's and humanity's behalf as idealistically as yourself. I ask your forgiveness for sending you my medal. It is of no use to you whatsoever, but I have nothing else to offer.'[23]

Less than a week later, Goebbels sent a letter of thanks. He felt humbled and could not have accepted this mark of respect 'if I had thought it was intended for myself and my own public duties, but I see it as an expression of your allegiance to our fight for a new Europe, and for a happy society'.[24]

The minister did not, however, make any mention of the possibility of a forthcoming meeting between Hamsun and the Führer; meticulously tight security surrounding the German leader meant that appointments could only be confirmed at the last minute, and it was strictly forbidden to discuss possible plans either publicly or privately.

On the very day Goebbels dated and signed his letter of thanks, Hamsun was already back in Berlin for the second time in a month.

He Shall Succeed!

On Tuesday, 22 June 1943, Hamsun flew from Fornebu, outside Oslo, to Tempelhof in Berlin. From there he was driven the short distance to the renowned Adlon Hotel where he would spend the night before travelling on to Vienna.

It was from this hotel that he wrote a letter to his daughter Victoria that broke a twelve-year silence. Just before leaving Nørholm, he had received news from her of Bergljot's death. 'I think of your poor dead mother,' he wrote kindly, 'and bless her for her heart's innocence, we have in all her admittance to Heaven [sic].'[25]

His letter was riddled with mistakes. It was not the result of grief or carelessness. A little over a year previously, Hamsun had been found slumped on the floor in the dining room after having suffered a brain haemorrhage. He had stayed in hospital for several weeks and made an amazingly speedy physical recovery; but he had been left with difficulties in finding the right words, both in speech and writing. Slowly he recovered the ability to spell correctly, but the aftereffects continued to hamper him. He generally eliminated most mistakes and weaknesses in style by taking his time and making several drafts of letters. But with his stay in Berlin being so brief and his reply to his daughter being so urgent, on this occasion he had not caught them all.

Arriving in Vienna the next day, he was received by an official delegation that included representatives of the German Propaganda Ministry, the Norwegian Reichskommissariat and the NS Party. After resting briefly at the Hotel Imperial, he was brought to the Wiener Hofburg Theatre. Here, Otto Dietrich, Hitler's press chief, escorted him to the place of honour at the front of the hall while the five hundred-strong assembly greeted the grand old man of literature with a long standing ovation. Once everybody was seated, Dietrich introduced the guest of honour. As Hamsun rose, the applause broke out again before settling into hushed silence as he began to speak.[26] Hamsun delivered a shortened variation on the speech he had given when accepting his Nobel Prize almost twenty-three years before. He apologised for his great age, but hoped that those present, representing all the peoples of Europe, would accept the greetings of a writer from the far North. He had written books before he had grown too tired, and since he was no great orator he would have to count on their benevolence.

His words were translated for the audience, and another long round of applause broke out. Then Arnt Rishovd, editor of *Fritt Folk*, the main publication of the Norwegian NS Party, came to the platform and read the strident, uncompromising political message of the man who moments earlier had joked about being so old and tired.

Hamsun had come to give his testimony: 'I am deeply and fervently anti-Anglophile, anti-British, and I cannot remember being anything else.' Throughout his long life he had registered how the greater part 'of all the unrest, the troubles, the oppression, broken promises, violence and international conflicts have England as their source. We can even thank England for the present war and worldwide misery. England is the source. England must be brought to her knees!'

He went on to express his unconditional love for Germany: 'One country withstood the poison of England's politics, a great and powerful land, Germany.' Germany had, he said, been dragged against its will into World War I. It had fought bravely against four continents, but had suffered defeat from within: 'Little by little with the passing years, the German people were infiltrated by foreign elements that infested and weakened the Germanic spirit – it suited England well, Germany had to be weakened. An overflow of unGermanic peoples and races gorged themselves in the country and exploited the population who had been exhausted after the war.'

He described how dark years had followed. Then the era of National Socialism had dawned in Germany; 'a revelation, a miracle of will and Germanic power. Adolf Hitler was indeed "der Führer".'

On this first day of the conference, Hamsun had already proved over-whelmingly that he should be given access to the Führer. The next day his testimony appeared in all the newspapers in Germany, as well as across the rest of Europe, under the title that Hamsun himself had fed the journalists in the final rallying words of his speech: 'England must be brought to her knees!' The Nobel Prize winner's unshakeable conviction that the Führer would ultimately be crowned with glory was commented on everywhere.

Propaganda Minister Goebbels was no doubt glowing with pride as he showed the newspapers' commentaries and extracts of Hamsun's speech to the leader of the Nazi Party: 'Adolf Hitler, that remarkable man who has steadily pushed the entire world on end – and is now turning it over onto its other side! He shall succeed!'[27]

Marie Hamsun had not accompanied her husband on this trip. Owing to the politically sensitive nature of any meeting with Hitler, neither she nor Tore was considered suitable to act as Hamsun's translator. The two men who had travelled with Hamsun from Oslo to Vienna were, however, amply qualified: Herman Harris Aall, a doctor of law and philosophy; and Egil Holmboe, who worked for the Justice Department. Both were experts in international law.

In fact a meeting with Hitler was far from certain. Not even Goebbels was in a position to guarantee Hamsun such an opportunity, although he must surely have had his eye on its potential propaganda value. Hamsun, on the other hand, must have been under the impression that this meeting was a fore-gone conclusion, otherwise he would never have agreed to making two visits to Germany, nor put himself through the ordeal of attending the congress. Indeed while he had been in Vienna, he confided to the Swede Leon Ljunglund that the sole purpose for his journey to Germany was to meet Hitler and to ensure the removal of Terboven.[28] Besides, Hamsun could hardly have imagined the dictator having anything against meeting him. But despite Hitler's weakness for royalty and state leaders, he had no interest in writers, and certainly none in meeting a deaf old man. And as far as Hitler was concerned, Hamsun had received ample reward by being entertained by Goebbels. When the gauleiter of Vienna, Baldur von Schirach, a keen Hamsun admirer himself, also suggested to the Führer that he might find it interesting to meet Hamsun, Hitler's reaction was, a secretary noted, far from positive.[29]

It was not until 24 June that Goebbels was given final confirmation that the meeting would take place.

You Understand Nothing!

On the morning of Saturday, 26 June 1943, Otto Dietrich, Egil Holmboe and Knut Hamsun drove out to Aspern, where Hitler's private plane, a Focke-Wulf 200 Condor, stood waiting. The journey lasted forty-five minutes, during which Dietrich tried to yell into Hamsun's ear the names of all the impressive mountaintops they flew over. There was time for refreshments, and Hamsun took a large glass of cognac.

A large Mercedes drove the party the 15 kilometres up to Berghof itself. Hamsun sat in the front of the car. Dr Aall had not been invited to join them; Hamsun's hosts felt it would be easier to ensure the meeting retained the tone of a courtesy visit without the presence of this prominent member of the NS and friend of Quisling.

Hamsun had been granted a meeting with Hitler at the lowest point in the latter's time as Führer so far. The Third Reich had reached its zenith the previous summer, when Germany occupied twenty-four European cities and the swastika fluttered over three continents. But by the end of January 1943, Roosevelt and Churchill had met in Casablanca and declared that the Allies would stop at nothing less than the surrender of the Axis Powers.

The eighty-three-year-old author on his way to meet Hitler was hard of hearing, had a right hand that trembled, and was still suffering the effects of his brain haemorrhage. Yet the fifty-four-year old who met him was probably in a worse condition. Hitler was now taking strong antidepressants and a dozen other medications prescribed by his doctor. He was unable to tolerate strong light, and frequently suffered from giddiness. A biographer describes him thus: 'With the defeats he lost the energy he needed for striking poses. Once he had dropped his monumental attitudes, the changes in him showed all too plainly: he moved through the scenery of headquarters wearily, with hunched shoulders, one foot dragging, eyes staring dully out of a pasty face. His left hand had a slight tremble. Here was a man obviously on the verge of physical collapse, a bitter man, who admitted he was plagued by melancholia.'[30]

Hamsun entered the hall at Berghof where he was met by uniformed men. He did not have to wait long before his host appeared, although in the interim his eyes may well have glanced up to read the words written over the door that Hitler led them through: 'Meine Ehre heisst Treue' (My honour is my truth), the motto of the SS. The two men shook hands.

'I feel, if not completely, then very deeply, connected to you, since my life resembles yours in certain ways,' began Hitler, after asking his guest a little about how he worked when writing. He preferred to write at night too, he explained.[31]

The Führer led the writer through to his study. In front of the 10-metre-wide panoramic window stood a 6-metre-long worktable. The walls were white above the half-metre-high larch panels, and the ceiling was dark oak. Hitler guided Hamsun and Holmboe over to the seating area closest to the window, where they were served tea.

Of course, Hitler granted Hamsun's request for Holmboe – who was presented as the legation's adviser – to act as his interpreter. Hitler's own interpreter, Ernst Züchner, then pretended to leave the room. In reality, however, he placed himself behind some drapery where, hidden from view, he and Christa Schroeder, one of Hitler's secretaries, recorded everything that was said. In another area of the room close by sat Otto Dietrich and Walter Hewel, one of Ribbentrop's men.

Hitler wanted to keep the conversation on the subject of writing but, as he rapidly discovered, Hamsun had come to talk politics. Having assured his host that he had the greatest faith in Germany, Hamsun turned the conversation swiftly to the occupation policies in Norway, and to the problems with Terboven: 'The president of the Norwegian Shipowners' Association, Stenersen, has asked the Reichskommissar for a freer hand in shipping and shipbuilding. But the Reichskommissar shows no understanding about this. In fact, he has mocked the Norwegians, telling them they can pursue their shipping on the Baltic Sea and in their own lakes.'

Hitler had to make it clear to his guest that it was impossible to engage in overseas shipping in wartime.

'But the Reichskommissar believes that this will continue after the war too', replied the old man.

Hitler was keen that visitors should lift his spirits. He wanted less than ever to be challenged or upset. He had doubtless convinced himself that the author might be a source of inspiration, perhaps conversing with him on the subject of genius, a theme that interested Hitler. But it was clear that the Norwegian – whom Goebbels had described as one of the world's greatest epic poets – had no intention of discussing art.

Hitler tried to close the subject of shipping and German policies in Norway, remarking that it was impossible to give any definite statements about the future. But the man sitting before him refused to be derailed: 'But this is Norway they are talking to, the third largest shipping nation in the world. Besides, the Reichskommissar has said several times that there will no longer be a Norway in the future!'

First the attack on Reichskommissar Terboven and now this. Hitler had no intention of pulling out of Norway. Quisling's repeated proposals that Norwegians should take over the defence of Norway themselves had been an *idée fixe* that it had been impossible to drive out of the minister president's head. As early as the beginning of 1941, Hitler had given Albert Speer and the Navy Command the task of developing Trondheim so that it could house a quarter of a million people. The city was to be central to Germany's endeavours to secure the Third Reich's control of the seaways along the Atlantic coast.

Once more Hitler tried to quieten Hamsun, pointing out as he had to Quisling in the past that Norway had been treated with special leniency: 'But unlike other occupied territories,' he said, 'Norway has been allowed its own government.'

But that was not enough for Hamsun. 'Everything that happens in Norway is decided by the Reichskommissar!'

Hamsun then went on to describe how the Reichskommissar had failed to listen even to true and loyal supporters of the Nazi occupation; he had planted obstacles, for example, in the path of prominent NS member Herman Harris Aall's attempts to counteract British sympathies among his fellow countrymen.

The host, already impatient, suddenly realised that Holmboe was continuing to talk after he had finished interpreting for Hamsun, voicing opinions of his own. Holmboe told Hitler that NS Party members were considered traitors by their own people in Norway. He reminded the Führer of a suggestion, originally mooted by Aall, for a commission that would show the Norwegian people that their king and government had betrayed them prior to, and during, the first phase of the occupation. The appointment of such a commission might, Holmboe suggested, help turn public opinion. He also asked that Terboven be ordered to release certain papers that Aall and others had had difficulty gaining access to.

Hitler expressed his displeasure at the interpreter acting on his own initiative, reprimanding him so sharply that Züchner, behind the drapes, made a note of it. Hitler moved onto the offensive and launched into a discussion of the impracticalities of such a commission.

Then the unheard-of happened. Hamsun refused to back down and interrupted Hitler: 'The Reichskommissar's methods do not suit our country, his Prussian ways are intolerable. And then all the executions. We can't take any more!'

From behind his curtain, Züchner did not fail to record Hamsun's extremely emotional state. He also noted that Holmboe had not translated the writer's last remark, doubtless because it hinted at rebellion, and even treason. The two Norwegian-speaking Germans hidden behind the drapery would no doubt have sent a grateful thought in Holmboe's direction for this, since Hamsun was certainly on the verge of detonating the Führer's rage. Dietrich and the others, all of whom knew Hitler from years of working with him, witnessed his attempts to collect himself while appeasing the old man with a long monologue. Its theme was close to his heart – the difference between a political and a military government – and he gave examples of how the obligations of war demanded sacrifice, both in Norway and elsewhere.

But just as Hitler was warming to his subject, Hamsun interrupted again. 'Terboven does not want a free Norway, but a protectorate. That is the future he has planned for us.'

Hamsun demanded to know if Terboven was ever going to be called back. Hitler saw his chance to bring the conversation to a close: 'The Reichskommissar is a man of the war. He is there exclusively for military reasons. He will eventually return to Essen, where he is the gauleiter.'

No one present would ever forget what happened next. While Holmboe was translating Hitler's words, Hamsun grew increasingly agitated, and when it was his turn to reply, he started to cry. 'It should not be thought we oppose the occupation. We probably still require it. But that man is destroying more for us than Hitler can build!'

Once more Holmboe avoided interpreting the most inflammatory part of Hamsun's outburst. Instead he turned from Hitler towards Hamsun, and advised him strongly: 'Don't talk about that. We have the Führer's promise.'

Hamsun had not come to this meeting for adulation, or to learn anything, or to have his belief in a German victory reinforced. He had taken the coastal ship from Arendal to Oslo, flown from Oslo to Berlin and on to Vienna, where he had performed his obligatory circus turn at the congress, and from there he had flown across the Alps, finally arriving in Berghof – and all this for only one reason. He had lent his name and his pen to an ideal of both historic and international import; an ideal that would lead to a new order for Europe, indeed the world, and to the creation of a new society for a new era. It was to this end that Hamsun criticised Terboven, and felt obliged to make Hitler understand that his brutal regime risked driving the Führer's great vision into the ground. Hamsun was not, as Hitler had clearly assumed, merely a delegate coming to ask a favour for his country. The man who sat before him on Saturday 26 June 1943 was a true pan-Germanist who stridently believed it was imperative that this 'unclean' influence be removed. Terboven was adulterating Hitler's true teachings. This was what the writer attempted to clarify for the dictator.

Hitler merely repeated that Germany's good will was evident in Norway's being allowed its own government.

'We're talking to a brick wall', Hamsun burst out frustratedly – and accurately. Holmboe did not translate. But Hamsun's body language could not be misinterpreted.

Four months earlier, Goebbels had spoken in the Sportspalast, and with ecstatic applause the masses had sanctioned a 'Total War' that would demand even greater blood sacrifices from the German nation. The Nazi leadership subscribed to endurance, willpower and unswerving ruthlessness; in contrast, Hamsun was begging for mildness and compassion for an occupied nation that persisted in resisting German dominance. This old man, who had even allowed tears to flow, was asking Hitler to remove the iron glove. Had the writer imagined that war was about giving speeches? How could the difficulties of an occupied nation compare to the hardships and sacrifice of lives that the German people were suffering? The Führer proceeded to detail the demands that the war had made on his nation.

Finally his guest managed to formulate what had always been at the heart of his concern: 'We believe in the Führer, but his will is being corrupted.'

In all those weeks in which Hamsun had sat preparing himself at Nørholm, he must in his most secret moments have seen himself as the chosen instrument of fate. Hitler would receive him. Hitler would understand him. Hitler would do as he asked when he understood how Terboven, with his excessive use of violence, was distorting the true Nazi message.

One of these two men was almost deaf, and the other chose to be so. The dictator's rhetoric had no effect on the writer; neither did the writer's words have any effect on the dictator.

But still, Hamsun's literary creations had regularly succeeded in turning failure into triumph at the last minute. The hope of one last lucky strike had probably sustained him throughout this conversation, and would keep him going until he finally had to acknowledge that he had lost, and the true extent of what he had lost. Casting care aside, he said: 'The approach in Norway is not right. It will lead eventually to another war.'

Holmboe did not dare to translate all of this, but it was more than Hitler could bear. 'Quiet, you understand nothing of this!' he snapped, rising from his seat, throwing up his arms and going out onto the terrace.

A Defeated Devotee

Hamsun had not been the chosen tool of providence after all. He wept, and was in such turmoil that he did not take leave of Hitler personally. He eventually managed to communicate the following to Holmboe: 'Tell Adolf Hitler this: we believe in you!'

As the meeting broke up, arrangements were hurriedly made behind the scenes.

The dictator asked Holmboe to calm Hamsun down, and Hewel ordered Züchner to accompany the guests in their car. When it arrived the two Germans sat in the back seat, with the Norwegians in the front. Dietrich stayed behind. 'I never want to see anybody like that here again!' screamed the furious host as the Mercedes drove the little party away.

Desperate to find some way of punishing the minister who had tempted him into meeting this vile Norwegian, he ordered Dietrich to cancel Hamsun's planned visit to see Goebbels. Dietrich, who had been close to Hitler since before his rise to power, had never witnessed a foreign guest interrupt the Führer's monologues as Hamsun had. Neither had he ever witnessed anybody contradict the Führer so openly.[32] Hitler's mood was affected by this episode for days.

Unaware that one of the Germans in the back seat could understand Norwegian, Hamsun talked openly with Holmboe during their car journey to the airport. He was concerned to know not only whether he had managed to make Hitler understand the terrible distress Norway was in, but also whether Holmboe had translated everything precisely. Holmboe assured him he had, but Hamsun was sceptical, and blamed him for having steered the conversation in the wrong direction.

Holmboe defended himself, saying it had been unnecessary to keep bringing the conversation back to the subject of Terboven, particularly after Hitler had reassured them he would be removed after the war. 'You idiot! What kind of rubbish is that!' Hamsun replied. 'The war will go on for a long time yet, a very long time! The Reichskommissar's methods cannot be tolerated any longer. Matters needed discussing without concern for propriety.'

Sitting in the back of the car, Züchner noted how Hamsun, his temper rising, struggled to find words to describe Terboven. He finally declared: 'The man doesn't suit our country. He is . . . uncultured.' When Holmboe objected that one could not attack such a high-ranking official appointed by the Führer himself, Hamsun choked on his tears: 'How will this all end?'

Holmboe reminded Hamsun that Norway had been allowed its own government, and this must be a sign of Germany's benevolence. 'You're taking their side. Denmark also has its own government', Hamsun retorted.

Holmboe tried to explain that the level of autonomy Hitler allowed them was far more generous than that given to the Danes, particularly considering the strength of the resistance that the Germans had encountered in Norway. Hamsun's answer was, noted Züchner, bitter. 'A government of our own, maybe. But there is no use in Quisling talking to Terboven. Terboven is the one who decides on everything that happens in Norway.' Filled with pain and scorn, he mused: 'Quisling. The man of few words. He cannot even give speeches.'

After a pause he burst out again: 'How will this end!'

On his return to the Adlon Hotel in Berlin that Wednesday evening, a message awaited Hamsun: Goebbels was unfortunately unable to receive him the following day. Farewell gifts had nevertheless been sent, and surrounded by them Hamsun exclaimed, 'I feel richer by the day!'[33]

His sense of irony was clearly still keen.

On Sunday, Hamsun was taken for a drive out to Potsdam to see Frederick the Great's palace, Sanssouci. On the Monday morning, he left the country. He would never return.

Was Hamsun still a supporter of Nazism after his experiences in southern Germany? It did seem that way. His parting oath of allegiance to the Führer – 'We believe in you!' – had not been empty rhetoric. He still believed in Hitler and the sacred mission of the Third Reich to create a new and better world. Hamsun was still a devotee, despite his angry complaints to Cecilia, when he stopped to see her in Copenhagen, that he had been made a fool of. Also despite the fact that Terboven arrived to greet him at Fornebu airport, to exploit him for propaganda purposes once again. Despite the newspapers' inflated reports of the magnificent welcome he had received from Hitler, and the lavish attention Goebbels had bestowed on him. Despite telling Tore that he had been less than impressed by Hitler, who said 'I' too often, and whose speech and appearance were, he said, as undistinguished as those of a handyman's apprentice.[34]

Having booked into a hotel in Oslo, Hamsun began to make notes for a letter of apology he would send to Hitler via Dietrich. 'I took great pains in writing this. I felt it important that the Reich's press chief should understand that I only heard Hitler's first answer to me much later. I asked him if Norway was still destined for the important position and the great future within the Greater Germany that he had promised – I have since heard that Hitler said: *Natürlich*. If I had heard that straight away, I would never have put him to the inconvenience of making a long speech.'[35]

Any cracks that might have threatened to appear in Hamsun's faith seemed to have sealed up again. He had never been so humiliated in all his life, but he had to see the insults he had suffered as a necessary personal sacrifice. The great pan-Germanic vision overrode everything. Hamsun, Quisling and his fellow NS Party leaders staggered on under the burden of the bloody regime that they blamed exclusively on the Reichskommissar. Meanwhile, people across Europe were discovering Nazism's gruesome core: the unadulterated ruthlessness exercised by true Nazis in sweeping aside any obstacle that stood in the way of their reaching their objectives.

We Will See Nothing But Destruction Now!

Nørholm was now the scene of a more personal but no less hostile conflict. More than ever, Hamsun and Marie's marital battles bore all the hallmarks of trench warfare. Neither of them wanted to move out. When Marie was at home, she assumed supreme control of her territory – the ground floor, the courtyard and the gates – while her husband held his ground in the large room upstairs. Here he kept his world map on the wall regularly updated, while an assortment of notes and press clippings were spread over the long mahogany table.

He held several discussions with his lawyer, Sigrid Stray, about filing for a divorce.

From his besieged headquarters, Hamsun followed the war's increasingly depressing progress. The Third Reich's propaganda chief was stretching his mendacity to unheard-of levels, but not even a liar of Goebbels's titanic proportions could hide the truth for ever.

It was not until February 1944, a full nine months after his meeting with Hitler, that Hamsun made any further political statements, expressing his support for the Finns when they allied themselves with Germany against the Soviets. In March, he made an appeal to Norwegian sailors serving with the Allied forces, asking that they break the bonds of slavery by which the Allies tied them to their convoy ships; those who did not, he declared, were betraying their fatherland.[36]

On his wall map he traced the Soviet forces' westward advance. On 6 January, the Red Army crossed the pre-war border of Poland. Hamsun told his son that 'the Germans will know what to do from here, they have not always been so wise in the past';[37] Germany, he acknowledged now (albeit briefly), had made mistakes before.

By the time Hitler's forces evacuated the Crimea in May, Hamsun was beginning to waver in his hitherto resolute belief in a German victory. A distinctly defeated tone crept into a letter written to his daughter Victoria on 3 June. She should be pleased, he wrote, that she had nothing more to do with Norway, 'for we shall see nothing but destruction here now, if the Germans fail to rescue us. God knows Germany is tremendously strong, but unfortunately it has all Europe to fight for.'[38]

Again and again in this letter he revealed his fear that Germany might suffer another defeat. He prayed to God that this should not happen – and that his daughter should teach her sons to do the same.

As his letter made its way to Victoria on the north coast of France, the Allies were putting the final touches to their invasion plans. Three days after he wrote to her, the beginning of the end of the war came: 155,000 soldiers on board more than 5,000 vessels, and supported by 11,000 planes, attacked an area not far from where Victoria Hamsun Charlesson lived with her family.

Hamsun's reaction appeared immediately in the newspaper columns: 'Just as the Eastern Front has remained unbroken to this day, so the Western Front will remain standing until the end. This is no idle hope, it is a matter of life or death for Europe, and Europe will choose life. In these times when the Anglo-Saxons are bringing death and destruction to us all, it is the Germans, the guardians of Europe, who hold our salvation in their hands.'[39]

Some weeks later Gyldendal published Hamsun's *Collected Novels* in twelve volumes. It was an opportune moment for Hamsun to appraise his entire literary oeuvre. 'Now and then, I may have aspired to deliver more than my writing talents allowed,' Hamsun conceded, 'but I have never delivered *less*. So, all in all, things have balanced out!'[40]

A neat statement. But was Hamsun letting himself off too lightly? His works had been evaluated throughout his career, riding the crest of criticism both positive and negative. During the 1930s, the connection between the aesthetic and ethical content of his work had increasingly been called into question. Most readers had allowed their love of the former to outweigh any doubts they might have had about the latter.

Hamsun had tried to influence public opinion long before the invasion of Norway on 9 April 1940. But on that day the political landscape changed fundamentally. From then onwards when Hamsun took up his pen to express pro-German opinions, he set himself on a potentially treasonable course that would eventually lead him into a legal minefield. In Norway's prison camps and in London's government offices, Hamsun's countrymen had long since begun to consider the parameters within which this great writer should eventually be brought to justice when the war was over.

If he lived that long, of course.

At the end of July 1944, Hamsun travelled to Oslo. With his eighty-fifth birthday looming fast he had reached a convenient agreement with the occupying forces. In exchange for a couple of photo opportunities, they would provide him with a place to stay, undisturbed by NS Party members and fans alike. Journalists would present no problem this time, since the press was now in the iron grip of the Reichskommissar. What proved more difficult for Hamsun's publicists was to get anybody to write signed articles of praise; there had been eighty-five in the Norwegian press in celebration of his eightieth birthday, but this time there were just seventeen. Some of those published were as exaggeratedly extravagant as most Nazi architecture.

Hamsun was given the use of Terboven's country cabin on the coast outside the capital. The chief of the German security police in Norway, Heinrich Fehlis, was responsible for keeping guard, and a cook was hired. Greetings arrived from prominent Nazis. Hitler, who had survived an assassination attempt only two weeks earlier, sent a telegram. Goebbels also sent his compliments, as did Nicolaus von Falkenhorst, the commander of the German forces in Norway, and Reichskommissar Terboven.[41]

But what had Hamsun offered in exchange? News footage was soon broadcast across Europe showing the eighty-five-year-old author inspecting a German armoured vehicle and a U-boat.

Paris was liberated on 25 August, and on 11 September Allied troops crossed the German border. Tore, a member of the NS Party and also, for a period, the party-appointed leader of Gyldendal, was nervous. Hamsun reassured him at the end of that month: 'Dear Tore, do not worry yourself about what you hear. Nobody knows anything. [. . .] The Germans have something in store, something for the Allies, Churchill said it himself, so we can believe and hope.'[42]

Hamsun still hoped for a lucky throw of the dice, but he was a good deal less optimistic than before.

He sat for long periods in his large upstairs room at Nørholm and longed for human contact. Tore's first child had been given her grandmother's full name, Anne Marie. Each time the little girl visited him, Hamsun would write to her afterwards sharing his loneliness with her.

Seeing his grandchildren reminded Hamsun of his own offspring when they had had that same innocence. Victoria was in France now, and father and daughter had resumed correspondence. Cecilia was in Denmark, making little use of the art training her father had paid for, and living a quasi-bohemian existence. Hamsun and Marie had brought Ellinor home from Germany; an alcoholic suffering from mental illness, she had to be nursed and watched over almost constantly. Arild had returned unharmed from the Eastern Front where he had been a war reporter, and back at Nørholm had made himself useful in running the farm, as Hamsun had intended – although he and his father did not always see eye to eye. Each time Arild attempted to change the way things were done, his father obstructed him. Tore struggled with money, marriage and art. And Marie had engaged her forces in a private civil war against her husband.

It was clear that the Second World War was drawing to an end. Arild, Tore, Marie and Knut Hamsun, who had all supported the NS Party and occupying forces, knew that they would be called to answer for their actions when peace returned to Norway and Europe.

At the beginning of November 1944, the Germans began razing Finnmark and Nord Troms in the far north of Norway. Hamsun's beloved Nordland was under threat from the German flames. There were no guarantees that the rest of the country would not be burned to the ground too.

The End of the Future

Some days into the new year of 1945, Hamsun stood in the outhouse chopping logs when he collapsed. Eventually he staggered to his feet and found his way into the kitchen. He had suffered another stroke.

He did not die, although there were many who thought it would have been better if he had. Hamsun and the Norwegian people would both perhaps have been spared a great deal.

He was too weak now to carry his own firewood up to his room, but he was still able to read. He had cancelled his subscription to *Politiken*, but otherwise continued to be well supplied with newspapers and magazines by means of which he followed the death throes of the Third Reich.

On 2 May, the announcement came over the radio and in the newspapers that Hitler was dead. *Aftenposten* described in heroic terms how Hitler had fallen at his post, fighting the Bolsheviks to the last; there was no mention of his suicide. One of the home helps later described the scene that day at Nørholm: 'It was as if Hamsun had been struck by lightning. He went into a state of shock and found it difficult to take in what had happened. A doctor was called, who gave him some sedatives. Marie was the one who kept things calm. It was not long before she said that they must send a telegram to the German authorities. It was done. Knut and Marie Hamsun then sent their condolences to the German people for the loss of their Führer. Marie wired the telegram through herself.'[43]

Hamsun still felt that he needed to do more: he must write an obituary. No doubt Marie tried to discourage him, since it was probably she who had thwarted the efforts of both the Reichskommissar and the Norwegian Telegram Bureau to speak to Hamsun when they telephoned Nørholm. 'You were told an untruth, I had not "fallen down the stairs" – somebody obviously wanted to prevent me from answering!' he complained to the *Aftenposten* editor when he was ready to formulate his words of remembrance.[44]

The obituary was so important to Hamsun that he went to the trouble of making a second copy, which he sent to the Reichskommissariat.

One of the very last actions of *Aftenposten*'s editor before his removal was to send Hamsun's short article, that had arrived that morning, to the printers for inclusion in the afternoon edition. The war was over, but nobody in Norway knew it yet. On 7 May 1945, Hamsun's obituary of Hitler appeared in the top right-hand corner of *Aftenposten*'s front page.

It was a very public declaration of devotion. The author knelt beside the dictator's bier. 'I am not worthy to speak Hitler's praises. Nor do his life and deeds invite sentimental outpourings. He was a warrior, a warrior for all mankind and a preacher of the gospel of rights for all nations. He was a reformer of the highest rank, and it was his fate to live in a time of unparalleled brutality, which ultimately felled him. Thus might any ordinary Western European look upon Adolf Hitler. While we, his closest supporters, bow our heads at his death.'[45]

'It was chivalry towards a fallen man of greatness,' he explained to Tore.[46]

In later editions of Tore's biography of his father, this quotation appears as 'It was chivalry, nothing else.' Tore attempted to edit out the intimations of his father's unwavering but misguided fidelity. But Hamsun was now, as ever, extremely precise in his choice of words.

The obituary was not a Nagel-like act that Hamsun had concocted in some masochistic frame of mind purely to make things impossible for himself. It was an honourable deed, and his message was twofold: he wanted to express his loyalty to his ideal, as well as to thank Hitler for having almost reached the goal.

Hamsun believed in heroic individualism. He viewed himself as an exceptional individual, and accepted that this was a privilege that came with obligations as well as freedoms. While everybody else jumped ship, Hamsun insisted on calling himself Hitler's close supporter. The sinking of the Third Reich did not take Hamsun's great vision down with it. Hamsun still believed that the natural order would ensure that, sooner or later, old England would go under, and another new Germany would rise to lead Europe. The armies of the Kaiser had surrendered in 1919, the troops of the Third Reich had lost again in 1945, and now, for one last time, Hamsun honoured the Führer who had almost managed, for a time, to turn the whole world around.

Hamsun did not fear the settling of scores that he knew lay ahead, but he did fear the political turmoil that was bound to succeed the last difficult years – years that had been meant to herald the tentative beginnings of the Thousand-Year Reich. On 5 May 1945, he wrote to an acquaintance: 'Besides – it seems there is no future for anybody here in Norway. Oh God, what are we moving towards? For myself, I am indifferent, I am too old for anything. But our children and our grandchildren, our descendants [. . .].'[47]

On 8 May, Terboven took his own life in the bunker at Skaugum. On 9 May, Quisling gave himself up to the Norwegian police. On the same day Arild

Hamsun was arrested on a train on his way to Nørholm. Three days later Tore was taken from his new home outside Oslo.

On 24 May, the question burning in the minds of many Norwegians was for the first time voiced publicly: 'What about Hamsun, our hero of the pen who bowed his head for Josef Terboven and – in spirit – bent his knee for Adolf Hitler?'[48]

Two days later the chief constable of Arendal came to Nørholm and put Knut and Marie Hamsun under house arrest. On the fourth day of incarceration Hamsun asked his lawyer, Sigrid Stray, for help. But almost immediately he sent a telegram rescinding this request; Marie, it seemed, had already been in contact with Stray. She had started to prepare her defence for her forthcoming trial for treason. Marie intended to cite her efforts to free imprisoned Norwegians – and, presumably, Hamsun's too. Marie's meddling, as Hamsun saw it, provoked his fury. He fumed to Stray: 'You have been contacted about events here on the farm, which *only* I have the right to speak to you about. If there is any hint about my failed attempts to help those who were sentenced to death, I can only feel embarrassed over the shame of it. It is not the first, and will not be the last, time, unfortunately.'[49]

Perhaps Hamsun felt it was beneath him to hide behind a few good deeds, and then kneel before his former enemies. Perhaps he felt that he had achieved so little that he was embarrassed to be reminded of his efforts. Perhaps the sheer number of rejected applications for clemency had made a chink in his political armour. Or perhaps he was trying to dethrone Marie.

Later, he said that he had sought clemency for over one hundred people condemned to death. The maids at the farm testified to both his and Marie's strong involvement in many such cases.

On 10 June, Marie was arrested as she was working in the garden. With her characteristic sense of pathos, and at the expense perhaps of a little truth, she described the scene: 'Then I shouted: "They can't do that, Knut, they can't take you from Nørholm!" He replied as calmly as ever: "They'll do what they want with us."'[50]

Four days later Hamsun was interned at the Grimstad Hospital, in the infectious diseases unit – somebody must have thought it appropriate. Hamsun, Marie and their two sons were among the sixteen thousand Norwegians who, during the course of the preceding three weeks, had been arrested on suspicion of betraying their country during the occupation.

I Plead Not Guilty

On 23 June 1945, Hamsun was brought before Grimstad District Court for a preliminary hearing.

The charges read against him were extremely serious. The first, under Section 86 of the Penal Code, applied to any person 'who at time of a war in which Norway is involved, or with such a war in mind, assists the enemy with advice and action, or weakens Norway's ability to defend itself, or the ability of another state committed to Norway's defence'. The punishment was anything from three years' to life imprisonment. Additionally he was charged under Section 140 of the Penal Code relating to the incitement of others to commit offences against the sovereignty and security of the state.

The judge, Peter Lorentz Stabel had been a guest at Nørholm before the war. Now he was asking the questions that many people, both in Norway and abroad, were impatient to have answered.[51]

Hamsun denied having been an actual member of the NS Party, although he explained that he had found 'many nice people among them'.

'Do you really think nice people have been members of the NS?'

'Yes, I do. Yes. One reads about all kinds of people who were members, even judges.'

'Yes, regrettably. But let us take the Grimstad District as an example. Are you really impressed with the group that belonged to the NS there?'

'No. But my residence is situated near the main road, and all kinds of people, Germans included, used Nørholm as a kind of stop-off point. I was drawn in. It was a real blow to me when our king and government abandoned the country. No, for my own part, I am only a farmer. I have my roots in Norwegian soil, I am not an immigrant arriving from outside. I am in favour of the monarchy, absolutely. One can't get around the fact that Norway has always been a monarchy. But things did not go well, with the war. I have never, by the way, been aware of any murders or torture taking place. I have known absolutely nothing of this until now.'

'Is that really true?'

'Yes, God knows it!'

'Would you have remained in the party if you had known of the Germans' conduct towards your countrymen, would you have written in *Fritt Folk*?'*

'That is a broad question. I sympathised with the NS, with head and heart, but I have not really looked into the detail. But three weeks ago, or

---

*   The NS Party magazine.

thereabouts, things certainly changed. It may look as though I want to trivialise my contact with the NS and the Germans, but I do not. I stand by what I have done, and I do not want to minimise my involvement, as I see some people have done.'

'Do you still think it was right for the Germans to oppress Norway?'

'I believed that everything that was done, was being done for the good of the country.'

'Could a man as intelligent as yourself believe the Germans would give us our freedom back?'

'There are greater men who believed it.'

'Have you read about and followed everything that happened?'

'No, my wife was unable to tell me much. No secret documents have ever come into my house.'

'Did you count yourself as being a member of the NS?'

'Yes, I must say I did, even though I did not attend many of their meetings in Grimstad.'

'You are accused of contravening Section 86 of the Penal Code: that is, you supported the enemy in the form of newspaper articles et cetera.'

'I cannot understand that at all. Yes, it is true that I have written a number of things, but that brings us back to my previous point: I believed we were neutral, the war was called off. I wrote a few scraps, and at one time a letter telling everybody that we should not oppose the occupation forces. It would only lead to death and execution. Everybody approved of what I wrote. I received many letters of thanks, even from the opposing camp. There were times occasionally when I was begged by the Reichskommissar to write in the Norwegian newspapers.'

'And so you wrote in the Norwegian papers?'

'The judge might perhaps suggest they were not Norwegian papers. I wrote in *Fritt Folk* and on occasion the Reichskommissar's office would ring me three times in one night.'

'The Germans presumably wanted your famous name backing them?'

'Yes, it was probably my name. They wanted me to support the German people. And when the Allies invaded France I wrote a little piece which went into several magazines.'

'Did you want to support the countries we were at war with?'

'I felt it was the right thing to do.'

'Don't you regret this, now that you've heard about the conduct of the Germans?'

'I shall modify my attitude, but not trivialise it. I think regret is a shabby thing. I wanted to comfort the German people with my scraps. Of course I also wanted to help Norway. But we had no need of comforting in Norway.'

The judge asked Hamsun whether he knew that the Norwegian people were being tortured by the NS and Germans:

'We lived under terror for four years, don't you understand that?'

'That was not my understanding.'

'We were terrorised by a villain by the name of Josef Terboven, whose corpse now lies in the vicinity of Oslo. Around three million Norwegians suffered under the rule of terror of this villain, who took his orders from Adolf Hitler. It is deplorable that you, with your famous name, should have behaved in such a way as to be charged with treason. The police authorities have demanded that you be imprisoned, but have nonetheless agreed to your remaining in the hospital.'

'Am I to continue living at the hospital? My farm is in a terrible state, and we need to get it back on its feet.'

Hamsun admitted that he had been pro-German:

'I wanted to serve the German people and thereby serve the Norwegian people.'

'Did you know beforehand that the Germans were going to make a naval invasion?'

'No, we were all taken by surprise when that happened.'

'It stated in the police report that you were delighted to be able to serve Germany.'

'The wording is not really right, but when the policeman interrogated me, I was frightened people might believe I wanted to play down my actions. I am a man after all, and will not back-pedal in any way. Such behaviour is not worthy of a man. One cannot just suddenly change the attitudes one holds in one's heart and soul.'

'Can't you acknowledge you were wrong now that you've heard about the Germans' barbaric actions? Don't you agree that you have championed a nation unworthy of your support?'

'I need to think about such a question.'

'Have you ever informed on anyone?'

'Who should I inform on? I have never done such a thing. I have received vast numbers of letters from prominent men, and from the judge's own circles, but have never handed them over to anyone. I'm used to receiving letters. In my opinion I have acted in Norway's best interests.'

'Do you remember the time you wrote about the Russians and used the expression "the Germans will beat them, they will beat them flat"?'

'I can't remember that, but it is not my intention to deny anything I have written.'

'Can you see how wrong you were now?'

'I don't understand the workings of war. The Germans, it transpires, did not manage to beat the Russians, not even in Kirkenes*.'

'Don't you regret your attitude to Norway during the war?'

'I don't know. I would prefer to wait before giving my answer. I don't think you would appreciate my being a turncoat, my lord. My sympathies were with the Germans to the very end.'

'The police have confiscated everything you own, and I am about to approve that decision, do you understand?'

'There's nothing to be done about that.'

'Have you heard the phrase "Vae victis"†?'

'Yes, but this situation can never repeat itself, it is wholly impossible. Therefore any punishment will be nothing but revenge.'

'Punishment serves as reparation, a fulfilment of justice.'

'I did not know it was punishable.'

'All of you in the NS must have known you were traitors. You must have seen how the Norwegian people reacted?'

'The English fleet laid mines. . . No, no, I shan't bother the judge by answering, it serves no purpose anyway.'

Like the majority of those put on trial in Norway, as well as in other countries that had been occupied by the Germans, Hamsun did not admit to any wrong-doing. On one essential point he lied to the judge, when he denied having known anything about Germany's rule of terror. He could hardly have forgotten Hitler's throwing him out of Berghof when he asked for Terboven's removal – and that this request had been born of his disgust at the Reichskommissar's violent and horrifying governance. Yet when the judge began lecturing him on Terboven's activities, Hamsun still failed to correct his statement. It seemed he was determined that his visit to Hitler should not be brought up. It had after all been the worst defeat of his life.

The Stakes in the 'Hamsun Case'

Norway's new coalition government was appointed the day before Hamsun was to appear at the magistrates court in the summer of 1945. The prime minister, Einar Gerhardsen, and the majority of those who now took their places as ministers were well aware of the need to handle the situation carefully.

---

*   In Finnmark.
†   'Woe to the vanquished'.

The previous November, Foreign Minister Trygve Lie and Justice Minister Terje Wold, both in exile at the time, had held a meeting with Molotov in Moscow. The Russian had expressed absolute hatred of the Nazis and their collaborators, and wanted to know how Norway planned to deal with its war criminals when Germany was defeated. Wold explained their planned policy. Molotov was dissatisfied, and clearly felt the Norwegian government gave far too much consideration to protecting the rights of the accused. Yet the instant Hamsun was mentioned, the fierce Molotov seemed almost to become a different man.

Lie later described the meeting: 'When Wold told him that Hamsun was perceived as a Nazi and a traitor, and that a trial would therefore be necessary, the Russian became very thoughtful. Molotov grew almost sentimental and requested that Knut Hamsun's life be spared. An author who could write *Victoria* and *Pan* was such a great artist that he had to be handled differently to the average Nazi. Besides, Molotov said, Hamsun was so old that he should be allowed to die a natural death. Wold pointed out that there might not be a call for the death penalty. Molotov was determined: a man who had created such great art must live the time he had left in peace.'[52] 'You are too soft, Mr Molotov!'[53] came the extraordinary answer, which would go down in all Norwegian history books.

Norwegian politicians undoubtedly faced a tricky predicament. The whole world would be watching their handling of Norway's famous Nobel Prize winner. Hamsun retained such symbolic power that he put the courts into a difficult position. Nobody else accused of treachery was as old as him; he would reach his eighty-sixth birthday in the autumn of 1945. Only Ibsen had brought greater fame to his country abroad. But nobody had ever fallen as low in the people's estimation. With his extensive pro-German articles, Norway's national bard had turned traitor to his own country. With the prevailing appetite for justice, it would have been unthinkable not to initiate proceedings against him, but how it should be done was something of a conundrum.

Even before the German invasion, there were those who felt that Hamsun's increasingly monomaniacal defence of Hitler in the latter part of the 1930s must be due to a decline in old age. As the war progressed this perception grew fixed; Hamsun may have been hated, but the majority also sought an explanation for his betrayal. When peace arrived, the leading newspapers pointed to his great age and possible senility, and also to the possibility that he been used and manipulated. Some suggested he should not be put in prison, but interned in some other way.

Two days after the appearance of an article promoting such a solution in *Arbeiderbladet*, the ruling Labour Party's main newspaper, Hamsun was detained in Grimstad Hospital.

The first difficult move had been made. The next was to specify what Hamsun should be charged with. The list of charges lodged against him were: membership of the NS Party; persistent propaganda on behalf of the NS and the Germans against the lawful Norwegian authorities; and the incitement of Norwegian soldiers and sailors to desert.

Hamsun's plea of innocence at the preliminary hearing could hardly have come as a surprise. But when word spread of the commanding impression he had made in court, it must have worried those who had hoped for a quick solution to the problem of bringing Hamsun to justice – or at least making him disappear. The report made by the journalist present, which was published in numerous newspapers, made it clear: Hamsun was obviously far from senile.

The 'Hamsun Case' was unique. He had been loved like nobody else. His works had not disappeared, but they were now temporarily locked out of reach – a mark of intense political disapproval.

Quisling, who would also be facing trial, may have perverted the symbols of Norway's proud past, but Hamsun had made three generations proud to be Norwegian. The former was in his prime, the latter an old man. The first had attempted to manipulate his nation, the second had been manipulated. Quisling deserved to be executed and struck from Norwegian history; Hamsun would soon die naturally, but would leave an enormous legacy behind him.

When Sigrid Undset was asked her opinion on the treason trials she gave her unequivocal support for the execution of the worst offenders. Regarding her Nobel Prize colleague, however, she was a little more lenient: 'He cannot be condemned to death for his actions. But he should be given a prison sentence and his property should be confiscated. He should be shut away in some institution or other.' When she was asked if she had expected this of Hamsun, she replied: 'Yes, this was exactly what I expected. He has never written about anything apart from his own inferiority complexes, the English nation of shopkeepers and the master race of Germany.'[54]

On 20 August 1945, the case was brought against Vidkun Quisling. The prosecution demanded the death penalty.

Several psychiatrists called for psychological assessments to be carried out on anybody who faced such a charge. Quisling, however, was not to be subjected to a complete assessment. Gabriel Langfeldt, chief psychiatrist of the University Psychiatric Clinic in Vindern, was outraged. But no one in a position of authority to reverse this ruling dared present the nation with the possibility that Quisling might be declared insane. If this happened, the foundation for all the treason trials could start to crumble.

In the case of Hamsun, however, the reverse was true: a psychological assessment might appeal to the nation's sensibilities. Langfeldt was without doubt the man to attach a suitable psychiatric label to Hamsun. Indeed, that summer the psychiatrist had written several articles in which he had described the National Socialist movement as a conspiracy of psychologically damaged individuals, and the impending trials for treason as a cathartic means of preventing 'our country [. . .] from ever again becoming a playground for the psychologically inferior'.[55]

At the end of September, the public prosecutor dealing with treason court cases in East Agder wrote to the district doctor in Grimstad requesting him to carry out a medical examination on Hamsun. The doctor delivered his written report: Hamsun's health was normal for his age and circumstances. The public prosecutor contacted the doctor again. More information was required about Hamsun's mental health. Their conversation was then reported back in a note to the public prosecutor's superior, Attorney General Sven Arntzen. The doctor's conclusion was that Hamsun was not now and never had been of impaired mental faculties or insane. There was no reason, in his medical opinion, for Hamsun to undergo a court psychiatric examination.[56]

It is hard to imagine a more unambiguous report than that delivered by this experienced district doctor, but it was clearly not the advice the authorities wanted to hear. Just four days later, the attorney general gave his approval for a forensic psychiatric assessment. A suitable diagnosis might salvage what was most important in this great man's fall from grace: the integrity of his works. Besides, there was always the possibility that by playing for time Hamsun might die, or indeed grow senile before legal proceedings could commence.

The Unshakeable Writer

Hamsun had wanted to get away from Nørholm since before the beginning of the war. Now, in the summer of 1945, his desire had materialised. It was not how he had wished it: Hamsun had been cut off from his farm, which had been temporarily confiscated, and also from Marie, who was in prison. In a large room in the hospital's infectious diseases unit, Hamsun established the hermit-like existence he had described with such zeal in several of his books.

During his travels through the Caucasus at the turn of the century, Hamsun had imagined what it would be like to be arrested as a dissident – to be taken in chains to St Petersburg and thrown in an underground cell, as many Russian authors had been. 'I'd make a hollow in my stone table with my bony elbow, as I sat there brooding with my head in my hands, and I'd cover the walls of my wretched cell with writings that would be discovered later and published in a book. I would receive all manner of reparation after my death; but what good would it serve? I have never been attracted to the honour that might come with big bronze statues of me in Norway's towns. Quite the opposite: each time I have thought of these posthumous statues, I have wished I could benefit from their value now – bring on the cash!'

Such were his fantasies in his travel journal *In Wonderland* at the turn of the century. Nearly fifty years later, concentric circles in his life and writing were completing themselves.

As a ten-year old he had been expelled from home; it had left him scarred, but it had also shaped his character, forming traits of his personality that would contribute, seventy years later, to him being expelled by his nation. Long ago he had stormed the literary world with a tale of personal catastrophe about a young man who refused to yield to either man or God; who might flee, but would never buckle. Now, a little over half a century later, he began to dream of his swan song to the literary world being a new tale of personal catastrophe. *Hunger* had been not only a literary but an existential triumph, and now for one last time he would prove that he was still unyielding. This was the unifying theme of the pile of notes that grew during the summer and autumn of 1945.

Perhaps the first thing he made notes on in the hospital was a rebuff from one of the nurses: 'I was asked by one of the young sisters in the hospital whether I wanted to lie down – it had, after all, been said in *Aftenposten* that I was "broken and needed nursing". Bless you, child, I'm not ill. There's never been a healthier person in this hospital than me. I am just deaf! Perhaps she took it for boasting, but she stopped talking to me altogether, and this silence was observed by all the sisters during my stay in hospital.'[57]

He transferred many of the humiliations he experienced during this time into literary sketches, just as he had done a lifetime ago in *Hunger*.

Hamsun was finally scrutinising himself again, rather than the figures of his imagination. And the closer he looked, the stronger grew not only his desire, but his capacity, for writing. After *The Last Joy* he had promised Marie that he would stop writing in the first person. He had kept that promise through twelve novels and thirty-five years. But now he was writing the book that would prove to be his very last, *On Overgrown Paths*.

At the beginning of September 1945, he was moved some 10 kilometres to an old people's home in Landvik. His lawyer, Sigrid Stray, visited him. She thought his room was shabby: a bed, a table, a couple of chairs, some hooks for hanging clothes on. He protested that he was perfectly content, though she found this impossible to believe. Even a police inspector who saw it found the standards unacceptable: 'The care is appalling, unclean and disagreeable in every way. It has also come to my attention that the place is infested with bedbugs.'[58]

Hamsun did not complain. He was writing again.

He revived the double viewpoint that he had used in *Hunger*, shifting continually between himself as object and subject. In so doing, Hamsun claimed a pre-eminent position from which to view both his actions and his motives. Subjectivity held no fear for Hamsun. It never had. He had always drawn his own conclusions about the world and judged it through his own senses. Now, as he reviewed events of the past few years, he felt he could only be held morally accountable for his own actions, and that he had nothing either to regret or to apologise for. Hadn't he been driven by a patriotism that was superior to that of those who had fled the country? Few, if any, had gambled like him; he had lost, but he had not yielded. He had refused to be bowed despite persistent efforts to break him.

This was what Hamsun wrote about now. Once more, the author could defend the dictator. But after a month in the home, Hamsun was torn away from this grubby, perfect literary existence. Under police escort he was taken on the night train to Oslo, and to a psychiatric clinic.

The Clinic

On 15 October 1945, some time between ten and eleven o'clock in the morning, Hamsun was met by what he would later describe as a swarm of nurses in white. They demanded he hand over everything he had in his pockets: keys, watch, notebook, penknife, pencil, glasses and two drawing pins. They also forced the lock on his suitcase and methodically checked all the clothes he had brought. All routine procedures at the psychiatric clinic at Vindern in Oslo.

From that moment forth Hamsun was locked behind three doors, and his behaviour was observed and recorded by the staff. Two types of journal were kept: one by the chief physician, Professor Gabriel Langfeldt, during his observations; the second by the nurses on the ward. The contents of these journals would be the basis on which Langfeldt would make his recommendations, which were due to be presented to the attorney general in barely two weeks. Langfeldt would have to deliver a verdict on whether there were grounds to believe that Hamsun was insane, or had been temporarily or permanently mentally impaired at the time he committed the illegal acts with which he was now being charged.

Hamsun was doubtless fully aware of what was at stake.

According to the hospital journal on his admission, he was calm, clear-headed and fully aware of everything that was happening. It was plain that he wanted things to be over as quickly as possible, and was therefore prepared to cooperate, despite the colossal readjustment that life in the clinic demanded of the eighty-six-year old. There is no indication that he thought Langfeldt could come to any other conclusion than that he was legally responsible for his actions. His challenge therefore was to hold out for the two weeks he knew Langfeldt had at his disposal.

On the morning of the second day of his stay, Langfeldt called Hamsun into his office for their first consultation. Hamsun was rushed and barely had time to dress properly. During this session he described how for thirty years he had written his books with his left hand gripped around his writing hand. He gave some information about his background. Langfeldt asked him to multiply some numbers; he managed his nine times table but not eleven times twelve. He talked about the aphasia that had followed his stroke, and the deterioration in his memory. Following this, Langfeldt wanted him to explain his political views. Judging by the length of the report, this went on for some time.

Langfeldt quoted from the nurses' log that day in his final statement: 'The patient is always angry and irritable and wants his demands satisfied immediately. He is impatient and irritable, and often makes sarcastic remarks.' But Langfeldt had omitted the reasons for Hamsun's irritation, as well as the more nuanced descriptions of his mood, that the nurses noted down:

> The patient ate a good breakfast and asked for the newspaper. When it failed to arrive, he lay down to sleep until the rounds, when he went to talk with the professor. Since then he has done nothing but nag about the newspaper. He says, 'I must see what's going on in the world'. First he was given yesterday's *Arbeiderbladet* and read it for a long time and with great interest. But as soon as he had finished, he asked in a very commanding tone if he could have today's newspaper brought. He lay and read *Aftenposten*'s morning edition until 5pm. Then he wanted to have the evening edition brought. He thinks time goes slowly. He burst out angrily that he has to hold his tongue and accept everything.[59]

Langfeldt included in his final statement the ward nurses' observations that, from the day of his arrival, Hamsun had a tendency to flare up about the least thing, and curse – passing over the reasons that might explain his behaviour: 'He says he cannot hear and that we have to write messages for him when we want something. He is annoyed that he isn't given his things, for example his watch and his tiepin. He eats well. He finds it cold in his room and says he is freezing. He was surprised when the nurse told him that the light would be switched off. He asked how such a thing could happen in a place like this.

When the nurse told him that there would be nightlights and that somebody would be on night duty he was pleased. "Ah, right," he said.'

Neither did Langfeldt feel any need to include the explanation for Hamsun's shock and ensuing anger when he realised where he would be expected to live; his room was the one usually allocated to the most disruptive patients. It was extremely narrow and had a peephole in the door. To go in and out he had to pass through another room, in which approximately ten patients, all suffering from varying degrees of mental illness, spent large parts of the day, sleeping or otherwise.

Langfeldt's lack of nuance in his report on Hamsun's condition was systematic.

On 20 October, he wrote only: 'Patient in good humour, polite and easygoing. Reads a lot', omitting the notes from the ward journal: 'When the nurse wanted to shave the patient, he became very annoyed and irritable, swore several times, and said he would shave on Sunday as always. The nurse pointed out to the patient that no shaving was done on a Sunday. All the same, he said, he would not be shaved now. He then continued with his reading.' From 29 October, Langfeldt noted simply that Hamsun was keeping his spirits up, whereas the ward journal details the difficulties Hamsun had in adapting to his situation, as well as how he overcame them: 'He received a parcel containing a pot of salve. The nurse asked for the string, since the patient wanted to keep it. He said there was something he wanted to pack. When the nurse told him that it was against regulations he laughed and said that he hadn't meant to hang himself with it. He asked if it would be possible to stay up a little longer in the evening, since the night seems so long for him. The nurse said that it was the rule that everybody should go to bed at 7pm. "Oh, well, in that case . . ." he said.'

In his observational interviews with Hamsun, Langfeldt tried to steer the discussion in a political direction. On 26 October, Hamsun spoke, among other things, about his uncle and his upbringing with him: 'I still bear the marks from where he pinched me', he said. Langfeldt had then moved the discussion on to politics: 'He found Hitler to be a self-important man, who only ever talked about "ME". Goebbels seemed to be a personality, a man of quality. Hitler came across as a handyman's apprentice.' The final interview of 31 October seems to have revolved solely around politics. Langfeldt pointed to evidence of contradictions of opinion that he found significant and later referred to in his statement: 'He began to have misgivings that the Germans might have been planning to control the whole of Europe as brutally as the English had tried to do. So he finished by saying that it might, all in all, be best that the German regime had been brought to an end. [. . .] "It may well be that I was kept in the dark, but there's no changing that."'

Langfeldt had run out of time. In fact, Hamsun had already been held beyond the legal limit when the psychiatrist finally sent his report to the attorney general on the first day of November. In it, he recommended that Hamsun undergo a full forensic assessment to find out how far his mental impairment had developed by 1940. The grounds were twofold. First, a neurological examination had revealed that Hamsun suffered from arteriosclerosis. Second, Langfeldt claimed that Hamsun's faculties seemed weakened, since he showed no interest in himself or current events, muttered constantly to himself, and often fell asleep in the middle of the day. No evidence from the journal was included that might have presented Hamsun's conduct in the clinic in a more detailed or multifaceted light.

There was a book in Hamsun's room, *Mañana*, written by his daughter Cecilia's new husband, Hans Andreasen. It was not until many years later that Dr Langfeldt would discover, to his surprise, that the eighty-six-year old had been hoodwinking all the hospital staff, himself included. On the blank pages at the back of his son-in-law's travel sketches, Hamsun had been keeping a diary.

Living in such close proximity to mentally ill patients, some with serious problems, began to take its toll on the author. On 29 October, Hamsun wrote: 'Two weeks here today. A patient discharged, worse than before, but happy.' The following day he had scrawled a few words that summed up his feelings about being watched by the nurses: 'Snooping, meddling.'

On 6 November, he noted his despair at being kept in the clinic longer than the two weeks expected: '3 closed doors to unlock in order to get out, 3 doors, the same closed doors to come back in. There are 3 cells here, one of them mine. A tiny little hole with glass in it. A patient is upset. Wants to ram his head in the wall.'

On 10 November, Langfeldt had informed him that he would be kept in the clinic for longer than previously stipulated: 'Not this side of Christmas!' the incredulous author scribbled in his notes. The next day he lamented his situation: 'Black Sunday, dreadful!'[60]

Hamsun was now at a very low ebb. His stay in the hospital felt worse than a prison sentence. He claimed he was being subjected to a kind of torture.

Battles and Treacheries

The authorities were evidently eager to have Hamsun declared mentally impaired.

There can be little doubt that the way Hamsun was treated contravened the principles of medical ethics and possibly broke the law. When Langfeldt informed Hamsun that his stay at the clinic was to be extended, he did so two full days before the courts had given official instructions to continue with the 'Hamsun Case'. Powerful people wanted the ticking bomb of Hamsun's political opinions to be defused and dismissed as merely a psychiatric condition.

To this end, another psychiatrist, Ørnulv Ødegård, was now appointed to give the second expert opinion required by law. Ødegård was chief physician at another psychiatric clinic in Oslo and probably rather less severe and authoritarian than his colleague Langfeldt. Hamsun had a few observational interviews with him, and the two men got on well.

But the relationship between Langfeldt and Hamsun was a contest of wills. Their clinical meetings were a long series of confrontations between two strong egos. Only one, of course, held the power to make the rules and demand they be followed to the letter. Langfeldt was the man in the white coat, free to let himself in and out of the locked doors with his bunch of keys, surrounded by his obsequious assistants. And Langfeldt had dozens of ways of reminding Hamsun that he was only one of many patients in his clinic – not the easiest role for Hamsun to adjust to.

In mid-December, Hamsun was moved to better accommodation. In *On Overgrown Paths*, he described it as 'not a cell, but a side room with a normal door that could be closed. [. . .] I was given a knife and fork to eat with, it was lighter here and more friendly, not quite so mad.'

More and more of the communication between Langfeldt and Hamsun was carried out in writing. Hamsun's hearing was now so poor that Langfeldt had to write his questions down, but that Hamsun should be required to write out his answers was both unnecessary and extremely stressful for the eighty-six-year old. It simplified Langfeldt's job, of course. Hamsun accused the chief physician, probably with some justification, of having destroyed his eyesight with this demand since the lighting in his room was abysmal.

Hamsun did not develop any respect for Langfeldt as a professional, despite the psychiatrist's high standing in his own circles. Hamsun felt as though he were being transformed into one of the one-dimensional characters he had demanded should be swept from the face of literature. When Langfeldt asked him one day to describe his own character traits, Hamsun was irritated and took him to task: 'Character traits! The so-called naturalistic period, Zola and his time, wrote about people with dominant character traits. They had no use for more nuanced psychology; for them people had "governing" characteristics that guided their actions. Dostoevsky and others taught us all something different about people. I do not think that in all my work, from the moment I began, I have created a single person with such a straightforward governing attribute. They are all without so-called "character", they are split and fragmented, neither good nor bad, but both things, nuanced, changeable in mind and action. As undoubtedly I am myself.'[61]

Hamsun felt a desire to defend himself on several fronts, although he also knew he was treading a tightrope. He did not want the courts to conclude that he was of diminished responsibility. He had to convince Langfeldt of the consistency of his political views, and that they were not the result of some mental deficiency. He also felt a need to defend his own dignity, while at the same time trying to curb his challenges to Langfeldt. Ultimately, the psychiatrist had the power to declare him incapable of running his own affairs.

This was therefore a rather different relationship from the one he had enjoyed with Dr Johan Irgens Strømme in 1926 and 1927, in which Hamsun had held the reins. Strømme and he had allied themselves against Marie. Now, when Hamsun refused to discuss his married life in any depth, Langfeldt took Marie's side against Hamsun.

On Langfeldt's orders Nørholm was searched and certain objects confiscated. The police forced the drawers in Hamsun's room. Two days later Marie was fetched from the prison in Arendal, and escorted by a policewoman to the psychiatric clinic.

Marie, now a sixty-four-year-old prisoner, faced the chief physician, who was sixteen years her junior. 'He asked and I answered. In the end there were some questions that caused me to fall silent. Must I answer? The professor told me it was extremely important if he was going to form a complete picture of Hamsun's psychology. To make it absolutely clear what his further examination meant, I told him: if my husband ever gets to know that I have told you, then I will never be able to live with him under the same roof again! The professor reiterated that my – I almost called it a confession – would remain confidential. Apart from the attorney general who would have to see it', wrote Marie many years later in her memoirs.[62]

Langfeldt gave quite a different version of events: 'I merely asked her how their relationship had been in their marriage, and then she spoke without pause, so any questions were almost superfluous.'[63] Marie's later claim that she had been cross-questioned about the intimate details of their sex life would be denied by Langfeldt and described as a gross distortion.

Marie asked to see her husband after her interview with Langfeldt. As soon as Hamsun set eyes on his wife, he became furious. The sound of them screaming at each other in the reception room could be heard throughout much of the clinic.

The main reason for Marie talking to Langfeldt had doubtless been regard for her husband, and an attempt to reduce his sentence. But she had probably also been lured by the opportunity to give her own version of their life together. 'When the interrogation was over, I felt far from well. I was on the point of taking it all back. If only I had', Marie wrote regretfully many years later.[64]

Her withdrawal would have been unlikely to change much of what happened between her and her husband, however. It was not the details of her confidences to the psychiatrist that caused Hamsun to fume; indeed, he would not discover what she had said until months later. The reason, Hamsun now bellowed, why he never wanted to see her again was what he saw as the treachery of his wife conspiring with his greatest adversary.

Marie did not take his histrionic parting too seriously. She had heard his threats before.

A Necessary Diagnosis

Early in January 1946, Hamsun managed to smuggle a note out to an old acquaintance and fellow writer, Christian Gierløff, who had visited him before Christmas. Hamsun wanted to talk to him again. On his arrival at the clinic, Gierløff was told to wait. Langfeldt appeared and refused him access to Hamsun. Gierløff tried to explain that his visit merely concerned a few practical matters, but Langfeldt did not budge. Demanding an explanation, Gierløff was told that it was 'due to the nature of the evidence'.

The answer did not impress Gierløff. He tried threats and pleas. 'When our examination is complete, access to him will be resumed', answered Langfeldt.[65]

Two weeks later Gierløff received a call from the clinic summoning him immediately. The minute he saw Hamsun he understood the reason for the haste. Hamsun was lying on the bed half-dressed, with his arms spread wide. He was extremely pale, his mouth half-gaping, his face soaked in tears. Gierløff leaned over him and tried to bring Hamsun round, talking and touching him gently. Hamsun did not respond. Gierløff tried unsuccessfully to lift his head and torso so as to ease him halfway out of bed. The will had been sucked out of the man who, only two months before during Gierloff's last visit, had displayed such devilish energy.

Gierløff had encountered Hamsun in this state before. He had been called to him during the last painful throes of his relationship with Bergljot in 1905. Then as now, Hamsun had lain utterly broken. Forty years before Gierløff had got him into a clinic; this time his task was to get him out of one.

On 5 February 1946, Langfeldt and Ørnulv Ødegård signed their final report:

1. Our findings are that Knut Hamsun is not insane, and that he was not insane at the time of his alleged offences.

2. We judge him to be a person with permanently impaired mental faculties, but do not consider there to be any danger of repeat offences.[66]

The politicians and attorney general had the diagnosis they needed. But not one of them was prepared for what would happen next. The old man would attempt to tear off their label of 'fool' with such vigour that not only the psychiatrist, but the whole of the Norwegian government and judiciary would stand to lose face.

On Monday, 12 February, Hamsun finally walked stiffly out of the door of the psychiatric clinic where he had been imprisoned for 119 days. Gierløff and Tore had to support him, but it seemed that with every step he took away from the great stone building, his strength returned. The moment the car's engine revved, Hamsun turned to look back and, as though uttering a curse, he mumbled: 'A three-storey state institution, with a zero at its top.' He was doubtless referring to the hospital's chief physician, Langfeldt.

Tore carried his father's suitcase onto the coastal ship that would carry Hamsun northwards, and took his leave of the old man and Gierløff.

Tore had been released that autumn after five months in detention. The thirty-four-year old had always lived off his father, never having had to learn how to earn his own money. Self-denial was an alien concept. Now his family of four had to survive on what he could sell as an artist. As far back as he could remember, the name Hamsun had always served him well. Now he bore one of Norway's most vilified nomenclatures.

A great deal of the unease and sadness in Tore's own life was owing to the members of his family leaning on him so heavily for emotional support. He was their 'wailing wall', the one to whom everybody turned: his sisters, his brother, his father and his mother, the latter being the bitterest of them all.

It is painful for any wife to suffer rejection, but for Marie Hamsun it had far greater ramifications.

Even before the war she knew that many people perceived her as a stronger supporter of Germany than her husband. During the war many Norwegians had blamed his pro-German articles on her, saying that Marie was misleading him, exploiting his deafness and old age. After Norway's liberation, ample column space had been given to such opinions in the newspapers. It was clear to Marie that she had been positioned to be used as the perfect scapegoat. Once again she felt she was being sacrificed on the altar of art, for the sake of the great writer.

Hamsun's writings were a legacy that must be saved for Norway at any cost. He could be packaged as a senile old man who had been manipulated by his wife. Her visits to Germany and contacts with prominent Nazis could be used against her. And now his refusal to have anything more to do with her, just as details of the German atrocities were emerging, acted as the crowning proof for those who were contriving to absolve Hamsun of responsibility.

As Marie saw it, the conspiracy to cast her as scapegoat had begun long before.

For some time Marie had been pondering her increasingly untenable position. It had become clear to her recently that a reconciliation with Hamsun would weaken the conspiracy against her. But she had also been mulling over another idea since the late 1930s. One of the most valuable assets she now owned was the life that she had shared with Hamsun. If she told the story of their years together – in a long article, or several articles, published abroad perhaps to begin with, and eventually in a book – her stature would be confirmed. It would also be a chance to present her own version of events rather than simply following the script that was now being written for her. She would probably be condemned by the courts. But in the years that followed, when the war had passed into memory, and Hamsun's works had survived as everyone was so determined they should, she reasoned that her own importance was likely to increase. She was only sixty-four. She would still be alive after Hamsun was dead – alive and able to write a unique account of this great writer which she knew would be in hot demand. Who had stood closer to him than she?

They had lost the war together. But the battle between husband and wife was far from over.

A Frozen Tap

The attorney general, Sven Arntzen, made an announcement in *Aftenposten* on 22 February 1946 that instantly provoked earnest and heated discussions among the Norwegian populace.

Hamsun would be eighty-seven this year, was almost deaf, and according to psychiatric reports was suffering from impaired mental faculties. The attorney general had therefore decided not to pursue the charges that had been laid against him. Instead, the state would consider whether a claim for financial compensation should be filed against him through Norway's post-war Compensation Directorate.

Hamsun's biographer and editor of *Dagbladet* Einar Skavlan rattled off the next day's editorial. He demanded that there be a criminal trial to remind everybody of the offences against the Norwegian people perpetrated by the author. 'Knut Hamsun committed this unpatriotic action from the shelter of his privileged position as the country's foremost writer, as one of the great leaders of Norwegian cultural life. Distinguished and admired as he was, nobody could have posed a more dangerous example to others than he did. Few bear more responsibility for aiding the Germans and traitors in arousing the sympathies of those who were easily influenced. None of the Germans' vile crimes caused him to turn. Knut Hamsun stood by Hitler all the way to his suicide.' Only a criminal prosecution could ensure that he would remain 'a discredited man' for all time.[67]

But many other Norwegian newspapers were prepared to accept the conclusions of the medical professionals and the attorney general: Hamsun's wartime activities could be blamed on the foibles of old age. Few, however, supported the attorney general's decision to drop all criminal charges against him. On this matter they shared Skavlan's view. Hamsun must be sentenced to imprisonment, and then either pardoned or held in special conditions that offered some degree of comfort. Out of regard for the people's need for justice, the writer should not be allowed to simply buy his way out of his misdeeds.

Hamsun himself agreed with the newspapers that called for a criminal prosecution. 'I am deeply angered and annoyed at the attorney general's decision. Starting with the magistrate, I have declared myself responsible and have stood by my actions. And then the attorney general strikes this weapon from my hand, just when I have spent four months answering <u>all</u> the charges in writing, and feel that I would have been acquitted or almost acquitted by an <u>ordinary</u> court.'[68]

Hamsun soon received the summons from the Directorate for Compensation. Under the so-called Traitor's Law he was accused of having been a member of the NS Party; it was this, rather than his actions, beliefs or pro-German articles, upon which the legal case against him would be brought. Hamsun was thereby accused of being partly responsible for the damage inflicted on the Norwegian people by Quisling's rule. State economists had calculated that the total cost of this came to 283 million Norwegian kroner. Hamsun was expected to contribute half a million kroner towards repaying this sum.

With the criminal charges formally dropped, Hamsun was freed from custody. There were now no legal obstacles to prevent his return to Nørholm – and Marie was still in her cell in Arendal. Nonetheless, he chose to return to the old people's home. It suited his needs perfectly. For years, and with neurotic meticulousness, he had cultivated a peculiar need to transform himself into a lonely, poverty-stricken and displaced creature when he wrote.

The few people who visited him in the spring of 1946 saw his squalid living conditions and were upset on his behalf. But he would brush off their concerns with a humorous remark on the congeniality of lice, or show them his invention for dealing with a sharply sloping floor: mittens placed on the legs of his chair, which stopped it from slipping. An old man's courage in the midst of tragedy, they thought. They did not know that, with every passing week, Hamsun found his living conditions increasingly well suited to his purpose.

Hamsun had brought with him the secret diary he had started at the clinic. The few words he had managed to jot down were invaluable. But he needed to build on them. The diary replaced the old game of patience he usually played with his little piles of notes. Hamsun would have liked to have the huge stacks of papers containing his own written answers to Langfeldt's questions during his forensic examinations. The problem was that these notes were kept in an institution run by a man he never wanted to meet again.

Years before, his other psychiatrist, Dr Strømme, had succeeded in opening not just one but many creative taps in the writer. Asked to compare the two, Hamsun would doubtless have said that Langfeldt had crushed any potential for creativity in him. But in the late spring of 1946, Hamsun described a feeling of a frozen valve having been dealt a sharp blow and loosened: 'I drip with delicate words. I am a tap that stands dripping, one, two, three, four –.'

The knowledge that he was once more able to write made him happier than he had been for years. 'I am tremendously absorbed in what I am writing. Not because I succeed at anything, no, practically nothing in volume. But I sit here with it, fully alert, day and night', he wrote to Christian Gierløff. At the end of June, he announced, not without some pride, that he had started on the forty-seventh page of his manuscript.[69]

Clearly Hamsun did not suffer from the inferiority complex that Langfeldt attributed to him since he spent the first week of July 1946 writing a long letter castigating Norway's attorney general. The first thing Hamsun pointed out was that he was not writing his letter for today, but for 'anybody who might read it after us. And I am writing for our grandchildren.'[70]

Hamsun accused Sven Arntzen of unpardonable treachery in handing over a poet of his calibre to a mere psychiatrist.

Somebody must have been able to inform you that I am not altogether inexperienced in the world of psychology, that during the course of an enormously long career as a writer, I have created several hundred characters – created them both internally and externally as living people, in every psychological state and nuance, in dreams and in action. You did nothing to inform yourself about me. Instead you handed me over to an institution and a professor who knew as little as yourself. He came equipped with the schoolbooks and scholarly works that he had learned by heart and sat his examinations in, but that was quite different from what confronted him. Since the attorney general was unqualified, the professor should have turned me away on my arrival. He should have known better than to come along with his expertise, where the task lay far outside his capacity.'

His rights, he felt, had been infringed by Arntzen on two counts: first, in sending him to Langfeldt; and, second, in dropping any charges against him. 'It didn't occur to you that I might be displeased by this decision. Until recently I was not just anybody in Norway or the world, and it did not suit me to spend the rest of my days in some kind of amnesty with you, without responsibility for my actions. But you, Mr Attorney General, struck my weapon from my hand.'

Arntzen must have felt rather uneasy as he read this lengthy letter from the old man who would soon be eighty-seven. It left little doubt that Hamsun was still more than capable of causing trouble, despite his having been declared permanently mentally impaired.

We Have Sinned So Greatly

Hamsun was led to believe that his case would go before the courts in September 1946, and he was satisfied. He wanted to explain himself, receive his sentence and get things over with so that he could concentrate on his writing. 'This rubbish has delayed me dreadfully', he complained to his son Tore on 20 August.[71]

He now announced his intention of representing himself, without a lawyer. It took the authorities by surprise, and they were rightly worried about the impression this might make: on one side of the court, a smooth-talking prosecution lawyer with neat stacks of documents in front of him, presenting complex legal and financial arguments on behalf of the state; on the other, an almost entirely deaf eighty-seven-year-old defendant who had been declared mentally impaired, perhaps sitting without a single note before him, with no legal advice to guide him from the empty lawyer's chair at his side, but with the capacity to say the most awkward things. Nobody in the witness box. And a room full of journalists.

They began to evaluate whether it would be better to declare Hamsun incompetent, thereby rendering him without legal capacity and eliminating the need for a court appearance altogether.[72] It was a tempting solution. There was certainly enough evidence to support the notion: his age, his hearing impairment and the psychologists' report. The drawback was that Hamsun could easily complain that a further injustice had been perpetrated.

However, there was another alternative which state, politicians and justice department alike might find more expedient: time. Let the case rest for long enough, they thought, and a bad cold might turn into pneumonia and resolve the problem for everybody. And if Hamsun did not die in eighteen months, before the deadline for completion of such compensation decisions, they could declare him incompetent immediately before the commencement of the court case. And so began an endless series of postponements.

Hamsun was only exaggerating a little when, in January 1947, he claimed that the case had been postponed some five or ten times already. He had seen through the plot: 'The purpose is of course to torture me to the end, when it seems I am too stubborn to die of my own accord! Of course I'm going down-hill, the arteriosclerosis is doing its business, and my eyesight is noticeably worse – which only a year ago was excellent.'[73] He was writing to the person he trusted more than anybody, his lawyer, Sigrid Stray. Writing to his daughter Cecilia, he was even more blunt: 'There's no doubt they are counting on my dying, so they can drop the whole case. But it's a question of whether they've taken into account what a tough old thing I am.'[74]

Journalists started to ask awkward questions. Pressure on the authorities was growing. But how long could Hamsun hold out?

After having been in prison for 325 days, Marie was released, albeit only provisionally.

Hamsun's feelings towards the woman he had once called his 'only love on this earth' were surely never as vicious as they were in May 1946. Six months after his hate-filled outburst at Marie in the reception room of the clinic, Hamsun sat at his rickety desk in the old people's home, surrounded by the papers detailing her interview with Langfeldt. He had received the enormous stack of documents in connection with his summons from the Directorate for Compensation. Everything Marie had told the professor about their marital life was there for him to read. And familiar with the judicial system as he now was, he was sure many other people would be revelling in Marie's intimate revelations.

Hamsun had built a 2-metre-high iron fence around Nørholm to keep out prying eyes. He had turned journalists away throughout his life. He had avoided situations that risked giving the public insight into his private life, booking into hotels and boarding houses under false names, and hounding those who threatened to invade his private sphere. Now it seemed that his own wife had behaved more abominably in her interview with Langfeldt than even Hamsun had suspected.

It was not until months later, in August, when she was visiting Sigrid Stray's house, that Marie would see the court documents. She was distraught. Everything she had said to Langfeldt was there, all her complaints about

Hamsun, and all her confidences about their woeful life together.[75] When she returned home she had to be comforted. Then Marie began writing a long letter to her husband which she posted on 18 August. He did not even open it. On the back of the envelope he wrote in his characteristic handwriting: 'I cannot bear to read this, and must be left in peace. The probable contents of this letter from you are neither here nor there to me.'[76] He then returned the letter to the sender.

Marie received this shattering rejection on 21 August, two days before she was due to appear in court. Like her husband, she was charged with having been a member of the NS Party, as well as with the appropriation of possessions of Norwegians fleeing the occupying forces, and the extensive dissemination of treasonous propaganda.

The prosecution was seeking a sentence of three years' hard labour, a fine of 75,000 kroner and the withdrawal of certain civil rights for ten years. Additionally, the Directorate for Compensation had calculated her proportional financial responsibility for the NS Party's actions at 150,000 kroner. She pleaded not guilty.

Marie was asked if she had anything to add before sentencing. Despite her lawyer's admonitory body language, she stood up and answered: 'I have no reason to apologise for my life and conduct during the war. My sentence has already been decided, thanks to the press. I therefore have nothing more to say.'[77]

The evidence she had amassed of her efforts to help Norwegians who had been arrested and convicted under the Nazi occupation, did nothing to soften the judges' attitude. Marie Hamsun was given the exact sentence demanded by the prosecution.

On the front page of *Dagbladet* that very day were the words: 'Knut Hamsun does not want to return to Nørholm!' It was a sentence that hit her harder than anything a court could have given her. The message Hamsun had written on the envelope had hinted at divorce. Now he was informing the world of the distance between them, and his conscious efforts to make that division permanent.

It confirmed Marie's position as the conspiracy's scapegoat. Those seeking to salvage Hamsun could now believe that his wife had been responsible for isolating him at Nørholm, and for manipulating him to turn his worthy pen to the service of the Germans and the NS authorities. 'A widespread belief – and a widespread lie', she would say of the conspiracy later.[78]

Incensed, Marie went into battle. She brought a serious complaint against Langfeldt, asserting that he had promised the information she had given during the interviews would be held in confidence. Langfeldt answered that he 'never made any promise to Mrs Hamsun that the information she gave would not be used. Of the information she gave, only part is used, and – in my opinion – very sensitively.'[79]

Whatever the exact details of the interview, the professor had certainly won Marie's trust. The intimate details she had confided to him were far from pleasant. Nor were the events that were to follow. The couple had slung the word divorce at each other for years, but only within the four walls of Nørholm. Less than two weeks after Marie had been sentenced so harshly, Hamsun told Christian Gierløff that he wanted to divorce her; it was the first time he had ever aired the idea to anybody apart from his lawyer. The reason was not, he said, on his own account, but for the sake of Victoria.[80]

The balance of power in this strange triangular relationship had been shifting for thirty-eight years and was about to shift again. As so often before, one woman would gain from Hamsun ousting the other. His plan was that Victoria should receive part of the income from the book he was presently working on – and Marie nothing. His divorce would put paid to their shared ownership of Nørholm.

The old man took walks every day, long walks of over an hour. Gierløff joined him on one occasion and was surprised by the distance Hamsun covered.

'What they're hoping is that I shall die. But I shall disappoint them. There's nothing goes as slowly in this world as wishing a man to die.'[81]

Hamsun had an iron grip on himself. He even took a trip to the capital, a pure demonstration of his strength. He intended to finish his book, force the court case through and be acquitted.

He also found strength in the Bible, a good and substantial book, he told Tore, that measured up against anything. 'But when it comes to it, I shall leave it to God to decide whether to save me.'[82] After his release from the clinic, he had also implored Ellinor, who seemed beyond cure, to entrust herself to God's hands. 'You are suffering now. Now is the right, indeed the only, moment to turn to our good and all-powerful Father and God in Heaven. Do it now, my very dearest Ellinor!'[83] His daughter must not think he did not do the same himself: 'It's your old papa writing this to you again: go to God in your sorrows, tell your brother Jesus Christ how you suffer, and ask the Holy Spirit for the guidance to endure it. Rest assured, I have been through it myself, otherwise I would not offer you this advice. It might seem quite strange to you, as it did to me. But you can be sure it will bring you solace and peace.'

Ellinor had fought her problems for many years, but her father wanted her to know that 'the Good Lord has helped many others apart from you and me; He will be willing to help us too in our appeal. But we must be in sincere and desperate need, we must beg earnestly for his mercy. We have sinned so greatly and have so much for which to ask pardon and forgiveness.'

He gave his eldest son a lesson too: 'I am not downhearted, but I am deeply tired of milling about with nothing but my own intelligence for guidance. And if nothing else, then at least our Father is there to complain to. There is some peace to be had from that.'[84] Ellinor must understand that only God could help them both. Yet Hamsun himself did not stop fighting.

My Conscience Is Clear!

People said that the summer of 1947 was warmer than usual, as though nature was signalling to the inhabitants of the North to unwind. The traitor trials had dragged on into their third year, and discussions were now taking place not only in Norway, but across the rest of formerly occupied Europe too, about how long they should be allowed to continue. Norway was prosecuting and sentencing a larger percentage of its population than any other nation.

Hamsun, who would be eighty-eight on 4 August, now entered a third summer of uncertainty as to when he would finally be allowed to stand in a courtroom and explain himself. Through the thin walls and rickety door of his room, the other residents in the old people's home could hear Hamsun talking loudly, even though he had nobody with him. The staff said it sounded as though he was giving a speech.

In fact, that was precisely what he was doing. He was rehearsing and honing the defence speech that he planned to present to the court. He needed to try it out on an audience.

One afternoon in the latter half of July, Hamsun tottered up the steps to Sigrid Stray's office in the centre of Arendal. His lawyer had gathered a small group together to help measure the effectiveness of his oration: among them were Hamsun's friend Gierløff; Max Tau, whom Hamsun and Tore had helped to obtain a Norwegian residence permit; his wife, Tove, who had helped refugees herself and had been engaged in the resistance; and her elderly mother, Laura Filseth, the wife of a prominent newspaper editor.

During the last two years the newspapers had published photographs of German gas chambers, piles of corpses, mass graves and the emaciated survivors of the Nazi concentration camps in Germany, Norway and other occupied countries. Every paper had carried extensive coverage of the Nuremberg Trials. The cases against Göring, Ribbentrop, Speer and other Nazi leaders had revealed how ideas of German expansion and belief in the master race had led to the development of a lethal war machine and a state-sanctioned ethnic cleansing programme that had claimed up to 55 million lives.

Hamsun remained extraordinarily unmoved by these appalling revelations. His perspective hardly seemed to have changed. In the book he was working on currently, he wrote matter of factly: 'Norway now has its own political prisoners. Long ago the political prisoner was a fairytale figure that we read about in Russian books – we never saw him – the whole concept was alien to us. [. . .] But today our country is filled with them, forty, fifty, sixty thousand individuals they say, perhaps thousands more.'[85] Under Terboven's rule, no fewer than forty thousand Norwegians had been arrested for their political activities. Many had suffered torture. Nine thousand had been sent to German concentration camps, and more than two thousand had died in German custody. Did these political prisoners not merit a place in Hamsun's consciousness?

'I am at peace, my mind spotless and my conscience clear. My balance sheet is in perfect order', he told the seven people present in his lawyer's office.

He explained what lay behind his support of Germany: 'We were led to believe that Norway would have a prominent and honourable place in the Greater German society that was dawning, and in which we all believed. Yes, in which we all believed.'[86]

But nobody in that room, apart from Hamsun, had ever believed in a Greater Nazi Germany, or that Norway would have a place in such a future society. Tove Filseth Tau had fought actively against Nazism in Poland, Czechoslovakia, Norway and Sweden. Her husband had lost almost his entire family and all his Jewish friends as a result of the Holocaust. Sigrid Stray had resisted the occupying forces and had been arrested for her efforts.

If those present expected him to renege on his beliefs, to apologise or even to confess to experiencing some doubt after his visit to Hitler, Hamsun defied their expectations. Instead, he began to weave an image of himself as a double agent of some stature:

It surely can't be difficult to understand that I had to write about the occupying forces. I had to avoid arousing their suspicions. Because the reality was, paradoxically, that I was under suspicion. I was surrounded by German officers and men in my house the whole time. During the night, yes also at night until daybreak, by observers who were supposed to keep an eye on me and my house. I received reminders twice, from quite high up in the German hierarchy, that I was not accomplishing as much as was expected of me – that I was not contributing as much as certain named Swedes. It was also pointed out that Sweden was neutral, which Norway was not. They were not pleased with me. They had expected more than they got.

He complained that nobody had told him that it was wrong to sit and write, nobody in the whole country. 'I sat year in and year out in my room writing alone, with nobody for counsel but myself.'

The fact that Hamsun had received anonymous letters expressing horror at his views seemed to have been forgotten. Friends, acquaintances, neighbours and others had also expressed their opposition to his ideas.

But Hamsun's version of events was that he had become isolated from the world: 'I didn't hear what people were saying to me – I was so deaf, it was impossible to engage with me. They used to bang on the stovepipe of the wood burner downstairs for me when my food was ready. I heard the noise. Then I would go down and eat and go up again on my own. That was how it was for years. No letters ever came for me. No little hint. I had a modest name for myself in the country, I had friends in both camps – but there never came the least little bit of good advice from the outside world.'

Many in the room were taken aback. Isolated in his own room for years? But they had seen photographs of him during the war travelling about by boat, plane and car, at home and abroad, even down in a German submarine, vigorous in appearance and sounding as robust as ever in his articles.

'I never got any information or help from my household or family. Everything had to be written down for me, and it was too much of a bother. I just sat there. All I had to refer to were my two newspapers, *Aftenposten* and *Fritt Folk*, and there was nothing in those to say that what I wrote was wrong. And it was <u>not</u> wrong. When I wrote it was the right thing. Let me explain. What did I write? Norwegian youths and men were behaving foolishly and provocatively towards the occupying forces, leading to their own destruction and death. <u>That</u> was what I wrote and expanded on in various ways.'

After about half an hour of talking, Hamsun's voice remained firm and unfaltering.

'Those who gloat over me now because they are outwardly victorious did not receive visits from families as I did, from the lowest upwards, who came and wept for their fathers, brothers and sons who sat behind barbed wire in camps and who were condemned to death. I had no power, but they came to me.'

Two women in the room must have felt these words hit home: Sigrid Stray and her daughter Anne Lise. The latter had come to Hamsun in Nørholm and cried over the imprisonment of her mother, begging for his help. She had received it.

'I appealed to Hitler and to Terboven and made indirect approaches to many men in positions of power. I sent endless telegrams to them. There must be an archive somewhere, where all my telegrams can be found. There were many – I was sending telegrams night and day. My telegrams did not always come to anything, any more than my scribblings in the newspapers served their intended purpose as a warning.'

And he had more to say. 'Perhaps I should have hidden away, gone over to Sweden. Or I could have crawled over to England, as so many others, and come back a hero.' Max Tau and his wife had both fled to Sweden, and they could not fail to notice his scorn as he continued: 'I did nothing of the kind. I believed that I owed it to my fatherland to continue with my farming at a time when everything was in short supply. And I sat there and pondered and telegrammed and wrote. I gained nothing from it. All I gained was that in the eyes of the world I betrayed the Norway I wanted to elevate. Be that as it may, they will blame me. That is the loss I must bear. In a hundred years this will all be forgotten. Even this honourable court will be utterly forgotten. All our names will be wiped from the earth – never to be heard of again. Now it seems that when I sat there and wrote to the best of my abilities and sent telegrams day and night, I was betraying my own country. It seems I was a traitor. So be it. But to this day I cannot see it that way. I was completely at peace with myself.'

The court might ask how he could be at peace with himself. Hamsun had prepared his answer: 'I hold public opinion in rather high esteem. I hold the Norwegian judicial system even higher – but I do not hold it as high as my own judgement of right and wrong, good or evil. I am old enough to have my own guiding principles. During what has turned out to be a long life, in many countries and among all kinds of people, I have always kept and honoured my homeland in my mind, and intend to keep it there while I await my <u>final</u> sentence.'

Hamsun, it now became obvious to everyone in the room, intended to apologise for nothing.

He went around the room shaking hands with each member of his small audience and thanking them for listening. Sigrid Stray had chosen them carefully. The Taus were close family friends, but there was a more pertinent reason: Max Tau had appeared as a defence witness for Tore Hamsun. And the lawyer knew something else: it had not been Tore who had prevented Tau's death in the extermination camp, but Knut Hamsun.

Tau could not help but be struck by the duality of this man, both enemy and saviour, politician and poet, as he listened to how Hamsun intended to defend his wartime actions. Sigrid Stray could not have been the only one in the room to wonder how the Jew, who had himself suffered under Nazism, would react to what he had heard.

Max Tau accepted the trembling right hand of the man to whom he owed his life.

A Glimmer of Hope?

Hamsun set about putting his house in order.

In the late summer of 1947, soon after the meeting in Arendal, he wrote a long letter to Victoria promising that the agreement of 1930 by which she had been bought out of Hamsun's inheritance was to be nullified.

Sigrid Stray drafted his new will, in which Victoria was to be given the same share of his estate as his four other children when it was eventually apportioned. There was no mention of his wife of thirty-eight years. The changes he had made to the will were intended to exclude her, as far as the law permitted. After his death she would be dependent on her children's good will.

Gierløff, Stray and others advised Hamsun against a divorce. It would be enormously long-winded, costly, and might entail the compulsory selling of Nørholm. Besides there was the risk that the divorce might be declared null and void, since the state had already intervened in several instances where it believed that traitors were trying to avoid responsibility for compensation payments.

Hamsun had been determined to go to court without any legal representative. He would, he had announced the previous summer, entrust his case to God's hands. Presumably he planned on making a grandiose farewell performance to the world.

Just after his eighty-eighth birthday, however, he changed his mind. Stray had perhaps managed to persuade him that his case was not beyond hope. She had explained that the state's case against him rested on two planks: first, the articles that he had written after the invasion on 9 April 1940, which Hamsun's speech in her office had proved could be dealt a challenging blow; and, second, his alleged membership of the NS Party. If reasonable doubt could be cast on his ever having actually joined the party, the Directorate for Compensation's case would be far weaker. A guilty verdict might not be a foregone conclusion. Hamsun needed the services of the sharpest lawyer he knew.

Sigrid Stray had just three weeks to prepare.

On 16 December 1947, Gierløff arrived early to fetch his eighty-eight-year-old friend from the old people's home. Hamsun had no intention of facing the world's media covered in cuts from a razor he wielded in his own shaky hand, so Gierløff took him to the barber's in the centre of Grimstad. Shortly afterwards Hamsun arrived at the town bank, where the court was to convene, wearing woollen gloves, a hat, a black suit, a white handkerchief in his breast pocket and a black overcoat. Not since the case against Quisling had the press come out in such force. The photographers raised their cameras, aimed and clicked, before racing up the stairs to take new positions.

There were fewer than thirty seats allotted to the public, and most were occupied by the press. The moment the district judge, Sverre Eide, ordered the usher to bring in the defendant, he lost control of the courtroom. The journalists and photographers jostled to capture what they all knew to be a historic moment, cramming themselves so close to the door that stood between them and Hamsun that the usher found it almost impossible to open it.

As he did, an explosion of flashbulbs went off in Hamsun's face, following him as he tried to turn away. The judge attempted to call order and demanded that the crowd let him through.

Hamsun shouted: 'Don't shoot! Don't shoot!'[87]

According to several journalists present, this barrage of flashes went on for several minutes. Eventually Hamsun was helped to his seat next to Sigrid Stray, but feeling very shaken he refused to sit down. He complained in a loud voice that he was unable to see and needed more light; his son Arild soon came with a paraffin lamp. Two photographers continued to ignore the judge's orders.

'Why are they standing there shooting at me the whole time?' Hamsun asked in the same loud voice. Nobody answered, and he continued to shout in what everybody soon understood to be the booming voice of a man who was extremely deaf: 'It is unfortunate that I'm alive.'[88]

Another explosion of flashbulbs.

Hamsun showed every sign of being in a temporary state of shock, and the flashes of light from the cameras had further weakened his poor vision.

The opening proceedings began, but they were soon interrupted by the author shouting to Sigrid Stray, who was sitting next to him: 'Where's the court sitting? Is it there?'[89]

When does a trial become a sham? Surely when a defendant is incapable of following proceedings. Sverre Eide was in his early thirties and perhaps a little green; a more experienced district judge would at least have adjourned the court for an hour in order to assess Hamsun's condition.

But with a blow of the hammer the court was in session.

The prosecution for the State of Norway, Odd Vinje, contended that there was sufficient evidence to show that Hamsun had been a member of the NS Party. Vinje referred to the party's membership cards, the completed questionnaire that was a part of the joining criteria, and also to Hamsun's own article 'Why I Am a Member of the NS'. The court could study all of these in the 216-page stencilled file that made up the case documents. Furthermore, he noted that Hamsun had worn an NS pin, even during the preliminary hearings.

During the prosecution's opening statement, the court was given further proof that the defendant was unable to follow his own trial. Hamsun suddenly began to speak as though he had been addressed.

The prosecution ignored him and continued: 'In my opinion there is no doubt Hamsun was aware that he was aiding the enemy, that there was war between Norway and Germany, and that Norway was participating in that war. Hamsun must also have known it was inappropriate to behave in this way towards his fatherland in this moment of crisis.'[90]

The judge then invited the defence to open. Sigrid Stray cast serious doubt on the sufficiency of the evidence that Hamsun had ever registered as a member of the NS Party. She also focused attention on the fact that Hamsun had tried to remove Reichskommissar Terboven in a meeting with Hitler.

When the court adjourned, they all went to the nearby Torvkafeen, the Temperance Society's restaurant. There was a transformation in the old man. After a doughnut and an alcohol-free beer, he began handing out cigars. Nobody, not even the district judge, two lay magistrates or even Vinje could refuse. The mood soon relaxed, and there in the middle of the circle sat the eighty-eight-year old. Hamsun was centre stage again – playing the role of the magnanimous benefactor, dazzling everybody.

A glittering interlude before his grand finale.

At almost half past one the members of the court and the defendant returned to their seats. 'Knut Hamsun may speak', intoned the judge. Hamsun did not hear him, so Stray had to indicate that it was his turn. Hamsun, of course, had failed to follow any of the proceedings, deaf to every word of Vinje's prosecution statement as well as to his own lawyer's arguments presented before the adjournment. Still wearing his overcoat, Hamsun now rose to his feet. Unlike the two lawyers, he stepped away from the table, placing himself directly before Eide and his fellow magistrates. The room was so tightly packed that from the viewing area it almost looked as though Hamsun was bearing down over them.

Two people in the room knew, from five months before, what he was about to say. Gierløff had made sure Hamsun had brought his notes with him. Stray had built her defence meticulously around its planned contents. It was imperative he deliver the speech to plan.

His opening sentences were rather more disjointed than at the dress rehearsal. After some fumbling and a pause, he seemed to gather himself; freeing himself from the script in his hand, he began to speak.

Bearing in mind the enormous pressure of the situation, it was impressive how rarely Hamsun departed from the speech he had practised. He made each point systematically, in the rehearsed sequence and generally using the same formulation – at least initially.

He informed the court that he had never been a member of the NS Party. He had grown increasingly isolated – even in his own home. He stood by the articles he had written. Nobody had told him it was wrong to write them and, in fact, it had been right: he had wanted to prevent Norwegians from being punished or even killed by the occupying forces because of their provocative behaviour. He explained how he had tried to find a balance between supporting the occupying forces and using his influence to help Norwegians who were in difficulty.

Soon the eighty-eight-year-old writer was speaking more like an inspired priest giving a sermon. But by this point his words were neither as tactical nor as guarded as he had planned them to be in his rehearsals. He came straight to the reason for writing in support of Germany which was, he said, 'because Norway was going be given a place of honour among the Germanic nations in Europe. The thought appealed to me from the start. Moreover, it inspired me, obsessed me. I don't think it ever left me in all that time, as I sat in solitude. I thought it was a fine idea for Norway, and to this day I still believe it is a fine idea for Norway; well worth fighting and working for.'

There it was. Knut Hamsun regretted nothing.

Then, with mounting emotion, he went on to explain how the flight of the king and the government had left him deeply confused. He had never regarded himself as a traitor, and neither did he now. Those accusing him of treachery would be totally forgotten in a hundred years. For his part, he could wait, he had time, alive or dead. He was completely at peace with himself, and his conscience was clear.

His rhetoric continued to gain in pathos and yet the real climax for his audience had undoubtedly already been reached when, twenty minutes into his thirty-five minute speech, Hamsun admitted he had been, and continued to be, obsessed with the idea of Germany as Europe's leading nation.

Odd Vinje was a measured man. Hamsun's speech was a gift to any prosecution lawyer, but Vinje chose not to exploit the free ammunition he had been handed. He already had more than enough. Stray, meanwhile, focused her energy on punching holes in the claim that Hamsun had been a member of the NS Party.

The prosecution summed up. 'In allowing his name to be used, Hamsun gave support and contributed to the illegal activities of the NS Party. It would be scandalous if he were not held responsible for compensation simply because he was not a signed-up member.'

Stray used her opportunity to reply. 'If we decide that Hamsun was not a member, but that he can be held responsible for compensation despite not being a member, then that is something quite new.' She pointed out that no other country had demanded compensation payments from anybody who had not been an actual member of a party that supported the occupying forces.

The district judge informed the court that judgement would be delivered by the end of the week. An article in *Verdens Gang* reflected the mood of most of the newspapers: 'The picture that emerged was this: a blind old giant raving through the forest – who senses the end is nigh as the undergrowth cracks under his heavy steps. Was he raving like this in the war too, when he did us such immeasurable damage? I think he most certainly was. His bombastic defence speech may seem to go against him, yet in my opinion it is the ultimate proof. The phrases and passages had a dramatic command, closely resembling the articles and quotations the Germans exploited so cleverly in their propaganda. [. . .] In my opinion this is the most significant thing to be taken from our experiences today: he must have been raving like this during the war, and it would be morally wrong to hold him responsible. For Hamsun himself, this is a tragedy – but for world literature it is a drama that has ended better than we thought.'[91]

That Friday, journalists waited impatiently for District Judge Sverre Eide to deliver his verdict. It was finally announced at five o'clock, and the reason for the delay soon became apparent.

The two lay magistrates serving alongside Eide, a district treasurer and a farmer, had opposed the judge's opinion that Hamsun should be acquitted. In their eyes, the fact that Hamsun had continued to be registered as a member of the NS Party after 1942 was his responsibility. Eide had clearly spent a great deal of time trying to educate the two men on the workings of the law: from a legal perspective, he argued, Hamsun had not done enough to be seen as having consented to membership.[92] The jurist found Hamsun not guilty. But the two lay magistrates thought differently, and as they were in the majority, it was their judgement that carried.

Sigrid Stray calculated that the Hamsuns' joint fines of 575,000 kroner would, in practice, leave them bankrupt. But a few voices in the press did not consider Hamsun's punishment severe enough; the word 'scandal' appeared in several instances.

Hamsun and his lawyer lodged their appeal on 29 December 1947.

The writer had never contested his support of Quisling's government, but during the spring of 1948 Hamsun repeated his assertions that he had never joined the NS Party, never received a membership card and never paid a membership fee.

Stray was at least heartened by the news that one of the five judges who would preside over the appeal proceedings in the High Court had already signalled a critical attitude to the hardline approach being taken in several of the traitor trials. Stray launched investigations in search of new evidence. She spoke to several people in the NS Party, at head office and local level. All the fresh information confirmed Hamsun's version of events. The office manager at the party headquarters gave a written statement categorically stating that Hamsun had not been a member; four procedures would have had to be completed for membership to be valid, and in Hamsun's case only one document existed.[93]

Stray would argue in her summary that, in Hamsun's case, the Norwegian State had changed the criteria governing the level of proof required to establish party membership, as well as the interpretation of the law. Two days before she was due to appear in the High Court, Stray compiled her appeal, sending a copy to Hamsun before leaving for Oslo. She was ready to refute the prosecution's accusations, one after another.[94]

On Friday, 18 June 1948, she put her case before the High Court. The following day it was the turn of the state prosecution; the chief of the Directorate for Compensation did not lodge any fresh evidence, but did withdraw an appeal for an increase in Hamsun's fine.

The following Tuesday an anxious Sigrid Stray was informed of the judgement: the High Court had come to the decision that Hamsun was, after all, a member of the NS Party. She was disappointed, she told the judges, and Hamsun would consider it a miscarriage of justice. She was also puzzled that Hamsun's fine had only been reduced by 100,000 kroner, to 325,000 kroner. Asking the judge what had convicted Hamsun, she was told it had been the sum of the parts.

When Hamsun was informed, he telegraphed his lawyer: 'Don't be disappointed. I thank you, in the name of posterity, for your excellent defence. You presented and upheld the truth. The rest cannot be blamed on you!'[95]

Strange to Be a Dead Man before I Am Dead

On the day he was notified that five judges in the highest court of Norway had found him guilty, Hamsun wrote the two sentences that would complete the manuscript he had worked on for almost three years: 'Midsummer 1948. Today the High Court has passed judgement, and I end my writing.'

He had accomplished the astonishing feat of finishing a book in his eighty-ninth year.

But nobody wanted to publish it. Even Harald Grieg, director of Gyldendal where Hamsun was still the largest shareholder, stood in the way of its release.

Hamsun had moved back to Nørholm the previous Christmas, 1947. His return had been motivated by several factors: his book had been nearing completion, Marie was still serving a long prison sentence and now he was set on fighting for his home.

With the Hamsun family's involvement with the Germans during the war, Nørholm had become a potent symbol of the Nazi years. The sheer magnitude of the fine imposed upon the couple was a sure sign that the authorities wanted to force the Hamsuns to sell up, and obliterate this symbol for good. It was a pleasure Hamsun intended to rob the victors of.

He had hoped that his publisher and close friend of twenty years, would be his most important ally in this demanding battle, and, after his release from the psychiatric clinic in early 1946, he had written to Grieg to ask for his help in a financial matter. Grieg had frequently helped him out in similar situations before the war. Indeed he had always claimed that it was a pleasure to assist Hamsun, as Gyldendal's principal writer and shareholder, professionally or otherwise.

This time Grieg was not so eager to help. Instead of sending a personal response, he passed the request on to his office manager. Hamsun was understandably upset, and wrote a second letter: 'Dear Grieg, I wonder what has come between you and me? It can't be my "national treachery", so it must be something else. I can't work it out myself, but I would be happy if you could tell me. Naturally I am a dead man in Norway and the world over, but this can hardly be what you are trying to tell me. So what is it? Let me ask you from the heart if there is anything I have done, or omitted to do?'[96]

Grieg took days to formulate an answer. He was troubled by questions of destiny, guilt and personal indebtedness: he owed a great deal to Hamsun. Without Hamsun's financial and literary power, Gyldendal's Oslo branch could not have bought its independance from the Danish company twenty-two years ago. He was also conscious of the boundless trust that Hamsun had shown in him over the years; and how Hamsun's backing, as the largest share-holder in the company had fortified Grieg's position relative to the Board and other owners. But, Grieg had also been an extremely effective publisher for Hamsun: they had done well by one another.

But there was something else: Grieg could not be sure whether he owed his life to Hamsun. The publisher been held in Grini prison camp, from where many prisoners had been sent to Germany, to face starvation and torture. But in the autumn of 1942 he had been released. Grieg knew that Hamsun had been asked to intervene on his behalf, but no one was sure what his actual involvement, if any, had been. Some claimed that the author had refused to help, others that he had furnished Marie and Tore with a letter of introduction and told them what to say to Terboven. It was Marie to whom Grieg had offered his thanks.[97]

Looking back, Grieg remembered his last meeting with Hamsun in 1941. The author had told him to be careful. At the time he had taken this as a sign of concern; now he thought it may have been a threat. And when his brother, the poet Nordahl Grieg, was shot down over Germany in 1943, it had done nothing to soften Hamsun's pro-German stance. Their differences, Grieg now concluded, were irreconcilable.

The days went by and Hamsun did not receive a reply. He was also looking over the past; the fact was that he had expressed a reluctance to intervene on

Grieg's behalf. But the only person that could have told Grieg this was Tore. After waiting for over a week Hamsun wrote to Tore, blaming him of breaking his trust, and thus causing the rift between Grieg and himself; 'Perhaps it is because I once expressed that I wasn't willing to apply for his freedom again? Perhaps you've told him this and tainted me so that you and mama can take all the credit for his release?'[98]

Grieg finally wrote back: 'Dear Hamsun. You ask "what has come between you and I". The answer is very simple. In a battle of life and death we stood on opposite sides – and still do. There are few people I have admired as much as you, and few I have been as fond of. None has disappointed me more profoundly.' Grieg concluded: 'I understand from your letter that it pains you that things should have turned out the way they have between us. I want you to know that it pains me no less.'[98]

Grieg had no idea at this time that the old man was in the process of completing a new script. Neither did he envisage any demand for Hamsun's previous books in the post-war years. Some time would have to pass before Gyldendal could think of trying to warm up the markets again for new editions of Hamsun's novels. Neither did it seem realistic that Hamsun would be able to hold on to his shares for long, given the vast fines that had been imposed on him and his family.

On the day Hamsun received his old friend's note, he wrote on the same envelope: 'Dear Grieg. I thank you for your letter. It was a gift. That is all I have to say. Your Knut Hamsun.'[100]

Grieg probably barely considered why Hamsun might thank him thus; although he must have noticed that the old man's capacity to hit home was still intact. Hamsun may well have been reminding Grieg of their mutual indebtedness. However, as Hamsun's apology to his son written on the same day shows, he might also have meant his thanks literally, since Grieg's letter reassured Hamsun that his son had not betrayed him as he had feared.[101]

Hamsun's relationships to his publishers had often been fraught, resulting in several breaks. But these conflicts had rarely resulted in negative outcomes for him; in fact they generally led to improved terms. It was not until the summer of 1947, that the full consequences of his rift with Grieg began to dawn on Hamsun: 'What use is it anyway that I write and write, he remarked to Tore, "I probably shan't even get a publisher. Funny to be a dead man, before I am dead."'[102]

The author who owned one-sixth of Norway's largest publishing house, was in reality without a publisher. Now that Grieg perceived him as a mortal enemy, he would try to kill him off as an author, both at home and abroad. Thus strangling him economically, and doubtless compelling him to give up his shares.

Hamsun faced a formidable opponent.

His first counter-move was to appoint Tore as his rights manager and equip him with the necessary powers to act. Hamsun was a hard task master. Only a few houses – Mondadori in Italy, José Janes in Spain – were actively interested in Hamsun now, and the Allied administration had closed down his faithful old publishers in Germany. Tore was instructed to find new ones, and soon there was some interest.

Later that year, Hamsun leaked the news to the press that he was writing a new book. Unsurprised, but nonetheless disappointed, he acknowledged that Harald Grieg had not shown the slightest interest in the bait. He could see that the time had come to exercise what weight he had as a writer.

In the New Year of 1948 he asked Sigrid Stray to help him make a complete break with Gyldendal, taking all his books with him. Grieg soon made it clear that if Hamsun was going to carry through this intention, he would have to buy himself out. Hamsun was furious. But a letter formulated by Hamsun and sent in Stray's name failed to make any significant impression on the publisher. Hamsun's confrontational approach was achieving nothing.

Sigrid Stray announced that she would visit Nørholm. Her delicate task following the judgment of the High Court was to rescue Hamsun from bankruptcy and the forced sale of Nørholm. If there was to be the least chance of success, she had to make Hamsun realise that he had to reach an agreement with Grieg.

Stray had received two shocking pieces of news in Oslo. The first had been the loss of Hamsun's appeal at the High Court. The second was that already some time ago, Harald Grieg had made secret moves to secure the two hundred Gyldendal shares presently held by the Hamsun family. She had discovered from the Directorate of Compensation that Grieg had already put in a bid, as he waited impatiently for the final decision of the High Court. Hamsun's publisher had shown his true colours; his insistence that political differences were all that separated the two men, had been untrue.

Stray contacted a bank to enquire how large a loan could be taken out on Hamsun's shares in Gyldendal. Hamsun would, she was told, receive a thousand kroner per share. She now made sure that Harald Grieg got the message, through a mutual acquaintance, that the shares were not for sale. His response arrived even sooner than she could have hoped. Grieg wanted a meeting with Stray.

It was a long time since Hamsun had tasted the sweetness of victory.

Grieg no longer had a clear idea of how his former poker partner would play his three trump cards: the rights to his past works, his shares in Gyldendal, and his new manuscript.

The value of the latter would soon be confirmed. Hamsun handed a copy of *On Overgrown Paths* to Stray, who in turn passed it to Max Tau for his opinion.

'I could not comprehend', Tau wrote later, 'how a person of his age, and after all he had gone through, could be capable of writing like this. It was as though the pages of the manuscript exuded a kind of magic, which revealed his creative force once more, in all its richness. . .'

The following day Tau rushed over to see Sigrid Stray. 'He has all his creative power and zest for life in tact, and the new book will be a success the world over!'[102]

Sigrid Stray was growing increasingly confident that their opponent Harald Grieg did not hold the strongest cards.

The Lion's Claw

On 20 July 1948, the irrepressible Sigrid Stray was back in Grimstad fighting on behalf of her client of eighteen years. This time the battle took place not in a courtroom, but in the hotel lounge where she met with Harald Grieg.

Stray returned to Hamsun satisfied with the negotiations. With his shares as security, Gyldendal was prepared to offer Hamsun a loan of 400,000 kroner. Grieg would pay him an annual advance on his royalties of 20,000 kroner for the rest of his life. But Grieg also stipulated that *On Overgrown Paths* would not be published until after Hamsun's death.

Hamsun was furious. His book must be published. He rejected the offer, telling Stray that he would rather pawn Nørholm, his shares and absolutely everything he owned. He was going to buy himself free of Grieg and Gyldendal – no matter what the cost.

Stray was hard-pressed to serve his best interests.

The Norwegian State was not known for its patience or understanding in the collection of fines. Hamsun owed 325,000 kroner, in addition to Marie's fine of 150,000 kroner. Now Hamsun wanted Stray to find a publisher willing to pay over half a million kroner to purchase his back catalogue from Gyldendal, while at the same time giving him a loan of several hundred thousand kroner. In her view this was impossible.

Stray was rational where her client was not. She knew that in reality there were only two routes to save Hamsun from financial ruin, now that he was so set on publishing his latest book: either he had to be persuaded to drop the idea of publication altogether, or Grieg had to be persuaded to publish it fast.

Stray should perhaps have seen Hamsun's reaction coming. She had known both Hamsun and his wife for a long time. For years the couple from Nørholm had been coming to her with their acrimonious complaints about each other. How often had Marie tried to explain, woman to woman, the huge price she and the children had paid for the way her husband always put his writing before everything else?

Stray now witnessed this uncompromising and merciless streak at first hand. She tried persuading Hamsun to back down, warning him that he risked financial ruin. She might just as well have tried to make her office chair perform a pirouette. She requested another meeting with Grieg, enclosing a copy of a letter Hamsun had written to her: 'The book will sell itself. Take my word for it. I shall not ask more of you in this life. I will not last beyond the winter, in a few days I enter my ninetieth year.'[104]

But having read the manuscript, Grieg was now doubly convinced that *On Overgrown Paths* should not be published. The strength of the writing certainly tore Professor Langfeldt's diagnosis to shreds, and there was no doubting Hamsun's sharpness of mind – 'One feels the ever-present lion's claw', Grieg concluded – but it also confirmed to the publisher that 'Hamsun still holds the same opinions today as those he expressed during the war. This not only is evident from his defence speech in court, reproduced here in its entirety, but runs like a red thread through his entire description of events.'[105]

Stray had to use every ounce of her strength, patience and cunning to stop Hamsun hitting the self-destruct button. Having suffered a rebuff from Grieg, and having also failed to ignite the interest of Aschehoug, Gyldendal's major competitor in Norway, Hamsun stated that he would send it to a minor publisher, or publish it himself. Stray managed to dissuade him, convincing Hamsun that it might send out the wrong impression and the public might think he had been relegated.

She persuaded him instead to go another round with Grieg, and she met the publisher again in Kragerø in mid-August.

Grieg was extremely concerned about the uncertain future of the Hamsun shares, which represented a considerable amount of power in his company. The publisher was privy to a few family secrets. After Hamsun had transferred some of his shares to Ellinor, she was now one of the largest shareholders in Gyldendal; Grieg, however, also knew that she had been admitted into a psychiatric institution in Oslo. Cecilia, who was on her way out of her second marriage, also owned a considerable number of shares, as did both Tore, who was likewise contemplating divorce and whose debts exceeded his income and assets, and ex-SS volunteer Arild, who would soon take over the loss-making Nørholm farm. Finally preying on the publisher's mind was Marie and the kind of control she might exert over her husband's shares, both before and after Hamsun's death.

Grieg and the board felt it was vital to secure these potentially loose cannons. When he received further confirmation that Hamsun would resist any sale of his shares to Gyldendal, Grieg decided to begin manoeuvres that might obtain indirect control over them for himself.

With security in Hamsun's one hundred shares, Gyldendal agreed to loan the writer 200,000 kroner and a further 150,000 in lieu of future earnings. In exchange, Grieg would hold voting rights over the shares held by the Hamsun family, as well as having first refusal if any of the children's shares were to be sold. The publisher also secured sole publishing rights on Hamsun's entire artistic output.

Having managed to hold onto Nørholm, retain his shares in the publishing house, and force Gyldendal to market and sell his past books, Hamsun was now in a position to pay the 325,000-kroner compensation fine. His only remaining goal was to get *On Overgrown Paths* published in Norway.

Despite his criticisms, Grieg had discerned the outline of the lion's claw in the manuscript. In the battle over the shares, Hamsun had demonstrated the cunning, strength and lethality of the king of cats. And Hamsun was not finished with Grieg yet. The final battle between Knut Hamsun and Harald Grieg had yet to commence.

One man, Christian Gierløff, tried to restrain the old lion. He would pay a heavy price for his attempts.

A Suicide Mission

Through the summer of 1948, Hamsun desperately sought a home for his latest work – even if that home was abroad. When the small Swedish publisher Ljus, partly owned by the publishing giant Norstedt, expressed interest, *Dagbladet* swooped in, making it known that Hamsun was to 'publish a book in Sweden. About his experiences during the Nazi years'.[106] The publishing house came under immediate fire and Ljus's interest cooled. Other approaches in Sweden, Denmark and Finland all came to nothing.

Hamsun and Stray continued to pursue Grieg. Some time in early 1949 Hamsun asked his lawyer to make contact with his old publisher. This year would see Hamsun's ninetieth birthday and, reminding Grieg of all the times in the past he had gone to such lengths to mark the various milestones in Hamsun's life and career, he suggested that it might be a good time to bring out *On Overgrown Paths*. Having courted Grieg's pity, Hamsun also added that a Swiss publisher was interested in putting the book out in the German-speaking countries, and that a Spanish edition was being planned.

For the first time since the question of publication had been mooted a year before, Grieg did not immediately reject the idea. He requested that the manuscript be sent to him again, and asked for a conference with Stray. Hamsun's suspicions were aroused. 'What is it about this time? Does he want to meddle with my manuscript? It is flawed, as you might expect from an old man, but I've already meddled with everything that is to be meddled with.'[107]

In March, Grieg and Stray met in Oslo, and the publisher capitulated.

It became clear to Grieg that Hamsun was not going to relent until the book was published. Genuine interest shown by publishers overseas, and now some independents in Norway, was adding to the pressure on him. Grieg remained adamant on one issue, however: public opinion meant it was out of the question that the book should be published in time for Hamsun's ninetieth birthday. Stray did manage to get him to concede to a press release just before 4 August, which would announce publication later that autumn.

Grieg realised that, when the content of the book was known, the conservative and generally more Hamsun-friendly press might well ask the author uncomfortable questions. Focus was bound to fall on the state's use of forensic psychiatry on an author who had managed to write such a book – particularly in the light of the way he had been treated and the diagnosis that had been made.

But Hamsun's attacks on Langfeldt were vitriolic, and publisher and lawyer now made another agreement which Hamsun was not party to: Hamsun's rancorous condemnations of the psychiatrist had to be toned down or removed. On this Stray was in wholehearted agreement, having already warned Hamsun that these put him in a precarious legal position. Christian Gierløff was of the same opinion, and Stray and Grieg now suggested that Hamsun's old friend should be the one to convince the stubborn old writer to moderate his words.

Both must have sensed they had given him a suicide mission.

For a month Hamsun read and commented on Gierløff's stream of letters, which suggested changes in passages relating to Langfeldt and his clinic. Then Hamsun stopped opening them. The pile of letters from his friend grew with each passing month. When he had left fifteen such letters unopened, Hamsun finally sent a reply, its four summary sentences not being addressed to Gierløff, but to his family: 'Mr Christian Gierløff knows that I no longer answer him. Yet he persists in pestering me with letters and parcels, which I never open. I have never heard or read of such shamelessness in a grown person. Now, I respectfully ask for the protection of his family.'[108]

Hamsun had written more than six thousand letters in his life. This must have been among the most unkind.

Hamsun was no less callous towards his wife. Marie had been released from prison on 19 August 1948, just as Grieg and Stray had been negotiating her and her family's fate. Tore had come to collect her in his car. She did not need to ask: his subdued concern told her that she would not be returning to

Nørholm. In the basement of Tore's house in Asker outside Oslo, next to a ceramics workshop he had set up for himself, there was a room she could have. It was so dark and cramped that her grandchildren didn't dare to venture down there alone. Tore suggested she might make a trip to Copenhagen in the new year, and stay with Cecilia for a while.[109]

Following Stray's advice, Hamsun had abandoned the idea of filing for a divorce. But he still intended to cut his wife out of his estate, now that the triangle had been realigned: it would be Victoria and Hamsun versus Marie.

Hamsun had been left with 17,000 kroner out of Gyldendal's loan and advance after paying the fine to the state. Almost a third was to be sent to Victoria, and quickly, as Hamsun instructed Stray: 'I have wronged her throughout her life.'[110] Hamsun had never been as critical of himself as this before, at least not in writing.

It was the week of Marie's release. The timing is unlikely to have been co-incidental.

Hamsun now also made preparations to pass on Nørholm, as had been his intention for many years. In October 1948, the former SS volunteer Arild had finally faced charges. His father had predicted a mild sentence – 'It won't be much to worry about. It would have been worse a few years ago – "justice" is not so cocksure of itself any more'[111] – and he was proved right: eighteen months' hard labour (minus the nine months already spent in custody), 700 kroner confiscated and payment of 10,000 kroner in compensation.

The day after the court ruling, Hamsun took Arild to Arendal, where Stray had prepared a document under his instructions. Now almost ninety years of age, the farmer was finally giving up his land and home to the next generation. His youngest son would take over Nørholm. His oldest child, Victoria, would have shares in Gyldendal, as well as a stake in the value of Nørholm's contents and author's rights equal to his other children. Marie would receive absolutely nothing, apart from an entitlement to stay at Nørholm after his death.

The scapegoat was herself desperate to point the finger at someone else. Marie Hamsun was in a rotten state. She spent a good part of the next eighteen months attempting to extract an admission of blame from Langfeldt. The professor, she averred, was the root cause of her misery: 'My husband has left me with nothing to my name, shut me out from Nørholm which was my home for thirty years, without a penny to live on. I am sixty-seven years old, I have angina and a stomach ulcer, and am so exhausted that I cannot work.'[112]

Marie stayed alternately with Tore and Cecilia, who pleaded her mother's case with Hamsun. His answer was brutal: 'I have told Mama that I never want to live a single day under the same roof as her as long as I live. Surely that's clear enough? [. . .] I understand it is painful for Mama and Ellinor and the boys – and neither is it a joy for me – that I'm still not out of this world, but here I am, unfortunately.'[113] Neither the children nor their mother needed to worry, he concluded, that he would live for ever; no doubt Marie was shedding tears of rage that he had not yet kicked the bucket.

. . . But No Martyr

The autumn of 1949 saw the publication of Aschehoug's *Who's Who?*, which contained references to 3,500 well-known Norwegians. Knut Hamsun's name had been removed.

Hamsun's ninetieth birthday was approaching, but efforts to organise a message of salutation from other Norwegian authors had led to nothing. Neither *Dagbladet* nor *Morgenbladet* gave the occasion a single mention. *Aftenposten* printed only an editorial note, in which readers were reminded, quite reasonably, that the German occupation was still too close for it to be possible to give as dispassionate an assessment of Hamsun as the quality of his writing might merit.

The author Sigurd Hoel, however, did not skirt the issue. His long article, published in time for Hamsun's birthday, appeared in both the Swedish *Dagens Nyheter* and the Danish *Informationen* – although only one small Trondheim newspaper carried it in Norway itself. Hoel looked back on Hamsun's eightieth anniversary:

> Already then Hamsun was a Nazi; but if this was mentioned at all, it was referred to in passing as a little blotch on a great writer's creative canvas. Now, ten years later, this blotch has, in most people's opinion, become the central feature of the entire picture. [. . .] What salvages most of Hamsun's writing is that his Nazism was after all only one streak in him. His writing flowed from quite different sources – sources of feeling and compassion, not harshness, arrogance and heartlessness. It has been said that Hamsun was an artist in every fibre. That is not true. In several of his novels [. . .] we can see how the poet's political opinions and agitation lie like alien objects in his books, like rocks in a field. But in the majority of his works we find absolutely no agitation in the pure sense of the word. They are simply works of art, created by a mind far richer than the one that made itself heard over the past few years.'[114]

Six weeks after Hamsun's ninetieth birthday, *On Overgrown Paths* came out.

Sigrid Stray's note to Harald Grieg after she had sifted through the reviews that day betrayed a note of triumph: 'They are bowing to his genius. No one is reacting negatively to its release. Quite the contrary.'[115] Grieg must have registered with some satisfaction that sales figures far exceeded expectations; the first print run of five thousand had sold out within days.

Writing in *Dagbladet*, a young reviewer, Philip Houm, observed that Hamsun had been no more reluctant to recognise the evils of Nazism in the 1930s than the post-war Moscow faithful were to admit to the evils of Communism now. In drawing this political parallel, Houm transformed Hamsun from merely a solitary voice in world history to one in a long line of artists and intellectuals who had supported despotic regimes.[116]

For all that, Houm did not venture into the hazardous territory of the attorney general's decision and Langfeldt's diagnosis. *Aftenposten*'s critic, however, did dare to step into the minefield: 'It is possible that the case against Hamsun was not dealt with correctly. Patience and mildness can be a dreadful mistake and lead to gruesome results, as was surely the case here.'[117] The reviewer was adamant that Hamsun would never have been cleared in a criminal court. Nor could he be morally excused: 'Hamsun was not only guilty of treason. [. . .] His actions and conduct were a betrayal of all human beings, ordinary human beings who just wanted to live their lives.'

With the exception of *Aftenposten*, the major papers were generally positive about *On Overgrown Paths*, their reviews focusing on the literary merits of the book. The few who were critical worried that this might be the first of many works that would defend the wartime actions of German sympathisers. Only two or three saw any evidence in the book that Langfeldt's diagnosis had been correct. The great majority of reviewers in fact took the opportunity to bring the author back in from the cold. The divide between Hamsun the writer-genius and Hamsun the political fool was now permanently established for the Norwegian public.

No one felt moved to complain on Hamsun's behalf that his incarceration in the psychiatric clinic had been an abuse of power. The critics went no further than to make Langfeldt's diagnosis the object of gentle irony.

Nevertheless, Langfeldt did publish a statement in the press excusing his diagnosis, stressing that in forensic psychiatry the term 'permanent' did not mean for ever, or unchanging. Hamsun's extraordinary memoirs, therefore, were completely conceivable; approximately half of all stroke sufferers make a recovery, said Langfeldt, 'and after so many years, it comes as no surprise that such an improvement took place as to allow him to write again'.[118] The professor's argument, however, was premised on his belief that Hamsun had not begun writing his book until years after leaving the clinic. In fact, he had started making his first notes immediately after the war during his internment in Grimstad Hospital. Most of the book had already been written by mid-1947.

Strangely, nobody questioned Langfeldt as to why his psychiatric report lacked clarity on one central consideration: whether Hamsun had been assessed by comparison with an average person of eighty-six, or with his younger self – and, if the latter, at what age and using what tangible facts. It was only years later that Langfeldt confirmed he arrived at his diagnosis by comparing Hamsun with his former self,[119] although Hamsun no doubt more than satisfied the criteria for a normal person of his age.

The intricacies of these issues remained undiscussed, although *On Overgrown Paths* had nevertheless focused a critical eye on the motives of the attorney general and Professor Langfeldt. But with memories of the German occupation still fresh, the public was hardly ready or willing to instigate investigations on Hamsun's behalf. Nor was there any surge of sympathy for him. As Ivan Pauli rightly observed in Sweden's *Morgon-Tidningen*, Hamsun's book had not succeeded in making him a martyr. For now, it would have to suffice that the author had been resurrected.

What every reviewer forgets, however, is that books outlive their time. Eventually, *On Overgrown Paths* would be employed to ridicule the psychiatrists' diagnosis of 'permanent mental impairment'. The fact that this term was in reality the only one available to Langfeldt and Ødegård at the time was increasingly ignored. They could of course have refused to put any diagnosis on Hamsun at all. But the question still lingers as to whether the professor, the attorney general and the Norwegian government itself had already decided on the diagnosis before any assessments had actually occurred.

The evidence certainly seems to indicate that such a politically, legally and ethically dubious dialogue did indeed take place.[120]

She Came with the Spring

Marie was given a copy of *On Overgrown Paths* as soon as it came out at the end of September 1949. She did not show herself again until she had finished reading it. She was greatly relieved. In the book's version of events, she had been definitively tricked by Langfeldt. Hamsun had gone to some lengths to excuse her.

The last pages, however, were painful. Hamsun had written beautifully of Maren Lægdslem, a local woman in Hamarøy who walked from farm to farm, begging for enough to survive on; he had betrayed not a single word of regret for having forced his own wife to do the same.

But it was another woman that Hamsun thought about that autumn: Marika Stiernstedt, the Swedish authoress who nineteen years before had left a burning red streak through him. Hamsun ensured a copy of *On Overgrown Paths* was sent to her from the Swedish publisher, and she, in turn, sent him her memoirs, *Mostly Truth*, in which she described their meeting in Oslo. He had contemplated giving her his Nobel Prize medal, but that had gone to Goebbels. Now he wrote to her: 'Dearest, thank you so much for your letter and the book. I am blind now and cannot read, not even your letter, only the big letters in the magazines. Oh, how your letter filled me with joy. I write this to you blind, but from habit and in a little light. [. . .] I have lived for too many years, but thank my God for having had a rich life. This is my last greeting for you – dearest – dearest.'[121]

A couple of weeks later he scribbled a last greeting to his daughter Victoria. 'I hope we have made good arrangements for you, dearest Victoria. Mrs Stray has been clever for you on my behalf. [. . .] Don't worry about me, I am fine. My dearest Victoria, live well. Your old Papa.'[122]

On 12 December, he asked Tore to visit him for Christmas. 'Come just this once, I beg you.' Four days later he reworded his plea. 'Don't worry that I asked you to come. Come when you want to yourself, and for the sake of Leif [Hamsun's grandson].'[123]

Hamsun was no longer in a position to make demands.

This would be his last letter to his son. Tore came to Nørholm for Christmas, bringing with him his children Anne Marie and Leif; two-year-old Ingeborg stayed in Oslo with her mother. Tore photographed Hamsun with his grandchildren. Their grandmother was alone in the house in Asker, just as she had been during Hamsun's ninetieth birthday celebrations.

The winter of 1950 passed into yet another miraculous season, a springtime that again drove all nature and its creatures to their extremes. It was at such a time, forty-two years earlier, that Hamsun had ended his novel *Benoni* with the words 'Edvarda came with the spring'.

She had been a dangerous, desirable woman, and as though he had written his own future in the novel, he had met Marie on 17 April 1908. Now, as he shuffled about the rooms of Nørholm staring half-blind at the almanacs, he suddenly noticed the date: it was 17 April, exactly forty-two years later.

It was a Monday night. Brit, Arild's wife, had gone to bed. She heard Hamsun pacing up and down in the hallway. He stopped, knocked on the door and stood before her. 'You'd best get Mama home.'[124] Brit rushed downstairs to tell Arild, who asked his father if he should write to Marie. He was told he had to telegram immediately. It was already too late to send a message that evening, but Arild promised to go to the telegraph office first thing next morning.

'Ring immediately.' Arild telegraphed his mother, frightening her out of her wits.

Two days later Marie was aboard the coastal ship. Arild and Brit met her at the quayside in Arendal, together with their oldest son, Esben, who had not seen his grandmother since she had left them before Christmas 1947 to start her prison sentence. Her hair, he thought, was a great deal greyer.

Hamsun had clearly planned the scene of their reunion with great care. He sat in his tatty old wicker chair in his room next to hers, with the dividing door open. He had placed himself so as to be turned away from the door, making her walk around and stop in front of him. His beard made him look like an elderly patriarch, Marie thought. He drew up a chair for her and gave her his hand.

'You've been away a long time, Marie. In all these days you've been away I haven't had anyone to speak to but God.'[125]

It had been almost five years. Marie claimed later that these were the only words he ever said to her about the years of their separation.[126] She moved into her old room and, sitting there, worked on the notes she had brought with her in her suitcase. She wrote about their life together – with the door between their two rooms alternately open and closed – through the summer, autumn and winter 1950, and on into 1951, through the whole year and finally into 1952.

Marie described to Tore the cantankerous state in which she had found Hamsun, although towards her he had been 'kind and pleasant'.[127] He was extremely irritable with both Arild and Brit, making a long list of complaints about his daughter-in-law: Nobody had looked after his infected eyes, nobody had made sure he had taken his vitamins, nobody cared for his clothes. Not to mention his mostly sitting on a box in the corridor, wishing he were dead.

Their finances were in an abysmal state. Marie managed to secure a 20,000-kroner loan, while Sigrid Stray approached the Justice Department to ask for a refund of part of Hamsun's compensation fine. She argued that the sum had been too onerous; it had threatened the writer's entire assets, which was contrary to the intention of the law. Her request was dismissed, but she did manage to agree a reduction in Marie's compensation fine.

Early in 1951, heavy snow broke the roof on the outhouse. The couple contacted Stray to see if she could find a solution for their increasingly difficult financial situation. As she left for Nørholm, the lawyer received a letter from Harald Grieg which she brought with her. It would bring some cheer to her old client: the letter informed her that Hamsun's *Collected Works* had been given a prominent place in one of Gyldendal's latest catalogues. Stray found Hamsun to be a changed man. The giant had vanished. When Stray told him that the catalogue was to be sent to every bookshop in the country, he began to cry.[128]

That day Hamsun had further confirmation that he had regained admittance to the literary establishment; *Aftenposten* reported that Hamsun had been elected to the Order of Mark Twain. He was the first Norwegian to receive this honour.

However, there was little the lawyer could do to improve the finances of the family at Nørholm. On her journey home, she wondered if the real reason for her being invited there was to see how much things had improved between the couple. Perhaps it was this easing of marital tensions that motivated Hamsun, on 15 March 1951, to sign a document cutting Victoria out of the estate once more. She would receive no shares now: her part of Hamsun's estate was to go to Arild, and her share of the author's rights would now be divided between Marie's children.

The evil triangle had still not lost its terrible hold.

Victoria would contest the changes to his will after his death – and, after several rounds, win.[129]

That April, Marie worked on the memoirs that would eventually be published under the title *Regnbuen* ('The Rainbow'): 'The old lady that I see in the mirror when I turn my head a little, is myself. And next to me, in the tatty wicker chair that creaks so badly, sits my husband, bowed by destiny and advanced years.' She described how she had wept over the outhouse that stood in ruins. Hamsun had comforted her: 'Don't cry, Marie, it's not worth your tears. Soon we die, life is so short. And yet it often seems too long. [...] Life is so short, a mockery.'

Marie was only seventy. She intended to live for a while yet – but not, if she could help it, in these squalid conditions.

That spring, she wrote an angry article, printed in the German press and reported in several Norwegian papers, revealing how she and her husband were living in poverty. Later that summer she encouraged Tore to ask Grieg to republish her books and poems in celebration of her seventieth birthday in November. Money played some part, but more important was the idea that she might bask in the same emergent reacceptance that her husband had started to enjoy.

Grieg apologised to Tore that 'these excellent children's books are not available. But I think I would do her a disservice if we published them now. As you know, there is a widespread opinion that she was more active during the war than your father. Many seem to think that it was she who dragged him with her.'[130]

Marie, of course, rejected any claim that she had been the more active of the two: 'A widespread opinion – a widespread lie. [...] Blame was poured over me largely with the purpose of salvaging an asset – Knut Hamsun – for Norway. But naturally many people who prized Hamsun wanted to save him for themselves too. I was a convenient scapegoat in 1945. [...] You [Grieg] knew my husband yourself. I think you must know which of us was the most dominant. He was a man who never allowed his opinions to be dictated by anybody.'[131]

But she did not have her husband's capacity to force Grieg to retreat. And Hamsun no longer had the strength to fight for his only love on this earth.

Confirmations of Hamsun's works' rehabilitation by the establishment kept coming. In life, however, he was obviously fading away. He was almost entirely deaf, and only sentences of the simplest nature were repeatedly shouted into his left ear by his patient wife. He was blind. The only thing he responded to was the gentle touch of a hand on his arm, or Marie adjusting his pillow. He was like a child, once again struggling for his share of motherly attention.

This time he was competing with himself: Marie was writing about him, about their lives, in the room next door, continually disturbed and dragged away by the invalid's demands. Now it was his presence that interrupted her writing, when for so many years he had complained of her troubling him. His writing had shaped her entire life from the moment they had met.

Early on 19 February 1952, just after one o'clock, Knut Hamsun died. A few hours earlier Marie had sketched the final act in Hamsun's life in a letter to her daughter Cecilia: 'Hamsun is performed and read the world over, he is called the greatest living writer, but we don't actually have the money to give him a funeral. And he's wearing rags on his deathbed.'[132]

'Life is so short, a mockery. And yet it often seems too long.'

Notes

All references to Hamsun's letters are, unless otherwise specified, from the Norwegian *Collected Letters* in seven volumes: *Knut Hamsuns brev I–VII*, edited by Harald S. Næss (Oslo 1994–2001). A shorter two-volume edition exists in English, published by Norvik Press: *Selected Letters I* and *II*.

Abbreviations

AAA   Aust-Agder-Arkivet, Arendal. Archive belonging to Arendal County.

GA   Gyldendal's archive, Oslo.

HPA-NBO   Knut Hamsun's private archive, kept at NBO.

KBK   Kongelige Bibliotek, København (The Royal Library, Copenhagen).

NBO   Nasjonalbiblioteket, Oslo (The National Library of Norway, Oslo office).

PAM   Psychoanalytical material. Johannes Irgens Strømme's notes concerning the treatment of Knut Hamsun, 1926–27 (transcribed) and NBO (not transcribed).

RA   Riksarkivet, Oslo (Norway's national archive).

Part I

1. Letter from Peder Pedersen to Hamarøy Schools Commission 28/8/1865. See Larsen, *Den unge Hamsun.*
2. Hamsun's oldest son, Tore Hamsun, writes about his grandmother's psychological afflictions and strange behaviour in his book *Knut Hamsun – min far.* It is likely this information came from his father.
3. Hamsun's mother, Tora Pedersen Hamsund, was interviewed once, in *Verdens Gang* 6/3/1911. In this interview she explains how her son guarded the words he wrote, and how his siblings made fun of him and tried to mess them up.
4. Hamsun's mother explains in the interview (see previous note) how her son longed for home when he lived with his uncle. On the same occasion, Johannes Nicolaisen, the son of the priest at Hamarøy, was also interviewed. He lived by the same parsonage yard as Hamsun, and explained that Hans Olsen would beat his nephew until he bled, and that

Hamsun ran away several times. The boat episode is referred to in Olaf Øyslebo's book, *Hamsun gjennom stilen*, in which Tore Hamsun is given as a source. Knut Hamsun writes that he considered taking his own life in 'Et spøkelse' ('A Ghost'), under the section heading 'Opplevde småting' ('Lived Moments') in the short story collection *Kratskog*. He writes the same in *On Overgrown Paths*.

5. Hamsun claims several times that Hans Olsen and the housekeeper let him go hungry, for example in *On Overgrown Paths*.

6. Hamsun stated during his psychiatric assessment in 1945–46: 'My home was poor but incredibly loving, I cried and thanked God whenever I could return home from my uncle, who mistreated me.' Langfeldt/Ødegård, *Den rettspsykiatriske erklæring om Hamsun*.

7. All the evidence points to Laura Walsøe being Knut Hamsun's first serious love. He repeatedly returned to the tradesman's daughter in his stories during his teens, and he also used her name for several female characters.

8. The Norwegian title for *The Enigmatic One* is *Den Gaadefulde. En Kjærlighedshistorie fra Nordland*.

9. Information about Hamsun's time as a sheriff's assistant and teacher in Vesterålen taken from Lars Frode Larsen, *Den unge Hamsun* and Tore Hamsun, *Knut Hamsun – min far*.

10. Hamsun to Zahl 26/4/1879. The publisher Gyldendalske Boghandel is referred to by its current name Gyldendal throughout this book.

11. The original Norwegian title for *The Reconciliation* is *Et Gjensyn*.

12. The capital of Norway was known as Kristiania until its name was officially changed back to its much older name of Oslo in 1925. In this book it is referred to as Oslo throughout for consistency.

13. On the letter received from Hamsun, Zahl noted that he replied on 1/5/1879 and promised him 1,600 kroner. Hamsun thanked Zahl in a letter of 17/5/1879. On a receipt for 1,600 kroner dated 5/5/1879, Hamsun signed himself Knud Pedersen Hamsund. See also note 22 below.

14. Atle Austestad writes extensively about Hamsun's stay in Hardanger during the autumn and spring of 1879 in his book *Knut Hamsun i Øystese*. Hamsun himself tells his daughter Cecilia Hamsun, in an undated letter from 1948, that he owned a collection of a hundred books when he left Hardanger for Copenhagen. Manuscripts for *Sverdgny* and a novel, *Frida*, have never been found.

15. Hamsun to Zahl 16/8/1879, 20/9/1879 and 23/10/1879.

16. Hamsun described his two visits to Gyldendal in a letter to his publisher Harald Grieg years later, 30/8/1934.

17. Hamsun to Zahl 2/1/1880. The Norwegian writer whom Hamsun visited, Andreas Munch, wrote him a recommendation after reading his manuscripts. Hamsun refers to these in a letter to Zahl 24/2/1880.

18. Hamsun's visit to Bjørnson is described in Tore Hamsun's *Knut Hamsun – min far* and *Efter år og dag*, and also in Einar Skavlan's *Knut Hamsun*.

19. Tore Hamsun describes in *Knut Hamsun – min far* how his father followed the auctioning of his possessions closely.

20. Hamsun to Bjørnson 24/1/1880.

21. Hamsun refers to Skavlan's praise in a letter to Zahl 24/3/1880.

22. It was customary at the time in Norway for people to add the place or farm they came from as a surname when they travelled. Hamsun went through different spellings of his surname, both Hamsunn and Hamsund, until he finally settled on Hamsun.

23. Nina Thaulow to Bjørnson 5/5/1880. Bjørnson to Nina Thaulow 15/5/1880. Both letters NBO.

24. Information about Hamsun's time as a road worker comes from the magazines *Raufoss Blad* 26/2/1959, *Totens Blad* 12/10/1961, *Alle Kvinner* 13/2/1954, *Vestoppland* 31/7/1934, 27/7/1939 and 10/8/1944, *Oplands Tidende* 26/10/1957, *Gudbrandsdølen* 5/2/1916 and *Nationen* 31/1/1925.

25. Tore Hamsun describes his father's story about his meeting with the German shipowner in *Knut Hamsun – min far*.

26. Hamsun wrote about his experiences in New York and Chicago in a letter to Kyseth 19/2/1882. The biographer is much indebted to the wealth of information contained in Harald Næss's *Knut Hamsun i Amerika*. Professor Rasmus Anderson (1846–1936) gave an account of the meeting between himself and Hamsun in his autobiography, *Life Story of Rasmus B. Anderson*.

27. Hamsun describes this event and many others in America in *On Overgrown Paths*.

28. Hamsun gave his first lecture on 5/11/1882. This was reported, probably by himself, in the magazine *Skandinaven* 8/11/1882. Reports of another lecture held in Stoughton appeared in the same magazine 14/4/1883.

29. Hamsun to Harry Hart 28/12/1882.

30. Hamsun's roommate Willy T. Ager writes about several bizarre episodes in the magazine *Kvartalsskrift*, January 1916, which also records a number of amusing experiences with Hamsun.

31. Hamsun wrote to Svein Tverås 11/4/1884 about the closeness he and Drude Janson enjoyed.

32. Hamsun described his sexual desire and the relationship between Drude Janson and himself in a letter to Erik Skram 26/12/1888.

33. Hamsun to Frøisland 27/10/1884.

34. Hamsun's short story 'Et livsfragment' appeared in the newspaper *Dagbladet* 12/12/1884.

35. Hamsun to Frøisland 27/10/1984.

36. Hamsun to Frøisland 19/1/1886.

37. Hamsun's short story 'På turné' appeared in *Dagbladet* 4/7/1886 and 5/7/1886.

38. Hamsun to Arne Garborg 13/6/1886. Tore Hamsun includes Garborg's negative response to 'På turné' in *Knut Hamsun – min far*.

39. Hamsun to Frydenlund 20/8/1886.

40. Hamsun to Janson 16/6/1887.

41. G.E. Loftfield described his memories of Hamsun as a public speaker in the newspaper *Minneapolis Tidende* 11/10/1934.

42. Hamsun to Vetle Vislie, undated, summer 1890.

43. G.E. Loftfield, see note 41 above.

44. Hamsun to Yngvar Laws, undated, possibly August 1888. Carl Behrens described his meeting with Hamsun in the newspapers *Nationaltidende* 31/7/1929 and *Dagens Nyheder* 4/8/1934 and in his book *Erindringer*.

45. Hamsun to Edvard Brandes 17/9/1888.

46. See previous note.

47. Valdemar Vegel in the journal *Ny Jord*, August 1888.

48. See note 44 above.

49. Hamsun in the *Hunger* fragment printed in *Ny Jord*, early November 1888. This later became a part of the novel *Hunger*, published in 1890. Kristiania was the name of Norway's capital at the time, see note 12 above. The description of Hamsun's feelings about his bag comes from a letter to Johan Sørensen 18/12/1888.

50. Axel Lundegård refers to alleged conversations between Brandes and Hamsun in his autobiography, *Sett och känt*. Einar Skavlan uses information supplied by Hamsun himself for his biography, *Knut Hamsun*.

51. Hamsun describes his thoughts and feelings on visiting Philipsen in letters to Johan Sørensen 2/12/1888, 8/12/1888 and 18/12/1888.

52. Hamsun describes his life in Copenhagen in a letter to Johan Sørensen 8/12/1888.

53. Events at the Skrams' described by Herman Bang in the newspaper *Bergens Tidende* 29/3/1890.

54. Hamsun to Erik and Amalie Skram 19/11/1888. As this letter shows, Hamsun consistently presented himself as a year younger by this time.

55. Thommessen in the Norwegian newspaper *Verdens Gang* 19/9/1888.

56. Hamsun to Sørensen 2/12/1888.

57. Sørensen to Hamsun 6/12/1888, NBO. Hamsun to Sørensen 6/12/1888.

58. Hamsun to Sørensen 6/12/1888. Janson to Edvard Brandes 10/12/1888. KBK.

59. No newspaper reports exist about the two talks in America. However, Hamsun's *Fra det*

moderne Amerikas åndsliv (*On the Cultural Life of Modern America*) was based on the lectures he gave.

60. Hamsun to Sørensen 18/12/1888. Sørensen to Hamsun 20/12/1888, NBO.
61. Hamsun to Erik Skram 26/12/1888.
62. See previous note.
63. Hamsun to Nilsson 13/1/1889.
64. Hamsun to Georg Brandes 13/1/1889.
65. This and the following quotations are taken from *On the Cultural Life of Modern America*.
66. Hamsun to Yngvar Laws, undated, possibly August 1888.
67. Hamsun to Erik Frydenlund 9/4/1889.
68. Olaf Huseby describes the party given in honour of Hamsun in *Et festskrift*. Hamsun gives a similar account in letters to Philipsen 23/4/1889 and Erik Skram 7/5/1889.
69. Edvard Brandes reviewed *On the Cultural Life of Modern America* in the Danish newspaper *Politiken* 28/4/1889 and Georg Brandes in the Norwegian *Verdens Gang* 9/5/1889. The Norwegian papers *Dagbladet* and *Aftenposten* reviewed the book on 26/4/1889 and 10/5/1889 respectively.
70. This and the next few quotations are from *Hunger*.
71. Hamsun to Philipsen 17/9/1889 and 18/3/1890.
72. Hamsun to Erik Skram, undated, possibly May/June 1890. Hamsun describes in detail the episode in the restaurant. The exact date is not known, but Hamsun's informality in the letter precludes it dating from his first stay in Copenhagen, 1888–89. When Hamsun returns to Copenhagen for a third time in April 1892, he writes that he has tried in vain to get hold of Nils Nilsen Noraker at his old address in Gamle Kongevej, an address referred to in this letter. Thus, the evidence points to the episode with Winkel Horn and his wife taking place between April and early June 1890.
73. Hamsun to Janson, June 1890.
74. Hamsun to Georg Brandes, May/June 1890.
75. The reference is to Raskolnikov, the central character in *Crime and Punishment* by Dostoevsky.
76. Hamsun to Frydenlund, May/June 1890.
77. Hamsun to Bolette Pavels Larsen, undated, autumn 1890. His stay in Lillesand is described comprehensively by Lars Frode Larsen in *Radikaleren*.
78. Dunne's short stories *Keynotes*, which she dedicated to Hamsun, were published in 1893 under her married name of Egerton. She depicts their relationship in the story 'Now Spring Has Come'. See also Hamsun to Larsen and Garborg, both 10/9/1890.

Part II

1. *Hunger* is reviewed in the Norwegian newspapers *Verdens Gang* 7/6/1890, *Dagbladet* 12/6/1890, *Dagsposten* 21/6/1890, *Christiania Intelligentssedler* 14/7/1890 and *Morgenbladet* 12/10/1890, and the Danish newspapers *Politiken* 24/6/1890, *Morgenbladet* 14/8/1890, *Berlingske Tidende* 26/6/1890, *Nationaltidende* 3/7/1890, *Aftenbladet* 21/6/1890 and *Avisen* 7/7/1890.
2. Hamsun to Erik Skram 18/6/1890 and undated, July 1890. Skram's review was printed in the Danish *Tilskueren*, June 1890, with another appearing in the Norwegian *Samtiden*, July 1890.
3. Hamsun describes his reactions to Hjalmar Christensen's review, which he believed Bjørnson was responsible for, in letters to Garborg 9/7/1890, Philipsen 10/7/1890 and 18/7/1890, and Skram 28/7/1890.
4. Hamsun to Philipsen 18/7/1890.
5. Hamsun to Brækstad 11/7/1890.
6. Hamsun to Geijerstam, undated, July 1890.
7. Hamsun in the article 'Fra det ubevisste sjeleliv' in the Norwegian *Samtiden*, September 1890.
8. Descriptions of lectures based on contemporary Norwegian press reports. Also in *På*

Turné: 3 foredrag om litteratur av Knut Hamsun, a collection of Hamsun's lectures edited by Tore Hamsun.

9. Bolette Pavels Larsen to Arne Garborg 27/7/1891, NBO.
10. Hamsun to Ole Johan Larsen 11/8/1891. Hamsun twists Ibsen's statement: he did not say he was not satisfied with the North Cape, but rather with his *trip* to the North Cape.
11. See note 8, above.
12. Ibsen's reaction is described in Francis Bull, 'Hildur Andersen og Henrik Ibsen', *Edda,* 48 (1957).
13. Quoted from *ibid.* After completing his next play, *The Master Builder,* Ibsen explained to Ernst Motzfeldt: 'I don't write symbolically, I only describe the life of the soul, as I know it – I write psychology, if you like. [. . .] I depict real, living people; anyone with some personality of substance will in their inner lives also represent the general, the thoughts and ideas of their time. The descriptions of these inner lives may therefore appear symbolic. These are the people I describe. And I have rich opportunity to do so, I have studied human beings and observed their souls.' See Meyer, 'Henrik Ibsen og Ernst Motzfeldt' in *Aftenposten* 23/4/1911.
14. Bolette Pavels Larsen in the Norwegian newspaper *Dagsposten,* October 1891.
15. Hamsun in his lecture 'Psykologisk litteratur', see note 8 above.
16. Hamsun to Henriette Lofthus 31/12/1891.
17. Dostoevsky's *The Insulted and Humiliated* is also known as *The Insulted and the Injured.*
18. Hamsun letters to Hans Martin and Sofie Neeraas 10/2/1892. Also to Caroline Neeraas, probably early 1892, and to the Larsens, probably January 1892. In all these letters Hamsun describes having strong emotional experiences during the writing of *Mysteries.*
19. In 'A Ghost', printed in the collection *Brushwood,* Hamsun describes being regularly plagued by visions of a ghost.
20. Hamsun to Caroline Neeraas, undated, spring 1892.
21. Hamsun to Hans Martin Neeraas, undated, summer 1892.
22. See previous note.
23. See Part I, note 78, concerning Dunne Egerton and Hamsun.
24. Hamsun to Marie Herzfeld 25/6/1892.
25. Hamsun to Nilsson 5/9/1892.
26. Hamsun to Philipsen 21/9/1892.
27. Reviews of *Mysteries* in the Norwegian newspapers *Dagbladet* 22/9/1892, *Verdens Gang* 20/9/1892, *Morgenbladet* 18/9/1892, *Aftenposten* 25/9/1892 and *Bergens Tidende* 22/9/1892, and the Danish *Berlingske Tidende* 13/10/1892, *København* 13/9/1892 and *Politiken* 21/9/1892.
28. The script for the talk 'Litt om litteratur' is in NBO.
29. Hamsun mentions this embarrassing episode himself in a letter to Brandes 24/12/1898. Jeppe Aakjær mentions the talk in *Før det dages.* See also the Danish newspapers *Politiken* and *København* 29/3/1893.
30. Frejlif Olsen describes the circumstances relating to the journey to Paris in his memoir *En kjøbenhavnsk journalist.* See also Åge Welblund, *Omkring den litterære café.*
31. Bjørnson wrote about *Editor Lynge* in the Norwegian newspapers *Oplandenes Avis* 25/4/1893 and *Dagbladet* 26/4/1893. Reviews appeared in *Dagbladet* 14/4/1893, *Christiania Intelligentssedler* 15/4/1893, *Morgenbladet* 16/4/1893, *Bergens Tidende* 21/4/1893, *Verdens Gang* 22/4/1893 and *Aftenposten* 23/4/1893, and the Danish *Politiken* 30/4/1893 and *Berlingske Tidende* 15/7/1893.
32. Hamsun to Erik Skram 10/5/1893.
33. Nils Vogt in *Morgenbladet* 27/10/1893.
34. Hamsun to Larsen 30/10/1893.
35. Hamsun to Larsen 31/10 and 5/11/1893, to Adolf Paul November 1893, to Birger Mörner 1/11/1893, to Bjørnson 18/11/1893 and to Nilsson 1/11/1893.
36. Hamsun to Larsen 12/11/1893.
37. Hamsun to Larsen 12/5/1894.
38. Reviews of *Pan* 7/12/1894 in the Danish *Politiken,* and in the Norwegian *Bergens Tidende* 14/12/1894, *Verdens Gang* 7/12/1894 and *Dagbladet* 13/12/1894.

39. Edvard Beyer, *Hans E. Kinck. Livsangst og livstro*, vol. 1 (Oslo, 1956); and Kinck to Hamsun 22/12/1894, NBO.
40. Hamsun to Elisa Philipsen 26/12/1894 and to G. Philipsen 28/2/1895.
41. The appeal was placed in a number of Norwegian papers, including *Dagbladet* 11/3/1895. Information about the rift between Hamsun and Strindberg from letters from Hamsun to Langen 31/3/1895 and 4/4/1895. Hamsun to Philipsen 5/4/1895 and 10/4/1895. Hamsun to Kinck 16/4/1895. Hamsun to Lie 17/4/1895. Strindberg to Lie 17/4/93. Cf. Strindberg's letters, Torsten Eklund (ed.), *August Strindbergs brev X. Februari 1894–april 1895*.
42. Fröding on *The Master Builder* in the Swedish newspaper *Karlstads-Tidningen* 4/2/1893. Fröding's opinions on the meeting in Lillehammer are taken from Mentz Schulerud, *Norsk Kunstnerliv*.
43. The poem 'The World Tilts' is taken from a collection of Hamsun poems that was unknown until recently, *En fløjte lød i mit blod*, ed. Lars Frode Larsen.
44. Hamsun to Langen 10/2/1894.
45. Bjørnson in the Norwegian *Kringsjaa*, (1896). Tore Hamsun describes events from Munich in *Knut Hamsun – min far*. He must have been told about them by his father.
46. The short story 'Life's Voice' also appears in *Brushwood* (1903).
47. Cf. Aldo Keel, *Bjørnstjerne Bjørnson*.
48. Hamsun to Bjørnson 8/6/1896.
49. Review of *The Game of Life* in the Norwegian newspapers *Dagbladet* 3/5/1896 and *Verdens Gang* 10/6/1896.
50. In Norwegian newspapers *Morgenbladet* 19/12/1896 and 22/12/1896, and *Aftenposten* 19/12/1896 and 24/12/1896.
51. Hamsun in his article 'Mot overvurdering av diktere og diktning', in the Norwegian newspaper *Aftenposten* 7/2/1897, based on a talk given at the Norwegian Students' Union 30/1/1897.
52. In Norwegian newspapers *Verdens Gang* 25/5/1897 and *Dagbladet* 25/5/1897 and 14/6/1897.
53. Anna Munch, *To mennesker*. The National Archive (RA) holds sixty anonymous letters and the police reports. Cf. Robert Ferguson, *Enigma – The Life of Knut Hamsun*.
54. Hamsun to Larsen 29/11/1897 and to Welhaven 4/8/1897.
55. In a letter to his second wife, Marie, 7/8/1909, Hamsun explains how the passion went out of his relationship with Bergljot, how he gave her the chance to call the marriage off and why he felt honour-bound to proceed with it.
56. Hamsun to Hagerup 14/12/1897.
57. Hamsun to Ullmann 26/3/1898 and to Chief Superintendent Jelstrup 22/3/1898.
58. Ingolf Kittelsen describes the veranda episode at Egertorvet, Oslo, as well as the couple's subsequent stay at Ås in a signed document 14/1/1957, NBO.
59. Hamsun to Gerda Welhaven 23/8/1898.
60. Hamsun to Frydenlund, late autumn 1898, and to Larsen 19/9/1889.
61. Nils Vogt in the Norwegian newspaper *Morgenbladet* 18/11/1898. Hamsun to Nils Vogt, undated, possibly November 1898.
62. Hamsun to Langen 25/11/1898, GA. Hamsun to Georg Brandes 26/11/1898. Brandes's reply no longer exists, but its contents are suggested by Hamsun's own reply. Hamsun to Georg Brandes 24/12/1898.
63. Johannes A. Dahle describes Bergljot and Hamsun's stay in Helsingfors in *Nordisk Tidsskrift* (1966).
64. Bergljot to Alette Gross 12/4/1899, NBO.
65. Hamsun to Larsen 22/8/1899.
66. All references to Hamsun's journey come from *In Wonderland*, published in 1903, and the short story 'Under halvmånen' from *Striving Life*, published 1905. The diary from Hamsun's travels is in AAA.
67. Hamsun to Hagelstam 9/1/1900.
68. Hamsun to Bergljot 24/5/1900.
69. Hamsun to Hagelstam 6/12/1900.
70. Hamsun to Larsen 6/12/1900.

71. Hamsun to Bergljot 18/7/1900.
72. Hamsun to Bergljot, January 1901.
73. Hamsun to Hagelstam 21/9/1901.
74. Hamsun to Bergljot, September/October 1901.
75. Hamsun to Hagelstam 13/10/1901.
76. Hamsun to Bergljot, October 1901.
77. Hamsun to Bergljot, October 1901.
78. Hamsun to Bergljot, late October 1901.
79. Hamsun mentions the planned trilogy in a book dedication to an American collector. Cf. Olaf Husby in the Norwegian journal *Kringsjaa*, 4 (1904).
80. Langen in Tore Hamsun, *Knut Hamsun – min far.*
81. Hamsun to Nielsen 19/12/1902.
82. Hamsun's struggle to get Hegel's help went on for some time and involved several people. See Hamsun to Bjørnson 20/1/1903, to Hegel 22/1/1903, to Nielsen 23/1/1903, to Bjørnson 26/01/1903, to Schibsted 23/2/1903, to Nygaard 9/3/1903 and to Peter Nansen 1/5/1903. See also *Aftenposten* 24/2/1903. Hamsun and Hegel's agreement signed 7/5/1903, HPA-NBO.
83. Hamsun to Peter Nansen, probably April 1904.
84. Hamsun to Næser, autumn 1904. Cf. Jeppe Aakjær, *Før det dages*, and Åge Welblund, *Omkring den litterære Café.*
85. Sten Drewsen, *En Kverulant ser tilbage* (1937).
86. Johannes V. Jensen in his poem 'Helled Haagen' in *Skovene* (1904) and in *Digte* (1906). Holger Drachmann in *Vagabundus* (1910).
87. Hamsun in the article 'Åpent letter til Bjørnson' in the Norwegian *Forposten* 5/12/09.
88. Hamsun to Hans Aanrud 12/12/1904.
89. Hamsun to Ragnhild Jølsen 20/11/1904, 22/11/1904 and 23/12/1904.
90. Hamsun admits infidelity to Bergljot in a letter to his second wife, Marie, 7/8/1909. There are strong indications that the woman was Ragnhild Jølsen.
91. Sven Lange in the Danish newspaper *Politiken* 18/12/1904. Hamsun to Hans Aanrud 20/5/1904.
92. Hamsun to Marie Hamsun 7/8/1909.
93. Hamsun's house plans, NBO. Hamsun to Langen 15/8/1905.
94. Tendering documents dated 1/4/1905, building expenses dated 23/10/1905 and completion document 7/12/1905, HPA-NBO.
95. Hamsun to Hans Aanrud 7/12/1905.
96. This extract is taken from the *The Last Joy*, the first three chapters of which appeared in the journal *Samtiden* in 1906.
97. The first three chapters of *Benoni* were serialised for the Norwegian daily *Posten* 3/2–9/2/1906.
98. Hamsun in 'At the Clinic' in *Posten* 1/3/1906. It has not been possible to verify beyond doubt that Hamsun was admitted into hospital. Christian Gierløff describes what a poor state Hamsun was in when he found him, in his book *Knut Hamsuns egen røst.*
99. Hamsun to Langen 4/3/1906.
100. Separation contract between Bergljot and Hamsun dated 20/3/1906 and 23/3/1906, HPA-NBO.
101. Hamsun to Peter Nansen 12/2/1907.
102. Coverage of Hamsun's lecture in the Oslo press, on the following day 27/4/1907. A debate continued in the papers throughout May. An extended version was published in the Danish newspaper *Politiken* and in the Norwegian newspaper *Verdens Gang* between 29/12/1911 and 21/01/1912.

Part III

1. The encounter is described by Marie Hamsun, *Regnbuen.*
2. Hamsun to Marie Hamsun 3/5/1908.

3. Hamsun to Køhler Olsen 5/5/1908.
4. Marie Hamsun to Hamsun early May 1908. Cf. Marie Hamsun, *Regnbuen.*
5. Hamsun to Marie Hamsun 7/5/1908.
6. Marie Hamsun's memoirs, *Regnbuen,* and Birgit Gjernes, *Marie Hamsun.*
7. Hamsun to Marie Hamsun 16/6/1908.
8. Marie Hamsun, *Regnbuen.*
9. *Ibid.*
10. *Ibid.*
11. *Ibid.*
12. *Ibid.*
13. *Ibid.*
14. Hamsun to Heinrich Goebel 27/12/1908.
15. Hamsun to Marie Hamsun 22/7/1909.
16. Hamsun in letters to Marie Hamsun, 24/7/1909.
17. Marie Hamsun to Hamsun, August 1909; cf. Marie Hamsun, *Regnbuen.*
18. Hamsun to Marie Hamsun 4/8/1909. He had used this abusive motif in his novel *Victoria,* but then as an example of entirely selfless affection.
19. Hamsun to Marie Hamsun 22–23/7/1909.
20. Marie Hamsun, *Regnbuen.*
21. *Ibid.*
22. Hamsun to P.E. Hansen 9/12/1909.
23. Mariya Blagoveshchenskaya to Hamsun 11/8/1909, 9/9/1909, 5/12/1909, 9/12/1909 and 15/12/1909, HPA-NBO. Hamsun to Blagoveshchenskaya 13/12/1909, (draft) HPA-NBO.
24. Hamsun in the article 'The Theologian in Fairyland' in the Norwegian newspaper *Morgenbladet* 5/1/1910.
25. Marie Hamsun to Hamsun, mid-May 1910; cf. *Regnbuen.*
26. Hamsun in the article 'A Word for Us' in the Norwegian *Verdens Gang* and the Danish *Politiken* 3/7/1910.
27. Hamsun to Dumreicher, July 1910, who printed an article about Hamsun in the Danish monthly magazine *Tilskueren II* (1910).
28. Marie Hamsun describes her arrival at Hamarøy in *Regnbuen.*
29. Hamsun to Storm, Bull & Co. 19/5/1911.
30. Quotation from Marie Hamsun, *Regnbuen.* An article based on interviews with Hamsun's mother, Tora Pedersen, Hamsun's brother Ole Pedersen, the local priest's son, Johannes Nicolaisen, and Hamsun himself appeared in the Norwegian newspaper *Verdens Gang* 6/3/1911.
31. Hamsun in his article 'Ærer de unge' in the Norwegian *Verdens Gang* and the Danish *Politiken* 29/12/1911.
32. Marie Hamsun, *Regnbuen.*
33. Hamsun to Marie Hamsun 23/3/1912.
34. Quotation from Marie Hamsun, *Regnbuen.*
35. Hamsun in 'A Word for Us' in *Verdens Gang* and *Politiken* 3/7/1910.
36. Bergljot to Hamsun 1/10/1912, HPA-NBO.
37. Hamsun to Marie Hamsun 19/9/1912, 24/9/1912, 26/9/1912, and 1/10/1912.
38. Marie Hamsun, *Regnbuen.*
39. Hamsun to Marie Hamsun 1/10/1912.
40. Swanström to Hamsun, early December 1912, HPA-NBO, and Hamsun to Peter Nansen 10/12/1912.
41. Sven Lange in the Danish newspaper *Politiken* 28/11/1912.
42. Hamsun to Køhler Olsen 20/12/1912.
43. Hamsun to Marie Hamsun 23/1/1913, 14/2/1913, 3/2/1913 and 28/2/1913.
44. Victoria Hamsun to Hamsun 16/6/1913, HPA-NBO.
45. Victoria Hamsun to Hamsun 22/9/1913, HPA-NBO.
46. Marie Hamsun describes her thoughts in *Regnbuen.* Hamsun to Einar Hilsen 26/6/1913. Marie Hamsun, *Regnbuen.*
47. Hamsun to Peter Nansen 19/7/1913.
48. Hamsun to Marie Hamsun 27/10/1913.

49. Swanström in a telegram to Hamsun 13/10/1913, HPA-NBO.
50. Hamsun to Marie Hamsun 27/10/1913.
51. Marie Hamsun, *Regnbuen.*
52. Ledgers from Gyldendal's accounts 14/3/1914 and Hamsun's bank statements 30/5/1914, both HPA-NBO. Hamsun to his friend Dybwad 31/5/1914.
53. Hamsun to Holm at Langen Verlag 10/9/1914, HPA-NBO.
54. Hamsun in the German magazine *Simplicissimus*, 19 (1914).
55. Hamsun to Holm at Langen Verlag 10/12/1914. Georg Brandes's article was printed in the Danish *Politiken* 1/12/1914. Hamsun's criticism of Brandes appeared in the Norwegian journal *Minerva*, 19 (1913).
56. Hamsun in his article 'Collin and the War' in the Norwegian newspaper *Tidens Tegn* 6/12/1914.
57. Hamsun in the article 'The Child' in the Norwegian newspaper *Morgenbladet* 16/1/1915.
58. Sigrid Undset in *Morgenbladet* 18/2/1915. Hamsun in *Morgenbladet* concerning the infanticide debate 4/3/1915.
59. Hamsun to Marie Hamsun 8/2/1915.
60. Hamsun to Marie Hamsun 28/2/1915.
61. Marie Hamsun to Hamsun, March 1915; cf. *Regnbuen.*
62. Hamsun to Kønig 25/8/1915.
63. Hamsun to Peter Nansen 5/11/1915.
64. Hamsun to Ola Christofersen 5/12/1915.
65. Hamsun to Axel Ebbe 2/4/1915.
66. Hamsun to Albert Engström 26/3/1915.
67. Henrik Cavling to Hamsun in a telegram 29/11/1915, HPA-NBO, and Hamsun to Kønig 2/12/1915.
68. Kristian Elster in *Aftenposten* 30/11/1915.
69. Hamsun to Kønig 4/12/1915.
70. Sven Lange's review in the Danish *Politiken* 16/12/1915.
71. Hamsun in 'A Word for Us' in the Danish *Politiken* and the Norwegian *Verdens Gang* 3/7/1910.
72. Marie Hamsun, *Regnbuen.*
73. Hamsun to his friend Erik Frydenlund 31/12/1916. Hamsun to Henrik Lund 5/10/1916.
74. Hamsun to Ola Christofersen 1/2/1917; cf. also Marie Hamsun, *Regnbuen.*
75. Hamsun to Georg Olsen 8/12/1917.
76. Hamsun to Harald Torp 17/12/1917.
77. Hamsun to Thorvald Aadahl 28/1/1918.
78. Hamsun to Langen Verlag 11/4/1918 and to Herman Hesse (draft) 28/8/1918, both HPA-NBO.
79. In Hamsun's lectures to the Norwegian Students' Union 30/1/1907 and 27/4/1907.
80. Marie Hamsun describes the first time she saw Nørholm and the day of their moving in, in *Regnbuen.*
81. Statements and letters from banks and publishers, HPA-NBO.
82. Hamsun to Nils Kjær, mid-November 1918, and to Kønig 19/11/1918.
83. Hamsun to Johannes Kraakmo 6/1/1919; cf. also the north Norwegian paper *Lofotposten* 4/7/1959.
84. Korfiz Holm at Langen Verlag to Hamsun 16/1/1919, Langen Verlag to Hamsun 11/3/1919 and 23/3/1919, HPA. Hamsun to Langen Verlag 2/2/1919.
85. Information about the early days at Nørholm taken from: Marie Hamsun, *Regnbuen*; Tore Hamsun, *Knut Hamsun – min far*; Tore Hamsun, *Efter år og dag*; Arild Hamsun, *Om Knut Hamsun og Nørholm.*
86. Kønig to Hamsun July 1919. Hamsun's draft reply 19/7/1919, HPA-NBO. See also the Norwegian newspaper *Nationen* 26/7/1919.
87. Articles in many newspapers including the Norwegian *Morgenbladet* 2/8/1919, *Verdens Gang* 4/8/1919 and *Tidens Tegn* 4/8/1919, the Danish *Berlingske Tidende* 4/8/1919, and the Swedish *Svenska Dagbladet* 2/8/1919.
88. Hamsun to Marie Hamsun 17/8/1919.
89. Sources concerning the discussions for the Nobel Prize are: the Nobel Association's

anniversary publications 1951 and 2001; Anders Österling, *Minnets vägar*; Harald Hjärne on the Nobel Prize and Hamsun, *Les Prix Nobel en 1919–20* (1922). See also John Landquist, *Hamsun* (1931); Helmer Lång, *Nobelprisen in litteratur 1901–1985*; Marie Hamsun, *Regnbuen*; Dag Nordmark in *Aftenposten* 4/8/1994 and in HS-7 (Hamsunselskapets skriftserie, No. 7, Tromsø, 1994); Terje Stemland in *Aftenposten* 19/2/2002; various material in HPA-NBO.

90. Hamsun to Albert Engström 7/10/1919.
91. Christian Kønig in a letter to Hamsun 4/11/1919, HPA-NBO. Hamsun to Kønig 15/11/1919.
92. Christian Lassen to Hamsun 8/11/1919, HPA-NBO.
93. Hamsun to Marie Hamsun 23/5/1920.
94. Hamsun to Marie Hamsun 23/5/1920.
95. Hamsun's article 'The Neighbouring Town' appeared in *Aftenposten* 8/7/1917 and 12/7/1917. He had already written a story in 1890 called 'Smalltown Life'. He reworked it radically in 1903, keeping the title. It appears in the collection *Brushwood*. In the 1903 version, he introduced the character Tønnes Olai, whom Hamsun may have used in the development of the central character in *The Women at the Pump*, Oliver Andersen.
96. Hamsun to Kønig 1/11/1916 and 23/7/1920.
97. Discussions between Kønig and Hamsun on these matters are partly sourced from correspondence between them during these weeks: Kønig to Hamsun 26/8/1920, 9/9/1920, 14/9/1920 and 25/9/1920, HPA-NBO. Hamsun to Kønig 10/8/1920. Also Curtis Brown to Hamsun 1/7/1920 and 20/8/1920, HPA-NBO.
98. From *The Women at the Pump*.
99. Kristian Elster writing in *Aftenposten* 11/11/1920, Sven Lange in the Danish *Politiken* 20/11/1920, Henning Kehler in *Politiken* 11/11/1920 and John Landquist in the Swedish *Stockholms-Tidningen* 16/11/1920.
100. See note 89 above.
101. From the Swedish newspaper *Dagens Nyheter* 16/9/1920.
102. Marie Hamsun describes Hamsun's reactions to being told about his winning the Nobel Prize in *Regnbuen*.
103. According to a letter from Hamsun to Erik Axel Karlfeldt 7/1/1922, Marie Hamsun helped him learn his speech, which is printed in Tore Hamsun, *Knut Hamsun – min far*.
104. Marie Hamsun's note is in Kungliga Biblioteket (The Royal Library), Stockholm.
105. Marie Hamsun describes Hamsun's reaction to her dress in *Regnbuen*.
106. Cf. Hamsun's almanac for 1921, AAA. Hamsun to Marie Hamsun 16/9/1930.
107. Hamsun to Holm at Langen Verlag 18/11/1920.
108. Hamsun to Marie Hamsun 26/8/1921.
109. Hamsun to Gunnar Gundersen 11/10/1921.
110. Victoria Hamsun (married name Charlesson) in a letter to Hamsun 19/8/1921 and a further eighteen letters up to 24/11/1922, when she stopped writing. A number of draft letters from Hamsun to Victoria Hamsun also survive. All in HPA-NBO. There are also a number of greetings cards sent by Victoria to her half-siblings in Hamsun's private archive. It must be assumed that Hamsun intercepted these, since they were still unopened in their envelopes when the biographer found them. They were opened in October 2001. Cf. HPA-NBO.
111. Carl Nærup in the Norwegian newspaper *Tidens Tegn*, May 1922.
112. Hamsun to Christian Kønig 18/5/1922.
113. Hamsun to Erik Frydenlund 8/5/1922.
114. Hamsun to Marie Hamsun 13/81922, 15/10/1922 and 28/10/1922.
115. Hamsun to Marie Hamsun 21/1/1923 and 26/1/1923.
116. Hamsun to Tore Hamsun 27/2/1923 and to Marie Hamsun 18/10/1922.
117. Hamsun to Marie Hamsun 2/2/1923.
118. Marie Hamsun, *Regnbuen*.
119. Hamsun to Marie Hamsun 27/6/1923. Marie Hamsun to Hamsun, June/July 1923. Cf. *Regnbuen*.
120. Hamsun to Henrik Lund 23/1/1923. Hamsun to Vilhelm Krag 10/3/1923. Telegram

from Almar Knut Hamsun to Marie Hamsun, undated, autumn 1922, HPA-NBO. Also Hamsun to the Norwegian newspaper *Nationen* 13/10/1921. Contextual information taken from correspondence between the lawyer Sam Johnson and Hamsun and Marie Hamsun 1921–23, letters from Hans Pedersen to Hamsun in 1922, and letters to and from a number of other individuals involved in the Hamsun name dispute. Also Hamsun's own evidence in court, originals of which are in HPA-NBO.

121. Reviews in the Norwegian newspapers *Dagbladet* 27/10/1923, *Nationen* 27/10/1923, *Fram* 1/2/1923, *Morgenbladet* 3/11/1923 and *Arbeiderbladet* 30/10/1923.

122. Christian Kønig to Hamsun 26/3/1923 and 19/3/1924, HPA-NBO. Sigurd Evensmo's *Gyldendal og gyldendøler* and Nils Kåre Jacobsen's *En forlegger og hans hus* have been invaluable sources of information surrounding the purchase of the publishing rights. Papers pertaining to Hamsun's finances in HPA-NBO.

123. Hamsun to Christian Kønig 5/12/1923 and 1/9/1924. Christian Kønig to Hamsun, undated, HPA-NBO.

124. Frederik Hegel to Hamsun 2/9/1924, HPA-NBO.

125. Hamsun to Christian Kønig 5/11/1924.

126. Nordahl Grieg in the newspaper *Oslo Aftenavis* 31/12/1924.

127. Sales ledgers for Hamsun's foreign sales are located in HPA-NBO.

128. The Hitler quotations in this section are taken from Joachim Fest, *Hitler*.

Part IV

1. Hamsun to Johan Sørensen 8/12/1888.

2. Correspondence between Hamsun and his lawyers is in HPA-NBO.

3. Hamsun to Sigfred Bugge 28/9/1925, to Hjalmar Pettersen 11/10/1925 and to Christian Kønig 4/11/1925.

4. Johan Irgens Strømme, *Nervøsitet* (Oslo 1925).

5. Hamsun in a draft letter to Marie Hamsun, early January 1926. Cf. Marie Hamsun, *Regnbuen*.

6. From Johannes Irgens Strømme's shorthand notes from the psychoanalytical treatment, Day 1. The original document is at NBO, partially transcribed material kept at Gyldendal publishers.

7. Hamsun to Marie Hamsun, probably late January 1926.

8. Hamsun to Marie Hamsun 29/1/1926.

9. Marie Hamsun, *Regnbuen*.

10. Hamsun to Marie Hamsun, probably late January 1926, PAM.

11. Hamsun to Marie Hamsun 4/2/1926.

12. Quotation from Hamsun in a letter to Marie Hamsun 4/2/1926.

13. PAM.

14. Hamsun to Marie Hamsun 28/2/1926.

15. PAM.

16. PAM.

17. During that spring, while undergoing psychoanalysis with Dr Strømme, Hamsun began working on material that would become the trilogy *Wayfarers*, *August* and *The Road Leads On*. Traces of this material are evident in Strømme's notes, PAM.

18. Thore Grøsle (ed.), *Bonde og menneske*; Tore Hamsun, *Knut Hamsun – min far*; and Arild Hamsun, *Om Knut Hamsun og Nørholm* contain much material on Hamsun as a farmer. The balance sheets from the farm are kept in HPA-NBO.

19. Hamsun to Müller-Langen Verlag 25/7/1926 and 2/11/1926.

20. Marie Hamsun, *Regnbuen*.

21. Marie Hamsun describes her first meeting with Strømme in *Regnbuen*.

22. Marie Hamsun, *Regnbuen*.

23. Hamsun to Tore Hamsun 29/8/1927.

24. Hamsun to Hans Pedersen 6/9/1927.

25. Hamsun to Christian Kønig 8/8/1927.
26. Reviews in Norway: Sigurd Hoel in *Arbeiderbladet* 1/10/1927, Carl Nærup in *Verdens Gang* 1/10/1927, Hans Aanrud in *Aftenposten* 1/10/1927, Ronald Fangen in *Urd*, 44 (1927), Helge Krand in *Dagbladet* 1/10/1927. In Denmark Tom Kristensen reviewed *Wayfarers* in several newspapers including *Lolland-Fasters Folketidende* 22/12/1927.
27. PAM.
28. Hamsun in the lecture 'Mot overvurdering av diktere and diktning' (Against the Overestimation of Writers and Writing), presented at the Norwegian Students' Union 30/1/1897, printed in *Aftenposten* 7/2/1897.
29. Hamsun to Christian Kønig 8/9/1927.
30. Sigurd Evensmo, *Gyldendal og gyldendøler*.
31. Background material: Harald Grieg to Hamsun 19/12/1927, 27/12/1927, 16/2/1928, 23/2/1928, all from HPA-NBO. Hamsun to Harald Grieg 21/5/1928 and 4/6/1928.
32. Hamsun to Maxim Gorky, February 1928 and February 1927. Marie Hamsun to Maxim Gorky 14/4/1927.
33. From *Overland Monthly*, 87 (1929).
34. Hamsun to Aleksandra Kollontay 10/9/1928.
35. Hamsun to Walter Berendsohn 24/4/1928.
36. Hamsun to Müller-Langen Verlag 27/4/1928.
37. Grethlein Verlag to Hamsun 21/5/1928 and 18/8/1928, both HPA-NBO. Hamsun to Grethlein Verlag, draft, 4/8/1928.
38. Hamsun to Ronald Fangen, and the journal *Vor Verden* 15/1/1929, and to Victor Mogens, *Vor Verden* 26/2/1929.
39. Review in *The New York Times Book Review* 21/10/1928.
40. Hamsun to Marie Hamsun 26/11/1928.
41. Hamsun to Trygve Braatøy 17/8/29. Sigrid Braatøy to Harald Næss. Cf. note to letter 2042, Harald Næss, *Knut Hamsuns brev I–VII*.
42. Trygve Braatøy, *Livets sirkel*.
43. Description from Tore Hamsun in *Knut Hamsun – min far* and Marie Hamsun, *Regnbuen*. Marie Hamsun to Harald Grieg 26/7/1929, GA, and other material in HPA-NBO. Information about birthday greetings in HPA-NBO.
44. Quotation from Joachim Fest, *Hitler*.
45. See previous note.
46. Hamsun to Marie Hamsun 18/3/1930.
47. Hamsun to Harald Grieg 31/5/1930.
48. Hamsun to Harald Grieg 4/6/1930.
49. Hamsun to Marika Stiernstedt 25/6/1930.
50. Victoria Hamsun to Hamsun 30/8/1930, HPA-NBO.
51. Hamsun to Victoria Hamsun 7/9/1930.
52. Marie Hamsun, *Regnbuen*.
53. *Ibid.*
54. The envelope with Hamsun's handwritten remark is kept in HPA-NBO.
55. The legal battle between Hamsun and his daughter over her inheritance is detailed in the following correspondence and drafts of letters: Victoria Hamsun to Hamsun 30/12/1930, 28/9/1931, 12/11/1931, 30/11/1931 and 31/11/1931, Hamsun to Victoria Hamsun 5/1/1931, 7/10/1931, 20/11/1931 and 8/12/1931, Marie Hamsun to Victoria Hamsun 7/12/1931, Hamsun to Bergljot Hamsun 8/12/1931, Bergljot Hamsun to Hamsun 14/12/1931 and Hamsun to Bergljot Hamsun 21/12/1931. All of the above are kept in HPA-NBO.
56. Tom Kristensen in the Danish *Tilskueren*, October 1930.
57. Sigurd Hoel in the Norwegian newspaper *Arbeiderbladet* 1/10/1930.
58. Tore Hamsun, *Knut Hamsun – min far* and *Efter år og dag*. Also Marie Hamsun, *Regnbuen*. The travel itinerary with Hamsun's amendments and comments, receipts and other material from the trip is kept in HPA-NBO.
59. Tore Hamsun, *Knut Hamsun – min far*.
60. *Ibid.*
61. *Ibid.*

62. Cf. Hamsun's article 'Et brev til Klassekampen' in the Norwegian newspaper *Klassekampen* 26/2/1916. Also Hamsun to Lyder Ramstad 24/11/1930.
63. Hamsun to Harald Grieg 2–4/3/1931. Hamsun to Stein Balstad 17/3/1927 and 21/3/1927.
64. Hamsun to Tore Hamsun 31/7/1931. The prostate operation Hamsun had undergone in 1930 is highly likely, according to medical opinion, to have left him impotent. This, however, did not prevent Marie Hamsun from accusing her husband of being unfaithful.
65. Hamsun in the preface to Hermann Harris Aall and Nicolai Gjelsvik's *Revolusjonspolitikk og norsk lov.*
66. Erich von Ludendorff to Otto von Hindenburg 2/2/1933. Cf. Joachim Fest, *Hitler.*
67. Quoted from Joachim Fest, *Hitler.*
68. Hamsun to Harald Grieg 5/11/1933.
69. After the court judgement in 1933 the family of the former owners of Nørholm continued to fight against what they considered to be a miscarriage of justice. Gunnar Svennevig, who took over from his father as sheriff, said in 1970 that his father must have given testimony against his better knowledge. Not until 1985 did the Office of the Prime Minister admit that 'The judgement might seem very unreasonable.' The following year, despite protests from the Hamsun family, the Department of Justice gave the descendants of Amalie and Johan Nørholm the right to use their old name. The then prime minister, Kåre Willoch, involved himself in the case.
70. Hamsun to Harald Grieg 10/6/1933.
71. Hamsun to Harald Grieg 17/8/1933.
72. Hamsun to Cecilia Hamsun 8/2/1934.
73. Tore Hamsun, *Efter år og dag.*
74. Adolf Hitler in the Reichstag 13/7/1934, quoted in Joachim Fest, *Hitler.*
75. Hamsun in *Aftenposten* 10/7/34. Johan Fr. Paasche was professor of European Literature at the University of Oslo. Heinrich Brüning was the Social Democrat Chancellor in Germany from 1930 to 1932.
76. Marie Hamsun in the newspaper *Nationen* 16/2/1934. Hamsun to Wilhelm Rasmussen 11/3/1934.
77. Hamsun to Christopher Vibe 18/6/1934. Christopher Vibe to Hamsun 19/6/1934. Cf. *Aftenposten* 30/10/1978.
78. Hamsun in the Norwegian newspaper *Fylkesavisen* 11/1/1934.
79. Tore Hamsun, *Efter år og dag.*
80. Quoted from Joachim Fest, *Hitler.*
81. Hamsun to a German bookbinder 14/1/1935, draft, HPA-NBO. Hamsun in the article 'Deutsch die Saar' in the German journal *Der Norden*, 1 (1935).
82. Hamsun's views here are a reflection of the sentiments expressed in his obituary on Hitler printed in *Aftenposten* 7/5/1945. The biographer feels that these views were in fact manifest in Hamsun from the early 1930s.
83. Carl von Ossietzky in the German journal *Die Weltbühne* 3/1/1933.
84. Hamsun in the article 'Ossietzky' in the Norwegian newspapers *Tidens Tegn* and *Aftenposten* 22/11/1935.
85. Heinrich Mann in *Paris Tageblatt* 5/12/1935. Erick Kuttner to Hamsun 6/12/1935, HPA-NBO.
86. Joseph Goebbels in 1933, quoted in Joachim Fest, *Hitler.*
87. Jørgen Bukdahl in the Danish newspaper *Politiken* 1/10/1936.
88. Alf Larsen, *I kunstens tjeneste.*
89. Goebbels 25/11/1936, German News Agency (*DNB*).
90. Heinrich Mann in *Pariser Tageblatt* 15/12/1936.
91. Cf. Tore Hamsun, *Knut Hamsun – min far.*
92. From Joachim Fest, *Hitler.*
93. Harald Grieg to Hamsun 29/11/1933, HPA. Hamsun to Harald Grieg 30/11/1933.
94. Hamsun to the editor of the Norwegian nationalistic journal *Nationalt Tidsskrift* 1/12/1925, 11 (1926).
95. Hamsun to Gustaf Ericsson, May 1927, quoted from Alf Larsen, *I kunstens tjeneste.*

96. Quotation from Tore Hamsun, *Efter år og dag*, in which Tore describes Hamsun's visit. See also Tore Hamsun, *Knut Hamsun – min far.*
97. Quotation taken from Tore Hamsun, *Efter år og dag.*
98. Hamsun to Niels Mürer 28/9/1938.
99. Inge Eidsvåg's lecture 'Dikteren og konsentrasjonsleirfangen' (The Writer and the Concentration Camp Prisoner).
100. Marie and Tore Hamsun confirmed that Hamsun worked on a sequel to *The Ring is Closed.* Hamsun to Tore Hamsun 4/5/1938, 8/6/1938 and 17/6/1938. Hamsun to Dybwad 5/8/1938.
101. Guest list marked with Marie Hamsun's comments. Letters from Nordische Gesellschaft to Marie Hamsun, May 1938, 10/6/1938 and 17/6/1938, and programme for 20–21 June 1938. All documents in HPA-NBO.
102. Hamsun to Mehle 7/1/1939.
103. Cf. telegram from the Norwegian Press Bureau printed in a number of Norwegian papers on 3 and 4 August 1939.
104. Hamsun to Grassmann 15/8/1939. Quoted in Karl Hans Fuchs, *Danzig har ordet.* Also in the newspaper *Nationen* 23/8/1939.
105. The description of Marie Hamsun's tour is based on her own itinerary, notes, press cuttings, letters and other material in HPA-NBO. Description of Marie's outfit in Birgit Gjerne, *Marie Hamsun – Et livsbilde.*
106. Marie Hamsun to Hamsun 19/11/1939. Further material in HPA-NBO, and from Arne Tumyr, *Knut Hamsun og hans kors.*

Part V

1. Hamsun to Johan E. Mellbye 14/12/1939. Writing to Tore Hamsun 18/1/1940, Hamsun boasts that he has stopped Mellbye's criticisms.
2. Hamsun to Arnt Rishovd 25/3/1940, printed in the NS Party newspaper *Fritt Folk* 30/3/1940.
3. Hamsun in the article 'Et ord til oss' dated 14/4/1940, printed in an occasional paper in Copenhagen 19/4/1940 and in the German journal *Pressedienst Nord*, 18 (1940). The occupying forces went to great lengths initially to deny that Norway and Germany were at war.
4. Anonymous letter dated 17/5/1940. A number of hate-letters from the war years are kept in HPA-NBO, along with some praising his efforts.
5. Hamsun in the article 'Norwegians!' published in the NS Party newspaper *Fritt Folk* 4/5/1940. It was also published in other newspapers and broadcast on national radio.
6. Gustav Smedal to Hamsun 29/5/1940.
7. Various Norwegian newspapers 2/6/1940.
8. Hamsun to Josef Terboven 8/6/1940.
9. Hamsun to Gustav Smedal 3/6/1940.
10. Tom Kristensen in the Danish *Politiken* 20/2/1952.
11. Hamsun to Victor Mogens 17/8/1940.
12. On BBC radio in December 1940. See Bjørn Fontander, *Undset, Hamsun och kriget.*
13. Hamsun in an interview with Norwegian State Radio recorded on 2/1/1941, broadcast 23/1/1941.
14. Reconstruction of meeting based on the following: documents relating the Knut Hamsun trial now found in RA and HPA-NBO; Tore Hamsun, *Efter år og dag*; Thorkild Hansen, *Prosessen mot Hamsun*, which includes Tore Hamsun's written evidence; Ronald Fangen, *I nazistenes fengsel.*
15. Hamsun's article 'Knut Hamsun Answers Two Questions' in the local newspaper *Grimstad Adressetidende* 30/1/1941.
16. Hamsun to Tore Hamsun 25/5/1941.
17. The article was based on a survey originally completed by Hamsun 16/10/1941 and

distributed to the press by Norsk Artikkeltjeneste 21/10/1941. It was published in *Aftenposten* 22/10/1941 and various other newspapers in Norway and abroad. The original has not been found, but in *Aftenposten* the article was called 'We Have Changed Track and Are Set on a Journey in a New Time and New World'. Other newspapers used the headline 'Why I Am a Member of NS'.

18. Hamsun in his article 'Manifest Companionship' in the German journal *Berlin – Rom – Tokio*, 2 (1942). The article was written before 7 December 1941. The Norwegian original has never been found.

19. Joseph Goebbels's diary 28/3/1942.

20. Dwinger quoted by Dag Skogheim, *Hamsunselskapets skriftserie* (The Proceedings of the Hamsun Society), no. 11.

21. Marie Hamsun, *Under gullregnen.*

22. Joseph Goebbels's diary, vol. II, 19/5/1943.

23. Hamsun to Joseph Goebbels, draft, 17/6/1943.

24. Joseph Goebbels to Hamsun 23/6/1943.

25. Hamsun to Victoria Hamsun 23/6/1943.

26. Hamsun in his speech in Vienna 23/6/43, printed in the NS Party newspaper *Fritt Folk* 24/6/43.

27. See previous note.

28. *Segelfoss Tidende*, 2 (October–December 1957). Both Leon Ljunglund and Marie Hamsun confirm that the Hitler meeting was preplanned.

29. Christa Schroeder, *Er war mein Chef.*

30. Joachim Fest, *Hitler.*

31. Account of meeting based on the following: Ernst Züchner's notes sent to the Office of Norway's Chief of Police 25/6/1945, RA; Christa Schroeder's *Er war mein Chef;* Sverre Hartmann's interview with Egil Holmboe in the newspaper *Aftenposten* 21/10/1978; Otto Dietrich, *12 Jahre mit Hitler;* excerpts in *Segelfoss Tidende*, January–March 1958. Quotations taken from above sources.

32. The description of the meeting's conclusion, Hitler's reaction and the return car journey is based on the following: Ernst Züchner's notes sent to the Office of Norway's Chief of Police 25/6/1945, RA; Sverre Hartmann's interview with Egil Holmboe in *Aftenposten* 21/10/78; Otto Dietrich's *12 Jahre mit Hitler;* Ulrich Freiherr von Gienanth's authenticated report from conversations with Dietrich, Lübeck, 1948. Cf. Thorkild Hansen, *Prosessen mot Hamsun.*

33. Thorkild Hansen, *Prosessen mot Hamsun.*

34. Tore Hamsun, *Knut Hamsun – min far.*

35. Hamsun in police interview 25/1/46 from among documents relating to Hamsun's trial, RA.

36. Hamsun on Norwegian State Radio, reported in the NS Party newspaper *Fritt Folk* 2/3/1944.

37. Hamsun to Tore Hamsun 16/1/1944.

38. Hamsun to Victoria Hamsun 3/6/1944.

39. Hamsun in the article 'Europa vil velge livet' in the NS Party newspaper *Fritt Folk. Aftenposten* and other newspapers 12/6/1944 and during the next few days.

40. Hamsun to Einar Schibbye, summer 1944.

41. Cf. various newspapers around the anniversary. Robert Ferguson, *Enigma: The Life of Knut Hamsun.* The Norwegian newspaper *Verdens Gang* 5/8/1998.

42. Hamsun to Tore Hamsun 28/9/1944.

43. Irene Berg quoted by Arne Tumyr, *Hamsun og hans kors.*

44. Hamsun to Doery Smith 4/5/1945. Hamsun writes that others at Nørholm, which can only mean Marie, attempted to prevent the news agency and the Reichskommissariat from getting in touch with him. In all probability a disagreement had arisen between the couple about the need and wisdom of publishing an obituary for Hitler at this time. See also Lars Frode Larsen in *Aftenposten* 16/7/1995.

45. Hamsun in *Aftenposten* 7/5/1945.

46. Tore Hamsun, *Knut Hamsun – min far.*

47. Hamsun to Ingeborg Andersen 5/5/1945.

48. Niels Christian Brøgger in the Norwegian newspaper *Morgenbladet* 24/5/1945.
49. Hamsun to Sigrid Stray 30/5/1945, 1/6/1945 and 2/5/1945.
50. Quotation from Marie Hamsun, *Under gullregnen.*
51. Birger Morholt was the only journalist present at the court 23/06/1945. He took notes in shorthand. Printed in the local paper *Grimstad Adressetidende* 25/6/1945 and 4/5/1996. See also documents relating to Hamsun's trial, 'Saken mot Knut Hamsun', held in RA.
52. Trygve Lie in his memoirs *Hjemover.*
53. Lie does not give this quotation in his book, but the Consular General Alf R. Bjercke, then an officer in the Norwegian army, confirmed Molotov's remark to this biographer in 2004.
54. Sigrid Undset in an interview in Norwegian newspapers, including *Morgenbladet* 8/9/1945.
55. Gabriel Langfeldt in the newspapers *Verdens Gang* 27/8/1945 and *Morgenbladet* 26/6/1945.
56. Magnus Benestad's evidence 4/10/1945, to be found among documents relating to Hamsun's trial, 'Saken mot Knut Hamsun', held in RA.
57. Hamsun, *On Overgrown Paths.*
58. Accompanying statement to the charge from Grimstad Police Authority. 'Saken mot Knut Hamsun', RA. Sigrid Stray describes visiting Hamsun in the old people's home in *Min klient Knut Hamsun.*
59. Account based on reports of Langfeldt and Ødegård, *Den rettspsykiatriske erklæring om Knut Hamsun*, and hospital journals archived at the Vindern Psychiatric Clinic, Oslo.
60. The copy of this book, *Mañana*, containing Hamsun's secretly scribbled notes belongs to Hans Andreasen's daughter, Irmelin Nohald, Berlin.
61. See note 59 above.
62. Marie Hamsun, *Under gullregnen.*
63. Gabriel Langfeldt in Norwegian newspapers, including *Aftenposten* 10/10/1978.
64. Marie Hamsun, *Under gullregnen.*
65. Christian Gierløff, *Knut Hamsun's egen røst.*
66. Langfeldt and Ødegård report, *Den rettspsykiatriske erklæring om Knut Hamsun.*
67. The newspaper *Dagbladet*'s editorial 23/2/1946.
68. Hamsun to Christian Gierløff 25/3/1946.
69. Hamsun to Christian Gierløff 10/3/1946, 26/3/1946, April to May 1946, 10/6/1946 and 30/6/1946. Hamsun to Tore Hamsun 27/3/1946, 21/5/1946 and 28/5/1946. Hamsun's reference to forty-seven manuscript pages corresponds roughly to the first thirty pages of *On Overgrown Paths.*
70. Hamsun to Attorney General Sven Arntzen 23/7/1946. However, Hamsun mentions having written this letter as early as 10/7/1946, in a letter to Cecilia Hamsun. It would have needed to be typed before being sent to Arntzen.
71. Hamsun to Tore Hamsun 20/8/1946.
72. Odd Vinje to the Directorate for Compensation 31/8/1946, quoted in Sigrid Stray, *Min klient Knut Hamsun.*
73. Hamsun to Sigrid Stray 20/1/1947. Stray to Hamsun 15/1/1947. Cf. Sigrid Stray, *Min klient Knut Hamsun.*
74. Hamsun to Cecilia Hamsun 8/4/1947.
75. Langfeldt and Ødegård, *Den rettspsykiatriske erklæring om Knut Hamsun.*
76. As well as writing a note on the letter to Marie, Hamsun wrote to Tore 20/8/1946: 'Yesterday I received a thick letter from Mama. I returned it unopened today.'
77. The quotation from the trial is taken from newspaper reports 24/8/1946. See also documents relating to Marie Hamsun's trial, 'Saken mot Marie Hamsun', RA.
78. Marie Hamsun to Harald Grieg 22/8/1951, NBO. See also Tore Hamsun, *Efter år og dag.*
79. Christian Stray on behalf of Marie Hamsun to Gabriel Langfeldt 30/8/1946. Langfeldt to Christian Stray 8/9/1946. Arild Hamsun to Langfeldt 10/9/1946. See Sigrid Stray, *Min klient Knut Hamsun.*
80. Hamsun to Christian Gierløff 4/9/1946.

81. Christian Gierløff, *Knut Hamsun's egen røst*.
82. Hamsun to Tore Hamsun 19/7/1946 and 28/7/1946.
83. Hamsun to Ellinor Hamsun 20/3/1946.
84. Hamsun to Tore Hamsun 27/3/1946.
85. Hamsun, *On Overgrown Paths*.
86. The depiction of what happened at the meeting in Sigrid Stray's office is put together from information in: Christian Gierløff, *Knut Hamsuns egen røst*; Sigrid Stray, *Min klient Knut Hamsun*; Max Tau, *Trotz Allem*. Extra material from HPA-NBO. Hamsun's speech is taken from Gierløff, *Knut Hamsun's egen røst*. Passages of this vary considerably from the speech Hamsun gave in court in Grimstad five months later. Gierløff's account of the test run in Arendal on 20 July 1947 is likely to be reliable. In a letter to Gierløff 7/8/1947, Hamsun thanked him for the shorthand account, which means Gierløff had been in possession of it and is likely to have kept a copy. Neither Sigrid Stray, Christina Gierløff nor Max Tau mentions a stenographer, so in all probability it was Sigrid Stray herself who took the shorthand minutes during Hamsun's speech in her office.
87. Quotation taken from the newspaper *Verdens Gang* 17/12/1947.
88. *Ibid.*
89. *Ibid.*
90. Quotations from Hamsun's speech, and other reports of what he and others said in court, are based on the court documents and the court proceedings, taken down by Sigrid Stray's secretary and stenographer. Cf. documents relating to Hamsun's trial, 'Saken mot Knut Hamsun', held in RA. Also various material in HPA-NBO.
91. Oskar Hasselknippe in *Verdens Gang* 17/12/1947.
92. See note 90 above.
93. H.R. Blom Sørensen to Sigrid Stray 31/1/1948, Stray's archive. The lawyers Cato Schiøtz and Anine Kierulf studied the High Court sentence on Hamsun at the request of this biographer and Gyldendal Norsk Forlag. See Schiøtz and Kierulf, *Høyesterett og Knut Hamsun*.
94. Sigrid Stray's case preparations sent to Hamsun 16/6/1948, HPA-NBO. Cf. Stray, *Min klient Knut Hamsun*.
95. Hamsun to Sigrid Stray, telegram, 24/6/1948.
96. Hamsun to Harald Grieg 22/3/1946.
97. Harald Grieg to Marie Hamsun 24/9/1942. NBO. In *En forleggers erindringer*, Grieg explains that he never fully understood Hamsun's role, but assumed that he had been involved in his release.
98. Hamsun to Tore Hamsun 5/4/1946.
99. Harald Grieg to Hamsun 31/3/1946, received 5/4/1946. Cf. Tore Hamsun, *Efter år og dag*. Harald Grieg's secretary, Bodil Thon, has told this biographer how Grieg worked for days to formulate a response to Hamsun.
100. Hamsun to Harald Grieg 5/4/1946. Cf. Tore Hamsun, *Efter år og dag*.
101. Hamsun to Tore Hamsun 5/4/1946.
102. Hamsun to Tore Hamsun 19/7/1946.
103. Max Tau, *Tross alt*. His remark to Sigrid Stray comes from his own account.
104. Hamsun to Sigrid Stray 26/7/1948. Cf. Stray, *Min klient Knut Hamsun*.
105. Harald Grieg to Sigrid Stray 31/7/1948, HPA-NBO. Cf. Stray, *Min klient Knut Hamsun* and Harald Grieg, *En forleggers erindringer*.
106. From the Norwegian newspaper *Dagbladet* 20/8/1948 and following days.
107. Hamsun to Sigrid Stray 17/3/1949.
108. Hamsun to Christian Gierløff 22/7/1949. Gierløff's daughter, Sølvi Sejersted, has said that her family never received this letter. Her explanation for the letter's existence is that Arild Hamsun may have held it back. This is unlikely, particularly as there are no other known examples of letters kept back by Arild or other family members. It is probable that Gierløff omitted to comment on this dreadful letter to his family out of regard for Hamsun. In his book *Knut Hamsun's egen røst* he portrays Hamsun in an entirely positive light. When the biographer and his team found Hamsun's private archive in the autumn of 2001, there were fifteen unopened letters from Gierløff.

These, along with all the other archive material, are now archived at the Norwegian National Library, HPA-NBO.

109. Marie Hamsun, *Under gullregnen.*
110. Hamsun to Sigrid Stray 18/8/1948, and Hamsun to Victoria Hamsun 24/8/1948 and 10/9/1948.
111. Hamsun to Tore Hamsun 26/10/1948.
112. Marie to Gabriel Langfeldt 17/4/1949. NBO. Quoted in Thorkild Hansen, *Prosessen mot Hamsun.*
113. Hamsun to Cecilia Hamsun 13/6/1949, Quoted in Thorkild Hansen, *Prosessen mot Hamsun.*
114. Sigurd Hoel's article in the Norwegian magazine *Nidaros* 3/8/1949.
115. Sigrid Stray to Harald Grieg 29/9/1949. Cf. Stray, *Min klient Knut Hamsun.*
116. Philip Houm in the newspaper *Dagbladet* 28/9/1949.
117. Sivert Aarflot in the newspaper *Aftenposten* 28/9/1949.
118. Gabriel Langfeldt in *Aftenposten* 8/10/1949 and the literary journal *Vinduet*, 2 (1952).
119. Gabriel Langfeldt in *Dagbladet* 25/9/1978.
120. Norway's first post-war prime minister, Einar Gerhardsen, denied in *Verdens Gang* 12/10/1978 that the 'Knut Hamsun Case' had been an issue for his government. However, a number of things indicate that there was heavy pressure at least on key people involved in the case to arrive at a particular result. Oscar Hasselknippe, a central figure in the wartime resistance and later editor of the newspaper *Verdens Gang*, was in no doubt when he wrote in this newspaper in October 1978 and on 9/7/1996 that the legalities involved in securing the desired psychological reports were questionable. Also, see an article by Cato Schiøtz, Lars Frode Larsen and the biographer, *Aftenposten* 12/12/2004, for a fuller assessment.
121. Hamsun to Marika Stiernstedt 10/10/1949.
122. Hamsun to Victoria Hamsun 31/10/1949.
123. Hamsun to Tore Hamsun 12/12/1949 and 16/12/1949.
124. Quotation from Tore Hamsun, *Efter år og dag.* Tore had this event described to him by his brother, Arild, and his wife.
125. Marie Hamsun, *Under gullregnen.*
126. A play written by this biographer about this period in Hamsun's life, called *I Could Cry Blood*, from Marie's return in 1950 until his death, premiered at the Riksteatret in Norway in 2004.
127. Marie Hamsun to Tore Hamsun, April 1950 and 28/4/1950, quoted in Tore Hamsun, *Efter år og dag.*
128. Sigrid Stray describes this meeting in *Min klient Knut Hamsun.*
129. Following Hamsun's death, Victoria Hamsun launched a case against Marie Hamsun and her half-siblings, which she won. Marie Hamsun and her children appealed, but settled out of court.
130. Grieg to Tore Hamsun, August 1951, quoted in Birgit Gjernes, *Marie Hamsun.*
131. Marie Hamsun to Grieg 22/8/1951. NBO. Three years later, Aschehoug, Gyldendal's main Norwegian competitor, began publishing her books.
132. Marie Hamsun to Cecilia Hamsun, 18/2/1952, KBK.

Bibliography

Works by Knut Hamsun
The novels *Sult* (*Hunger*, 1890), *Mysterier* (*Mysteries*, 1892), *Redaktør Lynge* (*Editor Lynge*, 1893), *Ny jord* (*Shallow Soil*, 1893), *Pan* (1894), *Victoria* (1898), *Svermere* (*Dreamers*, 1904), *Under høststjernen* (*Under the Autumn Star*, 1906), *Benoni* (1908), *Rosa* (1908), *En vandrer spiller med sordin* (*A Wanderer Plays on Muted Strings*, 1909), *Den siste glede* (*The Last Joy*, 1912), *Børn av tiden* (*Children of the Age*, 1913), *Segelfoss by* (*Segelfoss Town*, 1915), *Markens grøde* (*The Growth of the Soil*, 1917), *Konerne ved vannposten* (*The Women at the Pump*, 1920), *Siste kapitel* (*Chapter the Last*, 1923), *Landstrykere* (*Wayfarers*, 1927), *August* (1930), *Men livet lever* (*The Road Leads On*, 1933), *Ringen sluttet* (*The Ring is Closed*, 1936);
the collections of short stories *Siesta* (1897), *Kratskog* (*Brushwood*, 1903), *Stridende liv* (*Striving Life*, 1905);
the travel writing *I eventyrland* (*In Wonderland*, 1903);
the plays *Ved rikets port* (*At the Gates of the Kingdom*, 1895), *Livets spill* (*The Game of Life*, 1896), *Aftenrøde* (*Evening Glow*, 1898), *Munken Vendt* (*Friar Vendt*, 1902), *Dronning Tamara* (*Queen Tamara*, 1903), *Livet ivold* (*In the Grip of Life*, 1910);
the poetry collection *Det vilde kor* (*The Wild Choir*, 1904);
and the memoir *På gjengrodde stier* (*On Overgrown Paths*, 1949).
Knut Hamsuns noveller, Oslo 1959.
Livsfragmenter. Noveller, Oslo 1988.
Ord av Hamsun, Oslo 2000.
En Fløjte lød i mit Blod. Ukjente Hamsun-dikt, Oslo 2003.
Livets Røst. Noveller, Oslo 2003.

Juvenilia not acknowledged by Knut Hamsun
Den Gaadefulde (*The Enigmatic One*, Bodø 1877); *Bjørger* (Tromsø 1878); *Fra det moderne Amerikas Aandsliv* (*On the Cultural Life of Modern America*, Copenhagen 1889); *Lars Oftedal* (Bergen 1889); *Lurtonen* (1878–79, Oslo 1995); *Romanen om Reban. Et fragment* (Tromsø 1997).

Non-fiction by Knut Hamsun
Sproget i fare, Oslo 1918.
Artikler, Oslo 1939.
På Turné. Tre foredrag om litteratur, Oslo 1960.
Over havet. Artikler og reisebrev, Oslo 1990.
Hamsuns polemiske skrifter. Artikler og foredrag, Oslo 1998.

Collected volumes of Knut Hamsun's correspondence
Knut Hamsuns brev. I–VII, Oslo 1994–2001.
Brev til Marie, Oslo 1970.
Knut Hamsun som han var. Et utvalg brev, Oslo 1956.

Memoirs by members of the Hamsun family
Hamsun, Arild: *Om Knut Hamsun og Nørholm*, Grimstad 1961.
Hamsun, Marianne: *Eine Bildbiographie*, Munich 1959.

Hamsun, Marie: *Regnbuen*, Oslo 1953.
Hamsun, Marie: *Under gullregnen*, Oslo 1959.
Hamsun, Tore: *Efter år og dag*, Oslo 1990.
Hamsun, Tore: *Knut Hamsun – min far*, Oslo 1952.
Hamsun, Tore: *Lebensbericht in Bildern*, Munich 1956.
Hamsun, Tore: *Mein Vater*, Berlin 1940.

Archives consulted
Knut Hamsun's private archive, Grimstad (now given to the National Library, Oslo).
Norsk Gyldendal publisher's archive, Oslo.
Aust-Agder Arkivet, Arendal.
The National Library, Oslo.
Riksarkivet, Oslo. The Norwegian State Archive.
Det Kongelige bibliotek, Copenhagen.
Psykiatrisk klinikks arkiv, Oslo.
Victoria Hamsun Charlesson's private archive, France.
Tore and Marianne Hamsun's private archive, Nørholm and Gran Canaria.
Aftenposten's news archive, Oslo.
Dagbladet's news archive, Oslo.
Statsarkivet, Kristiansand.
Grimstad kommunes arkiv (Grimstad County Archives).
Sand Sorenskriverembede, Grimstad.

Other publications consulted
Aakjær, Jeppe: *Før det dages*, Copenhagen 1929.
Andenæs, Johs: *Det vanskelige oppgjøret*, Oslo 1979.
Anderson, Rasmus: *Life Story of Rasmus B. Anderson*, Wisconsin 1915.
Baumgartner, Walter: *Den modernistiske Hamsun*, Oslo 1999.
Berendsohn, Walter A.: *Knut Hamsun. Das unbändige und die menschliche Gemeinschaft*, Berlin 1929.
Bjøl, Erling: *Vår tids kulturhistorie*, I–III, Oslo 1979.
Braatøy, Trygve: *Livets sirkel*, Oslo 1929.
Brandes, Georg: *Hovedstrømninger i det 19de århundredes litteratur*, I–VI, Copenhagen 1872–90.
Dahl, Hans Fr.: *En fører blir til*, Oslo 1991.
Dahl, Hans Fr.: *En fører for fall*, Oslo 1992.
Egerton, George (Mary Chavelita Dunne): *Keynotes*, London 1895.
Eklund, Torsten (ed.): *August Strindbergs brev X. Februari 1894–april 1895*, Stockholm 1968.
Ferguson, Robert: *Gåten Knut Hamsun*, Oslo, 1988.
Ferguson, Robert: *Enigma: The Life of Knut Hamsun*, Farrar, Straus & Giroux, New York 1987.
Fest, Joachim C.: *Hitler*, Penguin Books, London, 1973.
Festskrift til 70-årsdagen, Oslo 1929.
Fuchs, Karl Hans: *Danzig har ordet*, Stockholm 1939.
Gierløff, Christian: *Knut Hamsuns egen røst*, Oslo 1961.
Giersing, Morten/Thobo-Carlsen, John/Westergaard-Nielsen, Mikael: *Det reaktionære oprør*, Copenhagen 1975.
Gjernes, Birgit: *Marie Hamsun*, Oslo 1994.
Goebbels, Joseph: *Die Tagebücher von Joseph Goebbels*, I–II, ved Elke Frøhlich, Munich 1987/1993–96.
Grieg, Harald: *En forleggers erindringer*, Oslo 1958.
Hansen, Thorkild: *Prosessen mot Hamsun*, Oslo 1978,
Hitler, Adolf: *Mein kampf*, I–II, Munich 1934.
Hobsbawm, Eric: *Ekstremismens tidsalder* (*The Age of Extremes*), Oslo 1997.
Janson, Drude (under the pseudonym Judith Keller): *Mira*, Copenhagen 1897.
Jørgensen, Johannes: *Mit livs legende*, Copenhagen 1916.

Karterud, Sigmund/Schlüter, Christian: *Selvets mysterier*, Oslo 2002.

Kersaudy, François: *Kappløpet om Norge* (*Norway 1940*), Oslo 1990.

Kirkegaard, Peter: *Hamsun som modernist*, Copenhagen 1975.

Kittang, Atle: *Luft, vind, ingenting*, Oslo 1984

König, Sven: *Die Rolle Knut Hamsuns in der Nationalsozialistische Propaganda*, Hamburg 1998.

Landquist, John: *Knut Hamsun*, Stockholm 1929.

Lange, Sven: *Meninger om litteratur*, Copenhagen 1929.

Langfeldt, Gabriel/Ødegård, Ørnulf: *Den rettspsykiatriske erklæring om Knut Hamsun*, Oslo 1978.

Larsen, Lars Frode: *Den unge Hamsun*, Oslo 1998.

Larsen, Lars Frode: *Radikaleren*, Oslo 2001.

Larsen, Lars Frode: *Tilværelsens utlending*, Oslo 2002.

Lie, Trygve Halvdan: *Hjemover*, Oslo 1958.

Løventhal, Leo: *Om Ibsen og Hamsun*, Oslo 1980.

Lundegård, Axel: *Sett och känt*, Stockholm 1925.

Marcus, Carl David: *Knut Hamsun*, Copenhagen 1926.

Meyer, Michael: *Henrik Ibsen*, Oslo 1971.

Muusmann, Carl: *Det glade København*, I–III, Copenhagen 1939.

Næss, Harald: *Knut Hamsun og Amerika*, Oslo 1969.

Olsen, Frejlif: *En kjøbenhavnsk journalist*, Copenhagen 1922.

Rottem, Øystein: *Guddommelig galskap*, Oslo 1998.

Saxtorph, J. William: *De to store verdenskrige*, Copenhagen 1978.

Schiøtz, Cato/Kierulf, Anine: *Høyesterett og Knut Hamsun*, Oslo 2004.

Schroeder, Christa: *Er war mein Chef*, Munich 1985.

Schulerud, Mentz: *Norsk Kunstnerliv*, Oslo 1960.

Speer, Albert: *Erindringer*, Oslo 1970.

Steffahn, Harald: *Hitler. Mennesket, makten, undergangen*, Oslo 1989.

Stray, Sigrid: *Min klient Knut Hamsun*, Oslo 1979.

Strømme, Johannes Irgens: *Nervøsitet*, Oslo 1925.

Tau, Max: *Trotz Allem! Lebenserinnerungen aus Siebzig Jahren*, Hamburg 1973.

Tiemroth, Jørgen E.: *Illusjonens vej*, Copenhagen 1974.

Tumyr, Arne: *Knut Hamsun og hans kors*, Kristiansand 1996.

Wamberg, Niels B.: *Digterne og Gyldendal*, Copenhagen 1970.

Index

NOTE: Works by Knut Hamsun (KH) appear directly under title; works by others under author's name.

Aall, Herman Harris, 281–2
Aanrud, Hans, 91, 112, 284
Aftenposten (Norwegian newspaper): reviews KH's works, 71, 154, 175, 228; prints petition against *The Game of Life*, 87; KH contributes article to, 173; on KH's nomination for Nobel Prize, 177; on award of Peace Prize to Ossietzky, 250; photographs KH with Terboven, 271–2; reports Hitler's death, 292; on KH's trial, 311, 337; KH reads, 320; notes KH's 90th birthday, 336; reports KH's election to Order of Mark Twain, 340
Ager, Willy, 21
Albert Langen Buch- und Kunstverlag, 77, 143
Andersen, Hildur, 63
Anderson, Sherwood: *Dark Laughter*, 230
Andreasen, Hans (Cecilia's husband): *Mañana*, 306
Arbeiderbladet (Norwegian newspaper), 299
Archer, William, 59
Arendal, Norway, 187, 321
Armour, Philip, 30
Arntzen, Sven, 301, 311, 313–14
Aschehoug (Norwegian publishers), 103, 192, 332; *Who's Who* excludes KH, 336
'At the Clinic' (KH, article), 113–14
At the Gates of the Kingdom (KH, play), 82, 87, 93, 95, 105, 121, 249
August (KH): writing, 223–4; publication and reception, 228–9; characters, 248
Austria: interest in KH, 59; Germany occupies, 254
Avisen (Danish newspaper), 57

Balzac, Honoré de, 16, 32
Bang, Herman, 15–16, 40; *Realism and Realists*, 16

Barth, Karl, 246
Basta (Norwegian magazine), 84
Beck, Josef, 159
Behrens, Carl, 34–5, 39–40
Benavente, Jacinto, 220
Benn, Gottfried, 243
Benoni (KH), 26, 117–18, 123, 133, 155, 171, 215, 239
Berendsohn, Walter, 216
Bergen, Norway: KH lectures in, 59–61; KH travels to, 68
Bergens Tidende (Norwegian newspaper), 61, 70
Berghof, 282, 285
Berlin: KH and Marie visit, 230; KH revisits, 243, 256; Olympic Games (1936), 246–7; Stadttheater stages *At the Gates of the Kingdom*, 249; city development, 250; Marie in, 256; bombed in war, 270; KH visits in wartime, 277–80
Berlin-Rom-Tokyo (German magazine), 274
Bjørger (KH), 13, 155
Bjørnson, Bjørnstjerne: influence on KH, 16–17, 36; KH visits at Aulestad, 17, 135; and Nina Thaulow, 18–19; KH lectures on, 21, 32–3, 60; Sørensen's admiration for, 46; KH competes with and criticises, 57–9; status, 57; KH meets in Germany, 83; attacks Langen over KH story, 84; thanks KH for *Festschrift* poem, 102; and KH's debts, 103; KH declines invitation to stay with, 104; favours union with Sweden, 105; wins Nobel Prize, 105; KH attacks, 107; death, 133; KH eulogises, 133; *Beyond Power II* (play), 83
Bjørnson, Einar, 83
Blagoveshchenskaya, Mariya, 131–2, 147

Bodpø, 146, 148
Boers, 97–8
Bolshevism: KH attacks, 274
Bourget, Paul, 38
Braatøy, Dr Trygve, 218–19
Brækstad, Hans Lien, 59
Brandes, Edvard: career, 34; reads and
   praises 'Hunger', 38–9; reviews *On the
   Cultural Life of Modern America*, 47;
   differences with KH, 58; reviews
   Mysteries, 71
Brandes, Georg: professorial appointment
   at Copenhagen, 16; lectures on
   Nietzsche, 34; writes on literary history,
   35; KH hopes to meet, 38; attends KH's
   lectures, 44, 72; relations with KH, 44,
   58, 93; reviews KH's *On the Cultural Life
   of Modern America*, 47, 52; rejects
   Hunger, 52–3; declines KH's request to
   support *Victoria*, 93–4; attacks KH for
   anti-British views, 150; nominated for
   Nobel Prize, 177
Britain: repression of Norway in
   Napoleonic wars, 5–6; KH's disdain for,
   6, 67, 95, 149–50, 152, 176, 196, 273,
   278, 280–1; and Boers, 97–8; KH attacks
   tourists in Norway, 134, 140–1; victory
   in Great War, 164, 176; KH's publishing
   difficulties in, 173, 251; agreement
   permitting expansion of German navy,
   245; Palestine immigration policy,
   251–2; and outbreak of Second World
   War, 258–9; KH's suspicions of during
   Second World War, 265–8
Brushwood (KH, stories), 105
Bukdahl, Jørgen, 247
Bull, Olaf, 217

Carl, prince of Sweden, 179
Casselton, Dakota, 30
Caucasus: KH in, 95–6, 301
Cavling, Henrik, 153
Chamberlain, Neville, 251, 258, 266
Chapter the Last (KH), 184, 190–1, 194,
   202, 203, 211–12, 216
Charlesson, Dederick (Victoria's husband),
   185
Charlesson, Dederick Knut (Victoria's
   son), 226
Charlesson, Erik (Victoria's son), 226
Charlesson, Victoria *see* Hamsun, Victoria
Chicago: KH in, 20, 29–30; Anarchists,
   31–2
'Child, The' (KH, article), 150

Children of the Age (KH), 146–8, 151, 160,
   171–2, 198
Churchill, (Sir) Winston, 245, 266, 274,
   282
Claussen, Sophus, 35
Collected Novels (KH), 290
Collected Works (KH), 117, 154, 160, 164,
   171, 173, 178, 183, 193, 196, 340
Copenhagen: KH in, 15–16, 34–6, 38, 46,
   50, 68, 96, 98, 104; KH lectures in, 42,
   44; KH treated in for skin infection, 70;
   Royal Theatre, 133; Cecilia in, 270, 288,
   291
Curtis Brown (literary agents), 173
Czechoslovakia, 258

Dagbladet (Norwegian newspaper):
   publishes KH's early writings, 26, 29;
   reveals KH as author of 'Hunger', 40;
   and KH's return to Oslo, 46; reviews
   KH's works, 47, 57, 70, 76, 80, 84; on
   KH's intention to abandon Nørholm,
   316; criticises KH for wishing to publish
   final book in Sweden, 333; on KH's
   embracing Nazism, 337
Dagens Nyheter (Swedish newspaper), 177,
   336
Dagsposten (Norwegian newspaper), 65
Daladier, Édouard, 258
Danzig, 258
Dawes Plan, 197
Dietrich, Otto, 282–8
Dostoevsky, Fedor, 29, 33, 36, 38, 216; *The
   Gambler*, 48, 59, 69; *The Insulted and
   Humiliated*, 66
Drachmann, Holger, 107
Drachmann, Mrs Holger, 106
Dreamers (KH), 108–9, 111–12, 117, 155,
   196
Drøbak, Norway, 106, 110
Dubrovnik, Yugoslavia, 254–6
Dumreicher, Carl Otto, 134
Dunne, Mary Chavelita, 54, 69
Düsseldorf: Schauspielhaus, 133, 135
Dwinger, Edwin, 277
Dybwad, Christian, 91

Ebbe, Axel, 152
Editor Lynge (KH), 71–2, 74–7, 82, 90, 95
Egersund, 234
Eide, Sverre, 226, 322–4
Einstein, Albert, 243, 246
Elroy, USA, 20–1
Elverum, Norway, 135

Emerson, Ralph Waldo, 42
England *see* Britain
Engström, Albert, 169–70, 180–1
Enigmatic One, The: A Love Story from Nordland (KH), 12
Ericsson, Gustaf: *Kreuger kommer tillbaka*, 253
Evans (KH's colleague), 31
Evening Glow (KH; play), 90–1, 93, 111

Falkenhorst, Nicolaus von, 267, 291
Fangen, Ronald, 271–2
'Father and Son' (KH, reworking of 'Hazard'), 99
Fehlis, Heinrich, 291
'Festina Lente' (KH, article), 217
Fett, Harry, 161
Filseth, Laura, 318
Finland: alliance with Germany against Soviet Russia, 289
First World War *see* Great War
Fischer, Samuel, 58, 69
Flaubert, Gustave, 32
'Fragment of Life, A' (KH, story), 26
France: victory in Great War, 164; and Versailles Treaty, 167; KH published in, 171, 215; KH travels in, 232; and outbreak of Second World War, 258–9; *see also* Paris
Frankfurter Zeitung (German newspaper), 59, 132
Freie Bühne (magazine), 58, 69
Freud, Sigmund, 254
Friar Vendt (KH, poetic drama), 101–2, 104, 111, 154, 251
'Frida' (KH, story), 14, 16
Friedell, Egon, 254–5; *A Cultural History of Antiquity*, 254–5
Fritt Folk (Norwegian NS newspaper), 280, 295–6, 320
Fröding, Gustaf, 81–2
Frøisland, Nikolai, 19, 26–7
'From the Unconscious Life of the Mind' (KH, article), 59
Frydenlund, Erik, 186
Frydenlund, Kari, 26

Galsworthy, John, 220
Game of Life, The (KH, play): writing, 84–5, 88; public petition against, 87; German publication, 135; women in, 141
Garborg, Arne, 28–9, 74–5
Geijerstam, Gustaf af, 59

Geisir (ship), 29
George Müller Verlag, 143
Gerhardsen, Einar, 298
Germanova, Mariya Nikolaevna, 131
Germany: generosity to KH and Norwegians, 20; *Hunger* published in, 58–9; interest in and regard for KH, 59, 171, 183, 196, 198, 216, 220–1, 244, 257, 271; and plagiarism charge against KH, 69; KH's fondness for, 83, 171; ends money donations to KH, 89; *A Wanderer Plays on Muted Strings* published in, 135; KH predicts defeat of English by, 141, 150, 152, 202; *Children of the Age* published in, 147; KH's earnings in, 148; KH supports in Great War, 149–50, 164, 169; attacks Norwegian shipping in Great War, 164; defeat in Great War, 164; post-Great War political activities and recovery, 165, 197–8, 202, 221–2; signs Versailles Treaty, 167; war reparations, 183, 221; economic decline after Wall Street crash, 221–2; rise of Hitler and Nazism, 222, 236–8, 243; KH revisits with Marie (1931), 229–30, 233; rearmament and compulsory conscription, 233, 245, 251; Cecilia criticises, 240; KH supports Nazi regime, 241–5, 247, 257, 288, 319, 325; Nazi repression in, 241; and Neo-Romanticism, 244; publishes *Wayfarers*, 247; stages and broadcasts KH's works, 249, 251; expansionist policy, 250, 254, 258; occupies Rhineland, 250; pacts with Italy and Japan, 250; persecution of Jews, 252–4; non-aggression pact with USSR, 258, 266; and outbreak of Second World War, 258–9; Marie lectures and speaks in, 260, 270–1; invades and occupies Norway and Denmark, 267; withdraws before Soviets, 289; defeat in Second World War, 293; death camps, 318
Gide, André, 220
Gierløff, Christian: finds KH weeping, 113; and success of *Wayfarers*, 213; visits KH in clinic, 309–10; and KH's resuming writing, 313; KH tells of wish to divorce, 317; hears KH rehearse defence speech for trial, 318, 324; advises KH against divorce, 322; and KH's dispute with Grieg, 333; KH rejects, 334
Gladstone, William Ewart, 67

Goebbels, Joseph: wins seat in Reichstag, 222; exploits KH's support of Nazi Germany, 243; resists modern age, 244; call to artists, 247; condemns award of Nobel Peace Prize to Ossietzky, 249–50; praises Hitler's rule, 250; congratulates KH on 80th birthday, 257; Marie meets, 259; visits Norway in war, 270; invites KH to meeting in Berlin, 271–3; KH sends Nobel medal to, 279, 339; and KH's prospective meeting with Hitler, 281; praises KH to Hitler, 283; Hitler cancels KH's meeting with, 288; sends gifts to KH, 288; and German defeats, 289; compliments KH on 85th birthday, 291; KH's view of, 305

Goebbels, Magda, 278
Goebel, Heinrich, 127–8
Goncourt, Edmond and Jules de, 38
Göpfert, Eduard, 86
Göpfert, Maria Bergljot ('Vesla'), 86, 89, 93
Göring, Hermann, 222, 247, 318
Gorky, Maxim, 133, 215, 219–20, 256
Great War (1914–18): KH supports Germany in, 149–50, 164, 169; outbreak, 149; ends with Allied victory, 164, 176
Greenland, 268–70
Grieg, Edvard, 63, 107
Grieg, Harald: arranges Norwegian buy-out of Gyldendal office, 192–5; heads Gyldendal's Oslo office, 192; succeeds Kønig as KH's publisher, 214–15; and foreign translations of KH, 217, 223; on Gyldendal's profits, 223; KH asks to buy china service, 224; and publication of The Road Leads On, 238; and Jewish refugee in Norway, 252; on sale of KH's books in Norway, 256; and KH's controversial political views, 257; requests KH's help for release of Fangen, 271; dispute with KH after war, 327–33; held in wartime prison camp, 328; agrees to publish On Overgrown Paths, 334, 336; rejects Marie's plea for republication, 341–2

Grieg, Nina, 63
Grieg, Nordahl, 195, 328
Gross, Alette (Bergljot's sister), 95, 225
Growth of the Soil, The (KH): writing, 156–9; theme of rural/farming life, 157–62, 172, 174; KH awarded Nobel Prize for, 170, 177, 243; sales, 171, 196, 251, 271; H.G. Wells contributes

commentary on, 173; Knopf publishes in USA, 173, 183; filmed, 189
Gudbrands Valley, 5, 7–8
Gustaf, Crown Prince of Sweden, 107
Gyldendal (Danish publishers): KH travels to Copenhagen to solicit, 13, 15; publish Siesta, 89; KH requests advance from, 102–3; persuade KH to write Dreamers, 109; lend money to KH to buy house, 112; KH requests better terms from, 115; new contract with KH, 116; KH's debt to, 143, 148–9; publish Children of the Age, 147; KH offers to sell farm to, 151; publish Collected Works, 154; payments to KH, 167; KH clears debt to, 171; and publication of KH in Britain, 173; mark KH's 60th birthday, 187–8; establish Oslo office, 192; and Norwegian resentment of dominance, 192–3; Oslo business purchased by Norwegians, 192–5, 328; KH buys back rights from, 251; publish KH's Collected Novels, 290; Grieg attempts to secure KH's shares, 330, 332; offer loan to KH, 331, 333; secure sole publishing rights on KH's works, 333; catalogue promotes KH's Collected Works, 340
Gyldendal's Nordic Library (series), 109

Haakon VI, King of Norway: elected king, 111; KH considers audience with, 243; absent from 1936 Nobel Peace Prize ceremony, 250
Hagelstam, Wentzel, 94, 96, 99
Hallström, Per, 169–70, 176
Hamarøy, Nordland: KH's early life in, 4–10, 14, 97; KH builds mill and dairy at, 152; KH leaves with family, 157; see also Skogheim
Hamburg, 20, 232–3
Hamsun, Almar (KH's nephew): KH takes to court, 189, 202
Hamsun, Anne Marie (Tore's daughter), 291, 339
Hamsun, Arild (KH–Marie's son): birth, 149; childhood, 163; 8th birthday, 184; KH snaps at, 184; schooling, 184; KH considers leaving farm to, 210; rivalry with brother Tore, 210; at school with Tore in Valdres, 217, 223, 234; character and style, 223; in Cannes, 240; attends Ellinor's wedding in Berlin, 259; returns to Norway in war, 270; returns safely from Eastern Front, 291; arrested at

war's end, 293–4; with KH in court, 323; owns shares in Gyldendal, 332; takes over Nørholm farm, 332, 335; sentenced, 335; and KH in old age, 339–40

Hamsun, Bergljot Bech (*earlier* Göpfert): KH meets and falls for, 85–6, 88; divorce from Göpfert, 87, 89; engagement and marriage to KH, 89–91; wealth, 91; marriage relations, 93–4, 96–8, 104, 108, 110, 112–13; trip to East with KH, 95–6; sends money to KH in Nordland, 97; travels alone to Nordland, 99; KH gambles away fortune, 100–1; pregnant by KH, 100–1; and baby Victoria's upbringing, 103; bank account restored by Gyldendal, 103–4; takes midwifery course, 105–6; moves into new house (Maurbakken), 112; divorce from KH, 114; defends Victoria against KH's criticism, 138; receives payment from KH for gambling debts, 160; death, 279

Hamsun, Brit (Arild's wife), 339–40

Hamsun, Cecilia (KH–Marie's daughter; *later* Andreasen): birth, 158–9; at Nørholm, 163; 5th birthday, 184; relations with brothers, 210; schooling, 217, 234; in Germany, 240; in wartime Copenhagen, 270, 288, 291; marriage, 306; owns shares in Gyldendal, 332; Marie stays with after release from prison, 335; letter from Marie on KH's death, 342

Hamsun, Ellinor (KH–Marie's daughter; *later* Schneider-Edenkoben): birth, 153; childhood, 163; 7th birthday, 184; relations with brothers, 210; early schooling, 217; at convent school in Germany, 234; in Cannes, 240; encounter with Hitler in Germany, 253; extravagance, 256; Nazis court in Germany, 256; marriage, 259; Marie visits in wartime Germany, 270; mental problems and return from Germany, 278, 291; KH advises to seek God's help, 317–18; admitted to psychiatric institution, 332; Gyldendal shares transferred to, 332

Hamsun, Esben (Arild's son), 339

Hamsun, Ingeborg (Tore's daughter), 339

Hamsun, Knut
FINANCES: improvidence, 15, 17–18, 27, 37, 46, 73, 105, 111; literary earnings, 39, 41, 43, 52, 134, 138, 148, 160, 167, 171, 183, 193, 196; debts, 50, 52, 103, 108, 129, 143, 148–9; acquires cash from others, 73; receives state stipend, 93; gambling losses, 99–102; improvement in means, 138, 148–9, 160, 196, 251; clears debt to publisher, 171; invests in Gyldendal's Norwegian publishing business, 193–5; pays off compensation fine, 333; money difficulties in final years, 340–1

HEALTH: tuberculosis, 23–5, 43; skin infection, 70; hand trembling problem, 76, 182, 190; in hospital with haemorrhoids, 102–3; admitted to clinic for mental state, 113–14; sciatica and ailments, 135; confesses to suffering neuroses, 143; takes electric treatment, 151; operation for sterilisation and anti-ageing, 182–3, 186; Strømme psychoanalyses and treats, 203–6, 208–9, 211–12, 224–5, 229; Braatøy psychoanalyses from writings, 218–19; hearing deteriorates, 223, 307, 320; urinary problems and prostate operation, 225–7; suffers brain haemorrhage, 279; suffers stroke (1945), 292; declared mentally sound, 301; in Oslo psychiatric clinic, 303–8; declared mentally impaired, 310, 313; leaves psychiatric clinic, 310

HONOURS & AWARDS: declines award of Knight of Order of St Olav, 134; nominated for and wins Nobel Prize, 161, 169–70, 176–9, 243; Nobel acceptance speech, 179–80; *Festschrift* for, 220; elected to Order of Mark Twain, 341

INTERESTS & ACTIVITIES: drawing, 21; buys books in Bergen, 34; interest in psychology, 36; drinking, 46, 73, 88, 107–8, 110, 118, 129; buys supposed Goya painting, 101–2; works to improve land, 138–9; art interests, 152; buys and improves Nørholm (farm), 161–3, 166–7; buys motorcars, 184, 186, 220; extends and develops Nørholm, 198

LITERARY LIFE: early story-writing, 12–13; international success and reputation, 14, 160, 171, 183, 196, 215–17, 220; early writings rejected, 15–20; lectures, 21, 27, 32–3, 42, 44, 59–64, 66, 72, 116, 161; writes articles and stories during illness, 24–7; adopts writing name, 26;

Hamsun, Knut: LITERARY LIFE (*Cont.*)
    literary technique, 27–8, 33, 36–7,
    117; and success of 'Hunger' fragment,
    40; inspirational episodes and
    creativity, 43, 48, 59, 146; plagiarism
    accusations, 48, 69–71; Langen
    acquires translation rights, 77; play-
    writing, 80–2, 84–5, 127, 131, 134,
    138; poetry, 92; suffers writer's block,
    97–8, 151, 167, 202–3, 256; resumes
    writing, 100–1, 206–8; speed of
    writing, 108; working methods and
    routine, 127–8, 146, 187–8, 235;
    reading, 134, 227, 230; dispute with
    German publishers, 143; revises
    writings for *Collected Works*, 154; Sven
    Lange assesses work, 154–5; controls
    characters in novels, 155, 172; and
    nervous struggle of writing, 201–2; on
    writer's role, 212; foreign publishing
    rights, 214–15; as subject of
    biographies and studies, 215–16; buys
    back book rights from Gyldendal, 251;
    declining readership in Norway, 257;
    obituary on Hitler's death, 292–3;
    keeps diary in clinic, 313; dispute with
    Grieg over publication and Gyldendal
    shares, 328–33; excluded from
    Aschehoug's *Who's Who*, 336
  PERSONAL LIFE: birth and baptism (as
    Knud Pedersen), 3; family
    background, 4, 8; schooling, 6, 8–9;
    lives and works with uncle Hans, 7–8;
    speaking and accent, 7, 14, 19;
    youthful rebelliousness, 7–8;
    confirmation, 8; moves to
    Jotunheimen, 8–9; returns to
    Hamarøy to work, 10–11; youth and
    employment in Nordland, 11–12;
    sensitivity to uncultured background,
    16, 94; life in Oslo, 17–18; conceit, 18;
    appearance and dress, 19, 32–3,
    121–2; works on road construction,
    19; contemplates suicide, 21–2, 43,
    100; declines Drude Janson's sexual
    offer, 23–4, 43; effect on women,
    43–4, 61; exaggerations and fantasies,
    44; affair with Mrs Winkel Horn,
    50–1; dalliance with Elise Jahnsen, 53;
    relations with Mary Chavelita Dunne,
    54, 69; attacked by Thommessen, 65;
    and Julie Amanda Lous, 66, 68;
    womanising, 68–9, 83, 108; sense of
    persecution, 76, 80, 90, 146; meets and

falls for Bergljot, 85–6, 88; persecuted
    by Anna Munch, 85–6, 88; reluctance
    to marry Bergljot, 89–90; slandered in
    Norway, 90; marries Bergljot, 91;
    marriage relations with Bergljot, 93–4,
    96–8, 104, 108, 110, 112–13; daughter
    (Victoria) with Bergljot, 100–1; denies
    suicide rumours, 102; fondness for
    baby Victoria, 103; outlandish
    behaviour, 106–7; builds and occupies
    house (Maurbakken) at Drøbak,
    110–12; divorce from Bergljot, 114,
    117; misses father's funeral, 116; takes
    daughter Victoria on holidays, 116,
    128; meets Marie Lavik, 121–4;
    confesses love for Marie, 123–4;
    engagement and marriage to Marie,
    125, 128; demands on Marie, 126–7;
    irritability, 126, 128, 304–5, 340; 50th
    birthday, 129; marriage relations with
    Marie, 129, 139, 142, 145, 171–2,
    187–9, 203–4, 214, 234, 249, 251, 289,
    309, 315; leaves Oslo with Marie, 130;
    moves to Skogheim (farm), Nordland,
    135–6; children by Marie, 137, 149,
    153, 158; threatens to sell and quit
    Skogheim, 140, 142, 145, 148, 151,
    156–7; devotion to children, 152–3;
    leaves Skogheim and farming, 157,
    160; and mother's death, 164; reads
    and talks to children, 166; admits to
    true age on 60th birthday, 168;
    banishes daughter Victoria for
    engagement to Englishman, 185, 189;
    anxieties and paranoia, 187–8, 203;
    nightmares and dreams, 188–9, 204,
    206, 211; takes brother and nephew to
    court for adopting name Hamsun,
    189–90, 202, 238; returns to farm after
    psychiatric treatment, 207–8; relations
    with growing children, 210; sense of
    ageing, 213, 219; 68th birthday, 213;
    portraits, 218; 70th birthday, 218–21;
    infatuation with Marika Stiernstedt,
    224, 235, 338–9; offers inheritance
    settlement to Victoria, 226–8; and
    children's education, 234; 80th
    birthday, 256–7; and outbreak of
    Second World War, 258; Goebbels
    invites to meet in Berlin, 271–3, 278;
    meeting with Terboven, 271–2;
    prospective meeting with Hitler,
    276–9, 281; meets Hitler at Berghof,
    282–6; loses favour in Norway, 290–1;

85th birthday, 291; resumes correspondence with Victoria, 291; arrest and internment at war's end, 294; charged and interrogated over wartime behaviour, 295–300; moved to old people's home in Landvik, 302–3; criminal charges dropped by state, 311–12; summons from Directorate of Compensation, 312; court case postponed, 313–14, 318; seeks divorce from Marie, 316–17; turns to religion for solace, 317; prepares court defence, 318–21; court appearance and trial, 322–6; redrafts will restoring Victoria to inheritance, 322; found guilty and sentenced, 326–7; loses court appeal, 326–7; 90th birthday, 333–4, 336; abandons idea of divorce, 335; cuts off Marie after release from prison, 335; reunion with Marie in old age, 339–42; death, 342

TRAVELS: to Copenhagen, 15–16; to USA, 19–22, 29–30; returns to Norway, 24; to Paris, 73–5, 78; leaves Paris, 81; in Helsingfors, 93–5; trip to Orient, 93, 95; revisits Nordland, 97; to Italy, 211; revisits Germany and European countries with Marie, 229–32; to Palestine, 251; visits Tore and Ellinor in Germany, 253; in Dubrovnik, 254–6; wartime visits to Germany, 270, 277–9; attends writers' conference in Vienna, 277, 279–80

VIEWS & OPINIONS: anti-British views, 6, 67, 95, 149–50, 152, 164, 176, 265–8, 273, 280–1; religious views, 8, 21–2; attitude to women, 13, 21, 26, 43, 75, 127, 130–1, 141–2, 151; on language, 35; on negroes, 45; criticises established Norwegian writers, 57, 60–1, 63–4; on 'psychological literature', 59, 64; attacks fourth commandment ('honour thy father and mother'), 116, 136, 150; on childless marriages, 129; attacks tourism in Norway, 134, 140; disparages old people, 136–7; on marriage, 148; on parents and children, 150–1; supports death penalty, 150; on death and reincarnation, 168–9, 213–14; political ideas, 175–6; hostility to book learning, 184; attacks city life, 191; supports and defends Nazi Germany,

233, 237–8, 241–5, 247, 255, 257, 267–9, 319, 325; admiration for Hitler, 245, 265, 273, 288; criticised for attack on Ossietzky, 246; attitude to Jews, 252; proposes Norwegian-German partnership, 273–5, 277; on German wartime reverses, 289–90

Hamsun, Leif (Tore's son), 339

Hamsun, Marie (*formerly* Lavik; KH's second wife): KH meets and falls for, 121–4; background, 123; and Lavik's death, 124–5; engagement and marriage to KH, 125–6, 128; and KH's demands and instructions, 126–8, 130, 139, 142; learns practical domestic skills, 126; KH leaves after honeymoon, 128–9; marriage relations with KH, 129–31, 139, 142, 145, 171–2, 187–9, 203–4, 214, 234, 249, 251, 289, 309, 315; desire to settle, 132; lives in country with KH, 134; fondness for Nordland farm (Skogheim), 135–6; moves to house in Elverum, 135; pregnancies and children, 137, 146, 151, 153, 158; visits mother-in-law, 137; life and work in Skogheim, 139–40, 146, 157–8; and KH's threat to sell Skogheim, 140, 142, 145, 148, 156–7; and KH's awareness of neuroses, 143; leaves Skogheim on sale of farm, 157; unmoved by Nørholm farm, 162; popularity at Nørholm, 163; reads to children, 166; and KH's 60th birthday, 168; informed of KH's Nobel Prize award, 177–8; at Nobel award ceremony, 179–81; and KH's irritability, 184; learns to drive, 186; writings, 186, 201–2, 217, 234, 271, 341; and KH's anxieties and nightmares, 187–9; assists KH with correspondence, 190; hopes of KH abandoning writing, 203; KH persuades to visit Dr Strømme, 204–5, 208–9; and KH's return to writing after psychiatric treatment, 208; resentment at KH's writing, 214, 218; and children's absence, 217; and KH's 70th birthday, 218; dispute with Victoria over inheritance, 226–7; travels abroad with KH, 229–33; suffers breakdown, 239–40; and children's departure, 240; supports German regime, 240–1, 310; participates in Nordic Day in Germany, 256, 260; attends Ellinor's wedding in Berlin, 259; meetings with Goebbels and Göring, 259–60, 278; first sees Hitler, 260;

Hamsun, Marie (*Cont.*)
  speeches and lectures in Germany,
  260–1, 270–1; wartime visits to
  Germany, 270; and KH's prospective
  meeting with Hitler, 277; and war's end,
  291; sends condolences on Hitler's
  death, 292; arrest and imprisonment,
  294, 301, 312; questioned by Langfeldt,
  308–9, 315–17; supposed influence on
  KH's political views, 310–11, 341;
  account of life with KH, 311; KH returns
  letter unopened, 315–16; released, 315,
  334; brings action against Langfeldt, 316,
  335; charged and sentenced, 316, 327;
  KH seeks divorce from, 316–17; KH
  excludes from will, 322, 335; and Grieg's
  release from prison camp, 328; relations
  with Sigrid Stray, 331–2; and control of
  KH's shares, 332; reads *On Overgrown
  Paths*, 338; reunion with KH in old age,
  339–42; raises loan, 340; complains of
  poverty, 341; *Ola in the City*, 217; *The
  Rainbow* (memoirs), 341; *Small Poems*,
  186; *Village Children: At Home and on
  the Farm*, 201
Hamsun, Thorof Oskar Almar (Thorvald's
  son) *see* Hamsun, Almar
Hamsun, Thorvald (KH's brother) *see*
  Pedersen Hamsun, Thorvald
Hamsun, Tore (KH–Marie's son): birth,
  137; childhood, 138, 143; KH's
  attachment to, 149; at Nørholm, 163,
  166; schooling, 184; 10th birthday, 185;
  KH warns of ageing, 187; character and
  style, 210, 223; in Valdres, 210, 217, 223;
  travels with parents, 230–2; joins SS in
  Germany, 244; arranges Tau's move to
  Norway, 253–5; KH visits in Berlin,
  253–4; returns to Norway, 255; attends
  Ellinor's wedding in Berlin, 259;
  interprets for KH at meeting with
  Terboven, 271–2; accompanies KH to
  Berlin to meet Goebbels, 273; and
  impending German defeat, 291;
  biography of KH, 293; arrested and tried
  at war's end, 294, 321; family depends
  on, 310; and KH's release from
  psychiatric clinic, 310; and KH's
  religious solace, 317–18; and Grieg's
  release from prison camp, 328–9;
  appointed KH's rights manager, 330;
  owns shares in Gyldendal, 332; collects
  Marie on release from prison, 334; KH
  invites for Christmas, 339

Hamsun, Victoria (KH–Bergljot's
  daughter; *later* Charlesson): birth, 101;
  babyhood and upbringing, 103, 110;
  moves into new house (Maurbakken),
  112; custody after parents' divorce, 114,
  128; spends time with KH, 116, 128; and
  KH's second marriage, 128; visits
  Skogheim, 138; meets KH on way to
  Oslo, 144; disappointed in attempt to see
  KH, 149; declines to accompany KH
  to Nobel ceremony in Stockholm, 179;
  KH sends to France for education, 185,
  190; qualities, 185; banished by KH after
  engagement to Englishman, 185, 189;
  defies KH's offer of reconciliation, 214;
  letter to KH seeking reconciliation,
  225–6; KH offers inheritance settlement,
  226–8; tells KH of Bergljot's death, 279;
  letter from KH on impending German
  defeat, 289; in Normandy, 290; resumes
  correspondence with KH, 291; KH
  revokes 1930 agreement and restores to
  inheritance, 322, 335, 359; shares in
  Gyldendal, 335; successfully contests
  KH's final exclusion from inheritance,
  341
Hamsund, Hamarøy, 14, 97
Hansen, Peter Emmanuel, 133
Hansson, Ole, 38
Harstad, 151
Hauberg, P. & Co. (publishers), 34
Hauptmann, Gerhart, 220
'Hazard' (KH, story), 47–8, 59, 69; *see also*
  'Father and Son'
Hedin, Sven, 111, 270
Hegel, Frederik, 13, 15–16, 18, 38, 89
Hegel, Jacob, 102–3, 194–5, 214
Heiberg, Gunnar, 40
Helsingfors (Helsinki), 93–5
Herzfeld, Marie, 59, 69
Hesse, Hermann, ix
Hesthagen, Tosten, 9
Hewel, Walter, 283, 286
Himmler, Heinrich, 256
Hindenburg, Otto von, 237
Hitler, Adolf: early political activities,
  197–8, 222; aggressiveness, 233; rise to
  power, 236–8, 250; persecutions and
  killings, 240–1; holds referendum on
  Saar, 244; resists modern age, 244; KH
  admires as natural European leader, 245,
  265, 273, 281, 288; repudiates Versailles
  Treaty, 245; opens 1936 Olympic Games,
  246; expansionist policy, 250, 254, 258;

forbids German acceptance of Nobel Prizes, 250; on aims of Nazism, 252; anti-Jewish measures, 252; encounter with Ellinor Hamsun, 253; congratulates KH on 80th birthday, 257; and outbreak of Second World War, 258; Marie first sees, 260; Quisling meets, 266, 269, 276; and strategic importance of Norway, 266; KH's prospective meeting with, 276–9, 281; KH meets at Berghof, 282–7; weakened condition, 282; and control of Norway, 283–4; telegram to KH on 85th birthday, 291; death and obituary by KH, 292–3; KH finds egocentric, 305; *Mein Kampf*, 197

Hjärne, Harald, 177, 179

Hoel, Sigurd, 192, 211, 227, 336; *Hærverk*, 228

Holland: KH published in, 171, 196

Holländer, Felix, 69–70, 216

Holm, Korfiz, 143, 216

Holmboe, Egil, 281–7

Holst, Lars, 26, 46

'Honour Thy Young' (KH, article), 136

Hornbæk, Denmark, 106

Houm, Philip, 337

Hungary: publishes KH, 171

'Hunger' (KH, fragment), 37–40, 46–7

Hunger (KH): and emotional states, 6, 62; autobiographical content, 19, 48–9, 52, 201; fame, 28, 302; writing, 37–8, 47–50, 155; publishing contract, 41; themes and characters, 48–9, 74, 141, 213, 239; printing, 51; Georg Brandes disparages, 52; reception, 52–3, 57–9, 61, 81; as psychological literature, 59; love affairs in, 86–7; copies unsold, 89; KH re-reads, 154; success in Hungary, 171; sales in USA, 196; success in Germany, 221; and KH's post-war detention, 302–3

Huntley (KH's colleague), 31

Ibsen, Henrik: leaves Norway, 17, 34; KH lectures on, 32; KH criticises and mocks, 57, 60–5, 67, 71–2, 103–4; KH's rivalry with and antipathy to, 57, 59, 80–1, 87–8, 127, 161, 177; returns to Norway, 62–3; attends KH's lectures, 63–4; silence over non-award of state subsidy to KH, 89; 75th birthday celebrations, 103; international reputation, 299; *A Doll's House*, 16, 37; *John Gabriel Borkman*, 87; *The Lady from the Sea*, 41; *The League of Youth*,

63, 65; *Little Eyolf*, 81; *The Master Builder*, 71–2, 81; *Peer Gynt*, 101

In the Grip of Life (KH, play), 132–4, 149, 155, 221

In Wonderland: Lived and Dreamed in the Caucasus (KH, travel book), 96, 103, 105, 302

Informationen (Danish newspaper), 336

Italy: KH visits with Marie and Tore, 231; Fascism in, 236; pacts with Germany and Japan, 250

Jahnsen, Elise Dorothea, 53

Janes, José (Spanish publisher), 330

Janson, Drude, 22–4, 43

Janson, Kristofer, 22–4, 30, 34–5, 43; on KH's 'Hunger', 42; *Mysteries of Minneapolis*, 33

Japan: pacts with Germany and Italy, 250

Jensen, Johannes V., 106–7

Jews: growing hostility to, 176; immigration in Palestine, 251–2; German policy on, 252–4; KH's attitude to, 252; deported from Norway in war, 275

Jølsen, Ragnhild, 108

Jørgensen, Johannes, 35

Jotunheimen, Norway, 3, 5, 8, 47

Junkerdal, Norway, 138

Kameradschaft der Deutschen Künstler, 253

Karlfeldt, Erik Axel, 176–7, 180

Kielland, Alexander, 27, 32, 57, 60

Knopf, Alfred (US publisher), 173, 183–4

Københavns Børs-Tidende (Danish newspaper), 57

Kollontay, Aleksandra, 220

Kongsberg, Norway, 116, 123

Kønig, Christian: and writing of *Segelfoss Town*, 151; and KH's rewriting of *Hunger*, 154; and KH's true 60th birthday, 168; and *The Women at the Pump*, 170, 175; and KH's German earnings, 171; visits Nørholm, 173; plans 3rd edition of KH's *Collected Works*, 178; promotes Marie's *Small Poems*, 186; and Norwegian bid for purchase of Gyldendal in Oslo, 192–4; wishes to return to Copenhagen, 194; and KH's writing difficulties, 203; KH delivers *Wayfarers* to, 209, 211; and KH's ageing, 213; returns to Copenhagen, 214

Krag, Thomas P., 108
Krag, Vilhelm, 118, 121, 133
Kringsjaa (Norwegian magazine), 84
Kristensen, Tom, 211, 220, 228, 269
Kristiansand, Norway, 78
Kristiansund, Norway, 65–6, 68
Kruger, Paul, 97
Kuhlefelt, Elias, 93
Kurella, Hans, 58
Kuttner, Erich, 246

Lægdslem, Maren, 338
Lagerlöf, Selma, 169, 177, 179, 279
Lamas, Carlos Saavedra, 250
Landquist, John, 175
Landvik, Norway, 302
Lange, Sven, 73, 109, 142, 154–5
Langen, Albert: KH meets, 77; publishes
    KH in German and French, 77, 80;
    payments to KH, 78; and support for
    Strindberg, 81; and KH's
    Germanophilia, 83; marriage, 83; and
    KH's not receiving state subsidy, 89; and
    KH's gambling debt, 102; provides KH
    with money, 112; KH sends 'At the
    Clinic' to, 114; publishes *The Game of
    Life*, 135; death, 143
Langen, Dagny (*née* Bjørnson), 83
Langen, Martin, 89
Langen Verlag, 149–50, 160, 164, 183; *see
    also* Müller-Langen Verlag
Langfeldt, Gabriel: psychiatric observation
    and report on KH, 300–1, 303–10,
    313–15, 332, 337–8; interviews Marie,
    308–9, 315–16; Marie brings action
    against, 316, 335; KH attacks in *On
    Overgrown Paths*, 334, 337–8
Larsen, Alf, 247
Larsen, Bolette Pavels, 61, 65, 70, 76–7, 88,
    95
Larvik, Norway, 157–9
Lassen, Christian, 171
Last Joy, The (KH), 112–13, 138, 140–2,
    150, 155, 191, 217, 302
Lavik, Dore, 121, 123–5
Lavik, Marie *see* Hamsun, Marie
Laws, Yngvar, 36–7
Lewin, Menartz, 133
Library for the Thousand Homes (series), 41
Lie, Jonas, 32, 50, 57, 77
Lie, Thomasine, 77
Lie, Trygve, 299
'Life's Voice' (KH, story), 84, 89
Lillehammer, Norway, 81

Lillesand, Norway, 53–4, 79, 165; *see also*
    Nørholm
Lillestrøm, Norway, 105, 144
Ljunglund, Leon, 281
Ljus (Swedish publishing house), 333
Locarno Treaty (1925), 198, 221
Lom, Norway, 5, 8–9
Lous, Julie Amanda (Lulli), 66, 68
Lübeck, 256, 260
Ludendorff, General Erich von, 237
Lund, Henrik, 218

Mackensen, Field Marshal August von, 253
Mann, Heinrich, 220, 243, 246, 250, 257
Mann, Klaus, 243
Mann, Thomas: praises KH, ix, 220;
    protests at non-award of state subsidy to
    KH, 89; KH denies influence, 216;
    deprived of German citizenship, 243;
    campaigns for Ossietzky, 246; in exile,
    257; on wartime Norway, 270;
    Buddenbrooks, 216
Masaryk, T.G., 220
Maud, Queen of Haakon VII, 111
Maupassant, Guy de: *Notre Coeur*, 62
Maurbakken (house), Drøbak, 112, 114
Mellbye, Johan, 266
Michaëlis, Sophus, 35
Michelsen, Christian, 193
Milan, 231
Miller, Henry, ix
Minneapolis, 30, 32
Molotov, Vyacheslav M., 299
Mondadori (Italian publishers), 330
Morgenbladet (Danish newspaper): on
    'Hunger' fragment, 41; and Holländer's
    accusation of KH's plagiarism, 70;
    attacks KH, 76; criticises *Pan*, 80; reviews
    KH's writings, 87, 93–4, 115, 192, 228
Mörner, Birger, 93
Moscow Art Theatre, 131, 133, 135, 149
Müller, Herman, 222
Müller-Langen Verlag, 208, 216, 247; *see
    also* Langen Verlag
Munch, Andreas, 16
Munch, Anna, 85, 88, 90
Munch, Edvard, 34, 71
Munich, 84–5; Deutsches Theater, 149
Mussolini, Benito, 236, 238
Mysteries (KH): character of Nagel, 66–8,
    110, 174, 213, 235; writing, 66–7, 69, 76,
    155, 201; cripple (Minutten) in, 67, 71,
    174; reception, 70–1; and craving for
    nature, 78; translations, 80; Bjørnson

praises, 83; financial failure, 89; women in, 141; Lange on, 154; Hallström on, 169–70; French interest in, 171; sales, 196

Naess, Harald, x
Namur, Belgium, 100
Nansen, Fridtjof, 111, 133
Nansen, Peter, 109
Narvik, Norway, 266
Nasjonal Samling (Norwegian political party; NS), 236, 241, 295–6, 322–6
National Theatre, Oslo, 118, 121, 133–4
Nationen (Norwegian newspaper), 241
Nazi Party Congress, 8th (1936), 247
Nazism: rise in Germany, 222, 236–7; aims, 252
Neeraas, Caroline, 68
negroes: KH's views on, 45
'Neighbouring Town, The' (KH, article), 173
Nemirovich-Danchenko, Vladimir, 133, 135
Neo-Romanticism, 244
New York Stock Exchange: crash (1929), 221
New York Times Book Review, 217
Nicolaysen, Peter, 226
Nietzsche, Friedrich, 45, 171, 216
Nobel Prize: Bjørnson wins, 105; KH nominated for and wins, 161, 169–70, 176–9, 243; award ceremony, 179; money prize, 183; awarded to Sigrid Undset, 217; for Peace, 246; Peace Prize awarded to Ossietzky, 249–50; KH sends medal to Goebbels, 279, 339
Nordische Gesellschaft, 233, 244, 256–7, 269
Nordland: in KH's novels, 77–9, 112–13; KH returns to, 97, 135; KH idealises, 132; KH's disenchantment with, 145; in KH's psychoanalysis, 212; Germans despoil, 292; *see also* Hamarøy
Nørholm (farm): KH buys and improves, 161–3, 165–7, 198, 207–8; explosion at, 167; harvest, 170; Kønig visits, 173; KH attempts to write at, 188; running costs, 196; KH returns to after psychiatric treatment, 207; photographed, 218; KH wins legal case against family owners, 238; KH leaves after war, 301; searched on Langfeldt's orders, 308; KH returns to (Christmas 1947), 327; Arvild takes over, 332, 335
Norway: KH criticises established writers,

57, 60–1; KH on politics in, 74, 141, 165, 175, 236; subservience to Sweden, 82, 105; refuses state subsidy to KH, 89; reconsiders and grants stipend to KH, 93; seeks independence from Sweden, 105, 107; declares independence (1905), 110–11; territorial disputes, 133; KH attacks tourism in, 134, 140; offers honour to KH, 134; social equality in, 145; social change and urbanisation, 147–8, 160, 172, 175, 191; rise of Labour Party, 165; dispute over purchase of Gyldendal's Oslo business, 192–6; disarmament policy, 233; Nobel Peace Prize committee, 246, 249–50; Jewish immigration, 252; waning interest in KH's writings, 257; neutrality at outbreak of Second World War, 259, 265–7; Germans invade and occupy, 267; administration under Nazi occupation, 269, 271, 284, 287; KH proposes partnership with Germany, 273–5, 277; as German strategic base, 275; Jews deported, 275; severe Nazi regime, 275–6; volunteers join German SS, 275; wartime resistance movement, 275, 287; hostility to KH's wartime views, 290; post-war coalition government, 298; traitor trials, 318; wartime arrests and deportations, 319
Norwegian Writers' Union, 89, 103, 115, 195, 234
Norwegian-German Society, 242
NS Party *see* Nasjonal Samling
Nuremberg Trials, 318
Ny Jord (Danish journal), 34–6, 39–40, 45–6
Nygaard, William (Norwegian publisher), 192–4

Ødegård, Ørmulv, 307, 309, 338
Olav, crown prince of Norway, 111
Olsen, Freijlif, 73
Olsen, Georg, 135
Olsen, Hans (KH's uncle), 3–9, 136, 182
Olsen, Ole (KH's uncle), 3
Olympic Ganes, Berlin (1936), 246–7
On the Cultural Life of Modern America (KH), 44–5, 47, 52, 265
On Overgrown Paths (KH), 302, 307, 331–3, 336–8
'On Tour' (KH, story), 28–9
Oscar II, king of Sweden, 107

Oslo: KH in, 17, 24, 29, 46–7, 49, 83, 205–7; in KH's writing, 75; Bergljot persuades KH to settle in, 99; earthquake (1904), 107; KH leaves with Marie, 130; KH moves to with Marie and family, 208–10; see also National Theatre
Ossietzky, Carl von, 245–6, 249–50, 255
Ostend, 99
Österling, Anders, 168
Øverland, Arnulf, 195
Øystese, 14–15

Paasche, Johan Fredrik, 241
Palestine: KH travels to, 251
Pan (KH): writing, 78–9, 201; plot and themes, 79, 85, 109, 118, 127, 235, 239; reception, 80; on nature, 83; love affair in, 87, 141; published in Russia, 111; Lange on, 154; special illustrated 25th anniversary edition, 167; sales, 196, 221; film version in Germany, 251
Papen, Franz von, 237
Paris: KH in, 73–5, 78; KH's breakdown in, 76; Jonas Lie in, 77; KH leaves, 81; liberated (1944), 291
Paul, Adolf, 93
Pauli, Ivan, 338
Pedersen, Anne Marie (KH's sister), 4
Pedersen, Hans (KH's brother), 210
Pedersen, Ole (KH's brother), 97, 136
Pedersen, Peder, Jr (KH's older brother), 4–5; KH meets in USA, 20
Pedersen, Peder (KH's father): farming and tailoring, 3–5; 75th birthday, 97; death, 116, 136
Pedersen, Sophie Marie (KH's sister): birth and childhood, 4–5, 7; career, 67
Pedersen, Tora (née Olsen; KH's mother), 4–6, 8, 36, 97, 116, 136–7, 152; death, 164
Pedersen Hamsun, Thorvald (KH's brother): KH takes to court for adopting Hamsun name, 189–90, 202
Pettersen, Hjalmar, 203
Philipsen, Gustav, 39, 42–3, 46–7, 50, 58, 71, 73–4, 80, 89
Philipsens Forlag, P.G., 39, 41
Pitoëff, Ludmilla, 220
Poland: publishes translation of KH, 77; invaded and partitioned (1939), 258–60
Polish Corridor, 258
Politiken (Danish newspaper): Edvard Brandes edits, 34; reviews On the Cultural Life of Modern America, 47;
reviews Hunger, 57; criticises Dreamers, 109; KH contributes article on effect of tourism in Norway, 134; reviews The Last Joy, 142; Georg Brandes attacks KH in, 150; Lange reviews Segelfoss Town in, 154; on KH's nomination for Nobel Prize, 177; criticises KH's support for Nazism, 247; KH cancels subscription, 292
Pollak, Oskar, 220
Polly (cook), 31

'Queen of Sheba, The' (KH, story), 88
Queen Tamara (KH, play), 104–5, 155, 183, 251
Quisling, Vidkun: KH supports, 236, 251; Paasche warns against, 241; meetings with Hitler, 266, 269, 276, 284; as wartime prime minister of Norway, 269, 276, 287–8; Sigrid Undset criticises, 270; proposes Norwegian control of defence, 283; surrenders at war's end, 293; trial, 300

Reconciliation, A (KH, poem), 13
Reinhardt, Max, 149, 221
Rhineland, 250
Ribbentrop, Joachim von, 257, 268–70, 318
Ring is Closed, The (KH), 247–8, 251, 255, 257
Rishovd, Arnt, 280
Road Leads On, The (KH), 235, 238–9, 257
Rode, Helge, 168
Roosevelt, Franklin D., 274, 282
Rosa (KH), 126–7, 155, 171, 196, 215, 235, 239
Rosenberg, Alfred, 244, 256–7, 260
Royal Theatre see Copenhagen
Russia see Soviet Union (and Russia)

SA (Sturm Abteilung, Germany), 237
Saar, 244
Samtiden (Norwegian journal), 58–9
Sarpsborg, 68
Schirach, Baldur von, 257, 281
Schleicher, Kurt von, 237, 240
Schneider-Edenkoben, Ellinor see Hamsun, Ellinor
Schneider-Edenkoben, Richard, 259
Schopenhauer, Arthur, 125–6
Schroeder, Christa, 283
Schück, Henrik, 177, 181
Second World War (1939–45): outbreak, 258; ends, 291

'Secret Pain' (KH, story), 88
Segelfoss Town (KH), 152–5, 160, 171–2, 182, 198, 235
Selmer, Jens, 17
Shallow Soil (KH): on women, 75–6; publication and reception, 76; published in Poland, 77; translations, 80; sales in USA, 196; extracts used in US textbook, 214
Shaw, George Bernard, 64
Sibelius, Jean, 94
Siesta (KH, story collection), 88–9, 95
Simplicissimus (German magazine), 83–4, 89, 149
Singer, Isaac Bashevis, ix
Skavlan, Einar, 311–12; Knut Hamsun, 217, 219
Skavlan, Olaf, 17
Skogheim (farm), Hamarøy: KH buys and occupies, 135–6, 143; management, 139; KH threatens to give up, 140, 142, 145, 148, 151, 156; KH and family leave, 157, 160
Skram, Amalie, 40, 43
Skram, Erik, 40, 43, 51, 57–8, 75
Slotte, Alexander, 94
Söderberg, Hjalmar, 220
Sørensen, Johan, 41–3, 46–7
Soviet Union (and Russia): KH visits, 52, 95; KH's publishing agreements in, 131, 138; translations of KH's works in, 133, 135, 147; KH's earnings in, 149; Axis pacts against, 250; non-aggression pact with Germany (1939), 258, 266; KH condemns, 274; Germany invades, 275; advance against Germany, 289; Finns oppose, 289
Speer, Albert, 284, 318
Spitsbergen, 133
SS (Schutzstaffel, Germany), 241, 244
Stabel, Peter Lorentz, 295
Stalin, Josef V., 236, 266, 274
Steinach, Dr Eugene, 182–3, 203
Stenersen, Johan Eckersberg, 283
Stiernstedt, Marika, 224, 235, 338; Mostly Truth, 338
Stockholm: KH and Marie attend Nobel ceremony in, 179–1
Stockholms-Tidningen (newspaper), 170
Stray, Anne Lise (Sigrid's daughter), 320
Stray, Sigrid: as KH's defence lawyer, 284, 318–24; KH discusses prospective divorce with, 289, 322; Marie requests support from, 294; visits KH in clinic,

302; drafts new will for KH, 322; attempts to secure KH's finances, 330–1, 340; and KH's dispute with Grieg and Gyldendal, 330–3, 336; and KH's attacks on Langfeldt, 334
Stresemann, Gustav, 197, 221–2
Strindberg, August: KH lectures on, 27, 32; Ibsen attends play, 64; KH meets, 80; mental problems, 81; KH admires, 216; Miss Julie, 43
Striving Life (KH, stories), 112
Strømme, Dr Johan Irgens: analyses and treats KH, 203–6, 208–9, 211–12, 224–5, 229, 308, 313; Marie visits, 208–9; KH leaves, 234; Nervøsiten, 203, 205, 209, 239
Stuckenberg, Viggo, 35
Svalbard, 133
Svenska Andelsförlaget (Swedish publisher), 171
Svenska Dagbladet (Swedish newspaper), 181
'Sverdgny' (KH, poem), 14
Svinhufvud, Eivind, 270
Sweden: hegemony over Norway, 82; Norway claims independence from, 105, 107, 110–11
Swedish Academy see Nobel Prize

Tau, Max, 253–5, 318–21, 331
Tau, Tove (née Filseth), 318–19, 321
Tavastjerna, Karl Adolf, 93
Terboven, Josef: and proposed Norwegian reclaiming of Greenland, 268–9; as Reichskommissar in Norway, 268; conflict with Quisling, 269; meets KH, 271–2, 278; and KH's visit to Goebbels, 272–3; KH criticises to German leaders and seeks removal, 278, 281, 283–5, 287–8, 297–8, 324; greets KH on return from Germany, 288; lends country cabin to KH, 291; suicide, 293; number of arrests under rule, 319; and Grieg's release from prison camp, 328
Thaulow, Harald, 18
Thaulow, Nina, 18–19
Thingvalla (ship), 33
Thommessen, Olaf, 40, 46, 48, 64–5, 70–1, 74
Tides Tegn (Norwegian journal), 150
Tilskueren (Danish journal), 39, 58
Times, The (London newspaper), 111
Tiraspolska, Raissa, 133
Tolstoy, Count Leo, 215
Torp, Dr (of Lillehammer), 81

Trondheim, 143–4, 284
Turkey, 95–6
Tverås, Svein, 22
Twain, Mark, 28, 33, 45, 117, 215

Under the Autumn Star (KH), 114–15, 117, 129, 196, 213
Undset, Sigrid: defends women against KH's criticism, 151; awarded Nobel Prize, 217; in USA during Second World War, 269; on Norwegian treason trials, 300
United States: KH first visits (1884), 19–22; KH's second visit to (1886), 29–31; industrialised farming in, 31; KH's disenchantment with, 32, 42; KH writes on cultural and social life, 44–5, 65, 217, 265; KH published in, 173; KH's sales in, 196
Urdal, Mikkel, 12

Valdres, Norway, 24, 27, 47, 91, 210, 217, 223–4
Vedel, Valdemar, 35–6, 38
Verdens Gang (Norwegian newspaper): praises 'Hunger' fragment, 40; and KH's return to Oslo, 46; prints Georg Brandes' review of *On the Cultural Life of Modern America*, 47; and publication of 'Hazard', 48, 69; reviews KH's works, 57, 76, 80, 84, 115, 211; attacks KH for critical lecture on Ibsen, 64–5, 70; depicted in *Editor Lynge*, 74; KH writes in, 134; interview with KH on return to Hamarøy, 136; on KH's trial, 325
Versailles conference and treaty (1919), 164, 167, 221, 233, 244–5
Vesterålen, 12
Victoria (KH): plot and themes, 91–2, 213; writing, 91; publication and reception, 93, 109; success, 95, 196, 271; published in Russia, 111; film rights, 165; Esperanto translation, 217; broadcast in Germany, 251

Vienna: KH attends congress in war, 277, 279–80
Vindern, Oslo: psychiatric clinic, 303
Vinje, Odd, 323–5

Walsøe, Laura, 10
Walsøe, Nicolai, 10–11
Wanderer Plays on Muted Strings, A (KH), 129–30, 132, 135, 142, 148, 213
War Resisters International, 242
Wassermann, Jacob, 20
Wayfarers (KH): KH's early experiences in, 11; writing, 207, 211, 213–14; plot and characters, 212–13, 248; on role of writer, 212; KH plans and writes sequel, 214–15, 228; sales, 221; published in Germany, 247
Wedekind, Frank, 89
Wells, H.G., 173, 220
Whitman, Walt, 422
'Why I Am a Member of the NS' (KH, article), 323
Wild Choir, The (KH, poems), 106, 127, 154
Winkel Horn, Erhardt Frederik, 50–1, 53
Wold, Terje, 299
women: KH's attitude to, 13, 21, 26, 43, 75, 127, 130–1, 141–2, 151; Strømme's theories of, 203, 209
Women at the Pump, The (KH), 169, 172–6, 181–3, 186, 196, 202, 217, 248
'Word for Us, A' (KH, article), 136–7, 156, 267
'World Tilts, The' (KH, poem), 81

Zahl, Erasmus: supports KH, 13–16; KH visits, 79; calls in KH loan, 87; KH released from debt, 91
Znaniye (Russian publishing house), 131, 133
Zola, Emile, 16, 32, 60
Züchner, Ernst, 283–4, 286–7
Zukunft (German journal), 84
Zweig, Stefan, 220, 254